'This collection of essays is a timely re-evaluation of the role and practice of the most senior police officers. Seen as an "impossible job" by many, the essays in this book describe the historical and modern contexts of the people who negotiated the changing policing landscape. It will be of great use and interest to political researchers as well as historians and criminologists.'

Professor Barry Godfrey, *Vice-President, Xi'an Jiaotong Liverpool University, China*

'This collection will, I am sure, become the essential reference work for police scholars seeking to understand the historical context of the role of Chief Constable. The editors and contributors have delivered an excellent balance of essays that provide much to advance our understanding of police leadership whilst simultaneously providing a highly engaging account of the shifting social and political contexts which shaped police organisations and their leaders.'

Dr Tom Cockcroft, *Head of Criminology, Leeds Beckett University, UK*

'There has been remarkably little historical exploration of police leaders in the UK and their relations with the police authorities. The essays here go a long way towards addressing the vacuum. Moreover, given the advent of PCCs and the debates about the varied tasks of policing, the collection is timely.'

Clive Emsley, *Emeritus Professor, Department of History, Open University, UK*

'The editors have assembled a team of authors who reflect the cutting edge of research on the ongoing issue of the tensions between autonomy, professionalism, and accountability in police leadership. The coverage of the entire British Isles provides invaluable insights into the topic as a whole. The long chronological scope allows the past to be considered both in its own terms, and as a source of inspiration for those grappling with the problems of the present.'

Dr Chris A. Williams, *Senior Lecturer in History, Open University, UK*

Leading the Police

In 2015 the College of Policing published its *Leadership Review* with specific reference to the type of leadership required to ensure that the next generation of Chief Constables and their management approach will be fit for purpose. Three key issues were highlighted as underpinning the effective leadership and management of contemporary policing: hierarchy, culture and consistency. Yet these are not just relevant to modern policing, having appeared as constant features, implicitly and explicitly, since the creation of the first provincial constabularies in 1835.

This collection reviews the history of the UK Chief Constable, reflecting on the shifts and continuities in police leadership style, practice and performance over the past 180 years, critiquing the factors affecting their operational management and how these impacted upon the organization and service delivery of their forces. The individuality of Chief Constables significantly impacts on how national and local strategies are implemented, shaping relationships with their respective communities and local authorities. Importantly, the book addresses not just the English experience but considers the role of Chief Constables in the whole of the United Kingdom, highlighting the extent to which they could exercise autonomous authority over their force and populace.

The historical perspective adopted contextualises existing considerations of leadership in modern policing, and the extensive timeframe and geographical reach beyond the experience of the Metropolitan force enables a direct engagement with contemporary debates. It also offers a valuable addition to the existing literature contributing to the institutional memory of UK policing. The contributors represent a range of disciplines including history, law, criminology and leadership studies, and some also have practical policing experience.

Kim Stevenson is Professor of Socio-Legal History at Plymouth University and joint general editor of the Routledge SOLON series. She is a former Police Sergeant serving with the Nottinghamshire Police and has published widely on historical and contemporary aspects of crime and the criminal law. She is currently leading a project on Everyday Offending in Plymouth.

David J. Cox is Reader in Criminal Justice History at the University of Wolverhampton, specialising in eighteenth- and nineteenth-century crime and policing history. He has been involved in such research for over two decades and is a Fellow of the Royal Historical Society.

Iain Channing is a lecturer in Criminology and Criminal Justice Studies at Plymouth University. He is an interdisciplinary scholar whose research crosses the fields of Criminology, History and Law.

Routledge SOLON Explorations in Crime and Criminal Justice Histories

Edited by Kim Stevenson, University of Plymouth; Judith Rowbotham, University of Plymouth; David Nash, Oxford Brookes University and David J. Cox, University of Wolverhampton

This series is a collaboration between Routledge and the SOLON consortium (promoting studies in law, crime and history), to present cutting edge interdisciplinary research in crime and criminal justice history, through monographs and thematic collected editions which reflect on key issues and dilemmas in criminology and socio-legal studies by locating them within a historical dimension. The emphasis here is on inspiring use of historical and historiographical methodological approaches to the contextualising and understanding of current priorities and problems. This series aims to highlight the best, most innovative interdisciplinary work from both new and established scholars in the field, through focusing on the enduring historical resonances to current core criminological and socio-legal issues.

3 Capital Punishment in Twentieth-Century Britain
Audience, Justice, Memory
Lizzie Seal

4 The Origins of Modern Financial Crime
Historical Foundations and Current Problems in Britain
Sarah Wilson

5 Transnational Penal Cultures
New Perspectives on Discipline, Punishment and Desistance
Edited by Vivien Miller and James Campbell

6 The Police and the Expansion of Public Order Law in Britain, 1829–2014
Iain Channing

7 Public Indecency in England 1857–1960
'A Serious and Growing Evil'
David J. Cox, Kim Stevenson, Candida Harris and Judith Rowbotham

8 A History of Forensic Science
British Beginnings in the Twentieth Century
Alison Adam

9 Leading the Police: A History of Chief Constables 1835–2017
Edited by Kim Stevenson, David J. Cox and Iain Channing

www.routledge.com/Routledge-SOLON-Explorations-in-Crime-and-Criminal-Justice-Histories/book-series/HCCJ

Leading the Police

A History of Chief Constables 1835–2017

Edited by
Kim Stevenson, David J. Cox and Iain Channing

Routledge
Taylor & Francis Group
LONDON AND NEW YORK

First published 2018 by Routledge

2 Park Square, Milton Park, Abingdon, Oxon OX14 4RN
605 Third Avenue, New York, NY 10017

Routledge is an imprint of the Taylor & Francis Group, an informa business

First issued in paperback 2021

Publisher's Note

The publisher has gone to great lengths to ensure the quality of this reprint but points out that some imperfections in the original copies may be apparent.

British Library Cataloguing-in-Publication Data
A catalogue record for this book is available from the British Library

Library of Congress Cataloging-in-Publication Data
Names: Stevenson, Kim, editor. | Cox, David J., editor. |
Channing, Iain, editor.
Title: Leading the police : a history of chief constables, 1835–2017 /
edited by Kim Stevenson, David J. Cox and Iain Channing.
Description: 1 Edition. | New York : Routledge, 2018. |
Series: Routledge SOLON explorations in crime and criminal justice
histories ; 9 | Includes bibliographical references and index.
Identifiers: LCCN 2017014518| ISBN 9781138217249 (hardback) |
ISBN 9781315441085 (ebook)
Subjects: LCSH: Police chiefs—Great Britain. | Police—Great Britain—
History. | Criminal justice, Administration of—Great Britain—History.
Classification: LCC HV7911.A1 L43 2018 | DDC 363.2092/241—dc23
LC record available at https://lccn.loc.gov/2017014518

ISBN: 978-1-138-21724-9 (hbk)
ISBN: 978-0-367-22726-5 (pbk)

Typeset in Times New Roman
by Florence Production Ltd, Stoodleigh, Devon, UK

Contents

Tables

Contributors

David Taylor has lectured for over 25 years and has written numerous books and articles on the history of crime and policing in the nineteenth and twentieth centuries. Books include *Policing the Victorian Town: The Development of the Police in Middlesbrough, c.1840–1914*, (Palgrave Macmillan, 2002), *Hooligans, Harlots and Hangmen: Crime and Punishment in Victorian Britain*, (Praeger, 2010) and *Policing in England and Wales, 1918–39: the Fed, Flying Squads and Forensics*, [with Keith Laybourn)], (Palgrave Macmillan, 2011) and *The Battle for the Roads of Britain* (Palgrave Macmillan, 2015). He is currently working on *Beerhouses, Brothels and Bobbies*, a history of the advent and impact of new policing in Huddersfield and its surrounding district.

David Smale served as a constable in Lothian and Borders Police working in both Edinburgh and the Scottish Borders. His Open University Doctoral thesis entitled 'The development of the new police in the Scottish Borders c. 1840–1890' was completed in 2008. He then undertook a Leverhulme Trust Postdoctoral Research Fellowship at Edinburgh University, 'Police and community in twentieth-century Scotland: A social history'. Publications include 'Police and community in twentieth-century Scotland: The uses of social history', [with N. Davidson *et al.*], *British Journal of Criminology*, 2017, vol.51:1, 18–30; 'Alfred John List and the development of policing in the Counties of Scotland, c.1832–77', *Journal of Scottish Historical Studies*, 2013, vol.33:1, 52–80.

Elizabeth Malcolm, MA, PhD, FRHistS, FASSA, is an Honorary Professorial Fellow in the School of Historical and Philosophical Studies at the University of Melbourne. She is currently writing books on violence, gender and memory in Ireland and on the history of the Irish in Australia. Her publications include: *The Irish Policeman, 1822–1922: A life,* (Four Courts Press, 2006); and '"What would people say if I became a policeman?" The Irish policeman abroad', in O. Walsh (ed.) *Ireland Abroad*, (Four Courts Press, 2003).

Richard W. Ireland works on the history of crime and the criminal justice system with particular emphasis on the Welsh perspective. Publications include *Land of White Gloves? A History of Crime and Punishment in Wales*. History of

Crime in the UK and Ireland, (Taylor and Francis, 2015); *Imprisonment in England and Wales: A Want of Order and Good Discipline: Rules, Discretion and the Victorian Prison* (University of Wales Press, 2007); co-editor in two volumes, *The Carmarthen Gaoler's Journal 1845–50* (Welsh Legal History Society, 2010); 'A second Ireland? Crime and popular culture in nineteenth-century Wales' in R. McMahon (ed.) *Crime, Law and Popular Culture in Europe 1500–1900*, (Willan, 2008).

Joanne Klein is Professor of History at Boise State University, and is active in the Criminal Justice network of the Social Science History Association. Publications include: *Invisible Men: Secret Lives of Police Constables in Liverpool, Manchester, and Birmingham, 1900–1939*, (Liverpool University Press, 2010); 'History of police unions', in Bruinsma and Weisburd (eds) *Encyclopedia of Criminology and Criminal Justice*, (Springer Verlag, 2014); 'Traffic, telephones and police boxes: Deterioration of beat policing in Birmingham, Liverpool and Manchester between the World Wars' in Blaney, (ed.) *Policing Interwar Europe: Continuity, Change and Crisis, 1918–1940*, (Palgrave Macmillan, 2007).

Judith Rowbotham is a visiting Research Fellow at Plymouth University and co-founder and director of *SOLON: Interdisciplinary Studies in Law, Crime and History*. She is also one of the general editors of Routledge SOLON: Explorations in Crime and Criminal Justice Histories and is well known for and has published widely on issues of crime and gender. Recent publications include *Public Indecency in England 1857–1960* [with D. J. Cox, K. Stevenson, C. Harris] (Routledge, 2015) and *Crime News in Modern Britain: Press Reporting and Responsibility 1820–2010* [with K. Stevenson and S. Pegg] (Palgrave, 2013).

Robert M. Morris is an Honorary Research Fellow, History Department, Open University. Home Office 1961–97, *inter alia* Home Office Liaison Officer with Met police, Principal Private Secretary to Home Secretary, and Bill team leader for the 1983 Police and Criminal Evidence Bill. Open University Doctoral thesis 'Metropolitan Police and Government 1860–1920', 2004; Editor, *Reforming the Police in the Nineteenth Century: The Making of the Modern Police 1780–1914*, vol.2, (Pickering and Chatto, 2014). He has also published on detective and criminal investigation history.

Marisa Silvestri is an Associate Professor in Criminology at Kingston University. Her work is focused on exploring the complex nature of police culture(s), the gendered nature of police work and critical diversities within the criminal justice system. She is Chair of the Women, Crime and Criminal Justice Network (British Society of Criminology) and is a steering group member of the Policing Network (BSC). She has a longstanding record of research on women and police leadership and has published extensively in the field. As a strong advocate of participatory action research with an emphasis on practitioner involvement, her work advances and informs theoretical, policy and practice understandings of gender and policing.

Joanne Murphy is a Lecturer in Organizational Change in the Management School, Queen's University Belfast and a Fellow in the George J. Mitchell Institute for Global Peace, Security and Justice. Her research focuses on leadership, organizational change and institutional transformation in societies emerging from conflict. She has written extensively on change after conflict, security sector reform and leadership. Her latest book is *RUC to PSNI: Conflict, Change and Community Confidence* (Palgrave Macmillan, 2013). Previously, she has been funded by a number of organizations including the IRCHSS, HEA, British Academy, AHRC and Santander.

Gareth Addidle is a Lecturer in Criminology and Criminal Justice Studies and Programme leader for Police and Criminal Justice Studies and Public Services (Policing) at Plymouth University. He is the secretary of the British Society of Criminology (South West) and a member of the Policing Network and the Scottish Institute for Police Research. He has recently been awarded his PhD entitled *Community Planning, Community Safety and Policing: a local case study of governance through partnership* Plymouth University, 2016.

Timothy Brain OBE QPM PhD was Chief Constable of Gloucestershire from 2001 until his retirement in January 2010, and had previously served in Avon and Somerset, Hampshire and the West Midlands. He was national lead on police finances and led several high-profile operations, notably Gloucestershire's response to the extensive flooding of 2007. He is an Honorary Research Fellow at Cardiff University and a Visiting Professor at the University of Gloucestershire. He is the author of two major works on policing, *A History of Policing in England and Wales from 1974* (Oxford University Press, 2010) and *A Future for Policing* (Oxford University Press, 2013), as well as a frequent broadcaster and contributor to police journals.

Preface

This book was inspired by the Everyday Offending in Plymouth project (*www.everydayoffending.org*) which revealed Plymouth's 'Youngest Ever Chief Constable': the charismatic Joseph Davison Sowerby 1892–1916, portrayed on the front cover photograph of Plymouth City Police Force in 1907 (second row, eighth from left). Sowerby's innovative strategies to tackle drunkenness and antisocial behaviour were an early form of zero tolerance policing which earned him the enduring respect of the town and his men. He provides a fascinating exemplar of some of the remarkable individuals who have held the office of Chief Constable but whose experiences have, from a historical perspective, often been undervalued. The office of Chief Constable is a unique, challenging and often invidious role requiring significant leadership skills, effective managerial strategies, diplomatic dexterity and political integrity. However, the role of Chief Constables in the past has not generally been afforded the same attention as the rank and file. *Leading the Police* aims to redress that balance presenting a series of chapters analysing the challenges and tensions associated with police leadership and exploring the wider contextual and historical developments.

Kim Stevenson is Professor of Socio-Legal History at Plymouth University, co-founder *SOLON: Interdisciplinary Studies in Law, Crime and History*, General Editor Routledge SOLON: Explorations in Crime and Criminal Justice Histories and is also a former Police Sergeant She has published widely on historical and contemporary aspects of crime and the criminal law including *Public Indecency in England 1857–1960* [with D. J. Cox, C. Harris and J. Rowbotham] (Routledge, 2015); *Crime News in Modern Britain: Press Reporting and Responsibility 1820–2010* [with J. Rowbotham and S. Pegg] (Palgrave, 2013).

David J. Cox FRHistS is Reader in Criminal Justice History at the University of Wolverhampton, co-director *SOLON: Interdisciplinary Studies in Law, Crime and History* and General Editor Routledge SOLON: Explorations in Crime and Criminal Justice Histories. He has published widely in the field of criminal justice history and the early history of the police: *Crime, Regulation and Control during the Blitz: Protecting the Population of Bombed Cities* [with P. Adey and B. Godfrey] (Bloomsbury, 2016); *Public Indecency in England 1857–1960* [with K. Stevenson, C. Harris and J. Rowbotham] (Routledge, 2015); *Victorian Convicts:*

100 Criminal Lives [with B. Godfrey and H. Johnston] (Pen and Sword, 2016); and *Crime in England, 1688–1815* [*History of Crime in the UK and Ireland* series] (Routledge, 2014).

Iain Channing is a lecturer in Criminology and Criminal Justice Studies at Plymouth University. He is an interdisciplinary scholar whose research crosses the fields of Criminology, History and Law. His publications include the monograph *The Police and the Expansion of Public Order Law in Britain, 1829–2014* (Routledge, 2015) which underlines his interests in police history, public order law and political extremism. These interests were established in his doctoral research on the legal responses to Sir Oswald Mosley's British Union of Fascists (Plymouth University, 2014). He has presented his research at various conferences across the UK and teaches across a broad range of areas which traverse crime history, contemporary policing and the criminal justice system.

Acknowledgements

We wish to express our sincere thanks to Graham Naylor, Development Manager at Plymouth City Library, for permitting the use of the photograph of Plymouth City Police 1907 on the front cover of this book and for the subsequent image of its Chief Constable, Joseph Sowerby. The various authors would also like to add their collective thanks to the respective staff at the numerous archives, record offices and libraries visited during the course of their research.

CHIEF CONSTABLE J. D. SOWERBY.

From a Photo. by Kelley, Old Town Street, Plymouth.

Chief Constable Sowerby

Source: *One Hundred Portraits from the 'Plymouth Comet' with biographical notes.* Published by James H. Keys at 7 Whimple Street, Plymouth, 1895.

Courtesy of Plymouth City Library

Introduction

Nearly 200 years after the creation of the Metropolitan Police force in 1829, Cressida Dick, a former Assistant Commissioner, was appointed as the first female Police Commissioner in February 2017 against a backdrop of political tension concerning the leadership of her predecessor Sir Bernard Hogan-Howe.[1] Dick's promotion was a ground-breaking appointment, not only in light of her gender but because it ended the longstanding tradition that appointees should have experience of leading other major conurbation forces; for example, Hogan-Howe was formerly Chief Constable of Merseyside before replacing Sir Paul Stephenson who had been Chief Constable of Lancashire. Outlining her reformist credentials and vision, Dick won the support of both the Mayor of London, Sadiq Khan, and the Home Secretary, Amber Rudd, to whom she is jointly responsible. Her appointment augurs a period of relative stability within a more controversial state of affairs where there has been talk of 'parachuting' in non-police leaders from the public and military sectors.[2] Starting her police career walking the beat and becoming head of the Met's counter-terrorism unit, Dick is well regarded by the rank and file and appears to have overcome the criticism concerning the 2005 operation she led where Jean Charles de Menezes was shot dead in the mistaken belief that he was a terrorist.

This revolutionary change in command of the largest police force in the United Kingdom also marked an unprecedented feminization in responsibility for the management of the criminal justice process and law enforcement. At the time of writing, Prime Minister Teresa May's Cabinet includes a female Home Secretary (Amber Rudd) and Minister of Justice (Liz Truss), Alison Saunders is the Director of Public Prosecutions, Sara Thornton (former Chief Constable of Thames Valley), one of the two female candidates of the four applicants shortlisted for the Commissioner role, is the first Chair of the National Police Chief's council

1 See 'Cressida Dick makes history as Metropolitan Police's first female Commissioner', *Daily Telegraph*, 22 February 2017, 'Cressida Dick appointed first female Met police commissioner', *The Guardian*, 22 February 2017.

2 'Former Admiral considered for top police job', *The Times*, 30 September 2016.

(formerly the Association of Chief Police Officers [ACPO]) and Lynne Owens (former Chief Constable of Surrey Police) is Head of the National Crime Agency.[3]

Such a significant shift in police leadership and accountability presents a timely cue to reflect on the historiographical framework of the role, function and importance of police leaders in the United Kingdom, past and present. The contemporary public face of police leadership is very different to that envisaged by the founding fathers of what we now regard as the modern police system. Chief Constables are much more publicly accountable for their actions (or inaction) than either the Fieldings or Peel anticipated, and the increasing politicization of the role of police leaders with regard to the appointment of Police and Crime Commissioners (PCCs) would seem similarly alien to them.[4]

Despite such reform underlining the rapid progress made during the last two decades, the whole concept of police leadership is currently under critical scrutiny as outlined in the College of Policing's *Leadership Review* published in June 2015. The report confirms that there has been increasing debate in recent years about 'the structure, status and culture of policing' and that while considerable efforts have been made to adapt 'to new social, economic and political realities' the diverse nature of the 43 separate forces in England and Wales have made it very difficult to achieve 'consistent cultural and structural reform'.[5] It concludes that fundamental changes in police management and supervision over the next 10–15 years are paramount in order to safeguard financial viability and public and political legitimacy. The report makes specific reference to the styles and type of leadership required to futureproof the police service and ensure that it and the next generation of Chief Constables will be fit for purpose. Three key factors were identified as central to the production of constructive outcomes in the effective leadership and management of contemporary policing: hierarchy, culture and consistency. This is reflected in Recommendation One which imposes essential responsibility onto Chief Constables: 'Existing police leaders should influence and drive the required culture change by demonstrating their own commitment to personal development and supporting the implementation of the review.'[6]

This edited collection details some of the numerous ways in which the tensions between Chief Constables and those in charge of the purse strings have played out. The authors, all noted experts within their respective field of research, provide a wide-ranging (though often surprisingly complementary and coterminous)

3 The National Police Chiefs' Council (NPCC) replaced the Association of Chief Police Officers formed in 1948 on 1 April 2015. The Police Reform Act 2002 requires that the Chair has held the post of Chief Constable, www.npcc.police.uk/Home.aspx

4 The world's first detectives, the Bow Street 'Runners' (see Cox, Chapter 2) were created by the half-brothers Henry and John Fielding in 1749, while the Metropolitan Police was created by Sir Robert Peel in 1829.

5 College of Policing, Leadership Review: Recommendations for delivering leadership at all levels, June 2015, College of Policing Ltd., www.college.police.uk/What-we-do/Development/Promotion/the-leadership-review/Documents/Leadership_Review_Final_June-2015.pdf. June 2015, p.5.

6 Ibid. p.21.

discussion of such tensions throughout a period of almost two centuries. As the contributors demonstrate, issues and concerns relating to the autonomy, hierarchy and consistency in police leadership are neither novel nor unique to modern contemporary policing.

'A dangerous set of men'?

In 1873 Henry Bruce MP, Home Secretary, stated in response to a question about the autonomous action of a particular Chief Constable that 'I have to remark that the Secretary of State has no direct means of censuring a chief constable of [a] county constabulary'.[7] Steedman argues that this statutory autonomy made them a 'dangerous set of men'.[8] Chief Constables remain autonomous unlike other public servants; although they can be held to account by the Executive they are only answerable to the law and enjoy statutory guarantees over their independence in operational matters.[9]

Since the passing of the Municipal Corporations Act 1835 questions have been asked (and often unsatisfactorily answered) concerning the structure, status and culture of police leadership in the form of Chief Constables in both boroughs and counties. Critchley, Emsley, Rawlings and Williams among others have examined their impact and influence on the day-to-day activities of the 'bobby on the beat' and his role and status in the force.[10] Similarly, Steedman, Taylor, Emsley and Cox have inevitably drawn on these factors when exploring the creation and development of modern police forces, provincial, county or borough, and from the Bow Street Runners to the formation of the Metropolitan Police.[11] But it is in relation to the history of Chief Constables specifically that the trilateral dynamics of hierarchy, culture and consistency are most significant. They are fundamental components in any discourse, including this volume, which seeks to compare and analyse the shifts and continuities in police leadership style, practice and performance. In consideration of the importance of individual leadership which has played (and continues to play) a vital role in how policing services have (and still are) delivered, the biographical detail of Chief Constables becomes critical.

7 HC Deb 25 April 1873 vol. 215 cc. 974–5.

8 C. Steedman, *Policing the Victorian community: The formation of English provincial police forces, 1865–80*, London: Routledge & Kegan Paul, 1984, p. 29.

9 *R v Metropolitan Commissioner, ex parte Blackburn* [1968] 2 QB 118, section 5 Police Act 1964, section 10 Police Act 1996 and equivalents

10 T. A. Critchley, *A History of Police in England and Wales*, London: Constable, 1978; C. Emsley, *The Great British Bobby*, London: Quercus, 2009, *The English Police: A Political and Social History*, 2nd edn Harlow: Longman, 1996; P. Rawlings, *Policing: A Short History*, Cullompton: Willan, 2002; C. Williams, *Police Control Systems 1775–1975*, Manchester University Press, 2014.

11 C. Steedman, *Policing the Victorian Community: The Formation of English Provincial Police Forces*, 1865–80, London: Routledge & Kegan Paul, 1984; D. Taylor, *Crime Policing and Punishment*, London: Macmillan, 1998; Emsley, *The Great British Bobby*; D. Cox, *A Certain Share of Low Cunning: A History of the Bow St Runners 1792–1839*, London: Routledge, 2012.

C. Wright Mills stated that 'Neither the life of an individual nor the history of a society can be understood without understanding both'.[12] This observation stresses the significance that profiles of individual police leaders can contribute to the analysis of these trilateral dynamics and offer a critical understanding of how they influenced the leadership styles of individual Chief Constables.

Leading the Police endeavours to incorporate such perspectives and also highlight the extent to which the impact of national and/or local political and social pressure could affect and influence the autonomy, discretion and authority of Chief Constables over their operational independence. The book therefore builds on the extensive work that Wall has already undertaken in his comprehensive and ground-breaking survey of this 'criminal justice elite' which we applaud and, together with Stallion, his encyclopaedic inventory of the 1,835 identified holders of this office that we have regularly dipped into and found invaluable.[13] As an edited volume, *Leading the Police* adds to and enhances such existing literature by incorporating a multiplicity of views on the subject enabling broader perspectives and critique, as well as covering the post-PACE (Police and Criminal Evidence Act 1984) landscape, developments and comparisons associated with the introduction of PCCs.

As Bruce presciently predicted, the problem of police accountability endured as essentially one of how to control Chief Constables as highlighted a century later by the Royal Commission on the Police in 1962, precursor to the Police Act 1964. The report identified one of the fundamental causes of the 'present uncertainty attending relations between Chief Constables and police authorities . . . [as] The lack of any widely accepted policy on the crucial question whether a chief constable ought to be controlled or supervised in some or all of his activities.'[14] The appointment of a Chief Constable cannot therefore escape its inherently political edge from either the central or local government agenda, thus a common factor in all the contributions included here is an examination of how certain Chief Constables managed their forces and communities within the particular political landscape of their tenure.[15]Authors consider how police chiefs were selected and appointed, the role and expectations placed upon them by the state and their respective police authorities, their style of leadership and the relationship they developed with their officers, the local community and those to whom they were answerable. Who were these Chief Constables and how did they function as leaders of what proved to be a constantly changing and evolving police service?

12 C. Wright Mills, *The Sociological Imagination*, Oxford University Press, 2000, p.3.

13 D. Wall, The *Chief Constables of England and Wales, The Socio-Legal History of a Criminal Justice Elite*, Aldershot: Ashgate, 1998; M. Stallion and D. S. Wall, *The British Police Forces and Chief Officers 1829–2012* (2nd edn) Bramshill: Police History Society, 2012, p.7.

14 Royal Commission on the Police 1962, Cmnd. 1728 London: Home Office, May 1962, para.80; also see T. Jefferson and R. Grimshaw, *Controlling the Constable: Police Accountability in England and Wales*, London: Frederick Muller, 1984.

15 N. Fielding, *The Police and Social Conflict* (2nd edn) London: Glass House Press, 2005, p. 29.

Thematic approach and methodology

Importantly, and again extending Wall's work, the book addresses not just the English experience but creates a decisively UK volume incorporating specific chapters that embrace the individual perspectives of the often overlooked home countries. Scotland provides two interesting case studies presenting a thought-provoking comparison between the formation of the first police forces in Glasgow which, established in1800, predated those south of the border and the controversial amalgamation, 200 years later, into one single 'nationalized' entity: Police Scotland. Historically, policing in Wales has been much neglected, it is hoped that the examination here of the role of Chief Constables in a Welsh rural constabulary will lead to additional work to supplement this narrative. Two further chapters investigate the more quasi-militaristic approaches utilized across the Irish Sea in light of the distinctive factors specific to Ireland and Northern Ireland concerning the policing of divided and conflicted communities within both a historic and contemporary context. We have also deliberately chosen to focus away from a London-centric (i.e. Metropolitan Police) bias in our choice of chapters, though we acknowledge, as Morris's chapter ably demonstrates, the often symbiotic relationship between senior Met officers and their provincial counterparts. This is in part an attempt to escape the confines of more traditional policing histories, in which the Met has often predominated, but mainly in order to provide readers with a more holistic view of the development of police leadership throughout the United Kingdom over the past two centuries.

The book adopts a loose chronological design covering the period from the enactment of the Municipal Corporations Act 1835 up to the present day. The chapters are divided into three thematic sections. With the explosion of new forces founded in the mid-nineteenth century Part One explores the experiences of the early Chief Constables as they took charge of their embryonic forces across the United Kingdom including Scotland and Ireland. Common to all were meeting the challenges they confronted in attempting to establish their new-found role and status, particularly in respect of the relationship with those 'above' – their respective Watch/Police Committee or local Justices. As the existing literature already confirms, the relationship with their respective governmental authorities was dominated by the tensions generated in assimilating the executive and administrative accountability demanded of their masters with the operational autonomy that effective leadership mandates.

By the late nineteenth century, arguably at the hiatus of local community policing, and following the respective Local Government Acts 1888, throughout the United Kingdom there were almost 90 county and some 181 borough forces albeit of disparate size and variable efficiency.[16] Part Two, entitled Chief

16 Stallion and Wall, *The British Police Forces and Chief Officers 1829–2012*, p. 20. This figure does not include Irish police forces, but the borough figures do include the various UK islands i.e. Isle of Man, Isles of Scilly and the Isle of Wight, and also Jersey and Guernsey (though neither are part of the United Kingdom).

Constables and their forces, focusses more on the ways in which Chief Constables led and managed their forces in the sense of those 'below' and how they were perceived and received by both their men and the local community they served. This section incorporates examples of how the preferences and personal beliefs of strong and often charismatic individuals could influence their operational strategies and consequently impact upon the command of their force, and the community it served.

The final section, Part Three, Chief Constables from the twentieth century onward, underlines the significant cultural and professional changes to the style and diversity of police leadership that had been building throughout the century but that could only be manifested once the prevailing social conditions were receptive. The appointment of the first women police leaders and the extent of ethnic representation are considered as well as the increasing politicization and corporatization of the role following numerous centralized decisions such as the appointment of PCCs, and the creep, both directly and indirectly, of regionalization and nationalization including the creation of national databases and nationwide agencies. These chapters complement research on contemporary police leadership, such as Jenny Fleming's edited collection *Police leadership: Rising to the top*. The current issues facing policing highlighted by Fleming's contributors, including austerity, community relations, gender and political influence, are also reflected here. Moreover, seen in the context of historical change offered by the approach of this volume, these concerns are also demonstrated as being reoccurring. Consideration is also noted to Robert Reiner's seemingly ageless and still seminal *Chief Constables*.[17] The increasing threat of centralization and the escalating bureaucratization of the role of Chief Constable highlighted by Reiner 26 years ago remains an ever-relevant topic. Indeed, two of the chapters in this section highlight the nationalization of the Northern Ireland and Scotland police services.

As a general caveat we acknowledge that a range of descriptors was used in the nineteenth century particularly to denote police leaders, but for the sake of convenience throughout both this Introduction and our Conclusion we use the term 'Chief Constable' generically to include where relevant: Superintending Constables, Head Constable (Liverpool being the only such example), Inspectors General, Commissioners of the City of London and Metropolitan forces and other similar descriptors of the head of a police force.

Synopsis

Starting with the early Chief Constables, David Taylor's detailed overview of what he refers to as the 'managerialism and morality' of some of Yorkshire's Watch Committees in the decades following the initial creation of borough forces clearly

17 J. Fleming (ed.) *Police Leadership: Rising to the Top*, Oxford University Press, 2015; R. Reiner, Chief Constables, Oxford University Press, 1991.

show the type of problems that beset the first Superintendents of Huddersfield. In particular, he highlights the fact that a combination of both inept Watch Committee members and leaders of the borough force was a recipe for disaster. There was clearly a complex trial and error system operating in many of the Yorkshire boroughs' police forces, with the role of Chief Constable (or Superintendent) and the respective Watch Committees being hammered out in an often ad hoc fashion, with the 'master and servant' attitude held by many Watch Committee members being hotly disputed by several of the leaders of the police.

This disjuncture between those who were responsible for doling out the financial wherewithal for the newly created police forces and those charged with its immediate executive implementation is similarly clearly seen in the often fraught and troubled relationship between the first Chief Constable of Northamptonshire, Henry Goddard, and his masters, the Police Finance Committee. David J. Cox's chapter recounts a somewhat sorry tale of the appointment of an extremely successful former Bow Street 'Runner' proving to be an unhappy marriage, with Goddard being faced with a vociferous minority determined to undermine his role from the start. Goddard's credentials, though impeccable in terms of his detective capabilities, ultimately proved wanting in regard to his ability to master the more mundane administrative duties associated with the post of Chief Constable. His social status (both in terms of his non-military background and his humble origins as the son of a fishmonger) also figured heavily in the heated debates about his suitability for the post; despite becoming a prominent member of the local Freemasons, he never appears to have achieved social acceptability among his peers.

David Smale's chapter on the role of Scottish Chief Constables in the first half of the nineteenth century provides a timely reminder that this book is designed to be a truly UK-wide historical and contemporary survey of the autonomy or otherwise of Chief Constables. Scotland's role in the creation of recognisably modern police forces has been too often overlooked by criminal justice historians; it is salutary to point out here that the Metropolitan Police of 1829 was predated by numerous other police forces, for example the Bow Street system pioneered by the Fieldings in the last half of the eighteenth century, and the various police forces that operated in and around Glasgow in the early nineteenth century. Smale argues that while the Glasgow police forces undoubtedly contributed to the subsequent development of other UK police forces, the particular model adopted in Glasgow followed a strict 'master and servant' ideal; the overwhelming aim being to employ police leaders who were dedicated to preserving the mercantile and commercial interests of those who funded it.

Traversing the Irish Sea, Elizabeth Malcolm's contribution recounts the development of a uniquely Irish form of police leadership: that of the Inspectors General. This was a national police force (arguably the only one in the United Kingdom if the much later foundation of the British Transport Commission [now British Transport Police] is excluded) that was created as a paramilitary force which faced unique problems throughout its existence. The religious and sectarian divides were exacerbated by the Great Famine in the 1840s, which together with later economic depressions, stretched the abilities of the Inspectors General to their limits. Malcolm argues that the paramilitary nature of the force has often been overstressed by historians and that a more nuanced interpretation is that of a 'highly centralized and bureaucratic political police force', going on to discuss the ways in which this adversely affected several of the Inspectors General, who had their hands tied and their decisions overruled by an absentee British political elite.

Returning to England, Kim Stevenson's chapter, which opens Part Two: Chief Constables and their Forces, concentrates on the role of Chief Constables as moral guardians. Focusing largely on the crusading zeal of Joseph Sowerby, one of the youngest ever men to be appointed as Chief Constable, Stevenson argues that his model of policing in late nineteenth century Plymouth can be seen as a prototype for the later Zero Tolerance Policing (ZTP) extolled and practised by Bill Bratton, Chief of New York Police Department 1994–6 and 2014–16. She also connects this type of policing to an earlier exhortation by Patrick Colquhoun, who thought that a main duty of a police leader was to inculcate moral fortitude in his men and explores the expected credentials that prospective applicants should possess in order to convince police authorities of their moral character. Stevenson also corroborates the view expressed in other chapters of this publication that the county judiciary and Watch Committees (overwhelmingly men of property and land) usually actively sought men of their own social standing and typically with military backgrounds to become leaders of police.

Richard Ireland's chapter takes the reader over another border to Wales. He argues that there was a fundamental tension in two aspects of a Chief Constable's duties: that regarding his responsibility to his employers and that towards the expectations of both his men and the wider community. The subsequent exemplars taken from the police leadership in Cardiganshire, West Wales, highlight the possible dichotomy between these two responsibilities, detailing what Ireland calls 'a protracted and painful process'. In contrast to the majority of other police historians, Ireland also offers the intriguing possibility that the reason for the preponderance of ex-military men appointed as Chief Constables in the early and mid-Victorian periods owed as much to their knowledge of their experience in mess-room culture as in their expertise in commanding men to carry out their wishes without question suggesting an early example of 'canteen culture'?

Joanne Klein's chapter focusses on the relationship between Chief Constables and their less senior officers. She argues that by the beginning of the twentieth century, a more educated workforce meant that police forces were now able to appoint leaders from their own ranks, replacing the more traditional system of recruiting largely from the military. This in turn created its own problems, with many constables being deeply suspicious of what Klein refers to as 'clerk constables', i.e. those men who furthered their police career in administrative rather than executive roles, with several of them not having much experience of life pounding the beat. This has close parallels with the current debate about direct entry appointments up to Superintendent level. The Chief Constable of Merseyside,

Andy Cooke, pointed out in his first Annual Lecture in 2016 that this was the equivalent of directly appointing a Colonel in the army.[18] He further argued that there should be more emphasis on an apprenticeship approach for all entrants and was not in favour of employing only graduates stressing that 'honesty and integrity' were the biggest qualifications required.

Judith Rowbotham takes us into less familiar territory (though one being increasingly investigated by crime historians such as Cox and Shpayer-Makov) in her chapter based upon the role played by Chief Constables in detective fiction.[19] She argues that in the earliest detective fiction, Chief Constables are largely noticeable by their absence, as the authors of such works usually sought to stress the superior middle (or upper) class nature of their privately educated amateur sleuth as seen against the bumbling professional. Such men (or less occasionally, women) would not normally have expected to mix in the same social circles as the working-class detective, but Rowbotham convincingly argues that the rise of regulatory motoring offences brought the two into a closer relationship. However, this often resulted in a rather negative depiction of Chief Constables as betrayers of their (newly acquired) social class, prosecuting their betters for middle-class offences such as speeding in their private motor cars.

Although this book is primarily concerned with the role of Chief Constables throughout the United Kingdom, Robert Morris's chapter states that leaders of the Metropolitan Police played an important role in the development of early provincial police leadership strategies, especially with regard to small rural constabularies, although very few county forces were established with senior ex-Met officers at their head. He argues that with the creation of Hendon Police College in 1934, this situation fundamentally changed, with the college providing hitherto unknown opportunities for bright Metropolitan Police officers to achieve senior rank within provincial county forces. In more recent years, Morris suggests that this trend has been somewhat reversed, with many senior provincial officers either returning to or joining the Met as high-ranking officers.

The increasing role of regulation in the daily activities of the police forms a central tenet of Iain Channing's chapter on public order policing. Channing details the attitudes and successes of the early Chief Constable of Birmingham in policing the various Chartist gatherings in the 1830s and 1840s through a deft blend of pragmatism and overwhelming police presence (cf. the recent failings of

18 Andy Cooke, Chief Constable of Merseyside's Annual Lecture, Liverpool John Moores University, 28 November 2016, www.ljmu.ac.uk/about-us/news/articles/2016/12/1/trust-key-to-future-policing.

19 See D. J. Cox, '"Elementary, my dear Wilton" – will the real Dr Watson please stand up?', British Crime Historians Symposium IV, University of Liverpool, September 2014 (unpublished conference paper) in which Cox suggests that the 1833 novel *Delaware or The Ruined Family* by George Payne Rainsford James is the first piece of fiction to feature a recognisable detective (in the form of a fictional Bow Street runner) and also possibly provided Arthur Conan Doyle with a prototype Dr Watson in the guise of a medic by the name of Dr Wilton; also see H. Shpayer-Makov, *The Ascent of the Detective: Police Sleuths in Victorian and Edwardian England*, Oxford University Press, 2012.

West Midlands Police when dealing with the riots of August 2011). He then discusses the less successful attempts to police public order during the suffragette campaigns in the early twentieth century, which resulted in a committee of enquiry to investigate the different police practices adopted when dealing with such insurrection. Public order policing again came to the fore in the interwar years with the rise of the British Union of Fascists (BUF) and Channing shows the range of methods employed by Chief Constables to police often violent demonstrations. He then further highlights the contrasting approaches and operational philosophies shown some 50 years later between John Alderson (Chief Constable of Devon and Cornwall) and Chief Constable James Anderton (Manchester). The accumulation of such case studies reveals the wide discretion and relative autonomy Chief Constables have yielded in the management of public order scenarios which has had wider implications on the consistency of policing responses throughout the country.

The final section on Twentieth Century Policing commences with Maria Silvestri's chapter as one of the most topical at the time of writing in the light of the recent appointment of Cressida Dick as the first female Commissioner of the Metropolitan Police. Her discussion of the early years of female policing at a senior level reflects the enormous advances made in gender equality within British policing (although a long journey remains). Concentrating on the lives and work of half a dozen of the most influential female police leaders: Nina Boyle, Margaret Damer Dawson, Mary Allen Sofia Stanley, Dorothy Peto and Barbara de Vitre, Silvestri provides us with an important reminder that while male-dominated, policing in Britain prior to 1973 was not exclusively male; females played an important (though still under-researched) role in the creation of the modern British police service.

The remaining three chapters bring the story of the development of British Chief Constables up to the present day. Joanne Murphy's examination of the Northern Ireland policing situation from the partition to the present day and how consecutive Inspectors General responded to the difficulties associated with policing divided societies, provides a salutary warning that the future of policing cannot be discussed without contemplation of the past. She states that 'there is nowhere in the UK where policing is subject to more significant scrutiny or individual police leaders are more heavily monitored', and explores the three major themes of continuity, conflict and change over almost a century. Murphy illustrates how the underlying conflict and tensions of the Troubles compelled leaders to reflect on the need to adopt a more modern and professional approach which paved the way for the transition of the Royal Ulster Constabulary into the Police Service of Northern Ireland (PSNI) formed in 2001.[20] The unique role of the PSNI in the ongoing peace process is a complex one, fraught with difficulties, and the recent collapse of the power-sharing agreement serves only to emphasize these particular problems.

20 Police (Northern Ireland) Act 2000.

Scotland also was to experience a major reorganization and split from centralized control once power had been devolved from Westminster in the Scotland Act 1998. Gareth Addidle's overview of the creation and development of the Police Service of Scotland details the attempts of the Scottish government's modernization and amalgamation of the eight existing Scottish police forces into a new, national service.[21] This major overhaul has significant and profound implications for local policing, with a centralized bureaucracy responsible for vast tracts of land ranging from some of the UK's most densely populated cities to areas of almost no habitation. From local representation through elected police authorities or boards, Scottish policing is now reliant on a centralized and unelected Scottish Police Authority, whose members are directly appointed by Members of the Scottish Parliament. Addidle shows how the 'Strathclydeification' of Police Scotland combined with a determined political agenda dominated and clouded the introduction of the newly formulated national force and the resultant loss of localism in terms of accountability and the premature resignation of its first leader. This centralization also appears to be a current topic of debate among some English police leaders with the Chief Constable of Merseyside recently suggesting that a reduction in the number of English police services would produce positive (financial?) benefits. He memorably described Chief Constables as 'a disharmonious collection of Machiavellian princes and princesses', with 43 princes in charge but no king or queen, and argued that fewer, larger forces would be more effective.[22]

Finally, Tim Brain (former Chief Constable of Gloucestershire) offers an 'insider's view of the changing role of Chief Constables in the post-PACE era. He argues that while the majority of Chief Constables coped admirably with the considerable administrative changes in training and procedure, some were less successful in inculcating a change in attitudes and practice among their officers. The introduction of fixed-term appointments for Chief Constables has, Brain argues, left Chief Constables reliant on the future continued goodwill of their police authorities. The increasing politicization of the police is also an area of concern with the introduction of PCCs leading to a confused understanding in the public's mind as to who actually runs the police, and a diminution in the status of Chief Constables with a concomitant problem of recruitment. This accords closely with the Chief Constable of Merseyside's experience that despite the incentive of an annual salary in excess of £160,000, he was the only candidate for the post at the time of his appointment in July 2016. This is a remarkable change in the fortunes of police leaders; in 1840, when Henry Goddard was appointed as the first Chief Constable of Northamptonshire, he successfully fought off almost two dozen candidates for the post.

The above chapters have been carefully selected in order to give a flavour of the various problems faced (and occasionally overcome) by some of the Chief

21 Police and Fire Reform (Scotland) Act 2012.

22 Cooke, Chief Constable of Merseyside's Annual Lecture.

Constables of the United Kingdom throughout the past two centuries. They each illustrate distinctive and separate aspects of what was and remains an undoubtedly difficult job, but also coalesce to form a coherent overview of the role of Chief Constable as leaders of the police. As editors we greatly enjoyed learning more about the most senior posts in UK policing; we sincerely hope that readers do the same.

Section 1

Early Chief Constables

1 'A fit man to be at the head of the police': Police Superintendents and Watch Committees in the first generation of 'new policing'

A Yorkshire perspective, c.1850–70

David Taylor

Introduction

There have been several detailed accounts of the first generation of 'new police' in the large cities of England. The city forces in Yorkshire have been well studied while the survival of the smallest has been noted, albeit in passing.[1] In contrast, the medium-sized boroughs, notwithstanding their socio-economic significance, have been largely overlooked. The main focus of this chapter is the borough of Huddersfield, which was governed by an Improvement Commission between 1848 and 1868. The fraught relationships between successive Watch Committees and Superintendents of police in the town highlight the considerable problems faced by local politicians and senior figures in their employ as they sought to develop an effective working relationship at a time when there were no clearly laid down guidelines or conventions regarding their respective responsibilities. Huddersfield had five police Superintendents, four of whom were dismissed or forced to resign, in less than 20 years. In contrast, in Halifax, incorporated in 1848, the first Superintendent, Thomas Spiers served for seven years and his successor, John Pearson, for two, while in Middlesbrough, incorporated in 1853, the first Superintendent, William Hannan, served for eight years and his successor, Edward Saggerson, served for 23.[2] A combination of managerialism and morality resulted in recurring

1 D. R Walsh, The reform of urban policing in Victorian England: A study of Kingston upon Hull from 1836 to 1866, unpublished Ph.D thesis, University of Hull, 1997; C. A Williams, Police and crime in Sheffield, 1818–1874, unpublished PhD thesis, Sheffield University, 1998 and D. C. Churchill, Crime, policing and control in Leeds, c.1830–1890, unpublished Ph.D thesis, Open University, 2012.

2 Details relating to Halifax are drawn from J. Posner, The establishment and development of the new police in Halifax, 1848–1914 unpublished PhD thesis, University of Huddersfield, 2015; details of Middlesbrough from D. Taylor, *Policing the Victorian town: The development of the police in Middlesbrough c.1840–1914*, Basingstoke: Palgrave, 2002 and of Huddersfield from D. Taylor, *Beershops, Brothels and Bobbies*, University of Huddersfield, 2016. Of the remaining fifteen

failures to establish an effective working relationship in Huddersfield. Particularly during the 1850s, leading Commissioners viewed the relationship between the town's Improvement Commission and various public agencies and servants, including the police, in terms of a business model with the Commissioners as the board of directors. Further, there was a continuing belief that the Superintendent of Police should be more an administrator, organizing and directing the work of the 'thief-takers' rather than being an active, hands-on 'thief-taker' himself (see Cox, Chapter 2 for an example of this causing problems between a Chief Constable and his committee). Finally, there was an ongoing emphasis that the Superintendent of Police should be a man of probity and unimpeachable moral standing without taint of drunkenness or gambling. In contrast, through a more pragmatic and flexible approach that recognized the experience and expertise of police Superintendents, a greater degree of success was achieved in the nearby (and similar) textile town of Halifax and also in the more distant (and contrasting) iron and steel town of Middlesbrough.

The Yorkshire context

In the mid-nineteenth century there were sixteen borough forces in the three ridings of Yorkshire, eleven in the West Riding alone. These forces fell into three categories (See Table 1.1). The sheer size of the forces, particularly in Leeds and Sheffield, but also Bradford and Hull, set these cities clearly apart from the rest.[3] In addition, these cities were more heavily policed, as their more favourable police: population ratios show. Although all borough forces faced some common problems, the largest forces had different organizational issues and, to a significant degree, their size impacted on the nature of the relationship between Watch Committees and their chief police officers.

The three towns studied had differing socio-economic characteristics. The two West Riding towns, Huddersfield and Halifax were both important textile centres

Yorkshire borough forces, only three (Scarborough, Dewsbury and York) saw their early Chief Constables serve for only a few years. In each case, a long-serving man followed. Elsewhere the common experience was of the first appointed Chief Constable serving for the best part of a decade, or more. In Wakefield McDonald served for 20 years, in Hull, McManus for 30 years. The first three Chief Constables of Bradford served for twelve, fifteen and 20 years respectively. Interestingly, the last James Withers, had served in Huddersfield, leaving for pecuniary reasons, as will be discussed later. See M. Stallion and D. S. Wall, *The British Police: Police Forces and Chief Officers, 1829–2000*, 2nd edn, Bramshill: Police History Society, 2013. Their information is not wholly accurate. The entry for Huddersfield makes no mention of the first two Superintendents, Cheeseborough and Thomas. While it would be naïve to assume that longevity guaranteed effectiveness in the force, the churning at the top of the Huddersfield force in the 1850s and 1860s was not conducive to the development of an efficient and effective force.

3 Bradford, Leeds and Halifax also had additional policing via the Worsted inspectorate. B. Godfrey and D. J. Cox, *Policing the Factory: Theft, Private Policing and the Law in Modern England*, London: Bloomsbury, 2013. Although not discussed by Godfrey and Cox, the Worsted Acts were also enforced in Huddersfield and the Huddersfield district via the Huddersfield and Holmfirth Manufacturers' Protection Association.

with a history dating back into the eighteenth century. By 1871 they were roughly similar in size (70,000 and 66,000 respectively), the former growing more rapidly between 1851 and 1861, the latter between 1861 and 1871. The policed areas were significantly affected by boundary changes in Halifax (1865) and Huddersfield (1868).[4] Middlesbrough was very different. It was a 'frontier town', built on iron and steel that had grown dramatically since 1840.[5] Attracting people, disproportionately young unmarried men and with one of the highest percentages of Irish in the country, it had doubled its size between 1851 and 1861 and doubled it again in the next decade to top 40,000 by 1871. Statistics relating to population and police numbers in these towns and cities is contained in Tables 1.1 and 1.2.

Table 1.1 Yorkshire Borough Forces (by size) 1872

	Population (000s)	*Size of force*	*Population per constable*
Large			
Bradford (WRY)	146	175	917
Hull (ERY)	122	172	706
Leeds (WRY)	259	315	822
Sheffield (WRY)	240	290	827
Medium			
Halifax (WRY)	65	65	1002
Huddersfield (WRY)	73	70	962
Middlesbrough (NRY)	39	43	917
Scarborough (NRY)	24	26	932
Wakefield (WRY	28	37	758
York (WRY)	44	47	931
Small			
Beverley (ERY)	10	10	1021
Dewsbury (WRY)	25	12	2064
Doncaster (WRY)	19	19	987
Pontefract (WRY)	5	6	895
Richmond (NRY)	4	2	2221
Ripon (WRY)			3402

(ERY =East Riding Yorkshire; NRY = North Riding Yorkshire; WRY = West Riding Yorkshire)

Source: Reports of Inspectors of Constabulary for the year ending 29 September 1873, *Parliamentary Papers*, 1873 (16).

4 The area covered by the Huddersfield Improvement Act 1848 was defined as being 'within a Radius of Twelve hundred Yards in every Direction from the Spot where the Old Cross formerly stood, in the Centre of the Market Place'.

5 The classic statement of Middlesbrough as a frontier town, the British Ballarat, is Asa Briggs, 'Middlesbrough: The growth of a new community', Victorian cities, London: Odhams Press, 1963. For an alternative view, comparing Middlesbrough to Melbourne (Bearbrass), see D. Taylor, 'Melbourne, Middlesbrough and morality: Policing Victorian "new towns" in the old world and the new', *Social History*, vol. 31:1, 2006, 15–38.

Table 1.2 Size of force, police population and police acreage ratios, Halifax, Huddersfield and Middlesbrough, 1858 and 1872

	1858 Police force	*1872 Police force*	*1858 Ratio police to population*	*1872 Ratio police to population*	*1858 Acres per constable*	*1872 Acres per constable*
Halifax	35	65	1:959	1:1002	1:34	1:54
Huddersfield	32	73	1:781	1:962	1:27	1:139
Middlesbrough	13	43	1:1143	1:917	1:58	1:42

Source: Reports of Inspectors of Constabulary for the years ending 29 September 1858 and 1872, *Parliamentary Papers*, 1859 (17) and 1873 (16).

Watch Committees and Chief Constables: some general issues

The responsibility for law enforcement in the boroughs of nineteenth-century England rested on local Watch Committees and justices, both of whom had statutory powers and Chief Constables, who retained the common law powers of constables. The relationship between these three elements was not spelled out in detail and, therefore, was a matter of local negotiation and compromise. This gave rise to considerable variations in practice, from very close supervision by a Watch Committee to a more hands-off approach in disciplinary and operational matters.[6] Recent discussion has focused on the notion of police independence and the enforcement of specific policies. The clashes between the Chief Constables of Birmingham and Liverpool with their local Watch Committees, in 1880 and 1890, dominate the literature. Despite some vigorous arguments by Brogden and Jefferson and Grimshaw,[7] the present consensus is that there was general agreement in the nineteenth century that Watch Committees had the power to instruct their chief police officers on matters of law enforcement policy.[8] However, the power to instruct did not, in itself, resolve the question of the appropriate day-to-day relationship between Watch Committees and their senior officials. To describe the relationship simply as one of master and servant, while not inaccurate in broad terms, overlooks the fact that the *nature* of that relationship was fundamental to a successful working partnership. A second source of tension, noted by several historians centred on expenditure with several Watch Committees cutting back the size of their forces in response to pressure from their electorates.[9] Demands

6 See M. Brogden, *The Police: Autonomy and Consent*, London, Academic Press, 1982; T. Jefferson and R. Grimshaw, *Controlling the Constable*, London, Frederick Muller/Cobden Trust, 1984; L. Lustgarten, *The Governance of Police*, London: Sweet and Maxwell, 1986 and R. Reiner, *Chief Constables*, Oxford University Press, 1992.

7 Ibid.

8 Reiner, Chief Constables, p.13.

9 See P. Rawlings, *Policing: A Short History*, Cullompton: Willan, 2002, p.130.

for 'economy' were important locally (the Huddersfield force was reduced by one for a brief period in the early 1860s) but of greater importance, and less well covered in the secondary literature, were considerations about the appropriate management model for policing in the town and the necessary personal qualities of a Superintendent of Police.

Conflict in the 1850s: Superintendent Thomas

The members of the newly formed Watch Committee of the Huddersfield Improvement Commission were very conscious of the fragmentation and weak leadership that had characterized policing in the town in the early and mid-1840s. The first problem was easily solved by establishing a single force, responsible for day and night policing, under a Superintendent of Police and responsible to the Watch Committee. Finding the right man to fill this post and developing an effective working relationship with him proved more problematic. The Commissioners' first choice, John Cheeseborough (a former Worsted Inspector), was incapacitated by a stroke within months of taking office but there appeared to be an appropriate successor in the figure of the Superintendent of night constabulary, John Thomas. Although his previous police experience was modest, he had been part of the two-man force created in Ripon in 1848, his early years in charge were largely successful in the eyes of the Watch Committee. He proved himself to be a positive, hands-on officer, playing an active role in quelling trouble in the Huddersfield's notorious Castlegate district and tackling the problems of immorality, disorderly beerhouses and cruel sports, which won him acclaim for his 'most praiseworthy' exertions.[10] Yet within two years he had been dismissed – twice!

The conflict that culminated in Thomas' dismissal in 1855 has to be set in a wider political context. Unlike in Halifax, where there was a strong radical and Chartist presence, Huddersfield had a less divided and more moderate political set up notwithstanding the presence of one-time Chartist, Joshua Hobson, though there were important (if at times overlapping) factions among its local politicians. The passing of the Improvement Act 1848 was a turning point in the town's local government as the old, oligarchic system that dated back to 1820 was replaced by one based on a property-based franchise. New political alliances, comprising strange bedfellows, were forged. Improvers, the victors of 1848, were led by Hobson now a sanitary reformer and Joshua Brook, one of the first Commissioners appointed in 1820 and a man of 'conservative principles'. Opposing them, under the banner of economy, were disgruntled members of the town's petty bourgeoisie as much angered by their loss of political power as by a determination to reduce rates, and Radicals, who felt both cheated by the complex property franchise that

10 *Huddersfield Chronicle*, [HC] 11 May 1850. For other examples of Thomas' actions see HC, 18 May and 14 September 1850, and 18 January, 1 February, 17 April, 26 June 1851, 7 February, 13 March, 17 April and 2 October 1852.

was less democratic than the old town vestry and betrayed by their erstwhile colleague, Hobson. In the run-up to the 1853 election of Commissioners 'economy' became a central issue. Addressing a public meeting in August 1853, local solicitor, J. I. Freeman, was unequivocal: 'many offices might be abolished; many salaries curtailed; and the whole affair [of local government] carried on upon a much more economical scale.'[11] The election was a triumph for the faction headed by C. H. Jones (later to become the first Mayor of Huddersfield after incorporation in 1868) and his right-hand man, Joseph Boothroyd.[12] Their impact was immediate and dramatic. An Enquiry committee was set up and chaired by Jones, who was determined to root out any lax book-keeping (and by extension waste of tax-payers' money and possible corruption) by the earlier Commissioners and the town's paid servants. Hobson, a major figure behind many of the reforms in the town after 1848, having been attacked in the pre-election campaign, found himself heavily criticized for negligence. John Jarrett, Superintendent of scavengers, was dismissed and then found guilty of embezzlement at the Quarter Sessions at Pontefract in the spring of 1854 (an incident which precipitated Hobson's resignation) and, significantly, in presenting the third and final report of the Enquiry Commission, Jones expressed his concerns about the police, being of the opinion that 'sufficient supervision was not exercised in the departments occupied by Superintendent Thomas'.[13]

Jones was clearly determined to exercise tighter control over financial matters but this was part of his wider vision of the role of the Commissioners in relation to their officials. He and his supporters adopted a business model of local government, likening their role to that of a company's board of directors.[14] Jones had no doubt that it was his responsibility to keep a close eye on all aspects of the work undertaken by the Improvement Commissioners and to intervene if necessary. He informed the Watch Committee that:

> he considered it the duty of the chairman to watch what was going on; and if he apprehended that any officer was liable to be damaged, or an office was likely to be damaged by the conduct of an officer, he was bound to look on and prevent the injury.[15]

In general terms, this meant asserting repeatedly the authority of the Commissioners over the town's police force, including its senior officer; more particularly,

11 *HC*, 13 August 1853.

12 There was little difference in socio-economic terms between the two, loose factions, though the 'economical' faction had more petty bourgeois figures. They also tended to be younger, had a significant number of Congregationalists in their ranks and voted Liberal rather than Whig. Reformers included more Wesleyan Methodists and Anglicans and tended to vote Whig or Conservative.

13 *HC*, 4 March, 8 April, 15 July 1854.

14 For example, see Commissioner Shaw's comparison of the members of the Watch Committee to company directors, *Huddersfield Examiner*, 4 August 1855.

15 *HC*, 4 August 1855.

it translated into taking an active role in the investigation of charges of improper behaviour and the disciplinary action that might be required, which, in turn, enabled him and his allies to elucidate the personal, moral qualities appropriate for a senior policeman (see Cox, Chapter 2 for an example of just such a conflict between a Chief Constable and his Finance committee).

As early as June 1854 Jones raised the (by now largely redundant) question of the relationship between the officials sworn in at the Court Leet and policing within the limits of the Improvement Act.[16] Of greater significance was his decision to 'originate a conversation [on] the necessity of keeping the efforts of the town police within the limits of the Improvement Act'.[17] In policing terms this made little sense. As the town's magistrates had observed, it was folly for the borough police to stop their enquiries or halt a pursuit simply because a suspect moved out of the area defined by the Improvement Act, all the more so as the town constables had a good working relationship with the Superintending Constable for the surrounding Upper Agbrigg district, Thomas Heaton.[18] Further, as the Holmfirth tragedy clearly demonstrated, it was important to leave 'some discretionary power . . . in the hands of Superintendent Thomas [because] many emergencies happened where there was neither time or [*sic*] opportunity for running after commissioners to grant permission.'[19] Initially, no others had joined the conversation but in January 1855 the Improvement Commissioners, spurred on by Jones, decided to instruct Thomas 'not to allow the night or the day police to act beyond the limits of the act without the previous joint sanction of two members of the [watch] committee.'[20] This decision had more to do with the politics than the practicalities of policing. Jones was determined to assert his authority and curb the independence that Thomas had shown on a number of occasions.[21]

The clash between the two men undoubtedly had a strong personal element. Jones, a gentleman and Congregationalist, 'a sturdy Nonconformist of the old-

16 It is not clear whether Jones' ignorance of the situation was real or feigned. He conveniently overlooked a decision made by the Commissioners and appeared more determined to assert his authority in matters of police jurisdiction. *HC*, 6 January 1855.

17 *HC*, 9 December 1854.

18 Part of Heaton's salary was paid in part by the ratepayers of Huddersfield, which meant that Thomas could call upon Heaton for assistance but not vice versa. For a discussion of Heaton's role and the importance of the superintending constable system see D. Taylor, '" No remedy for the inefficiencies of parochial constables": Superintending constables and the transition to "new" policing in the West Riding of Yorkshire in the third quarter of the nineteenth century', *Crime History and Societies*, 2015, vol. 19:1, 67–88.

19 Early in the morning of Thursday 5 February 1852 the Bilberry reservoir above Holmfirth burst its dam, killing 81 people and wreaking extensive damage. *HC*, 7 and 14 February 1852. The need for police discretion was recognized by Commissioner Thornton, *HC*, 4 November 1854.

20 *HC*, 6 January 1855.

21 At times Jones played fast and loose with the truth. He accused Thomas, on one occasion, of permitting two constables to assist the Hull force during the visit of the Queen, without the permission of the Commissioners. In fact, the Watch Committee had discussed and approved Thomas' proposal in response to a request from the authorities in Hull. *HC*, 4 November 1854.

fashioned type', had little in common with a man who had a reputation for drinking and gambling.[22] It was more than a matter of personal morality. Jones (and allies like Boothroyd) had a clear view of the qualities required of a public servant. Further, there were differences of opinion about the role of a Superintendent of Police. Thomas was not alone among early police Superintendents of small and medium-sized borough forces to combine his leadership role with active policing. In contrast, Jones, influenced by a Metropolitan-style of policing as practised in Manchester, had a more hierarchical view of the force as a whole combined with a more clear-cut managerial role for its Superintendent. 'Organization of system' was required, he 'wanted a directing superintendent . . . to direct and give orders to the whole [police] body'.[23] At no point did Jones doubt that the Metropolitan/Manchester model of policing could be transplanted to a significantly smaller borough force.[24]

While Jones did not approve of Thomas' 'hands-on', thief-taker style of policing, it was Thomas' conduct, on and off duty, that came to the fore from the spring of 1855 onwards when Henry Lord, a frequent critic of the local police, a teetotaller and part of the wider 'economical' faction in town made three allegations of misconduct against Thomas. Two were rejected, though Thomas was criticized for spending several hours drinking in the Cross Keys when his professional presence was not required.[25] More serious was the third accusation that Thomas had been drinking and gambling at the Golden Lion Inn, Pontefract, when he (and another officer) had accompanied a prisoner to the Quarter Sessions. The Watch Committee enquired into the allegation, upheld the charge and recommended the dismissal of Thomas for misconduct.[26]

A special meeting of the Commissioners was called to consider this recommendation. Political factionalism fuelled an often ill-tempered series of exchanges about the fitness of the town's police Superintendent. Dirty linen was washed in public but there was a widespread acceptance that Thomas was 'an officer of great talent.'[27] His defenders conceded that he had 'little venial peccadilos' [*sic*]

22 A. W. Sykes, *Ramsden Street Independent Church, Huddersfield. Notes and Records of a Hundred Years, 1825–1925*, Huddersfield, 1925, pp. 99–100 cited in E. A. H. Haigh, (ed.) *Huddersfield: A Most Handsome Town*, Huddersfield, Kirklees Cultural Service, 1992, p. 128.

23 *Halifax Courier*, 8 September 1855. In the same address to the Huddersfield Improvement Commissioners he made clear his wish to have a police system based on the Metropolitan model.

24 The attempt to reform policing in York in the 1840s and 1850s along London lines met with some difficulty but there is no evidence that Jones was aware of this. See R. Swift, 'Police reform in early Victorian York, 1835–1856', Borthwick Paper, 73, University of York, 1988, pp.10–11. The York force was deemed not to be efficient on its first inspection in 1857 and Superintendent Chalk, severely criticized by HM Inspector of Constabulary subsequently resigned.

25 Thomas was in the Cross Keys from the evening of Easter Monday to seven o'clock the following morning. *HC*, 19 and 28 May 1855; West Yorkshire Archive Service, Kirklees, Huddersfield Improvement Commission Minutes, KMT, 2/2/1, 6 June, 13 July and 1 August 1855.

26 Watch Committee Minutes, KMT, 18/2/3/13/1, 28 May 1855.

27 Messrs. Dransfield and J Brook, *HC*, 9 June 1855. For a fuller account see Taylor, Beershops, chap. 3.

but argued that it was 'sometimes necessary for a policeman to appear to be fit company for the bad characters they might have to associate with. Some had to get liquor in order to get others in a similar state'.[28] Such arguments cut no ice with the chairman Jones and his leading supporter Boothroyd. They conceded that Thomas had been an effective, 'thief-catching' officer but the central issue in their eyes was one of morality and fitness for position. Boothroyd in particular dwelt upon the details of Thomas' behaviour at Pontefract and argued that not only had this charge been proved beyond 'the shadow of a doubt' but also that this proof of his present drinking and domino-playing (albeit while off duty) 'quite removed the doubt entertained respecting former charges' dating back to 1849.[29] In similar vein Commissioner Shaw argued that 'they ought to have an upright and honest man' as police Superintendent.[30] An attempt to save Thomas' career failed as a motion to suspend him for a month was defeated by nine votes to five.[31]

Matters then became somewhat farcical. A new police Superintendent was needed, advertisements were placed, a shortlist drawn up, candidates interviewed and a decision made by the Watch Committee that the best man for the post was none other than John Thomas![32] The decision provoked a crisis in local politics. There were questions about the constitutionality of reappointing a man who had been dismissed by the Commissioners, further clashes between pragmatists and moralists, and heightened personal feeling. At another special meeting of the Commissioners tempers ran high with Jones specifically accused of 'vindictiveness and persecution'. When it came to the vote the Commissioners were evenly split (eight to eight), leaving the Chair, none other than Jones, with the casting vote. This he refused to use, notwithstanding the fact that he told the meeting that he could 'never act with him [Thomas] again [as] all my confidence in that officer is forfeited' and that should Thomas be appointed 'he should feel obliged to resign his office as chairman.'[33]

If the first special meeting showed the Commissioners in a bad light, the second was worse. Jones' resignation prior to the meeting further heightened personal animosity. In a lengthy and often vituperative speech, explaining his decision to resign, Jones became increasingly shrill as he listed all those who had made major errors of judgement: the magistrates who had 'decided wrongly' in the original case involving Lord and Thomas; the Watch Committee, with whom 'he entirely differed' regarding the *Cross Keys* incident and even the Commissioners 'now were in a wrong position'.[34] Jones continued his excoriating personal attacks on Thomas,

28 *HC*, 9 June 1855.
29 Ibid.
30 *Huddersfield Examiner*, 14 July 1855.
31 Watch Committee Minutes, KMT 18/2/2/1, 6 June 1855.
32 *HC*, 30 June 1855.
33 Watch Committee Minutes, KMT 18/2/2/1, 13 July 1855; *HC*, 14 July 1855.
34 *HC*, 4 August 1855.

accusing him of 'encouraging gambling and drunkenness' and condemning him as 'a violent worthless character'. Boothroyd was little less intemperate referring to Thomas as 'utterly incompetent'. 'The simple question', he asserted, 'was whether Thomas was morally qualified for the post.' Commissioner Shaw supplied the answer for the 'moralist' faction. 'How could [Thomas] properly carry out his duties?' he asked rhetorically. 'Would he not feel it necessary to wink at the faults of others or feel that he was acting unjustly towards them?' Clearly Thomas was not 'a fit man to be at the head of the police'.[35] Once again, the vote revealed the Commissioners to be evenly divided (9:9) but this time the new chairman, Thomas Firth, used his casting vote to seal Thomas' dismissal.[36] Thomas' enemies were united by a combination of morality and managerialism which set them apart from the more pragmatic arguments of his defenders.

There was little new in the second debate but Jones made his position very clear. He advocated an approach in which the primacy of the Watch Committee was translated into a form of micro-management that left little or no freedom of action for the Superintendent of Police. Further, in his managerial model, reinforced by recent discussions with the Chief Constable of Manchester, 'the chief constable ought to act as a Head Constable not as a thief-taker [and] ought to be the director of the thief-takers.'[37] Finally, Jones made clear the personal qualities he expected in a Head Constable. Thomas had demonstrated his 'improper conduct, including drunkenness [which] would be an encouragement to crime' whereas he should be 'superior to the vices he was employed to check'.[38] Thomas had his vociferous defenders who condemned the 'rancorous and vindictive feeling' with which Jones had pursued a 'system of espionage' against Thomas.[39] They took a more pragmatic view of policing, not simply recognizing that policemen were rarely teetotal, but also accepting the need to mix with criminal and semi-criminal elements. They were also supportive of an active, hands-on, thief-taking role for the Superintendent of Police but failed narrowly to win the vote.

Conflict in the 1850s: Superintendent Beaumont

The decision not to reappoint Thomas presented Jones with an opportunity to introduce his alternative, 'a new system, [with] new discipline, new orders [and]

35 Ibid.

36 Watch Committee Minutes, KMT, 18/2/2/1, 1 August 1855. Nineteen of the town's 21 commissioners voted in the two special meetings of 1855 and not one man changed his position. The two factions were similar in terms of economic background but differed in terms of religious affiliation, while Jones' most loyal supporters were three fellow Congregationalists (Joseph Bottomley, Titus Thewlis and Wright Mellor), he was also consistently supported in these debates by two Wesleyan Methodists (Benjamin Robinson and Josephus Jagger Roebuck) and an Anglican (Foster Shaw).

37 Ibid.

38 Huddersfield Improvement Commission Minutes, KMT, 18/2/2/1, 6 June, 4, 13 July and 1 August, 1855.

39 *HC*, 4 August 1855.

new men'.[40] George Beaumont, Inspector of the night police at Halifax, was to be the new broom. His relationship with many on the Watch Committee, and Jones in particular, was very close. Unlike his predecessor, Beaumont adopted an office-based managerial role. Constables deemed to be inefficient were dismissed, beats revised and police discipline tightened up. The changes aroused mixed feelings. The constables were unhappy with an order not to smoke on duty (not least because Beaumont continued to do so), and with another to touch hats when meeting Commissioners, which visibly encapsulated their subservient position. Others expressed concern at the high number of dismissals and resignations. In particular, the resignation of the long-serving Inspector Sedgwick aroused controversy. Jones was accused in the conservative *Huddersfield Chronicle* of fabricating charges against Sedgwick in particular and of 'pettifogging interference of every kind' and also operating 'a system of espionage'. Beaumont had powerful friends among the Commissioners particularly in the Watch Committee, which called a special meeting in November 1857 to discuss 'the management of the police . . . and its efficiency or otherwise'.[41] Constables were called to air their grievances but the Watch Committee members were 'disgusted' at the 'paltry' complaints of the constables. Such was their faith in Beaumont that they awarded him a salary increase and he even was able to ride out a sex scandal which had seen him found guilty of indecently assaulting a local woman in the police office.[42]

However, it was a financial scandal that ended Beaumont's career. Allegations (initially dismissed as malicious by the Watch Committee) had been made for some time but in October 1859 Police Constable Morton presented the Watch Committee with detailed information that demonstrated 'not a single or isolated offence but a series of petty but fraudulent acts' by the Superintendent over several months.[43] Beaumont admitted that monies had been received but not properly accounted for. The Watch Committee had little option but to dismiss him, though some members still defended their man by claiming that it was a case of 'gross carelessness' but with 'no evidence of intentional fraud', an opinion never tested in court. The failure of the Beaumont era reflected badly on the Jones' faction on the Watch Committee. Not only had the wrong man been chosen – his professed ignorance of the whereabouts of the notorious Castlegate in Huddersfield was the final straw – but a style of micro-management had been endorsed that proved to be counterproductive.

The advent of new policing in Halifax, in contrast, was relatively unproblematic. In particular, the relationship between the Watch Committee and the first two

40 *Leeds Mercury*, 3 January 1856.

41 *HC*, 7 November 1857. The Watch Committee minutes are silent on the matter.

42 The handling of the case was extraordinary. The complainant, Mrs Poppleton, was called to attend alone a special meeting of the Watch Committee where doubts were cast on her honesty and further evidence heard that led the members to recommend not dismissing Beaumont. *HC*, 16 October 1858.

43 Watch Committee Minutes, KMT 18/2/3/14/1, 11, 8 October 1859.

Superintendents of police was much less fraught. This cannot be explained in terms of a more hands-off approach. As in Huddersfield, so in Halifax the Watch Committee exercised tight control over appointments, conditions and discipline of the men as well as determining the main focus of police activity. Three factors, all related to personality, may explain the difference. First, both Spiers and Pearson were experienced policemen, in the case of the latter having specific experience of policing Halifax itself. Second, particularly under Pearson, the Watch Committee not only knew the man but 'trusted him to do his job under their guidance but without undue interference in the practical operation.'[44] Third, the development of this 'partnership . . . [was] helped by the continuity of the chairmanship of the Watch Committee.'[45] There was none of the personality clash that disfigured the Thomas/Jones years in Huddersfield but neither was there conflict over the style of management to be exercised by the Watch Committee.

Similarly, in Middlesbrough the introduction of 'new policing', following incorporation in 1853 was relatively smooth. The Head Constable, William Hannan adopted a positive approach, quickly apprising the Watch Committee of the need for more and better equipped full-time men and auxiliary constables for Saturday duty as well as improved street lighting. He had more in common with the hands-on style of Thomas but two other factors worked in his favour. First, the long-serving chair of the Watch Committee, Isaac Wilson, was responsive to Hannan's requests for more men and better pay. Theirs became a positive and productive relationship. Second, more fortuitously and short term, the provisions of the County and Borough Police Act 1856 were such that the Middlesbrough police force could be expanded but local costs reduced as government money was made available.[46]

Difficulties in the 1860s: Superintendent Priday

The dismissal of Beaumont and the departure from the local political scene of Jones and several of his leading supporters created another opportunity to put the management of the town's policing on a more secure footing. Although Jones was no longer a Commissioner, there were men who shared his vision of a Metropolitan-style police force for the town. The experienced Samuel Priday, Inspector of the Manchester B Division, was appointed in November 1858 and, in an apparent change of thinking, the chairman of the Commissioners, J. Freeman (the advocate of economy some years before) stated explicitly that the new Superintendent 'shall have a complete command of the policemen.'[47]

One of Priday's first concerns was to restore police morale after the bitterness of the Beaumont era but more important was the establishment of a workable

44 Posner, 'New police in Halifax', p.91.

45 Ibid.

46 For a more detailed account see Taylor, *Policing the Victorian Town*, chap. 3.

47 *HC*, 6 November 1858.

relationship with the Watch Committee. The decision of the Commissioners, concerned by levels of expenditure, to reduce the size of the town force in the early 1860s created tension but worse was the ongoing determination of the Watch Committee to be involved in matters of day-to-day management. Unlike in Halifax, where the Watch Committee effectively handed responsibility for all but the most serious disciplinary matters to their police Superintendent, in Huddersfield the Watch Committee interfered in a way that undermined Priday's authority. Matters came to a head in the summer of 1862 when the Watch Committee passed over a complaint by Priday against the wayward detective Partridge.[48] Priday made clear to the Watch Committee that he was seeking employment elsewhere, only to be effectively forced to resign by the chair of the Watch Committee, who informed him that 'the next business . . . was to consider . . . serious charges against his conduct'.[49] Priday complained to the local press that his reasons for resigning had been misrepresented in the Watch Committee minutes and, after a critical editorial in the *Huddersfield Chronicle*, an ill-tempered exchange of letters between Priday and the Watch Committee chairman, William Keighley, were made public. Priday was adamant that he had been badly treated and undermined by the Commissioners. There was 'a want of that cordiality and support which are essential to the effective working and discipline of the force' but, more significantly, he found himself in a 'very subordinate and anomalous' position in which 'the restrictions placed upon the exercise of my judgment are calculated unduly and prejudicially to limit the independent authority and action which in the interest of public justice a Superintendent of Police should have at his control.'[50]

Keighley argued the claims were 'utterly unfounded' provoking a further letter from Priday in which he spelled out an alternative model of policing to that of the Watch Committee:

> The prerogative of control which I consider essential to the due discharge of the functions of a Superintendent of Police has been limited in my hands. The principle of responsibility which proper control involves has thus been entrenched [*sic*] [encroached?] upon and in fact frittered away.[51]

Keighley's response to this 'more offensive' letter provoked Priday to a third missive in which he added more substance to his claim regarding his position viz-a-viz the Watch Committee.[52] Reminding Keighley of the promise that had been

48 Partridge was the most prolific 'thief-taker' in the Huddersfield force but regularly 'bent the rules', to such an extent that he was rebuked by the town's magistrates on a number of occasions. He also had a drink problem which finally brought his police career to an end. Taylor, *Beershops*, chap. 4.

49 Watch Committee Minutes, KMT 18/2/3/14/1, 25 August 1862.

50 *HC*, 11 October 1862. Letter dated 25 August.

51 Ibid. Letter dated 30 August 1862.

52 Ibid. Letter dated 2 September 1862.

made on appointment, Priday claimed that his access to the Watch Committee had been restricted and his recommendations regularly ignored but, more importantly, his authority had been undermined in two ways. First, an unnamed 'principal officer of the Commissioners . . . [had taken] upon himself to countermand my orders, thereby neutralizing my position and making me a nonentity in the eyes of the force'. Second, and more significantly, his authority had been undermined by the Watch Committee itself. 'Officers who have been brought before the Committee for improper conduct' he wrote, 'have been lightly excused and acts of insubordination almost entirely passed over.'[53] The incident with Partridge was the final straw. Members of the Huddersfield Watch Committee not only believed in (and exercised) their right to be involved in disciplinary matters notwithstanding the mixed success of such an approach, but also they showed no willingness to acknowledge the expertise of their senior police officer. Worse, they failed to appreciate how their interventions in disciplinary matters undermined the authority of this man.

Difficulties in the 1860s: Superintendent Hannan

Next the Commissioners looked to the boom town of Middlesbrough and its Superintendent, William Hannan, notwithstanding the presence of the strong, experienced local candidate, William Townend. Hannan was the founding father of 'new policing' in Middlesbrough and, initially, he made a positive impact in Huddersfield. The day and night police were amalgamated, record-keeping improved and new regulations introduced. He persuaded the Commissioners to introduce a superannuation scheme and, most importantly, took a strong and successful line against the scandal of beerhouses and brothels (see Stevenson, Chapter 5 for another example of a Chief Constable conducting a moral crusade against the twin evils of alcohol and prostitution). The high-profile and successful prosecution of two husband and wife beerhouse keepers for procuring young girls and keeping them as prostitutes brought considerable praise. His monthly reports in the mid-1860s were increasingly positive and the evidence he presented of improved police efficiency led to some warming of relations with the Watch Committee.

Nonetheless, there were complaints of police brutality under Hannan and his own personal conduct attracted criticism. The first sign of major trouble came following the 1865 Huddersfield election won, unusually by the Tories. Election day itself had been something of a triumph as Hannan and Chief Constable Cobbe of the West Riding County Constabulary acted together but the aftermath proved problematic. Complaints of intimidation by the losing candidate (Leatham) led to a parliamentary enquiry to which Hannan was called to give evidence. His performance before a Parliamentary Select Committee gave rise to criticism by some Commissioners, who accused him of acting for 'party purposes', giving false

53 Ibid.

evidence of violence by the Leathamites. Joel Denham, in particular, argued that the matter reflected on 'the character of one of the servants of the town'.[54] Although Hannan survived, when he appeared before the Watch Committee he ruefully noted that 'not one Superintendent had left Huddersfield to go to a better situation but had left in disgrace'.[55] Matters worsened in 1867, following the addition of a 'godly leaven of the Puritan element' in the Improvement Commission.[56] Hannan found himself under attack but this time on matters of morality rather than politics.

The first issue was the question of drunkenness in the town. Hannan was a long-time critic of beerhouses and had played an active role in prosecuting the proprietors of beerhouse-brothels but in the late summer of 1867 matters flared up, following the appearance of a report that purported to show that Huddersfield had one of the worst rates of drunkenness in the country. Hannan was asked to provide the Watch Committee with an explanation. His report was highly critical of the 'places of low amusement where obscene song, filthy comedy and degrading conversation . . . excite the worst passions', bemoaned the 'non-existence of any public park, or any place of public recreation' and made a plea for 'better educated [working-class] people.'[57] He also drew attention to the marked differences of recording from force to force. Unlike many towns, in Huddersfield all known cases of drunkenness were recorded thereby creating an exaggerated impression of the scale of the problem. As Commissioner Clough conceded: 'Huddersfield was not such an abominable place as has been represented.'[58] This was not good enough for those who believed that a solution could be found through the enforcement of the existing law and the passing of new legislation. Denham, again, was scathing in his criticism of Hannan's failure to improve the moral condition of the town. Hannan, not least with his knowledge of the extent of the problem in Middlesbrough, felt, not unreasonably, that he was being unfairly criticized.

The second issue also had to do with popular recreation. This time in the form of Guy Fawkes' night celebrations. Earlier in the century Huddersfield had gained a reputation for being one of the most riotous towns on 5 November. Attempts to clear the Market Square in the late 1840s had led to the humiliation of the police, notably the newly appointed Superintending Constable, Thomas Heaton, but there had been relatively little trouble in the town for over a decade. Hannan's approach was to take a low-key approach, not least because arrests were likely 'to result in conflict with the police, if not in riot'.[59] In terms of 'policing by consent', this was

54 *HC*, 7 July 1866.

55 Ibid. See also *HC*, 1 September 1866. Denham, a long-time supporter of Leatham, was also one of 'those local political agitators of the "advanced" or extreme Radical section.' *HC*, 8 September 1866.

56 *HC*, 9 November 1867.

57 *HC*, 7 September 1867.

58 Ibid.

59 *HC*, 9 November 1867.

a sensible stance on the part of the police but it was insufficient for the recently elected 'Puritans' under a chairman, who was a man 'who advocates the making of drunkards sober by Act of Parliament and the force of authority'.[60] The new Watch Committee rejected Hannan's advice not to change existing policy. As well as instructing the police to take firm action, members of the Watch Committee also took to the streets of the town, particularly St. George's Square, to arrest revellers, letting off squibs. The outcome was predictable. Bonfires were lit, fireworks set off and the 'over-zeal and frog-swelling pride of "authority" . . . [made them] the butts of fun, frolic and scorn of the assembled crowd'.[61] The events proved to be the final straw for Hannan whose health was deteriorating. In late October he had intimated that he was considering resignation but when he did so the Watch Committee had recommended that the Commissioners should not accept it. There was but a brief delay. Rumours swept the town that Hannan was about to resign and take over the Bull and Mouth Inn and on 6 November the Watch Committee resolved that 'the conduct of many of the Police Force . . . was very inefficient and deserving of the censure of the Commissioners.'[62] That was the end of Hannan's career as Superintendent of Police; he resigned to become a publican. Given his track record, as much in Middlesbrough as in Huddersfield, it is difficult to escape the conclusion that, once again, a Huddersfield Police Superintendent had been the victim of a campaign concerned more with personality, personal morality and political persuasion than with the practicalities of policing.

By this time the days of the Improvement Commission were coming to an end and the next new broom, James Withers from Preston, was brought in with an eye to the needs of the new, enlarged borough. His success is part of another story. However, there was evidence of a new outlook on the part of the Commissioners. The Watch Committee resolved that Withers would 'have the full charge and superintendence of the whole Police Force'.[63] This time words were backed up by deeds. Withers introduced a new system of policing, closely based on that of the Metropolitan Police and set about tightening up discipline. There was no evidence of friction between the Superintendent of Police and his masters, among whom was the influential figure of the town's first mayor C. H. Jones, the same man who had fought literally and metaphorically with a former Superintendent of Police in the mid-1850s. Despite his success, Withers left in 1874 when his request for an increased salary was rejected. The question of the salaries of public servants had been a contentious issue in the recent local elections and Jones was unable to convince his colleagues of rewarding a man with a proven track record. Withers moved to nearby Bradford where he served as Chief Constable with distinction for 20 years.

60 Ibid.

61 Ibid.

62 Watch Committee Minutes, KMT 18/2/3/14/2, 6 November 1867.

63 Watch Committee Minutes, KMT 18/2/3//14/2, 26 December 1867.

Conclusion

Although more research remains to be done, the evidence of certain medium-sized boroughs in Yorkshire points to the complex and differing ways in which 'new policing' developed in the third quarter of the nineteenth century. There was *in broad terms* a consensus regarding the relationship between Watch Committees and Chief Constables but that was (and is), not the conclusion, rather it is the starting point for analysis. Operationalizing the master/servant relationship, encompassing as it did the consideration of more specific questions of policing models, managerial styles and personal qualities, was a matter of local negotiation, through trial and error.

Huddersfield under the Improvement Act 1848 enjoyed 'an unenviable notoriety in regard to its police and their irregularities'. Successive Watch Committees were singularly inept. They chose the wrong man in Beaumont but it was not obvious that Thomas, Priday and Hannan, for all their rough and ready ways, lacked the ability to head up a relatively small borough force. A significant part of the failure to establish a working relationship was due to the Watch Committees (or certain of its members) who had a particularly managerial and moral view of what a police Superintendent should be, which resulted in a counterproductive form of micro-management of the police. Huddersfield Watch Committees were not unique in seeing themselves as masters and the police as servants but their strictness and inflexibility set them apart from their counterparts in Halifax and Middlesbrough as well as Hull. Undoubtedly Hull's Chief Constable, MacManus was a very able officer, it is also the case that successive Watch Committees viewed the police as competent professionals, who could be entrusted with the operational responsibility to police Hull and whom they would support in time of criticism.[64] Similarly, the first generation of 'new policing' in Halifax and Middlesbrough was characterized by a positive relationship between the Watch Committees and the town police.[65] The relationship between any borough Chief Constable (or Superintendent of Police) and his Watch Committee was one that had to be negotiated. The Watch Committee might 'hire and fire' and determine local policy priorities but there was a degree of operational control that had to reside with senior police officers. Drawing the line was not easy but, as more forces came into being and time passed, Chief Constables carved out a limited but recognizable degree of autonomy. There could still be problems, not least the spectacular clash between the Head Constable of Liverpool and the local Watch Committee, but in most boroughs a *modus vivendi* was established relatively smoothly in the first decade or so of a new force being

64 See particularly the robust defence by the Watch Committee of the town's police following accusations of misconduct made regarding the 1857 Blanket Row fire. Walsh, Reform of urban policing, pp. 338ff.

65 There were problems in Halifax in the early 1870s. The emergence of an increasingly powerful temperance movement and accusations that the Superintendent of police was too close to the local drinks trade led to the dramatic resignation of Superintendent Pearson in 1872. Posner, 'Establishment and development', p. 107ff. Also see Stevenson, Chapter 5 below.

established. This was not the case in Huddersfield. There several Commissioners held strong views about the extent to which local politicians should be directly involved in the management of the police and the personal qualities that a senior officer should have. Unsurprisingly, the various disputes were often acrimonious and highly personal. Managerialism and morality proved to be an unproductive, at times toxic, mixture. Ironically, even though the 'economical' faction exercised considerable influence in the 1850s and 1860s questions of manning levels and salaries were not major sources of conflict. Ironically, it was after incorporation, at a time when an effective working relationship had been forged between the council's Watch Committee and its indisputably 'fit man to be at the head of the police' that 'economy', the refusal to agree to Withers' request for an increase in salary, undermined the long-sought for success. The problems in Huddersfield contrast with the successes in Halifax and Middlesbrough and highlight the importance of recognizing the complex ways in which 'new policing' developed in the third quarter of the nineteenth century.

2 'The best Chief Constable in the kingdom'?

Recruitment and retention problems in an early English county constabulary

David J. Cox

Introduction

This chapter details the career of Henry Goddard, the only former Bow Street 'Runner' to have been appointed as a Chief Constable following the passing of the County Police Act 1839 (CPA 1839), together with the obstacles and objections that he faced from both Tory magistrates and a Tory press opposed to the Whiggish introduction of a county constabulary.

Henry Goddard was born in Southwark in 1800.[1] After initially following his father's trade of fishmonger, on 7 April 1824 he enlisted as a constable in the Bow Street Foot Patrol.[2] He was highly successful in his new choice of career, transferring by the end of 1826 to Great Marlborough Street Police Office as a plain-clothes Principal Officer (better known as 'Runners', though such officers rarely if ever referred to themselves as such, considering the term to be derogatory).[3] This was a significant achievement, as many London Police Office constables took over a decade to gain similar promotion.[4] In 1834 he followed the Chief Magistrate of Great Marlborough Street, Sir Frederick Adair Roe, to Bow Street (which was considered *primus inter pares* with regard to the London Police Offices), serving as a Principal Officer until the demise of the Bow Street policing system in 1839, a decade after Peel's creation of the Metropolitan Police.[5]

Goddard enjoyed an enviable reputation during his time at Bow Street, being praised on several occasions by magistrates in the provincial towns to which he had been despatched to investigate serious crimes including murder and arson

1 D. J. Cox, 'Henry Goddard (1800–83), police officer', *Oxford Dictionary of National Biography*, available online at www.oxforddnb.com/index/97/101097947/.

2 For further details of the Bow Street system of policing, see D. J. Cox, *'A Certain Share of Low Cunning': A history of the Bow Street Runners, 1792–1839*, Abingdon: Routledge, 2012 and J. Beattie, *The First English Detectives: The Bow Street Runners and the Policing of London, 1750–1840*, Oxford University Press, 2012.

3 Great Marlborough Street was one of the seven public or police offices created by the Middlesex Justices Act 1792 and modelled on the Bow Street public office.

4 Cox, *'A Certain Share of Low Cunning'*, p.39.

5 Roe had been appointed as Chief Magistrate of Bow Street in 1832.

(see Morris, Chapter 9 regarding the role of officers from the metropolis assisting other forces). In his *Memoirs*, he records that in 1836, following his successful investigation of an arson case, a magistrate of Tunbridge Wells sent a letter to the Bow Street Chief Magistrate containing the following laudatory comment:

> Considering the very slight clue we had as to the offenders, the conduct, activity and intelligence of Mr Goddard cannot be too much commended. I can only express my own appreciation and that of the principal inhabitants of this place of his exertions in this matter.[6]

In August 1839, the Bow Street 'Runners' were disbanded and the nine men either retired or sought other employment. While the majority left the field of law enforcement, Goddard (who received an annual pension of £100 per year following his enforced severance from Bow Street) decided that he wanted to stay within his profession. He consequently applied for the vacant position as Chief Constable for the newly formed Northamptonshire Police.

The creation of Northamptonshire Police

The creation of borough and county constabularies was an ad hoc and long-drawn out process over several decades. Section 76 of the Municipal Corporations Act 1835 required 'each chartered borough council to form a Watch Committee and within three weeks of their first election, to employ a sufficient number of constables to preserve the peace within the borough'.[7] Cowley states that the chartered borough of Northampton 'jumped at the chance to put its management and subsequently its policing on a more modern footing [and] the very first meeting of the Northampton Borough Watch Committee took place on Friday 8 January 1836'.[8]

However, it was not until the passing of the CPA 1839 that English counties were encouraged to form 'modern' county forces (there was no apparent will to enforce the implementation of the Act). Stallion and Wall comment that 'the idea of police reform in the counties was initially rejected by most of the Quarter Sessions (QS) magistrates who were responsible for the administration of the counties' due to the perceived increased burden on the ratepayers'.[9] Between 1839

6 H. Goddard, *Memoirs of a Bow Street Runner*, in P. Pringle (ed.) London: Museum Press, p.130.

7 M. Stallion and D. S. Wall, *The British Police: Forces and Chief Officers 1829–2012*, 2nd edn, Bramshill: Police History Society, 2012, p.12.

8 R. Cowley, *Policing Northamptonshire 1836–2013*, Kettering: Peg and Whistle Books, 2013, p.14. I am much indebted to Richard Cowley's ground-breaking research into both the Borough and County forces of Northamptonshire for invaluable information on the creation and day-to-day running of both constabularies.

9 Stallion and Wall, *The British Police*, p.13. The author would also like to take this opportunity to thank the extremely helpful staff at both Northamptonshire Archives and Northampton Library for their unfailing courtesy and knowledge imparted to him during his research.

and 1856 (when the County and Borough Police Act 1856 forced all counties to create such police forces), less than half did so voluntarily.

Cowley notes that Northamptonshire was the twelfth such county to create a county constabulary under the provisions of the 1839 Act.[10] In February 1840 advertisements were placed in the local and regional press (including the *Manchester Guardian* and *The Times*) requiring all 'persons desirous of becoming candidates for the situation . . . to send their testimonials to the Clerk of the Peace on or before the 30th day of March inst.'[11] There were certain conditions as to the eligibility of prospective candidates: they had to be under 45 years of age, be in receipt of a medical testimonial as to their good health and sound constitution, not to have been insolvent debtors and, finally, if they had previously been employed 'in any branch of the public service civil or military' they must 'produce testimonials from the proper authorities in such service as to general conduct while so employed'.[12] The attempt to ensure financial probity among prospective Chief Constables was prophetic; during the latter years of the nineteenth century at least one Chief Constable, Captain William C. Sylvester (previously Chief Constable of Rochdale Borough Police) was discovered to have been an undisclosed bankrupt with over £1,100 of debt three years after becoming Chief Constable of Salford Borough Police in 1866, while another Chief Constable of Salford, Captain R. W. Torrens, was forced to resign under suspicion of receiving bribes in early 1880.[13]

The minutes of the January 1840 PCM record that:

> Notice is hereby given that the Justices of the Peace for the county of Northampton will at the General Quarter Sessions of the Peace for the said county to be held on the 9th day of April next proceed to the appointment of a Chief Constable under the provisions of the Act of Parliament 2nd and 3rd Victoria Cap: 93. The salary will be £250 a year.[14]

In the event, almost two dozen candidates applied for the Northamptonshire vacancy, perhaps drawn by the attractive salary of £250 per annum.[15] This compared favourably with many other similar positions; the General Inspector of the Worsted Inspectorate in Yorkshire was paid £210 per annum in the 1850s, while

10 Cowley, *Policing Northamptonshire*, p.114.

11 Northamptonshire Archives QS/CC/353/1 Police Committee of Justices (or Magistrates) Minutes [NA PCM], January 1840.

12 NA PCM, January 1840; *Yorkshire Post*, 10 January 1880.

13 *Morning Advertiser*, 12 May 1869 and *Manchester Courier and Lancashire General Advertiser*, 7 February 1880.

14 NA PCM, January 1840. Constables were to be paid £52 per year, while the Deputy Constable received a salary of £75 per year.

15 The current annual salary of the Chief Constable of Northamptonshire Police exceeds £135,000 see www.policeoracle.com/pay_and_conditions/police_pay_scales.html. Goddard's annual wage of £250 in 1840 is equivalent in historic standard of living terms to £20,360, but the equivalent in labour earnings is £198,800 see www.measuringworth.com/calculators/ppoweruk/ for details of how such figures are calculated.

Bradford borough Chief Constable was paid £235 per annum in 1867. There had been considerable opposition to this generous emolument, Sir Charles Knightley, Conservative MP for Northamptonshire South, being particularly vocal in this respect.[16]

Although 'Peel clearly intended that the Metropolitan Police would offer the provinces both a model of reformed policing and a reservoir of trained officers from which senior officers for borough and county forces might be drawn', the Metropolitan Police had only been operating for a decade; therefore relatively few officers had gained the opportunity to rise to senior levels within its ranks.[17] Numerous of the candidates for the post of Chief Constable of Northamptonshire proved to be from either a military or policing background, with eight being former Army personnel and three being serving police officers; this largely accorded with the views of the proposer of the adoption of the 1839 Act, Colonel William Cartwright (Tory MP for South Northamptonshire, and the father of William Henry Cartwright, future first Inspector of Constabulary), who was of the opinion that only men with either a police background or who had been non-commissioned military officers would be suitable for the post (although all of the ex-military personnel were in fact junior commissioned officers; for more discussion on previous military experience see Stevenson, Chapter 5).[18]

Goddard's appointment and relationship with the Police Committee

Northamptonshire magistrates proved unique in their choice of candidate in that they decided to employ a former senior police officer in the shape of Henry Goddard, who had previously served as a Principal Officer with Bow Street Police Office.[19] He was the only former Bow Street Principal Officer to become a Chief Constable, though another, Joseph Shackell, joined the newly formed Metropolitan Police as an Inspector, with the promise of further rapid promotion.[20] A former member of the less senior Bow Street Patrol, Nicholas Pearce, became a Superintendent in the Metropolitan Police.[21]

16 *Northampton Mercury*, 11 April 1840.

17 D. Eastwood, *Government and Community in the English Provinces, 1700–1870*, Basingstoke: Macmillan, 1997, p.142.

18 *Northampton Mercury*, 11 April 1840. For a full list of candidates, see Cowley, *Policing Northamptonshire*, p.123.

19 It is extremely difficult to provide an exact equation of the rank of a Bow Street Principal Officer with that of a contemporary police officer, but elsewhere the author has argued that they could be regarded as equivalent to a Detective Superintendent; they were highly experienced and professional officers who had on average served at least a dozen years in the lower ranks see Cox, 'A certain share of low cunning', p.40.

20 TNA HO 60/3 Police Court Entry book 1836–39, letter dated 30 September 1839. This promise was not honoured; Shackell was still an Inspector in 1847; see OBP t18470405–991.

21 M. Fido and K. Skinner, *The Official Encyclopedia of Scotland Yard*, London: Virgin Books, 1999, p.67.

Goddard provided glowing testimonials from numerous magistrates from other counties and he was duly appointed as Chief Constable of Northamptonshire, beginning his duties on 25 April 1840. The Northamptonshire magistrates appear to have believed that a man with such a long and successful career at both Great Marlborough Street and Bow Street Police Offices was eminently suitable for the new position. As Goddard's biographer Pringle stated:

> The appointment is significant. It shows that the Bow Street Runners were not regarded with the suspicion and contempt they have had ever since Dickens debunked them in *Household Words*. If they had all been such rogues as Sir John Moylan has suggested, Northamptonshire would hardly have taken Goddard on. For the salary of £250 a year they could surely have got an experienced officer of the Metropolitan Police, whose rates of pay were relatively low.[22]

Goddard was no stranger to Northamptonshire, having visited the county on several occasions during his employment at Bow Street. He had successfully captured a deer-poaching gang in 1837, and revisited the county the following year to investigate the brutal murder of Elizabeth Longfoot at Easton on the Hill.[23] The 1841 census shows Goddard as living at Albion Place, Northampton with four of his children (the youngest of whom, Matilda, had been baptized in St Giles Church, Northampton on 25 November 1840). He clearly wasted no time in becoming involved in local society; described in masonic records as a 'Gentleman', he was initiated into the Freemasons on 18 March 1841, at Pomfret Lodge, Northampton.[24]

Emsley states that 'the forces established under the 1839 Act were not based on any one simple model drawn from the London experience', and it is clear that the Northamptonshire Police Committee did not simply seek to recreate the Metropolitan Police in a provincial setting.[25] (At least in the minds of the 'masters'), as Emsley has pointed out,

> the relationship between policemen and the municipal authorities was . . . different. The Metropolitan Police were directly responsible to the Home

22 Goddard, *Memoirs*, p.194. Sir John Fitzgerald Moylan was Receiver of the Metropolitan Police 1919–42, and was very critical of the Bow Street system – see J. Moylan, *The Police of Britain*, London: Longmans, Green & Co., 1948. Recent research into the Bow Street Principal Officers by Cox and Beattie has challenged the veracity of both Dickens' and Moylan's low opinion of this body of men; see Cox, '*A Certain Share of Low Cunning*' and Beattie, *The First English Detectives*.

23 Goddard, *Memoirs*, pp.137–140. The two men accused of Elizabeth's murder were subsequently acquitted, 'to the surprise and astonishment of the Judge and everyone in court', according to Goddard (*Memoirs*, p.146).

24 *England, United Grand Lodge of England Freemason Membership Registers, 1751–1921*, available at Ancestry.co.uk.

25 C. Emsley, 'Detection and Prevention: the old English police and the new 1750–1900', *Historical Social Research/Historische Sozialforschung*, 1986, no.37, 69–88, p.77.

> Secretary ... [whereas] municipal governments, through their watch committees, kept firm control of their policemen, and the relationship was very much that of master and servant'. [26]

A sub-committee, rather grandly entitling itself the Police Committee of Justice (PCJ), was duly formed (with a quorum of three members) and tasked with framing 'regulations for the management and establishment of the police force of the County', though in law their powers were effectively limited by the CPA 1839 to the appointment and dismissal of the Chief Constable; they had no official status with regards to the day-to-day running of the constabulary.[27] All other powers were at least theoretically placed in the hands of the Chief Constable, although it is clear from both QS minute books and the PCJ Minutes that the PCJ considered that their role was greater than that proscribed by the Act; they were the ultimate financiers of the venture and as such were determined from the start to exert financial restraint over their new Chief Constable. Surviving contemporary records detail the minutiae of such dealings; one of the PCJ's first edicts was to empower Goddard with the procurement of 43 staves, lanterns, rattles, red and white armlets and handcuff pouches, together with two leg-irons. Cowley states that similar armlets were sported by the Borough police (in that instance blue and white in colour) in order to indicate that the officer wearing the device was on duty; if an armlet was not present, the respective officer was off duty although still in his uniform.[28] He also states that 'unlike the Borough Police, the County Constabulary never adopted the armlet for some reason', so it is possible that the 43 armlets procured for the county force were never actually utilized.[29] The PCJ also ensured that they saw any bills and other charges to the county purse by the respective Superintendents and constables on a regular basis by insisting that such bills were submitted regularly to them and ultimately to the Court of QS for approval.[30]

Organization of the County Constabulary

Goddard's formation of the force was described in considerable detail in the *Northampton Herald*, (*Herald*) which reproduced Goddard's first quarterly report as Chief Constable: there were to be seven divisions, each with one Superintendent and five constables, with Goddard stating 'I have great satisfaction in stating that I have received all the support and assistance I could have hoped.'[31] In the same

26 Ibid. p.76.

27 NA PCM, January 1840 and section 6 CPA 1839. The appointment of Chief Constables also had to receive the approval of the Secretary of State.

28 Cowley, *Policing Northamptonshire*, p.40 and see p.38 for a photograph of a Borough constable wearing his armlet.

29 Ibid.

30 NA PCM, April 1841.

31 *Northampton Herald*, 11 July 1840.

report, Goddard laid out the rules of the new constabulary; the main ones are reproduced below:

- Each Superintendent and Constable was to 'devote his whole time to the service of the Police', and were to 'conform to the several regulations which may be made from time to time, by the Magistrates assembled at Petty Sessions'.
- The Constables were to be paid fortnightly by their respective Superintendent from a cheque sent by Goddard.
- Each Superintendent was also to be provided with an occurrence book to be produced at request of Goddard or a magistrate.
- One of the main roles of the new force was to maintain public order, and consequently, each Superintendent and Constable was to 'make themselves acquainted with the different houses of resort of bad character, and pay particular attention to all the public-houses, beer-houses, and public lodging-houses in their district, and report the time each is closed, and how such houses are generally conducted'.
- None of the Superintendents or Constables were to 'on any account, take up their permanent abode at any public house or beer-house'.
- An amendment to the original rules (dated 15 June 1840) stated that Constables were to be on duty from 5–10am and then patrol from 7pm until 'the beer-houses are closed, or longer if necessary, and report to the Superintendent any beer-house conducted in a disorderly manner, or found open after the hours regulated by the magistrates'.
- They were also to pay particular attention to, and remove 'all vagrants encamping or pitching tents, wherever found'.[32]

Rule 15 of the new Force was particularly interesting in that it stated that 'the Superintendents and Constables are on all occasions to cooperate with the Parish Constables, and, as far as they can, ascertain from them the state of crime in their districts'. Perhaps unsurprisingly, this somewhat idealized view of cooperation between the unpaid Parish Constabulary and the newly constituted county force was not realized. Northamptonshire was a relatively large county in terms of geography; it possessed nineteen hundreds (subdivided into 286 parishes) and at the time of the creation of the County Constabulary, each of these hundreds possessed two Chief Constables, together with a respective complement of parish constables.[33] A document printed in 1838 detailed some of the main duties of the parish constables:

> The most essential part of your duty is a general Superintendence over the Peace and good Order of your District: your powers for this Purpose are great and extensive and your Duty compulsory. . . . On reasonable suspicion you are to

32 Ibid.
33 NA PCM, January 1840.

> arrest Felons and Rogues of all kinds and carry them before a Magistrate. It is your Duty to keep a watchful Eye over Strangers of suspicious Appearance, who continue strolling about within your District; if such are seen out of their Lodgings at unseasonable Hours in the Night, and refuse to give an Account of themselves, you may detain them in Custody till the next Morning and carry them before a Magistrate. By your Attention in this particular, House-breaking, Felonies, and many other Crimes may be prevented.[34]

Perceived problems with the County Constabulary

These duties of parish constables were obviously similar to those expected of the new County Constabulary (although the parish constabulary was unpaid and severely limited in its ex-parochial power), and thereby illustrate one of the main reasons for the perceived lack of faith in the new force; ratepayers might reasonably suggest that the county already possessed a preventive police force and that the imposition of a county-wide force made up of less than 50 men was not good value for money. Cowley states that

> the county at the time had a population of just over 150,000 in an area of 546,277 acres with 43 Constables in the new force.[35] Therefore each Constable had about 3,500 people to look after in an area of . . . just over 20 square miles.[36]

A comparison of ratios of officers to population for all the county forces that were fully established by the end of 1840 is given below in Table 2.1.[37]

The ratio of one officer for every 4,633 inhabitants demonstrates that the Northamptonshire county force was understaffed in comparison to most other forces created as a result of the CPA 1839. To make matters worse, the force was not evenly distributed throughout the county; the *Herald*, 31 October 1840 carried a statement from Reverend Wetherall, who claimed in a QS meeting that Kettering (one of the largest divisions of the county) had a ratio of one county constable for every 4,728 inhabitants, while the three smallest divisions of the

34 NA QS/CC/184.

35 This varies from ONS figures see *ONS Northamptonshire Area Monitor*, available at www.ons.gov.uk/ons/.../northamptonshire/northamptonshire-area-monitor.pdf (which were taken from the 1841 census – these give a population of 199,228 and a total acreage of 646,810 acres). The discrepancy is due to the fact that the ONS statistics also include the Soke of Peterborough.

36 Cowley, Policing Northamptonshire, p.137.

37 For both Table 2.1 and Table 2.2, initial complements of county police forces are abstracted from Stallion and Wall, *The British Police* (except for Northamptonshire, where Stallion and Wall incorrectly record an initial complement of 29 officers). County populations and acreages taken from respective *ONS Area Monitor* pdfs available at www.ons.gov.uk. Several other counties partially created new forces, for example South Staffordshire created a police force in 1840, but the remainder of the county did not follow suit until 1842.

Table 2.1 County forces created in 1839/40 showing ratio of officers to population

County force created 1839/40	*Ratio of officers to inhabitants (1:)*
Wiltshire	1,287
Gloucestershire	1,726
Hertfordshire	2,214
Bedfordshire	2,297
Essex	2,974
Lancashire	3,334
Hampshire	3,349
Norfolk	3,685
Northamptonshire	4,633
Durham	4,913
Worcestershire	5,693
Leicestershire	8,365
Nottinghamshire	9,825
Shropshire	10,393

county enjoyed a ratio of 1: 2,731. The Northamptonshire County force was also understaffed in comparison to Northampton Borough force (which enjoyed a ratio of one officer to c.850 inhabitants by the time of the 1841 census).[38] This ratio compares broadly with other borough forces: for example, Bradford Borough police had an average ratio of one officer to 891 inhabitants in the decade from 1857 while Salford Borough police had a ratio of one officer to 929 inhabitants over the same period.[39]

With regard to the overall perception of the policing situation in Northampton and its county, it is interesting to note that the *Herald*, 26 December 1840 carried a notice for the forthcoming annual general meeting of the Northampton Association for Apprehending and Prosecuting Felons, which listed over 150 members (somewhat atypically including ten women) who each paid an annual subscription of five shillings, suggesting that a considerable number of inhabitants of the town or county were not satisfied with the existing policing arrangements. Such associations (the first recorded example of which was established in 1693 in Stoke on Trent) were extremely popular in the late eighteenth and early nineteenth century; Eastwood calling them 'the most significant components in a programme to deter crime in later Hanoverian England without abandoning traditional forms of communal policing', and research has shown that several associations were indeed active in prosecuting minor and occasionally more

38 Force complement taken from Cowley, *Policing Northamptonshire*, p.23. Population figure for Northampton Borough (21,242) taken from www.visionofbritain.org.uk/census/SRC_P/3/GB1841 ABS_1.

39 See www.familyhistorynorthants.co.uk/victorian%20northampton.html *for 1851* Northampton population figure 1851; Bradford and Salford Borough Police figures extrapolated from respective annual *Judicial Statistics*.

serious crimes.[40] Until the latter half of the nineteenth century the police were rarely responsible for the prosecution of suspected offenders; this was normally a matter left to the conscience (and purse) of the victim or his/her family/friends; such associations therefore helped defray the often considerable cost of any prosecution and also occasionally directly employed law enforcement officials.[41]The situation with regard to the County force was ameliorated slightly by an increase of seven officers in October 1840 (see below for the reasons given for this increase), but still resulted in a ratio of one officer for every 3,985 inhabitants.[42]

A comparison of ratios of officers to acreage for all the county forces that were established by the end of 1840 is given in Table 2.2 below. This shows that, as Cowley suggests, Northamptonshire County force was also undermanned in terms of the area that each officer had to cover as part of his duties. During the July 1842 QS it was minuted that Goddard was from now on required to state in his quarterly report the number of times he had visited each division in the interim period.[43]

Table 2.2 County forces created in 1839/40 showing ratio of officers to acreage

County force created 1839/40	*Ratio of officers to acreage (1:)*
Lancashire	2,235
Nottinghamshire	3,079
Gloucestershire	3,162
Wiltshire	4,319
Hertfordshire	5,369
Bedfordshire	6,333
Essex	8,440
Hampshire	9,609
Norfolk	9,717
Durham	10,296
Worcestershire	11,212
Northamptonshire	15,042
Leicestershire	20,454
Shropshire	37,581

40 Eastwood, *Government and Community in the English Provinces 1700–1870*, p.140. For details of the type and number of crimes prosecuted by one society, see J. Sutton, 'The Staffordshire Society for the Apprehension of Felons', *Staffordshire Studies*, 2002, vol.14, p.51. For an overview of the development of such societies, see D. Philips, 'Good men to associate and bad men to conspire: Associations for the prosecution of felons in England 1760–1860', in D. Hay and F. Snyder (eds) *Policy and Prosecution in Britain, 1750–1850*, Oxford: Clarendon Press, 1989, pp.113–70.

41 For details of a short-lived private police force employed in the 1810s by the Dorsey Association for the prosecution of felons, see B. Jerrard, 'Early Policing in Gloucestershire', *Transactions of the Bristol and Gloucestershire Archaeological Society for 1992*, 1993, vol.C, 221–40, 223. At least one Northamptonshire Association has been recently revived, albeit in a modern guise, see www.northantstelegraph.co.uk/news/keeping-an-eye-on-the-village-felons-1–728596 for details of the reconstitution of the Cranford Association in 2008.

42 *Northampton Herald*, 31 October 1840.

43 NA PCM, July 1842.

The County Constabulary was in a state of flux in the months following its creation; in October 1840 the horses of the seven mounted constables were sold and all constables were in future to patrol on foot.[44] This appears to have been a combination of a poor choice of mounts and a lack of forethought; one of the horses died shortly after its purchase, and two more were quickly deemed unfit for police service, while the mounted constables were soon considered to be an unnecessary expense.[45] The loss of mounted constables was to be compensated by the employment of seven additional constables, as Goddard had requested an increase to the force due to the fact that 'the local constables objected to patrol the districts with the police, and it was not safe for the policemen to patrol singly', thus exemplifying the hostility between the two types of law enforcement officers.[46]

Henry Sawbridge, a prominent Tory landowner and county magistrate (who had originally opposed the creation of the county force, but who seems to have been largely won over by it a decade later – see below), wrote a letter to the *Herald* on 7 May 1842 which was published a week later, suggesting that the way forward was for much closer cooperation between the professional county force and the established parish constables. He stated that:

> No-one would be satisfied to fall back upon the old way of proceeding unaltered. The parish constable, usually a person engaged in business, could seldom give an undivided attention to his official duties; his own affairs could not be neglected without serious detriment. Such an officer is not sufficient in the existing state of society, which requires active policemen, skilled from practice in the detection of crime and the apprehension of offenders . . . [but] it must be a force little short of an army which could patrol and watch the County of Northampton.[47]

His letter went on to suggest that the parish constable be regarded as the main source of information regarding the perpetration of an offence and that the County constable should subsequently act upon such information. He recommended the reorganization of the County force into 20 stations of two men, centrally stationed to ensure that no station was more than three-and-a-half miles 'from the most distant village', and that these officers should liaise regularly with parish constables, who should be made to keep entries of any reported crimes in an occurrence book.

Sawbridge's recommendations were not adopted by either Goddard or the PCJ, and the two constabularies appear to have continued in a state of mutual distrust, but it is interesting that Sawbridge's suggestions included one in which:

> the peculiar dress of the policeman should be laid aside; it impedes the performance of his duty; it is also objectionable, because it favours the notion

44 *Northampton Herald*, 31 October 1840.
45 NA PCM, July 1840.
46 *Northampton Herald*, 11 July 1840.
47 Cowley, *Policing Northamptonshire*, p.121.

> that policemen are to be distinguished from other respectable individuals; and that the responsibility of protecting the country is to be abandoned to them.[48]

This was an interesting proposition made at a time when very few police forces in Britain contained any officers who operated in plain clothes. The Bow Street Runners, the most famous (and earliest) of the plain-clothes detectives, had been disbanded in 1839, and while at least one Scottish police force (Glasgow, see Smale, Chapter 3) had employed a handful of plain-clothes officers from 1817, this was very much the exception to the rule.[49] At the time of Sawbridge's letter, even the Metropolitan Police was without a detective contingent, though following the farrago over the arrest of Daniel Good, who committed a brutal murder in April 1842 and whose subsequent escape had made a mockery of the Metropolitan Police's detective capabilities, a Detective Department was created shortly after his eventual capture and execution in late-May 1842.

Similarly, in 1848 several other magistrates called for the creation of a detective contingent within Northampton County Constabulary:

> To the Clerk of the Peace of the County of Northamptonshire
>
> Sir, Being of the opinion that it is desirable that the County Police force should be increased by the addition of four Constables, and who may act within any of the Divisions of the County, as necessity may require, as a detective force, we do hereby require you to give Notice that we shall . . . move the Court that an addition of four such Constables be made. Dated this fifth day of January 1848.[50]

There is no evidence that Goddard was part of this request, or even that he had prior knowledge of it; indeed, he appears to have made no attempt to introduce a detective element to the County Constabulary throughout his tenure. Considering his background as a senior Bow Street detective, this at first sight seems surprising, but it is clear from his *Memoirs* that old habits die hard; he was perfectly happy to continue his own detective work while employed as Chief Constable, and clearly did not feel the need to employ subordinates on such work, considering that his experience alone was sufficient. During his employment at Bow Street, Goddard would have worked on his own for the vast majority of cases that he investigated; previous research suggests that for provincial cases, the Runners worked independently on over three-quarters of their provincial investigations.[51] Even when

48 *Northampton Herald*, 7 May 1842.

49 D. Barrie, *Police in the Age of Improvement: Police development and the civic tradition in Scotland, 1775–1865*, Cullompton: Willan, 2008, p.154, and for further details also see A. Dinsmor, 'Glasgow police pioneers', *Journal of the Police History Society*, 2000, no.15. 9–11.

50 NA PCM, January 1848.

51 See Cox, '*A Certain Share of Low Cunning*' for further details of the provincial activities and working methods of the Principal Officers.

they did cooperate in investigations, they usually worked with another officer of equal rank (although there are few documented cases where less senior Bow Street personnel were also employed, perhaps to provide them with practical experience of how the Principal Officer carried out his work).

During his first year in office at Northampton, Goddard confirmed his detective capabilities by investigating and solving a murder on his own new doorstep. The *Morning Post*, 15 October 1840, gave details of a poaching attempt ending in the murder of one of the Marquis of Northampton's gamekeepers earlier that month, and stated that 'the promptness of Chief Constable Goddard and his men to apprehend the perpetrators of this horrid deed reflects great credit upon them'. His detective skills were again called upon in early 1841, after a bank clerk named John Haslock absconded from Whitworth's Bank, Northampton with 800 sovereigns.[52] Goddard immediately set out in pursuit, obtaining a passport and travelling to France, where after diligent detective work, he located Haslock in Tours. Goddard was, however, frustrated in his attempt to bring Haslock to justice in England; the French authorities arrested the suspect for travelling under a false name, and he was subsequently fined fifteen francs and discharged. The *Leicester Chronicle*, 13 February 1841, reported that

> the most interesting feature in the affair was the refusal of the French authorities to surrender him to an English police officer, 'as the English government could never be prevailed upon to deliver up a refugee from France under similar circumstances'.

Although Goddard failed in his attempt to return Haslock to face trial in England, he did manage to recover almost £500 from the suspect and return it to its rightful owners.

The PCJ also appear to have been content initially to allow Goddard a certain amount of leeway to pursue ongoing investigations instigated at Bow Street during the first year of his new post; he is recorded as giving evidence at several trials in both 1840 and 1841,for example, both the *Morning Post*, 29 June 1840, and his *Memoirs* contain details of Goddard appearing as a witness in a criminal conspiracy case that took him to Rouen and Paris while ostensibly also fulfilling his new role as Northamptonshire's Chief Constable.[53] In June 1842 he requested (and received) a leave of absence for ten days, presumably to investigate another non-county case.[54]

52 For Goddard's own account of this investigation, see Goddard, *Memoirs*, pp.189–94. Goddard mistakenly gives the suspect's first name as Thomas.

53 The criminal conspiracy case rumbled on until mid-1841.

54 NA PCM, June 1842.

Opposition to Goddard and the County Constabulary

The Haslock case serves to highlight two of the main problems that he faced while Chief Constable of Northamptonshire: Goddard's seeming inability to master the more mundane administrative aspects of the role of Chief Constable of what was a fundamentally preventive police force and the immovable and continued opposition of one of the most vociferous members of the Northamptonshire county magistracy, Reverend Francis Litchfield (1792–1876).[55] It is perhaps significant that Goddard chose largely to gloss over his time as Chief Constable of Northamptonshire; he only mentions one somewhat pathetic case – that of the deranged Sir Francis Mackenzie, who was found suffering from delusions in Northampton and who was eventually returned to the care of his brother by Goddard (who stated that 'a handsome present' was given to him by Sir Francis' brother); although employed by the local Police Committee, he clearly felt no qualms about accepting private recompense. In this regard, Goddard was not acting illegally; as Jennifer Hart states, the Municipal Corporations Act 1835 did not 'make it illegal for the police to receive fees or gratuities from private individuals or the public purse for services rendered or anticipated', although the Northamptonshire PCJ prohibited the receipt of rewards by County constables from March 1841.[56]

Regarding the latter problem, Reverend Litchfield was an ardent advocate of Poor Law reform and a resolutely High Church Tory, and therefore immovably opposed to the Whig-backed County Constabulary from the moment of its inception. His opposition to the County Constabulary was twofold: it cost the ratepayers too much for too little return, and although he conceded in a later missive that 'the police was a very good detective force', he argued that its preventive role would have been better served by a paid parochial constabulary.[57]

Despite his efforts to ameliorate the burden of the poor of his parish in Farthinghoe, where he initiated such enterprises as the Farthinghoe Provident Clothing Society, which aimed to 'convince the Poor that good conduct is in all respects their best policy' through the instigation of a subscription society to provide savings for necessary clothing, Reverend Litchfield does not appear to have gone out of his way to make friends; for example any member of the

55 For further details of Litchfield's life, see R. L. Greenall, 'Parson as a man of affairs: the Rev. Francis Litchfield of Farthinghoe, (1792–1876)', *Northamptonshire Past and Present*, 1990–91, vol.viii:2, 134–45. Despite professing himself to be of 'limited pecuniary means', Reverend Litchfield left over £15,000 in his will, a not inconsiderable amount in 1876 see *England and Wales, National Probate Calendar (Index of Wills and Administrations), 1858–1966, 1973–1995*, available at www.ancestry.co.uk. Goddard in comparison left £1,067 following his death in 1883.

56 J. Hart, 'Reform of the Borough Police 1835–1856', *English Historical Review*, 1955, vol.70, 411–422, p.419; and NA PCM, 19 March 1841. Discretionary rewards for exceptional service continue to this day (although funded by the public purse rather than private individuals); Section 31 Police Act 1996 states that: 'A police authority may, on the recommendation of the chief officer of police, grant out of the police fund to members of the police force maintained by that authority rewards for exceptional diligence or other especially meritorious conduct'.

57 *Northampton Mercury*, 12 April 1856.

Society whose husband or wife came before the magistrates for any misdemeanour or felony was to be expelled from the Society and his or her savings forfeit to the Society.[58] In her research into early-nineteenth-century Northamptonshire charitable provision Lewis states that:

> In a report to the Brackley Union, the Assistant Poor Law Commissioner, Richard Earle made the following observation: 'Mr Litchfield, whose insolent, energetic temperament led him to enforce in his parish sound principles of management in a mode little calculated to create good will, became if I am to believe the evidence of his Brother Magistrates, or indeed his own testimony, the object of detestation to all classes'.[59]

He was an ardent author of improving pamphlets and letters to both local newspapers and periodicals, and seems to have found something of a kindred spirit in the form of the Editor of the *Herald*, which never failed to support his views in print.

Not surprisingly, Reverend Litchfield remained a proponent of the traditional parish constabulary system (which continued throughout Goddard's tenure as Chief Constable) to the end; the *Northampton Mercury* (*Mercury*) 12 April 1856 (some seven years after Goddard had tended his resignation) reported that he stated:

> There was a new Police Bill before Parliament, and if they could get a clause inserted into it for a paid parochial constabulary, they might effect much good. . . . The parochial constabulary was one of the oldest institutions in the country, and it might now in his opinion be made one of the most useful.

Despite his constant cavilling, Reverend Litchfield proved to be in the minority regarding his views on Goddard's initial success as Chief Constable. Goddard's salary was increased from £250 to £325 in 1842, to £342 10s in 1846, and to £360 by June 1847.[60] It remained at £360 per year until his resignation in 1840, though there had been calls for it to be reduced, as it was considered over-generous by some members of the Police Committee.[61] There were sporadic public outbreaks of discontent with the new police force; the *Mercury* of 19 February 1842 carried a report of protests against Robert Peel, with an attempt being made to burn his effigy, during which Goddard was struck on the head by a stone.

58 F. Litchfield, Three years' results of the Farthinghoe clothing society, with a few remarks on the policy of encouraging provident habits among the working classes, Northampton: Freeman, 1832, p.4.

59 B. Lewis, Charitable Provision for the Rural Poor: A case study of policies and attitudes in Northamptonshire in the first half of the nineteenth century, unpublished PhD thesis, Leicester University, 2003.

60 *Northampton Mercury*, 22 October 1842, 14 February 1846 and 12 June 1847.

61 *Northampton Mercury*, 1 December 1849.

Reverend Litchfield's opposition to the new force was reflected and fully supported by the bitter Tory rival to the Whiggish *Mercury* – the *Herald*. An editorial in the *Herald* 31 October 1840 argued that the parish constabulary system, while admittedly imperfect was not necessarily bad. It argued that it was the magistrates rather than the system itself who were accountable for most deficiencies and reprinted part of a polemic published by a Leicestershire magistrate, who opined:

> To suppose that England can supply no middle class of sufficient intelligence, public spirit, and activity, to discharge the duties of a constable in a district of ordinary peacefulness, is an imputation disgraceful to the national character, and entirely inconsistent with any nation of political liberty.[62]

While the PCJ was happy to record by September 1840 that: 'so far as they have been able to make observation from the time the system has been in progress, they consider it to have worked beneficially as well in checking crime as in the speedy detection and apprehension of offenders', Goddard faced considerable opposition from the Tory-supporting *Herald* throughout his tenure as Chief Constable[63] The rivalry between the *Herald* and the *Mercury* often reached vituperative levels; for example an editorial in the *Herald* attacked the *Mercury* for being: 'the property of a magistrate and edited by his own pen. We wish the advocate of an expensive and inefficient Police all possible joy of such a supporter. He is worthy of the cause and the cause of him'. In the simplicity of our hearts we had supposed that the Police question, which involves the high question of morality as well as property, might have been treated by the *Mercury* proprietor without party malice or personal abuse.[64]

A week later, the *Herald* reported that a series of petitions against the continuance of the new police force had been received by the Northamptonshire QS magistrates.[65] This constituted one of the most serious attacks on Goddard's new force; the newspaper reported that there was a total of 97 petitions in favour of abolition of the County Constabulary and only three in favour of its continuance. Colonel Cartwright (a staunch supporter of the County Constabulary) reminded the magistrates that 'it should be remembered that "petition, petition, petition" had been repeatedly urged upon the rate-payers', but the Reverend Litchfield (who was probably the chief instigator of the barrage of petitions) replied that the use of such petitions was 'a very legitimate, constitutional and respectful mode of proceeding, and one to which the ratepayers of the county have very properly resorted'. He went on to state that:

62 'Observations of a Leicestershire magistrate', *Northampton Herald*, 31 October 1840.

63 NA PCM, 5 September 1840.

64 *Northampton Herald*, 9 April 1842.

65 *Northampton Herald*, 16 April 1842. Such petitions were not unique to Northamptonshire – as Clive Emsley remarks, there was quite widespread opposition to the new constabularies in favour of the new Parish Constables Act 1842 (see Emsley, *The English Police*, pp. 45–8).

> the result of his enquiries and reflections was, that the present police force, after a fair experiment, was inefficient, that the benefits derived from it were not commensurate with the cost, that it was not adapted to the wants and circumstances of the county and that a force differing in many respects from the one now existing was required.

He further stated that the force 'cost around £4,500 annually to maintain', arguing that it was simply cost ineffective stating that 'it could no longer be maintained that the police force was properly efficient'. Despite Reverend Litchfield's best efforts, the petitions were largely ignored by the majority of magistrates and the County Constabulary survived, although further petitions against its continuance were received in the following year (and in 1849), and disgruntled ratepayers continued to moan about the cost of the force throughout Goddard's tenure.

Throughout the remainder of Goddard's time as Chief Constable, there was intermittent debate concerning the future of the County Constabulary; the *Herald* continued its implacable opposition to both the continued existence of the County force in general, and (in more veiled terms) to Goddard's leadership in particular; his lack of social standing appears to have been a particular reason for the *Herald's* disdain. Matters concerning the probity of his officers did not go well for Goddard; in 1848 a Superintendent was discharged for improper financial conduct, while another Superintendent was reduced to the ranks for misconduct and a constable in Floore district forced to resign after 'a female of loose character had been seen to go into his house'.[66]

Resignation from post

In early 1849 Goddard suddenly and surprisingly announced his intention of resigning his post due to an 'internal injury' received during his duties. The *Herald* immediately seized upon this announcement with barely unconcealed delight. An editorial in the *Herald* strongly implies that Goddard had never been equal to the task, stating that:

> We feel ourselves justified in urging either that the Police force be abandoned at the next QS, as a failure, or that proper steps be taken to render it a very different body of constabulary, whether preventive or detective, from what it has hitherto been. We will take the liberty, also, of expressing our firm conviction that, unless some applicant of a different class should present himself, with proofs of most complete success as a Chief Constable in another county, no person but one placed far above the rank of Policemen by education and society, and that has enjoyed intercourse with gentlemen, should now be elected. Indeed, we will go further and say that, with so large a space as a county to divide and provide for, and with the absolute necessity that exists for methodical

66 *Northampton Herald*, 6 January 1849.

> arrangements, exact discipline and moral conduct, hardly any person is likely to be qualified for such an appointment except someone accustomed to military habits and command, and with that high sense of honour and those gentlemanly feelings which would lead him to resign his office, should he at any time perceive himself to have failed in the duties undertaken.[67]

Goddard's 'internal injury'; the explicit reason for his resignation, also came in for considerable scrutiny from the Tory press, with one purveyor of doggerel verse printed in the *Herald* suggesting that Goddard's hand had in fact been forced by the magistrates:

> But should men desire a useless Police
> No longer to live, and its cost to cease,
> Get someone to urge an improper increase;
> And, let such a step ignite a fire
> Of resistance that's mix'd with indignant ire,
> Persuade your Chief, as a ruse to retire.[68]

At the next QS (April 1849) Goddard received a gratuity of £150 for his injury; he claimed this was to support his family while he looked for new employment, and appears to have been paid with somewhat bad grace, perhaps due to the short notice that he had given of his intention to resign, which had caused the magistrates a considerable amount of problems and inconvenience. Reverend Litchfield stated flatly that 'he saw no proof that Mr Goddard had been injured in the service. The surgeon's certificate was not at all satisfactory to him'.[69]

At the same time as Goddard's resignation, the magistrates received another batch of petitions calling for the abolition of the county force, 'from 15 parishes, and signed by 1,789 names'.[70] Reverend Litchfield stated that he had a further 88 petitions to present, but the subsequent debate was somewhat overshadowed by Goddard's resignation. Mr Sawbridge strongly defended Goddard's record as Chief Constable, stating that:

> Mr Goddard had been brought from a situation – he believed he did not seek it – with a recommendation from the chief of the London police of the very highest kind – he believed his language was – If you have Mr Goddard, you will have the best Chief Constable in the Kingdom. If anybody now had a charge of neglect of duty to bring against him, let them bring it now.[71] It is

67 Ibid.

68 *Northampton Herald*, 20 January 1849. Goddard was not the only Chief Constable to have possibly used injury sustained on duty as an excuse to resign; the aforementioned disgraced Chief Constable of Salford, Captain R. W. Torrens, was allowed to resign ostensibly due to an arm injury in 1880.

69 *Northampton Mercury*, 7 April 1849.

70 Ibid.

71 Ibid.

> unclear in the report as to whom the 'chief of London police' referred to Sawbridge was; it is unlikely to have been either of the Commissioners of the Metropolitan Police, and was far more probable to have been the Chief Magistrate of Bow Street, Sir Frederick Adair Roe, who undoubtedly held Goddard in high regard.

Goddard's successor, Henry Lambert Bayly, perhaps unsurprisingly, given the criticism that Goddard had received from certain quarters, came from a landed gentry family and had a background as an able administrator in both the East India Company and the Irish Constabulary (which he joined as an officer in 1840). He served as Chief Constable of Northamptonshire for 26 years, the Reverend Litchfield's continued opposition to the county constabulary notwithstanding.[72]

Conclusion

The 1840s had proven to be a turbulent decade; it is debatable whether any other Chief Constable would have enjoyed more success (or support) from the Northamptonshire magistrates.[73] Northamptonshire was not immune to the various societal, political and economic pressures experienced by the country as a whole, the sharp political divide of Whigs and Tories over issues such as the Corn Laws, the aftermath of the horrific famines in Ireland, which had led to an unprecedented migration of the starving poor to England (and a perceived rise in crime), the rise (and eventual fall) of Chartism to highlight just a few.

Goddard, while undoubtedly having already proven himself to be a first-rate Bow Street Principal Officer, seems to have been ultimately ill-equipped to manage successfully the day-to-day running of a county police force; his had been up to then a fundamentally self-managed and detective style of policing, and he seems to have struggled with the more mundane aspects of provincial preventive policing. He clearly took every opportunity to continue his detective work during his employment as Chief Constable and this cannot have endeared him to his opponents in the county magistracy. His occasional absences due to this aspect of his work certainly caused a certain amount of friction; for example, he was censured in March 1841 by the PCJ for not having yet appointed a Deputy Constable who would perform Goddard's duties when *in absentia*.[74]

Goddard was further twice reprimanded in January 1848 for both allowing prisoners the unnecessary expense of receiving ale rather than tea or coffee and bread while in custody at the station houses and also not ensuring that strict records of such arrests were kept by the Superintendents.[75] In April of the same year he

72 For a brief biography of Bayly, see Cowley, *Policing Northamptonshire*, pp.145–50.

73 For a readable overview of the 1840s, see S. Bates, *'Penny Loaves and Butter Cheap': Britain in 1846*, London: Head of Zeus, 2014.

74 NA PCM, 19 March 1841.

75 NA PCM, January 1848.

was severely criticized over his failure to attend the Spring QS; 'having stated that he was on business in London and no satisfactory answer given for his necessary absence', he was required to report to the PCJ who would report their findings at the next QS.[76] The PCJ subsequently accepted that Goddard had provided a satisfactory explanation for his absence, but he was required in future to

> report such absences in advance to the Deputy Constable and also to report upon his return. Goddard was again criticized in the June 1848 sessions for not exercising sufficient oversight of the keeping of financial records by the Superintendent of Brackley Division.

Ultimately, Goddard's time in Northamptonshire was not a successful one; he faced continued opposition due to a combination of factors: his humble origins, the widespread Tory opposition to the imposition of a Whig-inspired model county constabulary and the vituperative attacks from both Reverend Litchfield and the editor of the *Herald*. While it is impossible to ascertain Goddard's feelings upon his resignation (whether willing or forced), it is perhaps not unreasonable to surmise that on his part a sigh of relief was involved.

Whatever the exact nature or extent of Goddard's 'internal injury' it did not stop him from pursuing a subsequent active career both as a private detective and a Principal Door Keeper at the House of Lords; Pringle states that 'he was certainly in practice [as a private detective] in October 1849 . . . but I think that probably he had begun taking cases again some time before this, possibly before he went to the House of Lords'.[77] He remained active until shortly before his death on 29 October 1883.

76 NA PCM, April 1848.
77 Goddard, *Memoirs*, p.xxiii.

3 Early Chief Constables in Scotland

Policing the city and the county

David Smale

Introduction

This chapter seeks to explain the role of Chief Constables in the first half of the nineteenth century in Scotland and their relationship with their political masters. This will be undertaken in four sections: first, the earliest Chief Constables in Glasgow from 1800 to the 1830s, second a review of Glasgow's suburban burghs formed in the city's shadow, and then the respective work of two men later in the century: James Smart in the city and Alfred List in the county. In fact, none of the men who took charge of early Scottish police forces were known as Chief Constables; they were Master of Police, Superintendent, Intendant or Captain, and these terms were often interchangeable. The rank of Chief Constable was proposed by the Police (Scotland) Act 1857 to be used by leaders of county forces. Under the Glasgow Police Act 1862, this rank was extended to their chief. Before continuing it is important to mention the current controversy over which force was the first 'new' police force in Britain. The Metropolitan Police model of 1829 dominates many histories of policing. I would simply add to the debate two contributions; Dinsmor has rightly objected to using '1829 as the historical base line' and emphasizes the example of Glasgow.[1] Barrie, however, offers a note of caution with the assertion that it is a debate that cannot be resolved because all of the new forces continued with components of the old system, notably the watchmen.[2] The diverse and complicated nature of the new police forces lead me to conclude that it was only with the establishment of Her Majesty's Inspector of Constabulary in 1857, with his insistence on 'efficiency' and his control of the purse strings, that most county, burgh and city forces moved to a recognisably new police model. Mention must also be made of the Scottish concept of the 'police'. Radzinowicz stated that the word was used loosely in Scotland and could involve regulation and administration, control of trade and economic policy, but

1 A. Dinsmor, 'Glasgow police pioneers', *Police History Society Journal*, November 2000, p. 9.

2 D. G. Barrie, *Police in the Age of Improvement: Police Development and the Civic Tradition in Scotland, 1775–1865*, Cullompton: Willan, 2008, p. 6.

essentially the concept of policing meant concern for the 'common good'.[3] The new police were part of a movement rooted in Enlightenment ideals of improvement with society progressing to be more orderly and better behaved, all for the common good.[4] Carson and Idzikowska agreed that in Scotland there had been a 'much broader conception of policing for the common good', and that policing referred to 'powers and regulations associated with urban improvement initiatives'.[5] This can be seen in the Glasgow Police Act 1800 where paving, lighting and cleansing are all mentioned before 'Officers and Watchmen'. By the early nineteenth century, policing in England and Wales 'took on an association with law and order rather than urban improvement'.[6] However, I think it is possible to detect a move in Scotland over the first half of the nineteenth century that demonstrates a similar emphasis.

The Glasgow police

In 1771 a visitor to Glasgow commented on the city's policing arrangements and that the inhabitants regularly undertook duty as the City Guard noting that, 'an excellent police is observed here; and proper officers attend the markets to prevent abuses'.[7] It was not a view shared by everyone. In the second half of the eighteenth century the population of the city rose from 31,700 in 1755 to 77,000 in 1801; Glasgow was rapidly transforming from a town built on international trade to a city that was a 'powerhouse of commerce and industry'.[8]

In 1779, following riots over the 'popish bill' calling for more toleration of Catholics, the council of Glasgow tentatively appointed James Buchanan, merchant, to be Inspector of Police. Two years later he resigned and the council 'agreed to abolish the said office in all time coming'.[9] By 1788 it was clear that the magistrates were still struggling in their attempts to detect crime and the city was wracked with disturbances by starving weavers, so another merchant, Richard Marshall, was appointed Intendant of Police.[10] He had eight officers and importantly the council required him to 'employ his officers in patrolling the streets

3 L. Radzinowicz, *A History of English Criminal Law and its Administration from 1750*, vol.3 London: Stevens, 1956, pp.3–4.

4 D. G. Barrie, 'Patrick Colquhoun, the Scottish enlightenment and police reform in Glasgow in the late eighteenth century', *Crime, Histories and Societies*, 2008, vol.84, p. 73.

5 K. Carson and H. Idzikowska, 'The social production of Scottish policing, 1795–1900', in D. Hay and F. Snyder (eds) *Policing and Prosecution in Britain, 1750–1850* Oxford: Clarendon, 1989, pp. 270–1.

6 Barrie, *Police in the Age of Improvement*, p. 13.

7 T. Pennant, 'Best of the second-rate', in A. Taylor (ed.) *Glasgow: The Autobiography*, Edinburgh: Birlinn, 2016, p. 27.

8 Barrie, 'Colquhoun', p. 62.

9 R. Renwick (ed.) *Extracts from the Records of the Burgh of Glasgow, Vol. VIII, 1781–1795*, Glasgow: Anderson, 1913, p. 5.

10 Ibid. p. 275.

. . . to detect and prevent crimes'. The Intendant was under the 'controle [sic] and direction of the Magistrates and Councill [sic] and ought to obey their orders'.[11] Within two years this force was also abolished. However, these two attempts at improving policing reveal a growing intolerance of crime and combined with the fear of public disorder created anxiety among both the middle-rank merchants and tradesmen and the city's elites fuelling the debate on forming a professional police force.[12] In 1793 the author who contributed to the *Statistical Account of Scotland* wrote that 'Great crimes were formerly very uncommon; but now robberies, housebreakings, swindling, pickpockets, pilferers, and consequently executions . . . [have] become more common'.[13]

These deliberations led to the Glasgow Police Act which received Royal Assent in July 1800. The enactment has been described as 'an epoch-making statute'.[14] This pioneering piece of legislation allowed some community control over the election of representatives to the Police Commission; the Act proved effective because it enabled the financial stability as provided by the imposition of rates on property in the city.[15] Another factor crucial to its success was the acceptance by the magistrates that the elected Commissioners should be pre-eminent in police affairs. The Act became a pattern for other towns to follow and the first quarter of the nineteenth century saw the growth of new police systems throughout Scotland's cities and burghs.

On 4 August 1800 Police Commissioners were appointed to the 24 wards in the city with places allocated for the Lord Provost, three Baillies, the Dean of Guild and Deacon Convenor of Guilds. The occupations of the Police Commissioners in August 1800 are illuminating; dominating the group were thirteen merchants, then four manufacturers and the remaining seven were shopkeepers or tradesmen.[16] These men, with vested interests in the city, sought to impose a body of police for economic and social reasons; the rapidly expanding city with accompanying social tensions had to be stabilised and regulated to allow trade to grow, indeed Glasgow's motto became 'Let Glasgow Flourish'.

On 29 September 1800, the meeting of the Police Commissioners considered the election of a Master of Police. Being pioneers they had no example to follow, so naturally enough, they elected one of their own number: John Stenhouse, a merchant. This was followed by the election of Sergeants and Officers of Police,

11 C2/1/1, Minutes of the City of Glasgow Magistrates Committee, 10 December 1788, Mitchell Library, Glasgow.

12 I. Maver, *Glasgow*, Edinburgh University Press, 2000, p. 51.

13 Sir J. Sinclair (ed.) 'Lanarkshire and Renfrewshire', in *The Statistical Account of Scotland, 1791–1799: Volume VII*, Wakefield: EP Publishing, 1973, p. 329.

14 J. Bell and J. Paton, *Glasgow: Its Municipal Organisation and Administration*, Glasgow: Maclehose, 1896, p.113.

15 I. Maver, 'The guardianship of the community: Civic authority before 1833', in T. M. Devine and G. Jackson (eds) *Glasgow Volume 1: Beginnings to 1830*, Manchester University Press, 1995, p.251.

16 E1/1/1 Minutes of Glasgow Police Commissioners, 4 August 1800, Mitchell Library, Glasgow.

among them an ex-Sergeant of the Argyllshire Fencibles and eight other tradesmen making a complement of a Master of Police, three Sergeants, six Officers and 68 Watchmen.[17] They also agreed that the Watchmen were to act as scavengers and sweep the streets, echoing the practices of the past. In a trend that was to be followed in police forces all over Britain, the large turnover of men leaving and joining the police started; one officer resigned before the force was mustered on 15 November.[18] The initial plan was for three shifts: one Sergeant and two Officers were to be on duty in the police office for 24 hours, one Sergeant and two Officers on patrol, and one Sergeant and two Officers on a rest day.

This new force took to the streets of the 24 wards of the city with the officers instructed to 'constantly patrol through such districts' to deter crime.[19] They also had the additional duty of keeping 'a sharp look-out after the Watchmen . . . [to] ensure that they are all sober'.[20] The majority of the servants of the establishment were Watchmen wearing greatcoats with their number painted on their backs and issued with a lantern and a stave. They manned sentry boxes at fixed points in the city and maintained elements of the old system of policing. From the very start the efficiency of the Watchmen was questioned. Within the first three months they had to be warned not to wander off their station or go home when on duty and particularly not to sleep on duty.[21] It is clear that many of these men were old and decrepit and proved to be easy targets for drunks, particularly students, who took great delight in fighting with them and overturning the boxes.[22] By March 1802 the Sergeants and Officers were instructed to keep an eye on the Watchmen to ensure they were sober. Their duties were restated: to apprehend vagrants and disorderly persons, look out for suspicious persons, inspect the lamps, turn out for fires, monitor road traffic and sweep the streets. The Master of Police reminded them, 'Watchmen . . . you have taken a great and solemn oath . . . to faithfully perform your duty as a Watchmen under the Police Establishment'.[23] In September 1802, Stenhouse was again elected as Master of Police against opposition from two merchants and two ex-military men.[24] He was informed that his uniform should be to dress in black with a cocked hat, a medal suspended by a ribbon and with a white rod or baton.[25] It appears that relations between Stenhouse and the Commissioners had deteriorated as they found it necessary to remind him that while he had 'charge of the other servants, Master of Police was their servant'.[26]

17 Ibid. 29 September 1800.

18 Ibid. 6 October, 1800.

19 J. Scott, *Abstract of the Police Acts with a Summary of the Powers and Duties of Special Constables*, Glasgow: James Hedderwick, 1821, p.9.

20 Ibid. p.10.

21 E1/1/2, Minutes of Glasgow Police Commissioners, 11 December 1800.

22 Ibid. 16 January 1801.

23 Ibid. 25 March 1802.

24 Ibid. 21 September 1802.

25 E1/1/3, Minutes of Glasgow Police Commissioners, 19 October 1802.

26 Ibid. 19 October 1802.

As will be seen, it is possible to assess what the Commissioners thought of their Masters of Police; however, it is more difficult to discover what the general public thought of this new institution. Correspondence in the *Glasgow Herald*, which did not reflect the musings of the working class, nevertheless displayed some support for the police. In September 1803 one writer had a suggestion to form a light infantry battalion to fight the French if they should invade. He continued with this theme:

> How honourable and independent would it be for this great city, if, in all time to come, the Civil Magistrate could . . . instantly rally round him, by sound of bugle, two or three hundred respectable citizens, all equally anxious with himself, for the maintenance of order, and the suppression of riot or sedition.[27]

The newspaper is peppered with examples of the police establishment failing in their duty with watchmen unable to hold onto prisoners, ignoring crime and of one lame ex-soldier working as a watchman, who broke into a shop and stole alcohol. He absconded and the Commissioners offered a reward of £10, this was matched by the watchmen, anxious to show their outrage at one of their number betraying the establishment.[28] The general population must have been aggravated by the imposition of petty regulations in the Police Act, but when the city did descend into riot, it was not aimed at the police but the economic conditions or to further political ambitions.

In August 1803, Stenhouse resigned and was replaced by another merchant, Walter Graham; however, after 21 months as Master of Police the Commissioners did not consider him a success and in June 1805 he was informed that they had 'no further occasion for his services after the first Monday of September unless re-elected'.[29] In that election James Mitchell, who had served in the Lanarkshire Militia replaced him. In a trend that followed the election of each new head, Mitchell, 'the tallest master of police we ever saw', set about improving the efficiency of the force.[30] He complained that on 'the whole officers have been very remiss in the execution of their duty'.[31] A committee made enquiry, agreed and reported a catalogue of failures by the officers; they were insolent, drunk on duty, unfit for duty or neglected their duty. Four were dismissed.[32] The Commissioners also received regular complaints about the Watchmen including failing to deter thefts, sleeping on duty and allowing prisoners to escape. They decided to inspect the Watchmen 'as a number of them appear old and infirm'.[33] They ordered them

27 *Glasgow Herald*, 5 September 1803, p.4.

28 *Glasgow Herald*, 4 April 1806, p.2.

29 E1/1/1, 3 June 1805.

30 P. Ellis and S. Mac a'Ghobhainn, *The Radical Rising: The Scottish Insurrection of 1820*, Edinburgh: Birlinn, 2016, p.17.

31 E1/1/4, Minutes of Glasgow Police Commissioners, 1 April 1806.

32 Ibid. 8 July 1806.

33 E1/1/6, Minutes of Glasgow Police Commissioners, 25 January 1810.

to march past the Watchmen and Lamps Committee and following an inspection the committee were satisfied that the Watchmen were all fit to do their duty. Nevertheless, the complaints continued and the Commissioners agreed not to employ Watchmen 'wanting an arm or otherwise disabled'.[34]

Criminal Constables, Special Constables and spies

In January 1811, the Police Commissioners asserted their privilege to intervene in police business and set up a committee called the Secret Service. This nascent criminal investigation department did not have any officers but met to try and formulate 'some Regulations for the more effectual detection of Robberies, housebreakings, etc.'.[35] The committee also held funds that could be released as payment for information concerning serious crimes and they rewarded 'police officers and others for finding out and apprehending great culprits'.[36] In September 1817, another committee which had been formed to consider whether there was a need to improve the investigation of crime decided 'it will be most expedient to employ two persons . . . to devote their time, solely to the criminal department', and the following month two Criminal Constables were appointed.[37] Two months later the Police Commissioners noted that the two men had been 'very active' and they considered rewarding them with five shillings each. It appears that much of the success of these officers was because they openly bought information regarding crimes. In just their first month they had paid out six shillings and eightpence 'procuring information'.[38] By 1820 the Secret Service Committee were so alarmed by an increase in crime and social unrest that two more Criminal Constables were appointed.[39] In 1842 the Metropolitan Police established a Criminal Investigation Department despite 'a latent distrust of undercover policing'.[40] The minutes of the Glasgow Police Commissioners do not reveal any debate over the morality of using detectives.

Throughout the early years of the force the Commissioners received a constant stream of complaints about the efficiency of the police and in April 1812 moved that they were 'not satisfied with the conduct of any of the Officers during the year' and proposed to dismiss them.[41] However, the conditions of service imposed by the Master of Police and the Commissioners also led to a large turnover in men. One of the officers, Henry Anderson, asked to be allowed to leave because of fatigue after night shift. A surgeon who supported his case expressed incredulity at the conditions officers were expected to endure:

34 E1/1/7, Minutes of Glasgow Police Commissioners, 1 November 1811.
35 Ibid. 21 November 1811.
36 Ibid. 15 August 1811.
37 E1/1/9, Minutes of Glasgow Police Commissioners, 18 September 1817.
38 Ibid. 6 November 1817.
39 E1/1/4, 3 February 1820.
40 H. Shpayer-Makov, *The Ascent of the Detective*, Oxford University Press, 2011, p.33.
41 E1/1/7, 23 April 1812.

> If the duty of an officer of police requires that he be kept constantly employed for thirty-six hours at a time without any interval for sleep and more especially if that duty is required of him twice a week I am decidedly of the opinion that he is totally unfit for it.[42]

Special Constables were employed from the earliest days of the force. In January 1812, their duties were defined and a campaign was started to increase their numbers in the various wards of the city.[43] These part-time men were expected to give information to the magistrates of the city of all crimes committed in their wards, apprehend vagabonds and vagrants and in time of social unrest assist the police in suppressing 'all mobs and riots'.[44] In January 1817, the Lord Provost announced a plan to increase the Special Constables to a force of 700 men and to 'procure small batons for them'.[45] The police needed this extra force to address the frequent disturbances, food riots, New Year celebrations and riots that accompanied the King's birthday. On the King's birthday in June 1819 all of the police establishment paraded supplemented by 40 of the local militia's Sergeants.[46] The magistrates pasted posters around the city requesting the public to show some restraint and prohibited 'all Bonfires, carrying of Burning Tar Barrels . . . and the Firing of Pistols and other Fire Arms, on the Streets and Public Places in the City'.[47]

Mitchell continued to eradicate drunkenness and improve efficiency as confirmed in the Police Commissioners' Minutes which are sprinkled with rewards given to members of the force. For example, 'one guinea be given to William Lennon, Watchmen for his activity in apprehending two persons carrying a dead humane [sic] body'.[48] Clearly the Watchmen were not all decrepit, infirm and ineffective. However, at the same meeting another committee on efficiency decided to sack one Head Constable, one Officer, eleven Watchmen and three Patrolmen, around 11 per cent of the force.[49] On 23 September 1819, in a move designed to remind Mitchell that he was their servant, the Commissioners decided that 'the Master of Police and his assistant shall not in future sit at the Board, but be in waiting in the adjoining room'.[50]

Glasgow in the decade following the Napoleonic Wars was the scene of much violent disorder and rioting. In November 1819, the Lord Provost was so concerned by the threat of revolution that he called on the police to assist in 'establishing an armed association . . . for the protection of the peace'. All police personnel were

42 Ibid. 24 September 1812.
43 E1/1/6, 9 January 1812.
44 John Scott, *Abstract of the Police Acts with a Summary of the Powers and Duties of Special Constables*, Glasgow: James Hedderwick, 1821, p.2.
45 E1/1/9, 9 January 1817.
46 E1/1/10, Minutes of Glasgow Police Commissioners, 31 May 1819.
47 SR22/62/1 King's Birthday Poster, June 1819, Mitchell Library, Glasgow.
48 E1/1/10, 9 September 1819.
49 Ibid.
50 Ibid. 23 September 1819.

armed 'to guard against any invasion of our established laws and constitution by the promoters of sedition and dissatisfaction'.[51] It is clear that the Lord Provost and his fellow merchants in the Commissioners had the most to lose from any disturbance whether it be a food riot or revolution. Nevertheless, Hugh Thomson, No. 1 Officer, refused to take up arms along with the rest of his colleagues and was immediately dismissed. [52] Mitchell's time in charge was affected by his response to the Radical Rising of 1820. It is generally agreed that there was great support for the rising and subsequent strike which was supported by over 60,000 workers in and around the city.[53] On Sunday 2 April, posters appeared proclaiming a provisional government with a view to establishing a Scottish Republic and a large part of the population took to the streets. Mitchell knew of the planned insurrection through a network of agents and 10 days earlier had arrested the entire radical committee. The uprising was fought with the use of government and police spies. The intelligence regarding the uprising was bought in three distinct ways. Spies infiltrated the radical organization, notably Alexander Richmond who reported directly to Kirkman Finlay, a local businessman and MP, or to James Reddie the town clerk of Glasgow.[54] The Lord Advocate, Sir William Rae, was concerned with the accuracy of the information obtained by payment. He employed Captain Brown, the Master of Police of Edinburgh, to try and infiltrate the radicals. This resulted in two Edinburgh policemen 'of Glasgow origin' serving on the committees of the reformers from August 1819 until January 1820, and Brown relayed their information directly to Rae.[55] From February 1820, the Criminal Constables of Glasgow police also had access to money for the purpose of buying information.[56] Mitchell certainly reflected the views of his Commissioners asserting that the Radicals were 'vipers' and 'vermin'.[57] James Hardie, Justice of the Peace, was unimpressed by Mitchell's actions; he had tried to tear down a poster but had been prevented by the crowd. In fact, Mitchell had ordered the police to ignore the crowds of people unless they were being assaulted or there was the chance of damage to property. Mitchell utilised a system of spies as a form of intelligence-led policing which restricted the revolt to the posting up of the proclamation and no large uprising occurred in Glasgow.[58] Even at this time of revolution normal

51 Ibid. 15 November 1819.

52 E1/1/11, Minutes of Glasgow Police Commissioners, 16 December 1819.

53 C.A. Whatley, 'Labour in the industrialising city, c.1660–1830', in T. M. Devine and G. Jackson (eds) *Glasgow Volume 1: Beginnings to 1830*, Manchester University Press, 1995, p.390.

54 G. Pentland, *The Spirit of the Union: Popular Politics in Scotland, 1815–1820*, London: Pickering and Chatto, 2011, p.30.

55 Ibid. p.91.

56 E1/1/11, 10 February 1820.

57 Ellis and Mac a'Ghobhainn, *The Radical Rising*, p.147.

58 Historians argue over the nature and extent of the uprising. In several places in the west of Scotland groups of men marched to support the declaration. At the 'Battle of Bonnymuir' a small group engaged in a skirmish with some Hussars. Eighteen radicals were arrested and later three were executed for treason.

policing continued with reports on the dirty 'state of the closses [sic]', beggars apprehended and three bakers charged with walking on the pavement with baskets on their heads.[59] This emphasizes the role of the police to ensure the imposition of a safe, clean, orderly environment where the wheels of business could roll along unimpeded.

It is clear that the long-serving Mitchell had fallen from favour, possibly because he had allowed disorder in the streets during the Radical Rising and not sent his small force to intervene. He was also charged with several minor 'scandals'; for example, in February 1820 he had provided lanterns and oil to 'private watchmen'. The Police Commissioners moved that he should 'pay for the expence [sic]', and that he would be reprimanded for his conduct.[60] In December 1820, he could not be contacted when two men arrived at the police office to report that placards were again to be put up around the city inciting a riot. This particularly enraged the Commissioners because 'the city was and had been for some months previous . . . in a state of agitation and alarm'. Mitchell appeared before them and simply stated that he had been in the office which was apparently accepted.[61] Nevertheless, in May 1821, the Lord Provost informed him that his services were no longer required and he was replaced by Hardie, the Justice of the Peace who had been critical of Mitchell's inactivity.[62]

The new Superintendent, James Hardie, seems to have endured a stormy relationship with the Commissioners. In June 1823, they demanded to know on what authority he had acted as Justice of the Peace at the Police Court only to decide a week later that was in fact his job. In October, they criticized him for acting without their permission in sending two men to Belfast to bring back a prisoner. A year later they discovered that he had appointed a man called Pinkerton as a Patrolman who had previously been dismissed by the Gorbals Police.[63] During a board meeting Hardie had been called to attend but he could not be found. The Commissioners admonished him and ordered him to attend all future meetings.[64] The criticism continued in February 1825 when the Committee on Officers and Watchmen reported to the Board that it was clear to them and to 'every citizen, that the establishment is perhaps in a more inefficient state . . . as regards the management of the servants . . . than at any previous period', and there was 'great dereliction on the part of your Master of Police'.[65] The Commissioners did not specify the details of his dereliction of duty but four days later, following a complaint against the Watchmen he was accused of showing 'a strong disposition to screen the servants when they commit any act of injustice or oppression on the

59 E1/1/11, 20 April 1820 and 8 June 1820.

60 Ibid. 10 February 1820.

61 Ibid. 7 December 1820.

62 Ibid. 10 May 1820.

63 E1/1/13. Minutes of Glasgow Police Commissioners, 9 October 1823 and 16 September 1824.

64 E1/1/14. Minutes of Glasgow Police Commissioners, 17 February 1825

65 Ibid. 24 February 1825.

citizens'.[66] The campaign against Hardie continued the next month when he was accused of abusing his powers in order to 'injure the character of' one of the Commissioners.[67] For the Police Commissioners this was a step too far; they set up an enquiry with which Hardie refused to cooperate.[68] The following month they attacked him for paying out the wages of the Superintendent of Weighing Engines despite the fact that the latter had been in Glasgow Jail for three weeks.[69] This oversight proved to be the final straw and the poor relationship between Superintendent and Commissioners came to an end when he was informed that he would be dismissed in May 1825.[70] Bizarrely, when the job was advertised, Hardie applied for it, suggesting he felt aggrieved by his dismissal.[71]

Hardie's replacement was John Graham, another merchant; yet again his first action was to clear out 'one-fifth of the servants' and reorganize the police body.[72] He proved to be a great success with his masters and the Board unanimously expressed their thanks for sorting out the mess he had inherited when appointed and 'for his excellent management of the establishment' presenting him with a medal engraved with his name.[73] In January 1832 Graham died and his successor F. G. Denovan, a Waterloo veteran with service in the Irish Police and at Leith Burgh, started his short time in charge. He also commenced a plan of improvement, weeding out the old and infirm Watchmen and submitting an extensive plan calling for, among other changes, three new Watchhouses, the discontinuance of the rank of constable and the introduction of the role of Lieutenant, and the ending of the practice of patrolling in pairs.[74] His proposal met a mixed response but it was on the matter of appointing Lieutenants that he fell out with the Commissioners. Denovan resigned in January 1833 citing his reason that the men had been appointed by the Board, not him, and that the three Lieutenants of Police 'were utterly incapable of exercising certain important duties'. He ended his letter of resignation with: 'Many other grievances equally influence me'.[75]

It is useful to summarize the previous occupations of the men who became Masters of Police or Superintendents in the Glasgow police in the first half of the nineteenth century.

29/09/1800–05/09/1803	John Stenhouse, Merchant
05/09/1803–02/09/1805	Walter Graham, Merchant
02/09/1805–05/07/1821	James Mitchell, Lanarkshire Militia

66 Ibid. 28 February 1825.
67 Ibid. 10 March 1825.
68 Ibid. 24 March 1825.
69 Ibid. 12 May 1825.
70 Ibid. 19 May 1825.
71 Ibid. 7 July 1825.
72 E1/1/15. Minutes of Glasgow Police Commissioners, 5 October 1826.
73 Ibid. 24 July 1828 and 11 December 1828.
74 E1/1/17. Minutes of Glasgow Police Commissioners, 28 June 1832 and 20 September 1832.
75 Ibid. 10 January 1833.

05/07/1821–21/07/1825	James Hardie, Justice of the Peace
21/07/182–??/01/1832	John Graham, Merchant
01/03/1832–24/01/1833	F. G. Denovan, Royal Irish Constabulary, Master of Police, Leith Burgh Police
24/01/1833–01/04/1936	John Watson, Police Commissioner, Glasgow
29/04/183–05/04/1844	Henry Miller, Superintendent of Prisons, Lanarkshire
25/04/1844–05/04/1847	Archibald Wilson, Superintendent of Anderston Burgh Police
05/04/1847–10/04/1848	William Pearce, Inspector of Royal Irish Constabulary
10/04/184–18/12/1848	Henry Miller, Superintendent of Glasgow Police (1836–1844) and Superintendent of Liverpool Police (Feb. to Oct. 1844)
18/12/1848–07/06/1870	James Smart, Superintendent Calton Burgh Police (1835–1846) and Assistant Superintendent Glasgow Police (1846–1848)

Glasgow's Masters of Police were dominated by merchants for the first 30 years, yet the longest serving and arguably the most innovative leader was Mitchell, an ex-military man. After 1833 most of the Superintendents had experience of leading police forces.

The number of men in the Glasgow Police grew in the first half of the nineteenth century and the Masters of Police often asked for more officers to deal with the increasing population and their increased duties. In 1800 there were 78 men and in 1846, following the amalgamation of the suburban burghs of Calton, Anderston and the Gorbals, it had increased to 360 men.[76]

The Gorbals, Calton and Anderston police forces

The three 'suburban' areas on the edge of Glasgow, that had also passed Police Acts: Gorbals Barony (1808), Calton Burgh (1819) and Anderston Burgh (1824) were a mirror image of their large neighbour and faced the same policing problems. It has not been possible to discover the previous occupations of the Masters of Police of these burghs but it is likely that these small forces attracted experienced policemen from Glasgow. Their Police Commissioners were composed of the same class of men as Glasgow; merchants, manufacturers, shop owners and tradesmen.[77] As previously noted, these forces on the edge of the city eventually amalgamated with Glasgow in 1846 despite the fact that much of the Police Commissioners' records for the 10 years prior to that were filled with plans to oppose the move. The three small forces were all concerned with the threat of riot and public disturbances, if anything the smaller numbers in the suburban forces made this

76 E1/1/1–21. Minutes of Glasgow Police Commissioners.

77 H-CAL/1. Calton Minutes of Burgh Commissioners, 3 September 1817, Mitchell Library, Glasgow.

apprehension more acute; in 1834 the Gorbals had 34 men, Calton 24 and Anderston 24. Like Glasgow there were dates throughout the year that could lead to disorder; New Year, the monarch's birthday, and any election. The Magistrates and Commissioners took a very 'hands-on' stance during these events. In the Gorbals, the New Year celebrations of 1818 were met with a force 'for preserving the peace' which comprised the whole force, two Commissioners and four 'additional hands'. Such regular events could be planned for; it was the frequent food riots and other violent disturbances that characterized the first quarter of the nineteenth century that brought fear to the burgh's leaders. In September 1819, concern about further disturbances led to the magistrates and Commissioners, both groups armed with batons, all of the police and a 'Military force consisting of Cavalry and foot' being mustered to face an expected riot.[78] A year later disturbances in the Gorbals had reached such a pitch that the Commissioners requested that a detachment of the army be stationed in the burgh, a 'Military Guard sufficient for the protection of the lieges'.[79] In all of the records of the small burghs there is a real sense of fear or apprehension of riot and tumult. Another theme that permeates the records is the frequency with which the Commissioners of these forces dismiss their Masters of Police for any indiscretion or failing.

In Anderston the relationship between the Commissioners and their Superintendents was extremely volatile. In the 10 years between 1836 and 1846 the force had recruited six Superintendents, three of whom were dismissed. In October 1836, George Lamb was dismissed after six months' service, with no reason given. His replacement, Daniel McLean, followed in another seven months after the Commissioners heard 'the report of the Provost and Bailie Jarvis as to the conduct of Daniel McLean Superintendent on Saturday last'. [80] Again, we do not know what he did, but the burgh enjoyed some stability for seven years under Alexander Findlater and Archibald Wilson. In April 1844, Wilson resigned to be the new Superintendent of Glasgow Police. His replacement, James Lawson, was not a great success lasting only 17 days when the Commissioners discovered that the Procurator Fiscal had issued a warrant for him for 'malversation in office'.[81] He was called to explain himself and his alleged corrupt conduct but was never seen again.[82]

The crimes and offences that these small burghs prosecuted show a distinct split between crimes including breach of the peace and drunk and disorderly, which dominate the lists, and regulatory type offences that we would not regard as police matters. In the Gorbals in one month in 1835, 19 per cent of the offences prosecuted

78 H-GOR/2/1. Minute Book of Gorbals Burgh Commissioners, 14 September 1819, Mitchell Library, Glasgow.

79 Ibid. 24 November 1820.

80 H-AND/1/1. Anderston – Minutes of Burgh Commissioners, 15 May 1837, Mitchell Library, Glasgow.

81 H-AND/1/3. Anderston Minutes of Burgh Commissioners, 29 May 1844.

82 Ibid. 30 May 1844.

were under the Police Act. In their mission to bring decorum and order to the city they charged people with leaving carts unattended, using horses without a bit, chimney fires, lurking, leaving flower pots on a window ledge, bakers carrying bread baskets on their heads, and a man answering the call of nature by 'exposing his nakedness and making his water'.[83]

James Smart, policing the city

The next generation of police chiefs produced two of the most important leaders in Scottish policing; James Smart and Alfred List.[84] There are striking parallels in their careers and they both formed part of the movement, noted by Reith and highlighted by Morris in Chapter 9 of this volume, of men of the Metropolitan Police who became leaders of forces throughout Britain.[85] Both men moved to Scotland in the 1830s, Smart to burgh forces and List to county constabularies.

After service and promotion in the London, Gorbals and Calton police, in 1846 Smart, along with Calton Burgh amalgamated with Glasgow and he became the Superintendent of the E Division of the new force. In 2009 at the James Smart Memorial Lecture, Keir Starmer, then the Director of Public Prosecutions in England, lauded Smart as 'one of the founding fathers of the Scottish Police', who had developed crime detection particularly in the fields of photography and the use of electric telegraph.[86] However, in 1848 Smart was involved in an incident which shook Glasgow and influenced his future approach to policing.

Glasgow in 1848 has been described as a 'powder-keg'. This was because of a number of incendiary elements and events: Chartism, the influx of poor Irish after the failure of the potato crop, Highlanders moving to the city and an outbreak of cholera. Add to this the continuing 'hungry forties' and a general depression in trade resulting in a downturn in employment, and the city was volatile. On Monday 6 March a gathering of the unemployed on Glasgow Green, also described as a bread riot, began to roam the city with cries of '*Vive La Ŕepublique*!' alarming the city fathers in that year of revolutions.[87] The mob ran amok forcing open shops and, more worryingly, gunsmiths.[88] There are different accounts of the reaction of the newly enlarged city police but it seems that initially the Chief Superintendent, Pearce, withdrew his officers indoors. The Police Board decided to employ the

83 SR22/66/1. Gorbals Charge Book, 23 April 1835–22 May 1835, Mitchell Library, Glasgow.

84 For a detailed examination of List's career, see D. Smale, 'Alfred John List and the development of policing in the counties of Scotland', *Journal of Scottish Historical Studies,* 2013, 33:1, 52–80.

85 C. Reith, *A New Study of Police History*, Edinburgh: Oliver and Boyd, 1956, p.212. Although Morris argues that relatively few former Met officers became provincial Chief Constables, see Chapter 9.

86 K. Starmer, 4 November 2009, 'James Smart Memorial Lecture: Criminal Justice: System or Service' www.gov.scot/Resource/Doc/254432/0099641.pdf.

87 A. Goldsmith, 'A local difficulty – The Glasgow bread riots of 1848', in *Strathclyde Guardian: The Magazine for Strathclyde Police*, 1994, 18:2, p.13.

88 *Glasgow Herald*, 28 May 1870.

military; cavalry, the 7th Regiment of infantry and a party of armed army pensioners, known as 'Old Foggies'.[89] The military showed no skill or inclination to control the crowd and in the general confusion, they opened fire on the rioters. Six men were killed, one of them a Special Constable trying to reason with the crowd, and many more were injured. At this point, Smart realized that the army would not quell the riot and he took control taking the police to the streets and with the aid of the soldiers managed to divide up the crowd into manageable groups arresting the ringleaders.[90] In the following days a large group of Special Constables was sworn in and the army withdrew. This action did Smart's career no harm and he received an accolade from Sheriff Alison, who had been present at the disturbance and had read the Riot Act; 'his conduct was . . . highly meritorious in trying circumstances'.[91] Smart entered Glasgow folklore and 64 years later a writer commented that his 'vigorous action . . . saved the city from pillage from the mob'.[92] A Glasgow newspaper reported that the police 'disciplined under a Chief from the Irish Constabulary . . . was nowhere to be seen in the riot . . . it barricaded itself for safety in its barracks'.[93] Apart from Smart's actions the police were generally regarded as ineffective.[94]

The businesses damaged in the riot claimed money from the Board and the Chairman of the Police and Statute Committee, was sent off to the Clydesdale Bank to obtain a loan of £8,150.[95] The Special Constable who had been killed, James Alexander, had 'left a family of seven children . . . who are orphans their mother being also dead'. They were given £150.[96] In the same year, Smart was injured as he tried to apprehend a thief. The man grabbed a shovel from a passing cart and struck Smart on the head with the sharp edge. Smart managed to arrest the man but retained the scar on the side of his head for the rest of his life.[97]

At the end of March, Chief Superintendent Pearce fell on his sword and in his resignation letter acknowledged that, following the riot, he did not enjoy the confidence of the Commissioners or the public.[98] Henry Miller, an ex-head of the city police took over until December when Smart became Chief Superintendent of the Glasgow Police.[99] He was an immediate success, the Lord Provost and the Watching and Fire Engines Committee commented after he had been in charge

89 J. Ord, *The Story of the Burgh of Calton*, Glasgow: Aird and Coghill, 1912, p.29.
90 Goldsmith, 'A local difficulty', p. 15.
91 *Glasgow Herald*, 28 May 1870.
92 Ord, *The Story of the Burgh of Calton*, p. 30.
93 M. Michie, *An Enlightenment Tory in Victorian Scotland: The Career of Sir Archibald Alison*, East Linton: Tuckwell, 1997, p. 88.
94 J. Saville, *1848 The British State and the Chartist Movement*, Cambridge University Press, 1987, p.89.
95 E1/2/3. Minutes of Police and Statute Labour Committee, 4 September 1848.
96 Ibid. 23 October 1848.
97 *Glasgow Weekly News*, 8 November 1905.
98 *Glasgow Herald*, 31 March 1848.
99 E1/2/3. 4 December 1848.

for a year: 'The Committee were satisfied with the general appearance of the whole force, which has been greatly improved of late, the men in general being strong and athletic persons'.[100]

Smart then began to lobby for policemen to be provided with houses in the city and actively sought to locate police houses including within a block of tenement flats as a sort of mini-barracks.[101] His experience of riots had led him to keeping his officers in houses on their beats or in barracks so that they could quickly be mustered to confront a disturbance. He made such residential requirement part of the Police Regulations; the constable 'will reside in the Section House, or in some other house near the Police Office of his Division'.[102] In 1859, Her Majesty's Inspector of Constabulary, Kinloch, speaking to a deputation from Edinburgh, commended the barrack accommodation in Glasgow 'and thought it was his duty to recommend it to them'.[103] Smart maintained this to the end of his service. In 1868 he allowed a Lieutenant to reside outside his division for a few months for personal reasons but he was required to move as soon as possible, 'into the Central District and, as near the office as possible'.[104]James Smart was undoubtedly a founding father of Scottish Policing, modernizing and introducing new technologies to aid detection. He died in service, having been Chief Superintendent then Chief Constable for 22 years, but the riots and disturbances of his early career cast a shadow throughout his tenure in charge.

Alfred List, policing the county

Alfred List, a Metropolitan Police Inspector, was placed in charge of the first county force in Scotland, East Lothian in 1832. The *Caledonian Mercury* reporting on crime in the county in 1834 decided that 'the newly appointed Superintendent ... has introduced a very efficient system of police'.[105] In 1839 List wrote an influential book *A Practical Treatise on Rural Police* in response to a competition. It was essentially an explanation of his methods and stated that 'the main duty of the Rural Police is the prevention of Crime and the suppression of Vagrancy'.[106] List realized that his small force of District Constables could not address what he saw as the key issues: crime and vagrancy. He introduced many more Parochial Constables scattered throughout the county who reported back to the District Constable. In 1840 List resigned as head of the police in East Lothian to set up

100 E1/9/2. Watching and Fire Engines Committee Minutes, 3 November 1849.
101 Ibid. 27 December 1849 and 18 February 1850.
102 SR22/60/2. *City of Glasgow Police Regulations, Orders and Regulations*, Glasgow: Anderson, 1857, 23. Mitchell Library, Glasgow.
103 *Glasgow Herald*, 11 August 1859.
104 E4/2/8. City of Glasgow Police. Chief Constable's Letter Book, No. 17. 20 August 1868. Mitchell Library, Glasgow.
105 *Caledonian Mercury*, 29 March 1834.
106 A. List, *A Practical Treatise on Rural Police*, Edinburgh: Fraser and Crawford, 1841, p. 4.

Midlothian Constabulary the 'metropolitan county' wrapped around the capital.[107] Upon the establishment of Her Majesty's Inspector of Constabulary in 1857, he quickly became a favourite of Colonel Kinloch who lauded his 'able administration' and particularly the paperwork in the force; 'The books and forms used in the office were very well kept and they have been generally adopted by other counties in Scotland'.[108]

However, it was not vagrants but another group of outsiders that were involved in the incident that influenced List's conduct. Railway building in the south of Scotland brought with it the navvies, and these men took exception to the formation of the Midlothian force believing the sole reason for its existence was to confront them. In June 1840, they rioted in Dalkeith protesting about the police. The impact of the new police was immediate when five men were arrested.[109] List's actions confirmed that the police were the natural enemies of the navvies; he ordered his men to keep up a surveillance on them and made himself even more unpopular by banning them from keeping dogs.[110] This state of mutual loathing continued as the North British Railway was constructed southwards from Edinburgh and into the Scottish Borders culminating in a riot in Gorebridge over the arrest of two Irish navvies. In response 300 Irish navvies marched on the police station to rescue their comrades and carrying 'bludgeons, pickaxes, hedgebills etc.' moved onto the works at Fushiebridge. A District Constable, Richard Pace, and a Railway Constable, unaware of the trouble in Gorebridge, met the mob on the road. In what must have been a terrifying scene the officers tried to escape and hide but Pace was attacked and beaten to death. List assembled policemen from his force and the City, and together with English and Scottish navvies, this body of over 1,000 men went in search of the culprits. They marched on the Irish encampment and some were arrested but most of the Irish navvies had made off to Edinburgh. This new mob set fire to the Irish huts with 20 policemen standing by apparently powerless to intervene.[111] Nobody was ever convicted of Pace's murder.

This incident hardened List's attitude to the navvies and in later dealings his response was extremely robust. In just one example, in July 1848, two years after the murder, it was reported that on their payday, Saturday, the navvies were going to riot in the village of Stow, as a response to what they perceived as heavy-handed policing. List led a body of 20 constables to the village and mustered them in the local schoolroom at midday, well before the navvies had started drinking. Later that day a riot erupted in an inn and then 'a general attack was made on the police', who responded with well-disciplined baton charges which sent the navvies

107 Her Majesty's Inspector of Constabulary (Scotland) annual report for 1863, 14. National Library of Scotland, Edinburgh.

108 Her Majesty's Inspectors of Constabulary (HMIC)(S) annual report for 1859, p. 18.

109 J. Handley, *The Navvy in Scotland*, Cork University Press, 1970, p. 29.

110 Ibid. p. 33.

111 Ibid. p. 287.

reeling.[112] No arrests were made and none of the police suffered any injury yet List maintained his heavy-handed approach to the navvies throughout their time in his county.

Unlike Smart, List's self-promotion and ambition did sometimes land him in trouble with his political masters. In 1853 he gave evidence to the Select Committee on Police and when questioned his responses suggest that he was either totally honest or got carried away with the occasion. He unwisely promoted his plan for a county force for all of Scotland, another plan to amalgamate the county of Edinburgh with the City force (both plans included him as the Chief Constable) complaining that the City police were not well disciplined and he was understaffed. Even more recklessly he suggested that the Commissioners interfered in police matters and that there was corruption that displayed itself in the contracts given to provide police equipment.[113] List was asked a question regarding how fit the city's Commissioners of Police were to serve. He unwisely answered honestly:

> They are respectable men in their sphere as shopkeepers, some publicans and brokers, but they are not calculated to have any knowledge of matters of police; in fact, it is their interference which causes the establishment to be not so effective as it otherwise would be.[114]

The Commissioners of the City police met to consider the accusations and then attacked List with stinging criticism that reinforced the fact that he was their servant. One of the Commissioners, Baillie Fyfe, found it strange that 'a person occupying the subordinate position of that gentleman took on himself to state facts and give opinions so materially about others who are above him in position'.[115] The Lord Provost of Edinburgh poured scorn on List's plan to amalgamate with the city and likened him and his small force of 30 constables to a 'petty German Prince, with a principality no larger than a good farm', demanding that the 'Emperor of Austria or the King of Prussia . . . put their forces under his management'.[116] List was mocked and abused yet he managed to hold onto his job for a further 24 years.

Conclusion

The appointment of the early Masters of Police in Scotland followed a pattern; the first leaders were members of the Police Commission or merchants, later ex-military officers are preferred, possibly to instil discipline and to toughen up the

112 *Border Advertiser*, 21 July 1848.

113 Police. Second Report of the Select Committee. Minutes of Evidence, appendix and index, 1853. Vol. XXXVI, (Sessional no. 715), 100–8.

114 Ibid. p.101.

115 *The Scotsman*, 24 August 1853.

116 Ibid. 14 September 1853.

men to face the ever-present threat of violence and riot, and finally they recruited experienced officers from other forces. Two of these experienced policemen, Smart in the city, and List in the county, were deeply affected by violent confrontations. The police model pioneered in Glasgow constituted a force to defend property and to ensure that industry and trade flourished. However, it has been argued that it was rooted in the Enlightenment and that the police were contributing to the common good and the creation of a more orderly, structured society.[117] The reduction of crime and rioting could be in the interests of all classes of the city, but it was the merchants, manufacturers and shop owners, who filled the ranks of the Police Commissioners, that ensured that the new police defended their interests. One feature permeates the workings of the Police Commissioners, Police Boards and the Commissioners of Supply; the Masters of Police were their servants and only remained as head of their police establishment at their pleasure.

117 Barrie, 'Colquhoun', p.73.

4 The Irish Inspectors General, 1838–1916

Leading Dublin Castle's constabulary 'machine'

Elizabeth Malcolm

Introduction

A national constabulary was established in Ireland following the Appointment of Constables, etc. (Ireland) Act 1822. This new force was at first a relatively decentralized body in that command rested with four provincial Inspectors General, while local magistrates retained their traditional right to appoint constables. But, during the late 1820s and early 1830s, a series of measures progressively transferred control away from the provinces and delivered it increasingly into the hands of the Irish administration based in Dublin Castle. This trend was consolidated and carried further by the Constabulary (Ireland) Act 1836, which in effect completed the creation of a highly centralized paramilitary police force, based on the model of a light infantry regiment. Under the Act, the Irish Constabulary was to be commanded from Dublin by one Inspector General, who would lead around 8,000 armed men quartered in some 1,400 barracks scattered throughout most of the country. Dublin city, however, retained its own separate, unarmed civilian force, the Dublin Metropolitan Police (DMP), modelled on the London Metropolitan Police. But, under the 1836 Act, the powers of the Inspector General were limited: appointments, promotions and dismissals, for instance, were vested in the Irish Lord Lieutenant. The first Inspector General's swift resignation in protest at this arrangement was to prove merely the first example of the tensions inherent in the relationship between the Inspector General and Dublin Castle – tensions that were almost invariably resolved in favour of the Castle.[1]

Colonel Duncan Mcgregor (1838–58)

It was in fairly inauspicious circumstances then that Scottish-born Colonel Duncan McGregor, following nearly 40 years' military service, embarked in July 1838 upon

1 S. Palmer, *Police and Protest in England and Ireland, 1780–1850*, Cambridge: Cambridge University Press, 1988, pp.243–5, 356–60; E. Malcolm, 'From light infantry to constabulary: The military origins of the Irish police, 1798–1850', *Irish Sword*, 1998, vol.21, 163–75; A. Dukova, *A History of the Dublin Metropolitan Police and its Colonial Legacy*, London: Palgrave Macmillan, 2016, pp.25–148.

his new career as head of the Irish Constabulary.[2] He had no previous experience of policing and little experience of Ireland either. When the position was offered to him, he had been hesitant to accept it. The fact that the first Inspector General, Colonel James Shaw Kennedy, also a Scot but one with far more policing experience, had resigned in acrimonious circumstances after less than two years in the post was hardly an encouraging sign. It is somewhat surprising then that the initially reluctant McGregor became the longest serving of the twelve Inspectors General, occupying the office for 20 years up until his retirement aged 70. His two decades as Inspector General were, however, hardly an undemanding period for Irish policing. On the contrary, they witnessed the most catastrophic event in modern Irish history, the Great Famine of 1845–50; and whereas Britain avoided an armed rebellion in 1848, Europe's 'year of revolutions', Ireland did not.

From the outset, McGregor was confronted with an array of major problems: some political, others organizational and operational. He had to establish a good working relationship with the Irish administration, while improving the recruitment, training and discipline of his policemen. More challenging was the problem of how to curb public disorder and agrarian crime in Ireland without totally alienating a population that was already deeply suspicious of British government interference in their lives. Related to this was the even more fundamental question of how a society, as bitterly polarized along political and religious lines as Ireland, could be policed successfully by a force composed of men born and brought up in the opposing Catholic nationalist and Protestant unionist camps.

The 1835–41 Whig government, headed by Lord Melbourne, had definite ideas about how Ireland should be policed. In 1836, it entered into a parliamentary alliance with Irish nationalist MPs led by Daniel O'Connell. This alliance facilitated a series of reform measures in Ireland, among them important changes to justice and policing.[3] The Irish administration, based in Dublin Castle, that implemented these changes was headed by a Lord Lieutenant, in effect a British Viceroy, and included a Chief Secretary, who was usually an English MP and often a Cabinet Minister, and an Under-Secretary, who handled the day-to-day operations of government and also oversaw policing. The latter position was filled in the late-1830s by a Scottish-born former army engineer named Thomas Drummond, who had worked during the 1820s for the Irish Ordnance Survey. Drummond knew Ireland well and had a particular interest in its law and order problems.[4]

The Irish Whig administration considered appointing more Catholics to the largely Protestant constabulary a priority. Drummond believed that, if the police

2 See 'McGregor, Duncan (General) Sir' in J. Herlihy, *Royal Irish Constabulary Officers: A Biographical Dictionary and Genealogical Guide, 1816–1922*, Dublin: Four Courts Press, 2005, pp.215–17. For McGregor's family life and the career of his son as a missionary and canoeist, see Edwin Hodder, *John 'Rob Roy' MacGregor*, London: Hodder Brothers, 1894.

3 A. Macintyre, *The Liberator: Daniel O'Connell and the Irish Party, 1830–47*, New York: Macmillan, 1965, pp.135–66.

4 R. B. O'Brien, *Thomas Drummond, Under Secretary in Ireland 1835–40: Life and Letters*, London: Kegan Paul, Trench and Co., 1889, pp.23–4, 29, 33, 74–7, 197–202.

were to be effective, they had to win public acceptance and, in order to do that, they had to reflect the composition of the general population in religious terms.[5] When Colonel Shaw Kennedy therefore wanted to dismiss a Catholic inspector, the Lord Lieutenant refused his request. Deciding this meant that he could not discipline the force he commanded, Shaw Kennedy promptly resigned.[6] In 1839, before a Select Committee on Irish crime established by the Tories and aimed to discredit Whig policies, he complained about Dublin Castle's preference for Catholics. McGregor, in evidence to the same committee, noted that of 3,000 men who had been accepted into the constabulary since 1836, 60 per cent were Catholic.[7] Shaw Kennedy's resignation had been politically embarrassing and Dublin Castle was determined not to make the same mistake with McGregor. According to Drummond, the appointment of constables, although still officially determined by the Lord Lieutenant, was by 1839 'practically' in the hands of the Inspector General, as were promotions and dismissals.[8]

Dublin Castle, as well as aiming for a constabulary whose composition was generally reflective of the Irish population, also aspired to create a force that was sufficiently well trained and disciplined to be able to suppress all forms of public disorder: a duty that a reluctant army had previously been forced to undertake. Large-scale gatherings at fairs and markets, election contests, religious festivals, race meetings and other sporting events – all attracted intensive policing. In this way, Drummond hoped to prevent crime as well as to detect and punish it. He was especially determined to curb Orange Order marches in the north and communal faction fights in parts of the south and west. Heavy policing, on occasion with army support, certainly reduced the number of Orange marches substantially during the late 1830s. In response to a questionnaire circulated by McGregor in 1840, many sub-inspectors and stipendiary resident magistrates in the south and west also reported a marked decline in faction fighting and public drunkenness, due in part to more active policing, although a major Catholic temperance crusade then underway had had a significant impact as well.[9]

Perhaps the most important achievement of Shaw Kennedy's brief period as Inspector General was the production in 1837 of a book of rules and regulations known as 'The Code', which in successive editions was to govern the Irish

5 M. A. G. Ó Tuathaigh, *Thomas Drummond and the Government of Ireland, 1835–41*, O'Donnell Lecture, Dublin: National University of Ireland, 1977, p.19.

6 E. Malcolm, '"The reign of terror in Carlow": The politics of policing Ireland in the 1830s', *Irish Historical Studies*, 2000, vol.32, 59–74.

7 Report from the Select Committee of the House of Lords Appointed to Enquire into the State of Ireland in Respect of Crime and Outrage, H. L. (486-I), xi, 1839, pp.13–15, 121–2; Palmer, *Police and Protest in England and Ireland*, p.362.

8 Minutes of Evidence taken before the Select Committee of the House of Lords Appointed to Enquire into the State of Ireland in Respect of Crime and Outrage, H. L. (486-III), xii, 1839, p.963.

9 Return of Orange Emblems and Processions, 12 July 1839, National Archives of Ireland, Chief Secretary's Office Registered Papers, 1839/103/6538 [NAI, CSORP]; Duncan McGregor, Circular, 12 March 1840, NAI, OPMA 131/10.

Constabulary until its disbandment in 1922.[10] Although not responsible for the Code, McGregor oversaw other important initiatives during 1838–47 that shaped the constabulary in fundamental ways, strengthening its training, organization and effectiveness. In 1842, a constabulary depot was opened in Dublin's Phoenix Park, which, according to Stanley Palmer, was the 'first police academy in the British Isles'.[11] The depot housed training schools for rank-and-file recruits and officer cadets. The training, which required men to familiarize themselves with relevant statutes and with the force's information gathering and reporting procedures, was heavily militaristic in character, with a decided emphasis on drill.[12] Whereas, before 1836, many officers had been promoted from the ranks, thereafter Dublin Castle selected outsiders for officer cadetships, although a small number of promotions continued. McGregor approved of officer cadetships since they were in line with army practice. But, in effect, they privileged class over experience, thus ensuring that the constabulary reflected Ireland's existing social hierarchy. Inspectors were drawn largely from the gentry and professional classes, which were strongly Protestant, whereas most constables were the sons of small tenant farmers, who were overwhelmingly Catholic.[13]

Also based at the depot was a reserve force that could be despatched via the rapidly expanding railway network to any part of the country at short notice in order to reinforce overstretched local police. From 1845, the depot also housed a riding school providing the basis for a mounted division.[14] In 1847, in response to an upsurge in crime, McGregor also cautiously instituted a scheme whereby small numbers of experienced constables were appointed as plain-clothes detectives, albeit on a part-time basis only and without the use of the title 'detective'.[15] In addition, beginning in 1841, the constabulary took on the job of collecting the information required for the decennial census. Its duty to gather census and other statistical data was to contribute to the force's popular reputation for being the omnipresent 'eyes and ears' of Dublin Castle throughout rural Ireland.[16]

10 Standing Rules and Regulations for the Government and Guidance of the Constabulary Force of Ireland, Dublin: Grierson, 1837.

11 Palmer, *Police and Protest in England and Ireland*, p.363.

12 For a description of the depot's military-style training under McGregor, see F. B. Head, *A Fortnight in Ireland*, London: John Murray, 1852, pp.56–65.

13 For analysis of the composition of the force, see W. J. Lowe and E. L. Malcolm, 'The domestication of the Royal Irish Constabulary, 1836–1922', *Irish Economic and Social History*, 1992, vol.19, 35–7; W. J. Lowe, 'Irish constabulary officers: Profile of a profession', *Irish Economic and Social History*, 2005, vol.32, 19–46.

14 For more information on these developments, see E. Malcolm, *The Irish Policeman, 1822–1922: A Life*, Dublin: Four Courts Press, 2006, pp.48, 68–93.

15 E. Malcolm, 'Investigating the "machinery of murder": Irish detectives and agrarian outrages, 1847–70', *New Hibernia Review*, 2002, vol.6, 75–8.

16 M. O'Callaghan, 'New ways of looking at the state apparatus and the state archive in nineteenth-century Ireland: "Curiosities from that phonetic museum": Royal Irish Constabulary Reports and their political uses, 1879–91', *Proceedings of the Royal Irish Academy*, 104C, 2004, pp.42–6, 48–56.

Most of the main organizational structures of the constabulary were in place before Ireland was first hit in the autumn of 1845 by a blight that destroyed the potato crop, ushering in five disastrous years of famine. The Great Famine put huge pressure on the constabulary. At perhaps its most basic level, the Famine led to hundreds of police deaths, largely due to the various contagious diseases that spread in its wake. The force's death toll during the years 1847–9, at nearly 600, was around double the annual average number of police deaths experienced throughout the period 1841–1914.[17] The Famine also produced a marked upsurge in crimes against property, and the homicide rate jumped as well, although with significant regional variations.[18] The constabulary had to guard agricultural food exports en route to ports to prevent them being plundered by hungry crowds. In addition, the police were required to keep order at mass evictions, when landlords instructed bailiffs to clear their estates of hundreds of small tenant farming families no longer able to pay rent. McGregor was appointed a member of the Central Relief Commission, established in November 1845, as the constabulary policed public works projects, soup kitchens and workhouses, which sometimes saw clashes over wages, food and shelter involving large groups of desperate people. Constables came mainly from tenant farming families, who, along with the rural labouring poor, suffered most during the Famine. Not surprisingly perhaps, resignations and retirements soared among the force. McGregor, studying these figures, believed that around three-quarters of those departing planned to leave Ireland altogether by emigrating.[19]

On top of the extraordinary demands of policing a famine, in 1848 McGregor had to deal with an armed attempt to overthrow British rule in Ireland. A campaign to repeal the 1801 Act of Union between Britain and Ireland had been actively underway in the years prior to 1845. The advent of famine, and especially Britain's grudging and inadequate response to the disaster, led the radical wing of the repeal movement to embrace rebellion. Given that the constabulary was already overstretched, the threat of a widespread armed uprising seriously alarmed Dublin Castle. There were fears that the loyalty of the constabulary could not be relied upon; some of the rebel leaders certainly expected Catholic policemen to rally to their cause. In the end though, when rebellion finally came in July 1848, it was a poorly organized and ineptly led affair, culminating in a clash between groups of police and insurgents at a County Tipperary farmhouse. Around 80 constables, led by two sub-inspectors, succeeded in dispersing a small group of rebels, killing and wounding a handful without incurring any casualties themselves.[20]

17 W. J. Lowe, 'Policing famine Ireland', *Éire-Ireland*, 1994, vol. 29, p.48.

18 Return of Outrages Reported to the Constabulary Office in Ireland during the Year 1860, with Summaries of the Preceding Years (NAI, CSORP, 1861/7273). See also R. McMahon, *Homicide in Pre-Famine and Famine Ireland*, Liverpool University Press, 2013, pp.20–3.

19 Lowe, 'Policing famine Ireland', 66–7; Duncan McGregor to Lord de Ros, 1 January 1848, National Library of Ireland, Larcom Papers, MS 7617, f.2.

20 R. Curtis, *History of the Royal Irish Constabulary*, 2nd edn, Dublin: McGlashan and Gill, 1871, pp.67–86.

McGregor appears to have been a rather unassuming, deeply religious man.[21] Perhaps this is partly why his two decades as Inspector General, served in sometimes exceptionally difficult circumstances, have largely been overlooked, whereas the brief tenure of his predecessor Shaw Kennedy has attracted more study.[22] But under his leadership the plans and procedures set out in the 1836 Act and the 1837 Code were brought to fruition, and the constabulary was enabled to successfully weather the severe storms of the late 1840s. The leading Irish historian of the Great Famine, Cormac Ó Gráda, in weighing up the performance of the constabulary, concluded that: 'the great majority of policemen who served during the Irish famine were honest and well informed' and proved 'very useful and reliable'. Whereas some of their duties, such as supervising evictions and protecting grain exports, may have increased mortality, in other instances they played an important role in collecting information on distress, in distributing relief to hard-hit and isolated districts and also in burying the dead.[23]

Yet McGregor's legacy was a decidedly mixed one. In keeping with his army background, he envisioned the Irish Constabulary as a paramilitary body dedicated to the enforcement of public order and peace in rural Ireland. In 1847, he wrote that he would be 'delighted' if Ireland no longer required its police to be 'armed with military weapons', but that time had certainly not yet arrived.[24] The training regime at the new Phoenix Park depot remained determinedly military in character. But, after the Famine, as both population and crime declined in Ireland, critics began to question whether the country really needed such a large military-style police force. Whereas outsiders complained about the huge cost of the constabulary, discontent began to grow within the force over pay and conditions. Police duties had expanded substantially since 1836, but McGregor made little attempt to champion pay rises, even though in the more prosperous years of the 1850s prices rose significantly. Indeed, the force did not receive a significant pay rise until 1866.[25]

McGregor's 'one anxiety', it was later claimed, was to create a constabulary free from both religious sectarianism and political partisanship.[26] On his retirement in September 1858, he informed his men that the good reputation they currently enjoyed had been acquired and could only be maintained by 'perfect impartiality' in the discharge of their duties. The constabulary, 'from the head downwards, should be utterly uninfluenced by sectarian or political feeling', insisted McGregor.[27] Yet,

21 For evidence of his faith, see [Duncan McGregor], *A Narrative of the Loss of 'Kent', East Indiaman, by Fire in the Bay of Biscay on the 1st March 1825*, Edinburgh: Waugh and Innes, 1825.

22 G. J. Fulham, 'James Shaw Kennedy and the reformation of the Irish Constabulary, 1836–8', *Éire-Ireland*, 1981, vol.16, 93–106. Shaw Kennedy also has an entry in James McGuire and James Quinn (eds) *Dictionary of Irish Biography*, Cambridge University Press, 2009, vol.5, pp.115–16, whereas McGregor does not.

23 C. Ó Gráda, *Black '47 and beyond: The Great Irish Famine in history, economy and memory*, Princeton University Press, 1999, p.58.

24 Duncan McGregor, Memorandum, 10 December 1847, NAI, OPMA 145/8.

25 Malcolm, *The Irish Policeman*, pp.75–8, 115–19, 131–3.

26 M. Brophy, *Sketches of the Royal Irish Constabulary*, London: Burns and Oates, 1886, p.19.

27 *Armagh Guardian*, 15 October 1858, p.3.

despite the Inspector General's public emphasis on impartiality, creating a police force perceived as neutral proved an impossibility in the political circumstances of Ireland under the union with Britain. Sections of both the nationalist and unionist communities remained deeply suspicious of the constabulary and very ready, particularly in times of crisis, to see it as a body accountable only to Dublin Castle, whose primary function was, not to protect the people, but to repress them. Dublin Castle's view of the police was in some respects not dissimilar. General Sir Thomas Larcom, Under-Secretary during 1853–68, praised his predecessor Thomas Drummond for transforming the Irish Constabulary into 'the most efficient police in Europe . . . an almost perfect machine, which . . . responded at once from the remotest part of Ireland, to his touch in Dublin Castle'. Indeed, even members of the force itself imagined themselves as 'part of a machine', their only duty being to follow unquestioningly the orders of 'those who controlled that machine' from within the Castle.[28]

Andrew Reed (1885–1900)

In 1859, the year after McGregor's retirement, a young law graduate from Galway town entered the constabulary depot to begin officer-cadet training.[29] His name was Andrew Reed and, during the following decade, he served as a sub-inspector in three counties before being posted in 1867 to Belfast. But this posting was cut short when he was invited in 1868 by the then Inspector General of the recently renamed Royal Irish Constabulary (RIC), Colonel John Stewart Wood, to become his private secretary. Reed filled this position for 11 years, first under Wood and then from 1876 under his successor, Lieutenant Colonel George Hillier. During these years Reed found time to continue his law studies and, in 1873, he was called to the Irish Bar. At Wood's request, he revised the constabulary's manual, a catechism of duties first issued to all members of the force in 1866, and produced his own *Irish Constable's Guide*, a useful handbook of statutes that went into multiple editions.[30] Having passed the examination for promotion to County Inspector in 1879, Reed was posted to County Donegal, where he looked forward to enjoying 'the pleasant outdoor life . . . of an Irish police officer'.[31] But, just two years later, he found himself back behind a desk in Dublin, recalled to head the RIC's new crime division, an office created specifically to deal with a major upsurge in agrarian and political crime.

28 Larcom in Curtis, *History of the Royal Irish Constabulary*, p.22; T. Fennell, *The Royal Irish Constabulary: A History and Personal Memoir*, R. Fennell (ed.), Dublin: University College Dublin Press, 2003, p.19.

29 For an outline of Reed's career, see M. Radford, 'Andrew Reed (1837–1914): A very civil policeman', *History Ireland*, 2005, vol.13, 31–5.

30 *The Constabulary Manual*; or, *Guide to the Discharge of Police Duties*, 2nd edn, Dublin: A. Thom, 1870.

31 A. Reed, *Recollections of My Life*, unpublished typescript, 1911, p.20. Original in possession of the Reed family; microfilm copy in author's collection.

During the late 1870s Ireland, along with Britain, experienced an economic depression that impacted agriculture severely. Bad weather and poor harvests aggravated the problem; famine loomed once again in Ireland; tenants were unable to pay their rents and landlords commenced mass evictions. Irish nationalists responded in October 1879 by establishing a Land League to support evicted tenants and to campaign not only for land reform but also for self-government, or home rule as it was called. During the resulting Land War, violence in the form of assassinations of landlords and their agents, arson, boycotts and intimidation spread rapidly through large parts of rural Ireland. In 1881 members of the Irish Republican Brotherhood (IRB), known as Fenians, used the land movement as an opportunity to pursue their armed struggle for an independent Irish republic by launching a bombing campaign in England itself.[32] As head of the RIC's crime division, Reed's principal task was to combat the activities of both the Land League and the IRB. By his own reckoning, between June 1881 and November 1882, he was absent from his office for only one day. He clearly stood up better to the strains of the Land War than did his superiors. Inspector General Hillier resigned for health reasons in May 1882, in the wake of the murders of the Irish Chief Secretary and Under-Secretary by Fenians near the RIC depot in Phoenix Park. His successor, Colonel Robert Bruce, fared even worse, departing abruptly in September 1885 amid allegations of incompetence and alcoholism.[33] The stresses of Land War policing also produced serious unrest among the rank and file of the RIC. In August 1882 a group of Limerick constables telegraphed a circular to hundreds of barracks around the country, setting out demands for increases in pay, allowances and pensions. Although those involved were swiftly sacked or disciplined, the government felt obliged, in order to forestall further constabulary unrest, to establish an inquiry, which in 1883 recommended modest improvements to pay and entitlements.[34]

When Hillier resigned in early 1882, Reed was appointed an assistant Inspector General and, in late 1885 after Bruce's departure, he was promoted, over the heads of two more senior colleagues, to the position of Inspector General. The two men passed over were both Catholics. Clearly Dublin Castle was not yet prepared to appoint a Catholic to head the largely Catholic constabulary. Reed's career might not seem that unusual in the context of policing today, yet it was unique in the history of the Irish Constabulary. He was one of only two Inspectors General lacking a military background who had risen through the officer ranks; he was the only one with legal qualifications; and, in addition, he was one of only four who were Irish-born.[35] Unfortunately for Reed though, his tenure as Inspector General

32 T. Garvin, *The Evolution of Irish Nationalist Politics*, Dublin: Gill and Macmillan, 1981, pp.59–88.

33 'Hillier, George Edward' and 'Bruce, Robert' in Herlihy, *Royal Irish Constabulary Officers*, pp.166, 75.

34 W. J. Lowe, 'The Constabulary agitation of 1882', *Irish Historical Studies*, 1998, vol.31, 37–59.

35 The other non-military Inspector General, Irish-born Thomas J. Smith, filled the post for only two months in early 1920. F. Campbell, *The Irish Establishment, 1879–1914*, Oxford University Press, 2009, pp.104–7; Malcolm, *The Irish Policeman*, p.164.

got off to a very inauspicious start. After 1885, owing to the ongoing campaigns for land reform and home rule, violent unrest continued. Two events in particular exposed serious shortcomings in the RIC's ability to handle mass protests and soured Reed's relations with Dublin Castle: one was the Belfast riots of 1886; the other the so-called 'massacre' at Mitchelstown, County Cork, in 1887.

The 1886 riots, which arose out of Protestant unionist protests at the attempt by the Liberal government of W. E. Gladstone to introduce Irish home rule, extended from early June into September. They were the bloodiest outbreak of violence in Ireland during the whole of the nineteenth century, with dozens killed and hundreds injured. The Protestant community was enraged by incidents in which Catholic constables, many hurriedly drafted into Belfast from the south, shot dead unarmed bystanders. Of those killed three-quarters were shot by the police. Many Protestants were convinced that the largely Catholic RIC was being used by the government to suppress opposition to home rule, and some inquest juries brought in verdicts of wilful murder against the police. A Royal Commission into the riots, which reported in 1887, largely exonerated the RIC from blame, but Reed, who in his later memoirs described the riots as the 'most arduous . . . duty' of his whole police career, had not proved a particularly impressive witness, offering contradictory assessments of the performance of his men.[36] The 1886 riots lived long in Protestant memory and played a significant role in undermining the credibility of the RIC's rank and file in the eyes of many Ulster unionists.

On the heels of the Belfast riots came the 1887 Mitchelstown incident, although by then the government in power was a Conservative one, firmly opposed to Irish home rule. Now it was the turn of southern nationalists to be outraged by police shootings. When Arthur Balfour became Tory Chief Secretary in March 1887, he was determined to suppress what was known as the 'plan of campaign': a concerted attempt organized by home rule MPs and Catholic clergy to force selected landlords to lower their rents. Backed by the draconian Criminal Law and Procedure (Ireland) Act 1887, Balfour ordered the police and resident magistrates to break up land reform meetings and arrest the leaders of the campaign. Over the following three years, 1,800 people were sent to prison under the Act, including 26 MPs and half a dozen priests.[37] But, in September 1887, during protests in Mitchelstown, where the first two Home Rule MPs were being tried, the RIC opened fire on a crowd. Only three died, but nationalist propaganda turned the event into a 'massacre'. In public, Balfour staunchly backed the RIC's action, but, in private, his views were very different. In letters to Prime Minister Lord Salisbury, his uncle, Balfour railed against police incompetence. As in Belfast, discipline had broken down and, instead of calming a dangerous situation, the

36 Reed, *Recollections of My Life*, p.81; M. Radford, *The Policing of Belfast, 1870–1914*, London: Bloomsbury, 2015, pp.99–121.

37 C. B. Shannon, *Arthur J. Balfour and Ireland, 1874–1922*, Washington, DC: Catholic University of America Press, 1988, pp.36–44; L. M. Geary, *The Plan of Campaign, 1886–91*, Cork University Press, 1986, pp.26–7, 71–81.

police had in fact enflamed it.[38] Balfour, having little faith in Reed or his officers, set about rewriting the rules governing RIC crowd-management himself, making clear that batons were always to be employed initially to disperse hostile crowds and firearms resorted to only if baton charges failed. These rules, which were incorporated into a new edition of the Code in 1888, combined 'humanity and efficiency', Balfour assured Salisbury.[39]

In the wake of both incidents, Reed had attempted to defend his men, but in doing so he only succeeded in alienating British officials. The Under-Secretary in 1886–7, General Sir Redvers Buller, a tough veteran of colonial wars, considered Reed and his senior officers 'effete and slack'. 'I could make a better man than Reed out of putty', Buller told one correspondent, while in a later letter to Balfour commenting on Reed's 'lamentable weakness', Buller asked if a 'nice colony [could be found] for him to govern' as his departure would be a 'first-class thing for Ireland'.[40] Although a colonial governorship was not forthcoming, Balfour obviously agreed, informing Salisbury in October 1887 that the 'Police want leading'. Balfour thought that Reed, as an Irish career policeman, was too inclined to cover up or make excuses for constabulary failings. Like Buller, Balfour would have preferred a non-Irish army officer in the role of Inspector General, but, having already lost two military Inspectors General prematurely in 1882 and 1885 and with the morale of the RIC under severe strain, the government was not in a position to sack Reed in 1887. Indeed, in May 1889 Balfour recommended a knighthood for Reed. By then, though, vigorous enforcement of the 1887 Crimes Act had successfully curbed the land agitation; and, moreover, Balfour made clear that the honour was intended to indicate government satisfaction with the performance of the RIC as a whole, not necessarily with Reed personally.[41]

Yet, despite incidents like these, violent clashes involving police and crowds that resulted in fatalities were actually becoming rare in Ireland by the 1880s, much less frequent than they had been before the Famine.[42] The 1890s also proved considerably less politically disturbed than the preceding decade. The implementation of land reform and rural development measures, along with intensive policing, eased unrest in the countryside, although it never ceased entirely. In addition, after 1890, the nationalist movement was distracted and weakened by

38 For a discussion of the problem of RIC weaponry and crowd control, see R. Hawkins, 'An Army on Police Work, 1881–2: Ross of Blandenburg's Memorandum', *Irish Sword*, 1973, vol.11, 80–81.

39 L. P. Curtis Jr, *Coercion and Conciliation in Ireland, 1880–92: A Study in Conservative Unionism*, Princeton University Press, 1963, pp.196–200; R. J. Q. Adams, *Balfour: The Last Grandee*, London: John Murray, 2008, pp.87–8.

40 Quoted in E. A. Muenger, *The British Military Dilemma in Ireland: Occupation Politics, 1886–1914*, University Press of Kansas, 1991, pp.96–7.

41 Arthur Balfour to Lord Salisbury, 27 October 1887, 14 May 1889 in R. H. Williams (ed.) *The Salisbury-Balfour Correspondence, 1869–92*, Cambridge: Hertfordshire Record Office, 1988, pp.219, 287–8.

42 S. Ball, 'Crowd activity during the Irish Land War, 1879–90', in P. Jupp and E. Magennis (eds) *Crowds in Ireland, c.1720–1920*, Basingstoke, Hampshire: Macmillan, 2000, pp.229–41.

bitter internal divisions. Analysis of per capita prosecution rates highlights the less violent character of the 1890s. Whereas there was an increase in summary offences during these years, after 1885 there was a marked decline in offences against the person, especially serious assaults, although offences against property in rural Ireland remained a problem. With fewer violent crimes to solve, the RIC turned to heavier policing of petty offences and, given that Andrew Reed was a strong supporter of the temperance movement, it is perhaps not surprising that prosecutions for drunkenness jumped dramatically.[43]

Thomas Fennell, who joined the RIC in 1875 and retired with the rank of Head Constable 30 years later in 1905, testified in his memoirs to how, after the strains of the Land War years, policing became increasing routine during the 1890s or, as he complained, a 'constant grind'. According to Fennell: 'Depot training went much more to the making of a soldier than a policeman . . . but, in time, men left it behind and in ordinary circumstances became more and more stereotyped policemen'. After the 1860s, constables normally only carried a truncheon when on routine duty and firearms drill was by no means always regularly or rigorously practised. Fennell believed that Reed's 'enlightened rule' as Inspector General had furthered this process of de-militarization, especially by giving more opportunities for promotion to long-serving Catholic constables like himself. In the face of strong opposition from the largely Protestant officer corps, which valued the RIC's military trappings as indicators of their superior social status, Reed had issued a circular in 1895 announcing that in future half of all district inspectorships would be filled by promotion.[44] He also softened the harsh military-style rules governing RIC discipline. Resignations declined to unprecedentedly low levels and the rank and file became increasingly characterized by Catholic family men like Thomas Fennell, who saw themselves, not as soldiers, but as typical civilian policemen.[45]

Colonel Neville Chamberlain (1900–16)

It is no doubt significant that Neville Chamberlain's entry in the *Oxford Dictionary of National Biography* sums him up as 'army officer and inventor of snooker' and that only one of the eight paragraphs in the entry concerns his 16 years as RIC Inspector General.[46] He was not held in high regard by many in Ireland and his police career ended ignominiously. The entry's author is probably right to consider

43 I. Bridgeman, Policing Rural Ireland: A Study of the Origins, Development and Role of the Irish Constabulary, unpublished PhD thesis, Open University, 1993, vol.2, pp. 242–52; M. Finnane, 'A decline in violence in Ireland? Crime, policing and social relations, 1860–1914', *Crime, History and Societies*, 1997, vol.1, 51–70.

44 Fennell, *The Royal Irish Constabulary*, pp.18–19, 96, 31–2, 50–1, 57.

45 Reed, *Recollections of My Life*, pp.77–9; Lowe and Malcolm, 'The domestication of the Royal Irish Constabulary', p.44.

46 T. R. Moreman, 'Chamberlain, Sir Neville Francis Fitzgerald (1856–1944)', *Oxford Dictionary of National Biography*, Oxford University Press, 2004; online edn, May 2006, www.oxforddnb.com/view/article/73766.

that, in retrospect, his alleged invention of the game of snooker has been of more lasting significance than his contribution to Irish policing. Nevertheless, Colonel Chamberlain's period as Inspector General was a crucial one for it culminated in the most serious rebellion Ireland had experienced in over a century. The British government, naturally, sought scapegoats for Dublin Castle's failure to prevent the 1916 Easter Rising and, although the Royal Commission into the Rising exonerated the RIC from blame, Chamberlain felt obliged to tender his resignation. It is hard not to assess his Irish years through the prism of the Rising. However, his shortcomings as Inspector General have to be viewed in the context of a much broader failure of British policy in Ireland during the early twentieth century.

Chamberlain, the son of an officer in the Indian army, joined the British army in 1873 and spent most of his career carrying out routine duties in India. He was a protégé of Field Marshal Earl Roberts for whom he worked first as a staff officer in India and later as private secretary in South Africa. A Tory and unionist in politics, Chamberlain was an avid sportsman, and his military career, although successful, was hardly stellar. His selection as Inspector General was due partly to George Wyndham, the recently appointed Conservative Chief Secretary. Wyndham, who had worked as Arthur Balfour's private secretary in 1887–9, appears to have shared Balfour's low opinion of Andrew Reed and was anxious to replace him with another Inspector General of military background.[47] Roberts, who had served in Ireland during the late 1890s, strongly recommended his old colleague Chamberlain for the post. Interestingly though, Roberts chose to highlight, not Chamberlain's leadership qualities, but rather that he was 'good looking', had 'charming manners' and displayed an 'unusual amount of common sense and . . . tact'.[48] But, in fact, Chamberlain's charm and tact won him no admirers in Dublin Castle.

While Wyndham aimed to strengthen the leadership of the RIC, at the same time, he took steps to reduce the force's size. He was committed to an expensive government subsidized land redistribution scheme and, in order to secure Treasury approval, he agreed in 1903 to major cuts in the Irish police budget. Appointments ceased and RIC numbers were allowed to fall during the next two years by over 1,000.[49] Wyndham worked closely with his Under-Secretary, Sir Antony MacDonnell, an Irish-born Catholic and a former senior Indian civil servant. Both men were convinced that Ireland was over-policed and that land reform would put an end to most rural unrest, thus obviating the need for so many policemen. When Chamberlain questioned his superiors' optimistic expectations, he found his views

47 E. O'Halpin, *The Decline of the Union: British Government in Ireland, 1892–1920*, Dublin: Gill and Macmillan, 1987, pp.21, 220 n.45; L.W. McBride, *The Greening of Dublin Castle: The Transformation of Bureaucratic and Judicial Personnel in Ireland, 1892–1922*, Washington, DC: Catholic University of America Press, 1991, p.96.

48 Quoted in C. Townshend, *Political Violence in Ireland: Government and Resistance since 1848*, Oxford: Clarendon Press, 1984, p.68.

49 O'Halpin, *The Decline of the Union*, pp.42–3, 57, 62–3.

firmly rejected. In December 1903, MacDonnell labelled a report Chamberlain had prepared on agrarian crime as 'much too gloomy' and 'coloured by prejudice', forcing the Inspector General to rewrite it until it better reflected the Castle's prevailing policies. In his next report Chamberlain took care to be 'ostentatiously . . . soothing', and his 1904 reports were uniformly 'bland'.[50]

It was not only differences over rural unrest that caused tensions between Chamberlain and MacDonnell; unrest within the RIC itself, especially in Belfast, added to the problems of their relationship. Among the nearly 1,000 RIC men who policed Belfast there was considerable discontent. For one thing, the RIC had not received a pay rise since 1883. When a long transport strike took place in the city in 1907, adding greatly to the work of the police, hundreds of RIC men ignored the force's regulations and organized meetings to protest about pay and allowances. The quick-tempered MacDonnell was furious, demanding 'punitive action' against those involved and rejecting any negotiation as 'fatal weakness'. But, he also blamed senior RIC officers for being out-of-touch with their men and failing to prevent trouble. Chamberlain, meanwhile, equivocated, sympathizing with the men's pay demands, yet, at the same time, seeking to shift much of the blame elsewhere by alleging that the *Constabulary Gazette* had been 'fomenting indiscipline in the force for years past'.[51] In the end, around ten men were sacked and over 200 transferred out of Belfast, but no improvements to pay were forthcoming. MacDonnell later claimed that this crisis had led him to recommend Chamberlain's dismissal, but the government rejected his advice.[52]

MacDonnell's six years as Under-Secretary (1902–8) not only saw the RIC's manpower reduced and unrest among the rank and file, but the force's ability to detect revolutionary activity was also seriously compromised – and this just at a time when the IRB was reviving in Ireland and new republican groups were emerging.[53] The main intelligence arm of the RIC was Crime Branch Special (CBS), established in 1882 as an office in Dublin Castle aimed at combating Fenianism by collating and analysing political intelligence gathered by designated RIC men from around the country and also abroad.[54] By 1907, however, MacDonnell was seriously contemplating scrapping CBS, although he desisted when London advised against such an extreme step. Nevertheless, CBS was starved of funds and personnel. Assistant Inspector General Samuel Waters, in his memoirs, recollected MacDonnell on one occasion 'dancing around the room in

50 W. F. Mandle, 'Sir Antony MacDonnell and Crime Branch special' in O. MacDonagh and W. F. Mandle (eds) *Ireland and Irish-Australia: Studies in Cultural and Political History*, London: Croom Helm, 1986, pp.179–83.

51 Neville Chamberlain, Report, 14 September 1907, NAI, CSORP 1908/20333. For a pamphlet by the *Gazette*'s editor attacking the RIC officer corps, see [William Harding], *The RIC: A Plea for Reform*, Dublin: Wood Printing Works, [1907].

52 Radford, *The Policing of Belfast*, pp.124–41; Malcolm, *The Irish Policeman*, pp.155–60.

53 F. McGarry, *The Rising. Ireland: Easter 1916*, Oxford University Press, 2011, pp.19–43.

54 Bridgeman, *Policing Rural Ireland*, vol.2, pp.223–33.

a rage', rejecting a CBS report and accusing the staff of having 'conspiracies on the brain'. Chamberlain, on the other hand, showed little interest in the branch's activities.[55] W. F. Mandle, who made the most thorough study of the CBS records, certainly found a 'marked diminution' in their number and usefulness beginning under MacDonnell and continuing under his successors.[56]

If Chamberlain encountered problems with Tories who believed that Irish unrest and violence could be ended by land reform, his relations with Dublin Castle worsened after 1905 when he had to deal with Liberals who were convinced that home rule was the panacea for Ireland's woes. The Liberal Chief Secretary from 1908 to 1916, Augustine Birrell, was contemptuous of the Inspector General, believing that his judgement was warped by his strong unionist sympathies. A 'True Blue' unionist was how Birrell described him in letters to Prime Minister H. H. Asquith in the autumn of 1913. Chamberlain's occasional warnings about political unrest invariably focused on the threat posed by nationalists rather than unionists. In evidence before the Royal Commission investigating the 1916 Rising, Chamberlain pointed out that in June 1914 he had warned Birrell about the rapid growth of the Irish Volunteer Force (IVF), a nationalist militia established in November 1913 to defend the home rule cause against unionist opposition. But, as his concerns about the IVF were accompanied by claims that the Irish were an innately lawless people who could only be governed by force, it is perhaps not surprising that Liberal ministers were inclined to doubt the soundness of his analysis. In a memo to his Under-Secretary in November 1914, Birrell wrote that he had 'no sort of confidence' in Chamberlain, as 'his judgment is nil'. In the event of civil war in Ulster over home rule, the Inspector General and many of his senior officers would have to be removed, Birrell believed, because their loyalty could not be relied upon.[57]

Birrell represented a government committed to the introduction of Irish home rule and was convinced that the land problem had been solved and Fenianism was largely a spent force. According to the provisions of the Liberals' first two unsuccessful Home Rule Bills of 1886 and 1893, the RIC was to have remained under British control indefinitely. But, according to the third Bill, belatedly introduced in 1912 and not finally passed until late in 1914, the RIC was, after a short interval, to become the responsibility of the new Irish devolved parliament.[58] Given the Liberals had decided to transfer the police to Irish control, it is

55 S. Waters, *A Policeman's Ireland: Recollections of Samuel Waters, RIC* in S. Ball (ed.) Cork University Press, 1999, pp.82–3.

56 Mandle, 'Sir Antony MacDonnell and Crime Branch special', pp.178, 185.

57 L. Ó Broin, *The Chief Secretary: Augustine Birrell in Ireland*, London: Chatto and Windus, 1969, p.68; P. Jalland, *The Liberals and Ireland: The Ulster Question in British Politics to 1914*, Brighton: Harvester Press, 1980, pp.134–5; Neville Chamberlain's evidence in *Royal Commission on the Rebellion in Ireland. Reports and Minutes of Evidence*, H. C., Cd. 8279, xi, 1916, p.7 [*Royal Commission on the Rebellion*, 1916].

58 Jalland, *The Liberals and Ireland*, pp.42–3.

understandable that they did not welcome the Inspector General's opinion that the Irish were unfit to govern themselves.

When war broke out in August 1914, home rule was postponed and the IVF split, with most members volunteering for service in the British army, as did many Ulster unionists. Consequently, Dublin Castle became fairly confident that the poorly armed surviving remnant of the organization no longer posed a serious threat. The war also impacted the RIC significantly in that some 750 men volunteered for military service. While the army welcomed RIC recruits, Chamberlain worried about declining police numbers. As a result, in 1915, resignations and retirements were severely curtailed. RIC recruitment also ceased, as did promotions, which only deepened the malaise already afflicting the force.[59]

On the whole, Birrell took little interest in policing and Chamberlain demonstrated no real capacity for initiative or innovation. The RIC continued to rely heavily upon tactics devised during the 1880s, such as 'shadowing' or following suspects and taking notes of speeches at political meetings. Large amounts of data were thereby collected, much of it trivial. The police had been ordered not to prevent IVF training exercises, while attempts to infiltrate the organization achieved little. The RIC therefore had limited insight into the councils of the Volunteers. The DMP collected political intelligence for Dublin city through its detective office, G Division, but the two forces did not always share information. Not until late in 1914 was an RIC inspector named I. H. Price appointed to the Irish army command and given access to RIC, DMP and also military intelligence. Price became in effect Dublin Castle's chief adviser on political subversion, superseding Chamberlain. Yet, although by the spring of 1916, he was warning that a rebellion was being planned, the police intelligence upon which he relied was not accurate or detailed enough to alert him, or the Castle, to the fact that a rebellion was actually imminent.[60]

As the Easter Rising largely took place in Dublin city, which was policed by the unarmed DMP, few RIC men were directly involved and the rebellion was put down after six days by the British army. But in rural areas the IVF launched a series of sporadic attacks on RIC barracks. In north County Dublin three barracks were captured. At Ashbourne, County Meath, the barracks came under concerted attack and was on the point of surrendering when RIC reinforcements arrived. During the gun battle that followed, two Volunteers were killed, but eight policemen died, including a district and a county inspector, and fifteen were wounded, before the surviving constables were obliged to surrender having exhausted their ammunition.[61] In terms of Irish police fatalities, this was the worst

59 J. Herlihy, *The Royal Irish Constabulary: A Short History and Genealogical Guide*, Dublin: Four Courts Press, 1997, pp.98–100; L. Ó Broin, *Dublin Castle and the 1916 Rising*, London: Sidgwick and Jackson, 1966, pp.51–2.

60 I. H. Price's evidence in *Royal Commission on the Rebellion*, 1916, pp.56–60; C. Townshend, *Easter 1916: The Irish Rebellion*, London: Penguin Books, 2006, pp.85–7, 143–4, 146; Ó Broin, *Dublin Castle and the 1916 Rising*, pp.72–3; O'Halpin, *The Decline of the Union*, pp.102–4.

61 Townshend, *Easter 1916*, pp.217–21.

single incident since the early 1830s. But it was not only the paramilitary character of the RIC that was found wanting during the Rising, so too was its morale and loyalty. At Ashbourne, the IVF had 'more stomach for the battle than the RIC', with some policemen fleeing the fight. And in County Galway, although attacks on at least three barracks were repulsed, six constables taken hostage by local Volunteers later refused to identify their captors, although they knew them well.[62]

What occurred in parts of rural Ireland in 1916 was an ominous pointer towards what was to happen in 1919–21 when, during a sustained guerrilla campaign for Irish independence, the RIC would prove incapable, in terms of both military effectiveness and morale, of defeating the Irish Volunteers, by then calling themselves the Irish Republican Army or IRA.

Conclusion

Histories of policing in the British Isles usually draw attention to the paramilitary nature of the RIC, considering that this distinguished it from the forces policing Britain, and also Ireland after 1922, and lent it a markedly colonial character.[63] It is true that Irish recruits and cadets received military-style training at the Dublin depot; Irish policemen in many instances carried firearms; most lived in barracks under strict discipline; and all but two of the twelve Inspectors General had military backgrounds. Yet, it is questionable as to how militarily effective the RIC actually was by the end of the century.[64] Some Irish police historians, though by no means all, have argued that the constabulary had gradually become 'domesticated' after 1850: that is, it had evolved into a largely civil force.[65] This was certainly the opinion held by the British army on the eve of the First World War. When, in 1912, the army command in Ireland was considering schemes for national defence, it concluded that the RIC would be of limited use in the event of war, because 'it cannot be regarded as a military force in any circumstances' due to its 'rudimentary training in firearms'. The RIC would therefore 'assist [the army] in the same way as all other civil police do in Great Britain'.[66] The inadequate military performance of the RIC in 1916 and again in 1919–21 fully confirmed this assessment. Reed had promoted the 'domestication' process, but it was to some extent simply a result of the changing nature of post-Famine Irish society and policing. Stationed mainly in small, relatively peaceful, rural communities, few policemen were required to

62 McGarry, *The Rising*, pp.230–46.

63 V. Conway, *Policing Twentieth Century Ireland: A History of An Garda Síochána*, London: Routledge, 2013, pp.25–45. For a critical assessment of the RIC as a model for colonial forces, see R. Hawkins, 'The "Irish Model" and the Empire: A case for reassessment', in D. M. Anderson and D. Killingray (eds) *Policing the Empire: Government, Authority and Control, 1830–1940*, Manchester University Press, 1991, pp.18–32.

64 [Harding], *The RIC: A Plea for Reform*, pp.23–4.

65 Campbell, *The Irish Establishment*, pp.99–103, 133–6.

66 Quoted in Muenger, *The British Military Dilemma in Ireland*, p.107; Lowe and Malcolm, 'The domestication of the Royal Irish Constabulary', p.27.

rely upon their military training. And if they did need to, as for instance in 1886–7 when attacked by large stone-throwing crowds, they demonstrated a lack of basic discipline by panicking and firing indiscriminately.

While at least outwardly paramilitary in character, the RIC was perhaps more fundamentally a highly centralized and bureaucratic political police force. Under-Secretary Larcom and Head Constable Fennell both envisaged the constabulary as a 'machine'. According to Sir Henry Blake, a former RIC inspector and later colonial governor, it was a 'machine' expected to deal with everything in Ireland, 'from the muzzling of a dog to the suppression of a rebellion'.[67] It operated under tight control, but that control originated, not from the Inspector General, but rather from the Irish administration in Dublin Castle, representing the British government in London. Unlike most British forces, local civic authorities exercised no power in connection with the police in Ireland. Instead Chief Secretaries and Under-Secretaries could, and frequently did, overrule the Inspector General, especially when it came to political matters, as the careers of Reed and Chamberlain amply demonstrate.

In 1909 R. Barry O'Brien, a nationalist writer, published a critical account of the Dublin Castle administration, including some astute observations regarding the RIC. According to him, the Chief Secretary was actually in 'supreme' charge of the RIC, and the Inspector General 'could not so much as dismiss a man in the ranks without the authority of the Castle'. While the police might at times 'act on their own responsibility' in routine matters, if there was any hint of politics being involved – as there often was in Ireland – they immediately became 'timid', unwilling to do anything without explicit instructions from the Castle.[68] O'Brien would doubtless have agreed with Under-Secretary Buller, who in 1886 had imagined the Inspector General as putty in the hands of Dublin Castle.

67 H. A. Blake, 'The Irish police', *The Nineteenth Century*, vol.9:48, February 1881, p.390; Malcolm, *The Irish Policeman*, pp.96–101.

68 R. B. O'Brien, *Dublin Castle and the Irish People*, Dublin: M. H. Gill, 1909, pp.124–6. For a very similar view from a unionist source, see C. Lloyd, *Ireland under the Land League: A Narrative of Personal Experiences*, Edinburgh: William Blackwood, 1892, p.57.

Section 2

Chief Constables and their forces

5 Chief Constables as 'moral heroes' and guardians of public morality

Kim Stevenson

Introduction

This chapter explores the role of certain Chief Constables in the late nineteenth century who were regarded as effective law enforcers because of the ruthless stance they adopted towards the policing of immoral behaviour within their communities. Often self-declaredly presenting themselves as standard bearers and guardians of public morality such individuals were exemplary models of irrepressible moral leadership, deploying operational strategies to control social behaviour that local elites regarded as essentially immoral: primarily drunkenness, prostitution, betting and gambling. Typically, such policing was reactive, responding to the demands of the local Watch Committee and magistracy by enforcing the established law using conventional policing practices. But some Chief Constables gained national prominence because they were particularly proactive in implementing policy-led initiatives that targeted types of everyday offending perceived as immoral. This prompts the question of whether such figures were simply highly effective conduits and managers who obediently implemented the wishes of their masters, or whether their own personal moral integrity and beliefs compelled and empowered them to lead the way by example effectively utilizing the law to curb such immoral practices and, as highly influential individuals, having a direct impact upon the wider popular consciousness and consensus.

Operational orders suggest that such 'moralistic' Chief Constables could be characterized as early proponents of a form of zero tolerance policing (ZTP) and 'tough on crime' rhetoric well before such late-twentieth century terms were even imagined. Their actions echo Punch's contemporary descriptor of ZTP as 'a catalyst for a more assertive style of policing' reinforced by the uniquely British "service and consent" paradigm' but they contrast sharply with his assertion that it operated more as a rhetorical device than a major policy shift.[1] These were in fact deliberate policy initiatives. For example, in 1876, Birmingham's recently appointed Chief Superintendent of Police, Major Edwin Bond, instigated a major crackdown against drunkenness in the city, ordering his constables to arrest all

1 M. Punch, *Zero Tolerance Policing*, Bristol: Policy Press, 2007 pp.ix–x.

'quiet drunks' found in public thoroughfares irrespective of whether they were disorderly or misbehaving.[2] This led to an inevitable conflict with the Watch Committee concerning his legal authority and jurisdiction to issue such commands and resultant calls for his dismissal.[3] In justifying an unsuccessful prosecution of a music hall manager for 'improper performances' he claimed his office granted him the independent right to institute such prosecutions as 'the guardian of public morality and order' which again was not well received by the Committee and local justices.[4] In 1893, Plymouth's new Chief Constable, Joseph Davison Sowerby, an avowed temperance supporter, earned acclaim from the Mayor and local dignitaries for his widespread moral campaign and policing plan to tackle alcohol-fuelled offending and curb drunkenness. Similarly, his innovative leadership and deliberate introduction of ZTP-style techniques, which provide a case study for this chapter, cannot simply be dismissed as mere 'rhetoric' as together they clearly evidence a shift in law enforcement policy and crackdown on 'bad behaviour' operationalized by Sowerby with the support of the Watch Committee and local elites.[5] Such operational direction enables an informative and detailed analysis of one force's strategic approach to policing immorality and the issues generated by such responses. While certain examples of such pre-emptive and proactive policing garnered plaudits for successfully meeting Watch Committee expectations in achieving agreed social objectives, some pioneering tactics such as the use of surveillance techniques to help secure convictions, proved more controversial. So how were such strategies received by the public and local police committees, especially given Pike's assertion that in relation to the exercise of discretion in respect of public morality it is 'often difficult to assess the boundaries of public indignation or public tolerance'?[6] What legal authority justified such initiatives and what was the judicial response? To what extent were leaders like Sowerby self-determined 'moral guardians of the law' desirous of and able to impose their own moral perspectives and values on the local populace, and are there any indications that they possessed any distinctive character traits that could motivate such moral evangelism? Before examining Sowerby's leadership and endeavours in more detail, the chapter starts with a brief prosopographical profile of the requisite personal characteristics and previous career experience that prospective Chief Constables were generally expected to demonstrate to justify their credentials as the potential moral figurehead of both the local community and their men.

2 *Manchester Courier and Lancashire General Advertiser*, 19 August 1876.

3 The friction between Bond and the Watch Committee endured for the six years he held the post until he was dismissed in 1882 and was raised in Parliament in discussions about his subsequent appointment as a police magistrate in Ballingarry, Tipperary, *Birmingham Daily Post*, 11 February 1882, *Leeds Times*, 7 January 1882.

4 See N. Fielding, *The Police and Social Conflict*, 2nd edn, London: GlassHouse Press, 2005, p.29.

5 *Plymouth Comet*, 1 July 1893.

6 M. Pike, *The Principles of Policing*, Basingstoke: Macmillan 1985, p.69.

Leading by 'moral' example

Colquhoun's 1796 blueprint on how to prevent crime explicitly stressed the importance of morality in respect of both the official role and personal conduct of the police recommending that not only should it be 'the business of the parochial Chief Constable to instruct petty constables in their duty', but that they should also 'impress upon their minds the necessity of purity, vigilance and attention to orders, and of being humane, prudent and vigorous in the execution of their duties'.[7] Peel confirmed that the new Metropolitan Police must maintain high standards of individual professionalism, honesty and integrity.[8] The police constable, as Emsley notes, was 'the "domestic missionary" charged with bringing civilisation and decorum' to his community.[9] Chief Constables therefore needed to lead by example but how did Watch Committees when appointing a borough chief officer, and the local magistrates on recommending a county Chief Constable to the Home Secretary, ensure that potential applicants met such moralistic expectations?

The County Police Act 1839 stipulated that justices could only recommend the appointment of a county Chief Constable provided he was under 45 years, fit to perform the duties of office, not a declared bankrupt and was of general good character and conduct. A Home Office Circular in 1857 authorized by the County and Borough Police Act 1856 reduced these stipulations to fitness to perform and general good character and conduct.[10] Borough and city Chief Constables were directly recruited by the Watch Committee under the Municipal Corporations Act 1835 which was less restrictive in its appointment criteria and typically more influenced by local party politics and mutuality. Their police forces were a symbol of civic pride to which power and authority was delegated to the Chief Constable as the public-facing representative of idealistic moral dignity. This is reflected in Kleinig's description of the modern equivalent of ethical policing referring 'not so much to the morality of police officers and their institutions but to that morality as it is refracted through various roles and institutional purposes.'[11]

Both types of police authority 'sought Chief Constables whose backgrounds and social qualities were similar' to the district's social, economic and municipal elites with inevitably 'various hidden [and] social agendas at play'.[12] Fielding notes that in many small forces Chief Constables were often cowed by strong Watch Committees undermining their authority and there was often 'conflict between the high-minded morals of lowly constables and the venal self-interest of their

7 P. Colquhoun, *A Treatise on the Police of the Metropolis*, London: J. Mawman,1806, p.407.

8 See Pike, *The Principles of Policing*, p.42.

9 C. Emsley, *The English Police: A Political and Social History*, Abingdon: Routledge, 2014, p.74.

10 These provisions were not revised until the Police Act 1919.

11 J. Kleinig, 'Ethical policing', in A. Wakefield and J Fleming (eds) *Sage Dictionary of Policing*, London: Sage, 2009, p.107.

12 D. Wall, *The Chief Constables of England and Wales: The Socio-Legal History of a Criminal Justice Elite*, Aldershot: Ashgate, 1998, pp.97, 101.

superiors'.[13] As Taylor confirms in the opening chapter, Watch Committees could instruct Chief Constables on law enforcement policy but Chief Constables retained their original authority under the common law, thus it was the nature of the relationship between the two and the composition of the committee that were fundamental to any effective policing policy. This is also demonstrated in Cox's chapter concerning the somewhat fraught career of Henry Goddard, Chief Constable of Northamptonshire 1840–9. The county justices in particular were closely connected with the local aristocracy therefore the formative years of most county forces were dominated by the influence of gentry and clergy. Justices usually recruited individuals equal to themselves in social standing and outlook, typically the 'scions of gentry families' experienced in military command; this is reinforced by both Cox and Ireland in their respective chapters.[14] Such appointments increased significantly after the 1856 Act as conflicts throughout the Empire meant that senior military personnel could prove the necessary criteria of good character and conduct. A stereotypical example is Colonel Walter Raleigh Gilbert CB who, with 23 years' service in the Royal Horse Artillery, was invited to be Chief Constable of Cornwall (1857–96). Gilbert could trace his family lineage back to Edward the Confessor and later Sir Humphrey Gilbert (half-brother of Walter Raleigh). Bodmin Beacon, a 150-foot memorial costing £1,500, had been recently erected in honour of his uncle Lieutenant General Sir Walter Raleigh Gilbert's distinguished service in the 1845 India campaign, and his father was a Prebendary at the Cathedral.[15] It is therefore highly unlikely that there could have been a more 'suitable' candidate.

Wall estimates that prior to 1920 and the changes wrought by the Desborough Review, 95 per cent of county Chief Constables had previous military experience in the rank of captain or above, 50 per cent of whom had held the position of Major or higher.[16] Among other examples, he cites the Standing Joint Committee's selection process for the new Chief Constable of Buckinghamshire in 1896 which attracted 61 mainly upper-middle and middle-class applicants comprising 80 per cent middle-ranking military officers, 15 per cent with no military rank but with strong local connections, and 5 per cent who were serving officers. To give a sense of the importance of military service, testimonials were received from two field marshals, 27 major generals, 35 lieutenant generals, three brigadier generals, 102 colonels, 35 lieutenant colonels, fifteen majors and six captains. Four majors and one commander were shortlisted. The successful applicant, Major Otway Mayne, was another stereotypical exemplar who possessed the requisite military

13 Though he does not provide any supporting examples, Fielding, *The Police and Social Conflict*, p.32.

14 See T. Jefferson and R. Grimshaw, *Controlling the Constable: Police Accountability in England and Wales*, London: Frederick Muller, 1984, p.38; Wall, *The Chief Constables of England and Wales*, p.91.

15 Obituary, *The Times*, 19 October 1896.

16 Wall, *The Chief Constables of England and Wales*, p.275.

background, support of a serving Chief Constable and a 'preferred social profile' with connections to leading local and national politicians.[17]

Further evidence of the importance of military service can be gleaned from a qualitative assessment of the obituaries of Chief Constables who served between the mid-nineteenth century and the early years of the First World War published in *The Times* 1894–1942.[18] Wall suggests that a Chief Constable's 'military status was typically more significant than his military achievements, especially before the First World War'.[19] But the obituaries indicate that individual courageousness could be an equally compelling factor in establishing moral character and strength. Predictably, the ranks of Colonel, Lieutenant Colonel, Major and the more junior rank of Captain are well represented. Not only had these men commanded troops and fought for Empire with active service in a range of major conflicts but many were recipients of awards for bravery or had been mentioned in despatches including a recommendation for the Victoria Cross,[20] Khedive's Star,[21] and medals and clasps from the Crimea,[22] Ashanti, Cabul, Punjab, Lucknow, Burma, Sudan, etc. Otway Mayne had received medals in Afghan, Yawaki and Burma and was remembered for 'his tactfulness, shrewd judgement of character and his power of leading and inspiring his men'.[23] These were genuine, proven heroes including many nationally known figures who, if they had served in the troublesome domains of India or Ireland, epitomized the 'face of empire'. An unblemished military background automatically endorsed a man's status as a loyal and positive leader and the bestowal of an award proved he had the moral integrity to put others before himself. Rowbotham underlines how such military leaders were portrayed as hagiographic heroes in popular literature to encourage 'manliness' and moral responsibility and that any 'personal heroic characteristics highlighted are generally revealing of the priorities and prejudices of the period'.[24] She states that between 1850–70 there was an 'air of confident British masculinity' underpinned by a set of complex stereotypical expectations predicated on respectability and morality essentially mandating that 'heroes' and 'good leaders' must demonstrate proof of moral courage.[25] Therefore it was critical that Chief Constables were appointed

17 Ibid., pp.101–3.

18 Survey based on 53 obituaries covering a wide range of 46 county and city forces in England and Wales. There is evidence that 66 per cent had previous military experience, of those who served between 1850–1915 the figure was 79 per cent.

19 Wall, *The Chief Constables of England and Wales*, p.272.

20 James Kellie-Macullum, Northamptonshire (1881–1931), the longest serving of all Chief Constables, *The Times*, 15 September 1932.

21 Captain Williams-Freeman, Shropshire, (1890–1905), *The Times*, 28 December 1905.

22 Captain Robert Sterne,Wiltshire (1870–1908), *The Times*, 6 June 1927; Captain Francis Perry, Derbyshire, (1873–92), *The Times*, 21 February 1905.

23 (1896–1928), *The Times*, 4 November 1939.

24 J. Rowbotham, '"All our past proclaims our future": Popular biography and masculine identity', in I. Inkster (ed.) *The Golden Age: Essays in British Social and Economic History* 1850–1870, Aldershot: Ashgate, 2000, p.264.

25 Ibid., p.262.

who could be endorsed by their committee as moral protagonists able to inspire the men under their command and be relied upon to lead from the front while at the same time obeying the wishes of their committee. Interestingly, while many obituaries highlight individual military exploits, apart from a few notable exceptions such as Sir Robert Peacock, Chief Constable of Manchester and Sir Charles Rafter, Chief Constable of Birmingham,[26] they rarely reference any aspects of their police role and (often significant) achievements. This implies that there was a general public expectation and trust of what Chief Constables were required to do and that while in the smaller borough forces many tended to be regarded as symbolic figureheads, in the larger forces they needed to promote themselves as established and effective leaders.

Managing drunkenness and immorality

In advocating the moral responsibility of the police Colquhoun also proposed that legislation should be enacted enabling them to deal with:

> THE PREVENTION OF THE PRESENT CORRUPTION OF MORALS, as originating from ill-regulated Public Houses, Tea-Gardens, Theatres, and other places of Public Amusement; indecent Publications; Ballad-Singers, Female Prostitution, Servants out of Place, the lotterry[*sic*]; Gaming, Indigence and various other causes.[27]

The trope of immorality permeated society throughout the nineteenth century generated by the dogma of the social purity movement and moral campaigners including the Society for the Reformation of Manners and Society for the Suppression of Vice (later the Public Morality Council) who self-determined what conduct was 'socially immoral' and should be prohibited.[28] Activities perceived as immoral had been largely controlled by the common law on a case-by-case basis, but by the mid-nineteenth century the police had gained a range of powers to deal with undesirable behaviour through the generic Vagrancy Act 1824 and Town Police Clauses Act 1847 which created new statutory offences that conferred powers on the police to arrest violators. But increasingly, despite such regulation, the allure of alcohol magnetized immoral conduct and bad behaviour, triggering public demands and political pressure to curb drunkenness and restrict drinking. However, the police had no specific powers to deal with individuals who were drunk and incapable or drunk and disorderly until the Licensing Act 1872 authorized the issuing of summons for such offences. In the early days of the Metropolitan Police, Commissioners Rowan and Mayne had been reluctant to

26 Both died in post having served 40 and 36 years respectively in the rank.

27 Colquhoun, *A Treatise on Policing*, p.617.

28 For a more detailed discussion on this see D. J. Cox *et al.*, *Public Indecency England, 1857–1960*, Abingdon: SOLON Routledge, 2015, chap.2.

police licentiousness, fearing that it could undermine their reputation and public support, particularly as there was no legislative or judicial backing.[29] Conversely, as with the example of Major Bond cited in the introduction to this chapter, some chief officers were prepared to push the boundaries of the statutory provisions and direct their officers to crack down on the problem utilizing their more nebulous common law powers of public protection. Therefore, as Miller notes, police chiefs found themselves in an invidious position caught between the religious fervour of Sabbatarianism aided by the growth of the temperance movement and teetotalism but reliant on the respect of the working classes and libertarians to maintain order.

By the last quarter of the nineteenth century political concern intensified about public drunkenness and how it undermined moral discipline spawning prostitution, gambling, violence and general disorder. As Yeomans notes, the 'People could not be coerced into sobriety' but the State could make it more difficult for them to become intoxicated.[30] The 1872 Act, sponsored by the Home Secretary Henry Bruce, granted magistrates more control over the management of licensed premises and the police more powers to enter and inspect them in order to 'persuade' citizens to 'self-improve' by summonsing licensees to appear before the court. Individuals were allowed the legal freedom to drink but within 'officially designated moral parameters' and censure.[31] Yeomans applies Ruonavaara's model of persuasive moral regulation to the growing temperance movement, arguing that there was a synergy with the Act's legal regulation as both sought to engender rather than force, behavioural reform.[32] The Home Office keenly monitored the impact of the Act and alcohol-related policing generally as underlined by the specific references of HM Inspectors of Constabulary in their annual reports. These included comparative comment and rankings in relation to the annual statistical returns from each force area on the number of licensed premises, type of liquor sold and convictions for drunk and disorderly offences.[33] Cox's research explains why the Home Office were so concerned because nationally the number of convictions for drunkenness between 1885–1905 generally increased.[34] Plymouth, however, provides an interesting comparator. Compared to the larger borough forces such as Birmingham, Liverpool and Manchester discussed elsewhere in this book, Plymouth was a relatively small force with approximately 100 men. But as a naval port they had to contend with similar and significant alcohol-related problems. Once notorious for its overcrowded public houses which encouraged inebriacy,

29 W. Miller, 'Never on Sunday: Moralistic reformers and the police in London and New York City', in D. Bayley (ed.) *Police and Society*, London: Sage, 1977, pp.130–2.

30 H. Yeomans, *Alcohol and Moral Regulation*, Bristol: Policy Press 2014, p.83.

31 Ibid., p.85.

32 Ibid., p.87 citing H. Ruonavaara, 'Moral regulation: A reformulation', *Sociological Theory*, 1997, vol.15:3, 277–293.

33 See Parliamentary Papers, *Reports of the Inspectors of Constabulary 1896–1897*, Paper 379, London: Home Office, 1898, pp.6, 73, 258–63; *Reports of the Inspectors of Constabulary 1897–1898*, Paper 157, London: Home Office, 1899, p.73.

34 Cox *et al.*, *A Serious and Growing Evil*, p.162.

prostitution and illicit gambling among its residents and visiting sailors, the town experienced a reverse in this trend directly attributable to the policy shifts introduced by the appointment of its new Chief Constable in 1892. Five years later, Joseph Sowerby proudly informed the 1897 Royal Commission on Liquor Licensing Laws that as a result of his resourceful efforts and extensive monitoring of the town's 350 licensed premises 'there is less drunkenness than there used to be. Drunkenness is decreasing.'[35]

Sowerby was an atypical appointment and unlike the more well-known leaders of the larger forces, he had no previous military experience. In 1881, aged eighteen, he followed his father who had moved from Everton to Leeds to become a publican, and joined the Leeds City Police as a clerk. Leeds had already secured a reputation for employing a robust approach to drunkenness initiated by its former Chief Constable, James Wetherell (1866–74). Storch notes that the Chief Constables of Leeds 'saw themselves as natural allies of the temperance movement, with whose local leaders they corresponded'. Wetherell expressed his support for the extended closing of public houses and the complete closure of beerhouses on the Sabbath 'as long as the working classes imbibe the . . . decoctions of Beer sellers there will not only be drunkenness and poverty but crimes of open violence among us.'[36] Such a standpoint was continued by Sowerby's two superiors, the Nott-Bower brothers: Captain Sir William Nott-Bower (1878–81) who would become Head Constable of Liverpool and then Commissioner of the City of London,[37] and Arthur Nott-Bower (1881–90). Sowerby quickly moved through the ranks making First Inspector within three years and Chief Inspector two years later, in 1891 he was credited with bringing to justice Walter Lewis Turner, executed for cutting the throat of six year-old Barbara Waterhouse, thereby establishing his investigative skills.[38]

Sowerby held no military honours to prove his moral courage but he had regularly taken charge of the fire brigades in Leeds and attended some 400 fires. In January 1892 he nearly died in the notorious 'Dark Arches' fire underneath Leeds railway station which took 20 hours to control and caused £200,000 damage. According to the *Leeds Times*, Sowerby and a colleague found themselves 'IN CONSIDERABLE PERIL' and had to dive into the Leeds and Liverpool canal.[39] Sowerby 'being an expert swimmer, managed to keep afloat, in spite of the fact that the conflagration raged all around him, and that the water had somewhat the consistency of ink.'[40] Hauled out and with a quick change of clothes he was

35 Royal Commission on Liquor Licensing Laws [1897] c.8523 p.217.

36 Cited by R. D. Storch, 'The policeman as domestic missionary: Urban discipline and popular culture in Northern England, 1850–80', in R. J. Morris and R. Rodger (eds) *The Victorian City*, London: Longman, 1993, pp. 281–306 at 288.

37 His son was Sir John Nott-Bower, Metropolitan Police Commissioner (1953–8).

38 *Dundee Courier*, 13 June 1891; 'Shocking discovery at Leeds', *Nelson Evening Mail*, 11 September 1891.

39 *Leeds Times*, 16 January 1892; *Leeds Mercury* 14 January 1892.

40 *Plymouth Comet*, 1 July 1893 (marking the twelve-month anniversary of his appointment).

immediately back in action (while his colleague opted to remain at the infirmary) proving as equal a hero as any of his former military counterparts and substantiating his credentials of a 'good leader'.

Plymouth's Chief Constable, Arthur Frederick Wreford, a Freemason and Anglican conformist, had led the force for 26 years until his unexpected demise in 1892. Watch Committee records single out drunkenness and demoralizing exhibitions in the town's notorious Union Street, the display of indecent advertisements in public houses, swearing and obscenity in public and low-level violence as ongoing problems.[41] Such concerns chimed with a reinvigoration and 'multifying' of the number of local temperance associations[42] including the Plymouth Police Temperance Association. Wreford pleaded for another eleven constables to increase the force establishment to 103 and more severe fines from the magistrates to help 'greatly minimize the evils' but acknowledged 'I do not think a complete remedy is possible' as the only locations where 'the class of people who create the difficulties can resort' were licensed premises.[43] This prompted Plymouth's Watch Committee to seek a more commanding replacement, ideally an outsider and a nonconformist, to clean up the town and impose a solution.

The publican's nemesis

In July 1892, aged just 29, Sowerby's moral integrity and promise to eliminate drunkenness, prostitution and gambling clearly impressed the Committee; 'his testimonials were of the highest possible character, and his appearance and general behaviour told much in his favour'.[44] He quickly made his presence felt ordering his constables to fill the petty sessions registers with lists of offenders charged with drunk and disorderly, drunk and incapable, using profane and obscene language, keeping disorderly houses and harbouring prostitutes. He immediately instigated 79 proceedings against licensees for unlawfully permitting drunkenness, opening premises during prohibited hours and harbouring thieves and prostitutes, convincing the magistrates to close 60 public houses. This instantly triggered arguments at town council meetings between teetotallers, temperancers and the Licensed Victuallers' Protection Association who claimed its members were being harassed and were suffering significant financial loss. Sowerby then decided to review the management of all licensed houses and openly confirmed his sympathies, and bias, when he joined the Plymouth Methodist Temperance League.[45] He personally visited over 300 licensed traders, notably entering 40

41 See E. A. Dickaty, *From Rattles to Radio; A History of the Plymouth Police Plymouth* (original typed manuscript, 1977) Plymouth and West Devon Record Office (PWDRO), 922. p.37.

42 *Western Weekly News*, 19 November 1887; see *Western Weekly News*, 7 October 1893 for reference to the Plymouth Temperance Societies.

43 Dickaty, p.41. Wreford did get his extra men.

44 *Plymouth Comet*, 1 July 1893.

45 'Local gossip', *Trewman's Exeter Flying Post*, 6 August 1892.

premises on the same day asserting, in another example of moral direction, that he could not trust his constables as the licensees were supplying them with liquor while on duty.[46]

Plymouth's elite welcomed Sowerby's strong leadership. To mark his first twelve months in office the *Plymouth Comet* reported that 'In connection with the suppression of immorality in Plymouth, and in other ways where law breakers are concerned, our Chief Constable has shown himself equal to any emergency'. The editorial confirmed that 'the local papers have on several occasions highly eulogized Mr Sowerby for his zeal and discretion'.[47] Sowerby's crackdown on licensees was reinforced by the press with reports of prosecutions highlighted by-lines such as 'IMPORTANT POLICE PROSECUTION'.[48] As a temperance advocate, Sowerby, was as equally concerned about the causes of alcohol as its effects and made no distinctions across class boundaries.[49] But his main aim was to reduce the consumption of alcohol believing this would in turn diminish the problems associated with immorality and sexual impropriety. Sowerby's success, aided by the magistracy and Watch Committee, would have been less effective without the support of other local agitators such as Isaac Foot, a fellow member of the Methodist Temperance League.[50] Foot was also a Guardian and no doubt acted as a conduit between Sowerby and the other temperancers on the Plymouth Board of Guardians who lobbied hard to prohibit alcohol being used as a 'medicinal measure' in the workhouse.[51]

Meanwhile the local breweries were smarting after being castigated by Sowerby because the exorbitant rates they demanded from their licensees encouraged the practice of 'rack renting' where whole families rented spare rooms in public houses resulting in some housing more than 20 adults and children. Sowerby was deeply troubled by such social problems and disturbed by the fact that children had to enter the bar to access their rooms and could peer into the 'snugs' where men and women (often prostitutes) would engage in sexual behaviour that was beyond the gaze of the landlord. Heavitree Brewery challenged Sowerby's enforcement initiative in a contested appeal at Exeter Quarter Sessions in 1896. The Brewery appealed a decision of the Plymouth Justices (based on a prosecution by Sowerby) to refuse to renew the licence of the Royal Exchange Inn because the former tenant had received two previous convictions courtesy of Sowerby's campaign.[52] The

46 Royal Commission on Liquor Licensing Laws [1897] c.8523 p.215.

47 *Plymouth Comet*, 1 July 1893.

48 *Western Weekly News*, 16 October 1893.

49 See examples of prosecutions reported in *Exeter Flying Post*, 2 December 1893.

50 Father of the future Liberal MP Isaac Foot and grandfather of the Labour party leader Michael Foot.

51 A Home Office report published in 1887 detailing the spend, in 1885, of every Workhouse in the country showed that Plymouth had the highest spend per inmate in the county and one of the highest nationally by a significant margin, *Return of Quantity of Spirits and Wine consumed in Workhouses in England and Wales, 1885*, House of Commons Papers, 18 June 1886.

52 Heavytree Brewery v Plymouth Justices, *Western Times*, 23 October 1896.

Justices called Plymouth's Chief Collector of Rates to testify as to the excessive number of licensed premises in the vicinity and the chaplain of the Seaman's Mission to depose that the Exchange was frequented by a certain 'low' class of person. His Honour Judge Edge upheld the appeal asserting that the Justices' argument that there were too many public houses was irrelevant to the refusal of the licence although he did reject the brewery's application for costs. Despite this setback Sowerby continued with his enforcement policy. In 1893 he prosecuted 28 publicans for breaching licensing regulations and in 1897 just nine, informing the Royal Commission that this was because licensees generally had become more cooperative and responsive to police advice although he retained the view that there was still an unnecessary number of public houses in the town.[53]

In 1903 Sowerby published an extensive audit of all 347 licensed premises to support his claim that in '1902 drunkenness has considerably decreased in the Borough.'[54] The number of public houses had reduced by 59 since 1875, the conviction rate for drunkenness was now one of the lowest nationally and the average population per licensed premises one of the highest. Sowerby modestly informed the Royal Commission that he attributed these successes to the 'improved social condition of the people' brought about by the police supervision of public houses and 'enlightened attitudes of the young'.[55] He continued to introduce innovative ideas to curtail drinking; a keen photographer, after the Licensing Act 1902 gave the police the power to arrest anyone found drunk and incapable, he personally photographed all habitual drunkards in the town, i.e. those convicted more than three times a year, confidentially distributing the images among licensed victuallers who could then alert officers to apprehend regular inebriates.[56] However, even Sowerby struggled to manage Plymouth's notorious Union Street; its eighteen public houses, 22 beerhouses, six off-licences and numerous brothels were an irresistible magnet drawing sailors and marines on shore leave, describing it in 1904 as 'the most difficult street in Plymouth to manage', a reputation it is only just starting to recover from today.[57]

'Moral' connexions

Pike cautions that 'where a chief officer of police adopts a moral stance in relation to selective enforcement' of the law, they are on difficult ground as ultimately they are responsible for enforcing the law and 'any professional judgement on moral issues may become an expression of personal moral values which are

53 Royal Commission on Liquor Licensing Laws, p.219.

54 PWDRO, 274/678, Plymouth Chief Constable's Report, Public Houses and Licensed Premises (1903).

55 Royal Commission on Liquor Licensing Laws, p.217.

56 *Photographic News*, 2 January 1903 and see 'Drunkenness and the law', *The Spectator*, 17 January 1903.

57 *The Western Times*, 6 April 1904.

out of step with public morality.'[58] This is particularly pertinent when considered in the context of late nineteenth century associations with prominent morality campaigners who lobbied for police cooperation and assistance to prosecute individuals they believed had committed 'immoral' offences. The establishment of the National Vigilance Association for the Repression of Criminal Vice and Public Immorality (NVA) in 1885 increased social purity efforts to educate the 'degenerative' classes and improve the health of the nation, framing an agenda that demanded the prohibition of all things 'indecent' including literature, advertisements, dramatic performances, mail communications, lotteries etc. Such moralistic activism intensified considerably in the 1890s as 'Middle-class campaigners enjoyed greater influence, co-opting newly empowered local councils, magistrates, and the now-ubiquitous police to the cause'.[59] Enlightening in this context is American research conducted among police officers in New Jersey in the 1970s that showed how the enforcement of law involving moral issues can be affected by their perception of a community's values, precipitating a 'sensitivity to local attitudes, beliefs and expectations' producing a response 'governed less by legal definition of what should be done and more of a personal value judgement of the situation'.[60] And it was those Chief Constables with strong moral instincts who found themselves in the awkward position of determining which community values to police without compromising their operational independence.

A number of Chief Constables from the larger city forces, disturbed by the seemingly intractable levels of everyday offending in their poorer wards, were persuaded by the rhetoric of the NVA. Mort's examination of the NVA's eleventh *Annual Report* published in 1896 confirms that some had become active members of the Association and were willing to collaborate with local branches, exchange information and reciprocally refer cases to ensure a greater likelihood of conviction. Mort references Birmingham's Joseph Farndale, Liverpool's Captain Sir John William Nott-Bower, and Manchester, Leeds, Sheffield and Cardiff as other cities where such mutual cooperation was evident.[61] The Sunderland Vigilance Association spoke positively of their local Chief Constable, William Huntley, who acted on complaints made by the branch without divulging the names of informants and in successfully closing several immoral houses.[62] Such societies could be equally critical if they perceived any reluctance on the part of Chief Constables to enforce their agenda as illustrated in the comment made by the secretary of the Leeds Vigilance Association regarding A. W. Nott-Bower 'declining to interfere with notorious houses' despite the issue of seventeen such summonses in the previous twelve months, twelve warrants for failing to answer and fifteen warnings.[63]

58 Pike, *The Principles of Policing*, p.73.

59 Cox *et al.*, *Public Indecency England, 1857–1960*, p.46 and chaps.3 and 4.

60 Pike, *The Principles of Policing*, p.70 citing research conducted by Finckenaur.

61 F. Mort, *Dangerous Sexualities: Medico-moral politics in England since 1830*, London: Routledge, 2000 p.105.

62 *Sunderland Daily Echo*, 16 May 1889.

63 *Leeds Times*, 4 February 1888.

Birmingham City Police were on particularly good terms with the NVA. In 1894 its local chairman stated that 'their work had been very much lightened, by the way in which' Chief Constable Farndale and his officers had helped them in 'doing so much to suppress bad houses.'[64] In 1900, William Alexander Coote, the vociferous national co-secretary of the NVA praised the 'splendid' Birmingham Police Force 'who had long assisted in the social and moral life of the city . . . creating a sweeter and purer Birmingham'. Farndale's successor, Sir Charles Rafter appointed in 1899, was lauded for securing the conviction of Robert Wells for obscene libel in publishing his book *Marriage Physiologically Considered*. Then already in its twentieth edition with thousands of copies sold the prosecution raises questions, however, about whether Rafter was sensitive to the interests of the whole community or was acting primarily from his own moral perspectives and beliefs.[65]

The NVA had lobbied hard, and for some time, to cultivate alliances with police leaders in the provinces beyond the Metropolis, especially the larger cities. The NVA actively sought the views of Chief Constables, for example on the criminalization of incestuous relations which was highly controversial at the time. Almost all were in favour despite considerable opposition from lawyers and magistrates who feared it would be counterproductive suggesting that many Chief Constables supported the conservative tendencies of the NVA.[66] In 1900, Samuel Smith MP, the NVA's parliamentary spokesman, informed its fifteenth Annual Meeting that in 'the past 20 to 30 years the moral tone of other cities had been advancing, but that of London had been going back.' He attributed this difference to the fact that as the Metropolitan Police were under the control of the Home Secretary they were less able to administer the law as 'vigorously' as those forces supervised by the County Councils.[67]

Back in Plymouth, Sowerby, with the backing of the Watch Committee was one of those NVA sympathizers able to rigorously enforce the law. As a maritime town Plymouth had a considerable number of immoral houses; in 1865 it was noted that in Stonehouse there were over 100 prostitutes in Fore Street alone servicing some 2–3,000 soldiers at the local barracks.[68] Although Stonehouse was outside Sowerby's jurisdiction (as a division of the Devon County Constabulary), the proximity of the boundaries between Plymouth and Stonehouse presented identical problems for both forces. There had been numerous attempts to prosecute beerhouse and brothel keepers but many 'unfortunate' and 'immoral' women who had lost their husbands at sea had no means of financial support other than

64 *Birmingham Daily Post*, 27 April 1900.

65 *Birmingham Daily Post*, 16 February 1900, also J. Reilly, *An Account of 150 Years of Policing Birmingham*, Birmingham: West Midlands Police 1989.

66 Mort, *Dangerous Sexualities*, p.105. Such fears were justified with the subsequent Punishment of Incest Act 1908, see K. Stevenson, '"These are cases which it is inadvisable to drag into the light of day" Disinterring the crime of incest in early twentieth century England', *Crime Histories and Societies*, 2016, vol. 20:2, pp. 6–28.

67 *The Times*, 23 June 1900.

68 *The Royal Cornwall Gazette*, 14 December 1865.

engaging in illegal prostitution. Beerhouse keepers claimed the presence of prostitutes was necessary to attract male customers and that 'it would be unjust to deprive' the women of their 'refreshments'.[69]

Sowerby was in the fortunate and authoritative position (long before the days of the Crown Prosecution Service) of being investigator, enforcer and prosecutor and could more easily express his concerns to the Bench and offer more informed and practical suggestions for disposal than could ever be the case today. In 1901 he started a campaign in association with the National Social Purity Crusade against the keepers and owners of disorderly houses leading the local press to by-line reports of such prosecutions as 'The Sowerby Crusade', the 'Plymouth Purity Crusade', 'a Policy of Worrying' and 'the Plymouth Agitation'.[70] Such rhetoric reflected the pervasive 'indecency agenda' of the new moral activists, middle-class Liberals and Conservatives, who invoked the concept of the Christian crusade to fight immorality, indecency and intoxication to turn the tide of 'degeneration' at the end of the nineteenth century.[71] In one such 'crusade' Sowerby and the Mayor of Plymouth visited his home town Liverpool, his former workplace Leeds, and the cities of Cardiff, Manchester and Portsmouth to see how other forces dealt with the suppression of vice. Undoubtedly Sowerby was familiar with this idea of knowledge transfer from his time at Leeds as referenced in Churchill's review of such fact-finding missions and sharing of police expertise among the main cities and towns as the development of what would become more formalized 'municipal networks'. And in contrast to the early influence of the Met as explored by Morris in Chapter 9, his foray substantiates David Barrie's argument that by the end of the nineteenth century 'British boroughs were more likely to look to each other for guidance on police administration than to seek answers from London.'[72]

Visiting Liverpool one of the reasons why Plymouth appeared to have a problem quickly became apparent. In 1890 there had been a dispute over the Head Constable William Nott-Bower's deliberate policy not to prosecute brothel keepers leading to vociferous complaints from purity campaigners. Nott-Bower believed that indiscriminate prosecution would spread prostitution across the city but succumbed to the demands of the Watch Committee and local justices instructing his officers to prosecute all known brothels. He instigated 443 proceedings which subsequently led to complaints from the Committee about the dispersal of prostitutes into more respectable areas, just as he had predicted.[73] To retrieve the situation Liverpool City Police adopted its own form of ZTP employing 64 plain-clothes constables to watch houses of accommodation with the result that when Sowerby visited the city in 1901 no brothels were visibly evident, also any prostitute who simply

69 Ibid.

70 PWDRO, 854/2 Plymouth Temperance Society booklet.

71 Cox *et al.*, *Public Indecency England, 1857–1960 p.*58 and ch.4 generally.

72 D. Churchill, 'Local initiative, central oversight, provincial perspective: Governing police forces in nineteenth-century Leeds', *Historical Research*, 2015, 458–81.

73 See Fielding, *The Police and Social Conflict*, p.30.

accosted three or more men was immediately convicted by the stipendiary magistrate.[74] Sowerby did not have such manpower and in Plymouth a conviction required proof that a prostitute had in fact made an invitation of an improper character, this not only required the police to enter a house to obtain evidence to show it was a place resorted to by known prostitutes but also witness testimonies to confirm the solicitation. In Cardiff, he found that for the past fifteen years the police had exercised strict vigilance and prosecuted every case they could; 'localities that were hotbeds of vice and crime have been entirely cleared of both'. On his return to Plymouth, Sowerby advised that the Watch Committee approve similar strategies and requested that the current force be strengthened in order to do so.[75] Despite his best efforts and securing extra men to act as watchers of houses of ill-repute Sowerby never managed to completely control the problem largely because of the naval presence in the town and he must have been frustrated when, in 1907, a representative from the NVA came down to Plymouth as locals had raised concerns about the ongoing 'flagrancy of immoralities' in Plymouth and Stonehouse.[76]

Moral protector or 'spoiler'?

Not content with eliminating sexual immorality on licensed premises, Sowerby's next target was to tackle premises that allowed betting on the basis that it encouraged more drinking. He invoked the Suppression of Betting Houses Act 1853, which had not been used in Plymouth for over 30 years, and started to watch suspected houses to gain evidence on which to conduct a number of raids between 1893–96. These were widely reported in the press nationally as such legislative tactics had not been used by other forces thereby promoting Sowerby's reputation. Readers of the *Birmingham Post* and *Bristol Mercury* were informed that 'Chief Constable Sowerby had raided a public house' and seized evidence of betting, his police officers had dressed as labourers to avoid recognition and all classes were involved from fishermen to tradespeople.[77] Was this simply a matter of public record or was it perhaps a warning from the respective editors to their readers that they might find themselves subjected to similar raids? On 18 April 1894 Sowerby led 60 plain-clothes officers to raid twelve licensed premises including a chemist, tobacconist and bowling alley, arresting all the proprietors and 50 men found to have laid bets at the various locations.[78] The following week a further eighteen men were arrested after Sowerby, of his own volition, paid two undercover agents a weekly wage to monitor licensed premises in the town over a two month period, he also gave them money to act as agents provocateurs to place bets in public

74 PWDRO 854/2 Plymouth Temperance Society booklet.
75 Ibid.
76 PWDRO 94/2 Plymouth and Stonehouse Vigilance Association.
77 *Birmingham Daily Post* 30 March 1893, 6 April 1893; *Bristol Mercury*, 30 March 1893.
78 *Nottingham Evening Post* 19 April 1894; *Western Gazette* 20 April 1894.

houses in order to secure evidence for prosecutions. Interestingly, the accused were termed 'victims' in the newspaper report emphasizing the views of the editor and readers who regarded such methods as unacceptable 'foreign' or 'Continental' policing. The defence were highly critical of Sowerby's 'underhand' tactics especially when Sowerby acknowledged he had allowed one of the men to keep his winnings in lieu of any wages.[79] In another case against Philip Curzon, the landlord of the Spirit Vaults, where a number of racing chronicles, guides and sporting papers were seized by Sowerby's stooge, the defence counsel protested to the magistrates that 'If on such evidence the magistrates held there was a *prima facie* against the defendant, no citizen of Plymouth would at any time be safe.' The magistrates agreed and dismissed the case because of the use of an agent provocateur amid much public applause.[80]

There is evidence of a consciousness that in conducting these raids Sowerby was aware that he was not arresting the usual criminal types but ordinary respectable people whose confidence he needed to retain. When one defendant, Brock, tried to destroy some gambling papers during a raid on his tobacconist shop, PC Voysey immediately slapped on the handcuffs. Brock later complained, and amid much laughter in court Voysey stated, 'That's nothing to losing your head.' However, Sowerby stepped in and offered an apology:

> It was not my wish that violence of any kind should have been used to anybody, but from what I have heard, you have been greatly to blame in this matter. The matter, however, shall be inquired into, and you shall have an opportunity of being present at the inquiry. I am sorry that the handcuffs have been used at all.[81]

Betting and gambling have of course always attracted concern, but whist drives? In the early twentieth century winter whist drives were enormously popular in raising money for charitable causes often combined with evening dances. Sowerby announced that he would prosecute anyone who organized a whist drive where there was a fee for entry or participation saying he had no choice but to enforce the law and apply it. Unsurprisingly, this led to a 'lively agitation' especially when 20 bookings at the Corn Exchange were suddenly cancelled. For Plymouth's respectable class this was a step too far, prompting a number of groups to protest and defy the ban and prosecutions to collapse.[82]

Conclusion

Chief Constables like Sowerby were able to exert considerable influence on the expected moral behaviour of their local community by imposing, or as in the case

79 *Devon and Exeter Daily Gazette* 28 April 1894; *The Western Times* 24 and 25 July 1894.

80 *Western Morning News*, 10 May 1894.

81 *Western Morning News*, 9 May 1894.

82 *Derby Daily Telegraph*, 27 September 1912.

of attempting to prohibit whist drives, their own views and standards. In 1910 a number of Chief Constables gave evidence to the Royal Commission on Divorce and Matrimonial Proceedings Commission about whether local courts should be given jurisdiction to permit divorces in respect of the poorer classes as they could not afford to initiate divorce proceedings at the High Court. Spouses subjected to domestic violence or whose partner had left the matrimonial home could make applications to the Police Court for separation orders and maintenance payments but securing such orders was something of a 'postcode lottery'. While the Chief Constable of Worcester was sympathetic to such cases, Sowerby believed that 'Separation of that kind was not conducive to good morality.' In support he cited statistics that in the previous three years 69 applications for separation orders had been made in Plymouth, 35 were granted of which fourteen couples were still living apart and ten were back together. The Chief Constable of Hull agreed that 'divorce for desertion would ruin the national character' and the sanctity of marriage was 'the greatest national asset'.[83] Sowerby also reprised his concerns about the poorer classes living in public houses.[84] But he was also pragmatic and was one of the first Chief Constables to recruit women as Special Constables to look after the morals of young girls found wandering the streets at night.

There is no question that Sowerby proved to be an effective moral evangelist, diplomatic and politically astute he genuinely believed in social change and justice for all not just the few. The temperance agenda provided the context for his campaign against drunkenness, betting and gambling and its success is largely attributable to the concerted moral judgements he and his associates made about individual conduct but more significantly in targeting those who supplied and sold intoxicants. Sowerby's approach and strategies confirm Innes' ZTP model that traditional policing functions resided more 'in the veiled nature of the available coercion – an iron fist in a velvet glove' rather than the 1990's 'tough on crime' rhetoric.[85] Innes also concludes that late-twentieth century ZTP strategies were simplistically deceptive in appearing to address the underlying and complex causes of crime by targeting the problems of disorder, ultimately tending to deal with the effects rather than its roots[86] whereas Sowerby genuinely tried to understand and tackle those underlying causes informed by his own moral compass.

Sowerby's broad police experience and qualification, as administrator, fire-fighter, leader and prosecuting officer in court is very different to that of his modern-day counterparts. As a case study Sowerby offers a useful comparator in respect of the contemporary and ongoing debate about whether it is necessary and/or desirable that ACPO ranks be required to work their way up from the 'uniform copper on the beat' or be directly parachuted in at senior levels from

83 *The Times*, 19 March 1910.

84 *Aberdeen Daily Journal*, 10 March 1910.

85 M. Innes, 'An "iron fist in an iron glove": The Zero Tolerance Policing debate', *The Howard Journal*, 1999, vol.38:4, 397–410 at p.398.

86 Ibid., p.401.

other internal departments and external organizations. Other leading figures have also, albeit more controversially, sought to impose their moral perspectives on the local populace through various early forms of ZTP such as 'God's cop' James Anderton of Greater Manchester Police in the 1980s and former soldier Captain Popkess of Nottingham City Police in the 1960s but arguably neither commanded the same respect from both the local authorities and the public. Sowerby retained the confidence of the Watch Committee until his retirement in 1917, celebrated by the *Plymouth Pictorial and Western Figaro*. The paper lauded Sowerby on its front page 'Open letter to Local Celebrities' feature on behalf of the town by-lined 'Sowerby: An English Gentleman'. This encapsulates the response to Pike's query referred to at the beginning of this chapter regarding the difficulty of assessing public reaction and acceptance to the policing of public morality:

> I have searched all over Plymouth – the Three Towns and have not been able to find a single man who had a word to say against you. You are well respected. You have, I am told an unblemished record and your retirement is generally and unanimously regretted. The town, whatever its libellers say, is a much more moral, clean and better behaved borough than when you came a quarter of a century ago and I knew it to be something, well different.

6 'A nonconformist must be Chief Constable'

The historical challenges of policing in rural Wales[1]

Richard W. Ireland

Introduction

That the office of Chief Constable is a responsible one is unquestionable, but the nature of that responsibility requires further consideration. Historically, the Chief Constable was obliged to look upwards, to the wishes of lawmakers, the influence of the Government (national and local) and the requirements of the Inspectorate: he had, in other words, 'responsibility to' others. But he also had to look downwards, to the conditions of his force, the expectations of his community, the nature and extent of local criminality: the elements which made up his 'responsibility for' others. Once we begin to examine the complexities of this notion of responsibility we find tensions may arise between its two elements, while the easy identification of its terms ('community'?) becomes increasingly problematic. In this chapter I will examine a series of disputes illustrative of these problems within the County of Cardiganshire in West Wales in the late nineteenth and early twentieth centuries before discussing a similar dispute over the role of the Chief Constable in the 1950s which eventually led to the disestablishment of the Cardiganshire Constabulary.

This then is not a comprehensive review of the office in Wales. Nor could it be, for Wales as a country contained the urban and industrial areas of the South and the North East, the rural fastnesses of the West and North West. The relations between these and the conditions within them changed considerably in the period of around a hundred years (from the 1850s to the 1950s) which form the boundaries of this study, as indeed do the relations with its immediate neighbours, Ireland and England. Moreover, although the experience of Wales, as I have argued elsewhere, has been frequently overlooked, it may not be in all respects exceptional.

1 I would like to thank Ffion Llewelyn, Nerys Llewelyn Davies, Heledd Hâf Evans, Hannah Williams and Helen Palmer and the staff of Ceredigion Archives for their assistance in the writing of this chapter. The title is taken from an article by the Welsh Correspondent of the *Independent* during the 1890 controversy to be discussed within this chapter. That comment is quoted and roundly condemned ('the cloven hoof of Dissenting despotism is no longer concealed') in the *Carmarthen Journal*, 14 November 1890.

Many of the problems which will be encountered in the following narrative, particularly as relating to the challenges of policing small, tight-knit rural communities, would not, I suspect, be found only to the west of Offa's Dyke. Others, however, such as the significant question of language, clearly have a specifically Welsh dimension.[2]

One general point that needs to be addressed at the outset is that no matter what cultural and structural elements may have had a bearing on the experience of Chief Constables in Wales, the more specific details of their individual characters and personalities, and those of others with whom they interact, must necessarily be a factor in structuring that experience. History may be explicable through wider social forces, but it is not populated by them, though the importance of social background in underlying character cannot be understated. This will become clear in the narrative which follows, but the influence of individual actors has wider importance. Without the reactionary, red-fearing intensity of the polo-playing Chief Constable of Glamorgan, Lionel Lindsay, the policing of significant industrial disputes such as the Tonypandy Riots of 1911 and the social legacy which such disputes left might have been rather different.[3] Similarly, Rachael Jones has argued that a clampdown on drunkenness and prostitution in Montgomeryshire in the 1870s was a result of an initiative by the Chief Constable John Danily.[4]

Just as significant as individual character was the issue of social class, indeed in the case of Lionel Lindsay it is impossible to distinguish their relative influence. Evidence of such class relation can be seen in the particular events related below, but again it seems wise to pause at the outset to reflect more generally on this dynamic. In occupying an intermediate position in terms of responsibility the Chief Constable is also obliged to deal with the dynamic of both social superiors and social inferiors. The relationship between the old county gentry who formed the local Quarter Sessions bench to whom the Chief Constable initially reported and that figure himself, might differ as between the ex-army officers who often took charge of the early constabulary forces and those promoted through the ranks of the police whose appointments became more consistent at a rather later period

2 See R. W. Ireland, *Land of White Gloves? A History of Crime and Punishment in Wales*, London: Routledge, 2015, *passim*, but particularly the Introduction.

3 For Lindsay and more generally for policing in South Wales see D. J. V. Jones, *Crime and Policing in the Twentieth Century: The South Wales Experience*, Cardiff, University of Wales Press, 1996, especially chap.4. See his comment on p.188: 'The Glamorgan police had a conservative, even backward image, which owed something to the fact that for almost a hundred years (1841–1937) it was run by Chief Constables of a military-gentry lineage. Henry (1867–91) and Lionel Lindsay (1891–1937), father and son, with a family estate at Glasnevin near Dublin, mixed naturally with the Glamorgan gentry at race meetings, shoots, shows and clubs, and displayed an old-fashioned paternalism'. C. Emsley, *The English* [*sic*] *Police: A Political and Social History*, London: St Martin's Press, 1991 also considers Lionel's relations with both local coal owners and his Standing Joint Committee. For Lindsay's polo, see *Glamorgan Gazette*, 18 June 1909.

4 R. Jones, Crime, Courts and Community in Mid-Victorian Montgomeryshire, unpublished PhD thesis, Aberystwyth University, 2015, p.139. For another individual see Anon, *Chief Constable Mackenzie: Cardiff's Reformer*, South Wales Police Museum, History Notebook 15, nd.

(see Stevenson, Chapter 5). It is tempting to speculate that one of the reasons such military men were in demand was as much their experience of the mess as their powers of leadership.[5] That the tide began to turn against such men is evident from a piece in the *Cardiff Times* of May 1889, which, having highlighted specific problems attributable to ex-army men in charge of both Glamorgan and Cardiganshire forces, continued:

> Chief Constables who have been appointed from among military men carry with them into the force which is intended to preserve peace, all the weaknesses and arrogance, and tendencies to appeal to brute force of those whose duty is war. . . . It is full time that the custom which has cost the country so much in broken heads and ruined homes should be put a stop to, and the principle be universally adopted that the most fitting man for the post of a Chief Constable should be sought for in the ranks of the force itself.[6]

If the vector of change seems a natural one it is not uncomplicated. The man who had worked his way up from the rank of constable was emblematic of the new breed of professional 'expert' whose experience demanded respect from those, such as Justices of the Peace (JP), whose qualifications lay in such general accomplishments as tenure and rank were assumed to confer. Nevertheless he might lack the social status of those to whom he might in other circumstances be expected to defer.[7] A couple of examples illustrate the complexities of this relationship.

In addressing the Select Committee on Police of 1853 Sir Baldwin Leighton's evidence speaks of an effortless superiority. Leighton was a JP in both Shropshire and Montgomeryshire, living on the border between the two. He readily volunteered the fact that an agreement had been reached 'to do away with the boundary of the counties and to draw a line'. He himself instructed '*My* Shropshire policeman . . . and *my* Montgomery policeman' (i.e. local constables, emphasis added) and remarked on the cordial relationship between the forces:

> I attribute it in a great measure to my being myself an influential magistrate over both the Chief Constables and if they were not to work well they would know that I should report them to the quarter sessions; my office would carry considerable weight with it in either county. I am bound to say that the Chief Constables are working very well; I think that the knowledge that there is a person interested in both counties is a very great tie over them.[8]

5 Carmarthenshire Constabulary in the 1840s employed a Superintendent, Kennett Alexander de Koven, who subsequently became a baron. See R. W. and R. I. Ireland (eds) *The Carmarthen Gaoler's Journal 1845–1850*, Bangor: Welsh Legal History Society, 2009, Part II, p.387.

6 *Cardiff Times*, 25 May 1889.

7 A similar situation emerged elsewhere in the criminal justice sphere: for the position of the prison governor see R. W. Ireland *'A Want of Order and Good Discipline': Rules, Discretion and the Victorian Prison*, Cardiff: University of Wales Press, 2007, pp.127–8.

8 Evidence to the Select Committee on Police 1852 (603) vol. xxxvi, paras.2470 *et seq*.

Contrast this attitude to the testy response of Colonel Scott of Carmarthenshire in 1870 when asked by the Quarter Sessions for an explanation of the distribution of police in the county. Scott's boldness may have been due to his military background, but his wrath is explicitly based on the challenge to his particular expertise:

> As for my reasons for the existing distribution I might almost as well be asked how I learned to eat and speak. I think a quarter of a centuary's [*sic*] experience of the County its inhabitants and the Police and the quantity of Crime would entitle me to form a pretty correct opinion of where the Police are required in each Petty sessional Division . . . [9]

It will become apparent later in this chapter that questions of the relationship between the increasingly specialist role of Chief Constable and the body to whom he was locally responsible might be made more complex by the introduction of local elected officials onto that body, alongside the appointed JPs, a move which could also serve to heighten the tension between local and central government in their claims to exercise control over the appointment and conduct of the officer.

There is, of course, no suggestion here that the vagaries of individual personality and negotiations over the barrier of class were issues unique to Wales. Yet the question of language was a much more specific one. Though there were variations in the usage of Welsh in the period surveyed by this chapter, variations dependent on temporal, geographical and social class context, the language remained an important element of practical policing, leaving aside any national sentiment. The intermediate position of the Chief Constable as a conduit between the Home Office and the population (to use the starkest dichotomy, the variant linguistic capacity of local government officials and members of the force only adds to the confusion) might be complicated by the fact that in passing through that conduit the messages would have to be translated into another language. From the outset, notwithstanding that senior policemen had sometimes been imported from outside Wales, the language problem was a genuine one. We will see it rumbling through the Cardiganshire disputes examined here but linguistic concerns were by no means restricted to that county. The 1870s saw the issue arise in a number of appointments to forces. Welsh was regarded as essential for the head of the Anglesey force, but apparently not so in Denbighshire. The Chief Constable of Carnarvonshire was criticized in 1879 for apparently having to use a dictionary to help with his Welsh, while in 1907 the requirement of proficiency in Welsh was considered by the Standing Joint Committee (SJC) of Merionethshire who confirmed, by a majority of seven to six, that it should remain an element of selection.[10] If language was a

9 *Chief Constable's Report*, 29 March 1870, Carmarthen Record Office QS Box 12.

10 See H. C. Birch, *The History of Policing in North* Wales, Pwllheli: Gwasg Carreg Gwalch, 2008.

primary marker of community in some areas so too was religious affiliation.[11] Again, clear evidence of this will be seen in the Cardiganshire controversy, but the tension between the Anglicanism espoused by many of the elite and the nonconformism of many of their social inferiors (a tension sufficiently marked, after all, to lie behind the serious public disturbances of the 1880s and 1890s known as the 'Tithe Wars') was visible elsewhere too. In 1891 the Chief Constable of Denbighshire was obliged to defend his request that referees for candidates seeking to join the force should include a clergyman as not being designed to exclude nonconformists.[12]

Personal character, class and employment background, linguistic ability and religious affiliation were all, therefore, individually and collectively, elements which could be productive of discord in the tripartite relationship between Chief Constable, the persons to whom he was locally administratively responsible and the broader community in which both operated. If we add to that mixture the potentially combustible dynamic which marked the nexus between central and local government and the faint, but noticeable, shade of Welsh exceptionalism, then the possibility of conflict seems inevitable. Such conflict ignited in Cardiganshire in the 1880s and was to smoulder for another 20 years.

The Local Government Act 1888 and the Cardiganshire controversy

The legislation concerning the establishment and spread of the 'new police' in the nineteenth century has been well documented and much discussed. One late provision, however, seems to have escaped analysis in the general histories of policing, possibly because it looks, frankly, boring, marking an apparently unexceptional administrative change. The Local Government Act 1888 established County Councils. Before then the Chief Constable made his reports to, and was answerable to (on a local level), the Justices of the Peace at the county Quarter Sessions which dealt with both judicial and local governmental business. So, when the new County Councils were instituted it made sense, since policing might be understood to straddle the line between these two functions, to divide the responsibility for the force between the new body and the old. Hence section 30 of the 1888 Act, while leaving the precise function of the new bodies impressively vague, provided that:

11 The proportions of the speakers of the different languages and practitioners of the different religions change across time and locality and the data are inevitably of varying reliability. The best source for statistical data on population, language, religion, etc. is D. Jones, *Statistical Evidence Relating to the Welsh Language 1801–1911*, Cardiff: University of Wales Press, 1998. But note too, the interesting case from 1838 when the assistance of a Welsh speaking officer was requested from the Metropolitan Police to investigate a case of arson from Llandovery, Carmarthenshire; see D. Cox, A *Certain Share of Low Cunning: A History of the Bow Street Runners 1792–1839*, London: Routledge, 2012, pp.155–6.

12 *Denbighshire Free Press*, 28 February 1891.

> For the purpose of the police . . . there shall be a standing joint committee of the quarter sessions and the county council consisting of such equal numbers of justices appointed by the quarter sessions and of members of the county council appointed by that council as may from time to time be arranged . . .

The admirable Clive Emsley sees little immediate impact on policing as a result of this measure, arguing that up until at least the First World War councillors came largely from the same social background as the magistrates and conducted themselves similarly, and Philip Rawlings arrives at a similar conclusion about this early lack of change and its social explanation.[13] 'Move along, there's nothing to see' seems to be the academic response to this functional legislative measure but it was not a response that reflects events in Cardiganshire.

The provisions of the Act were stated to commence in January 1889. By October of that year Cardiganshire's Chief Constable of fourteen years' standing, Major Bassett Lewis, had had his pay suspended and in February 1890 he was dismissed. Yet in April 1890 the Quarter Sessions passed a motion congratulating Lewis on his work and a Committee was set up which decided to refer a case stated for determination by a court as to the powers conferred on the Standing Joint Committee (SJC) by the 1888 Act, and therefore on the legality of the dismissal, which had been condemned by the JPs as unlawful. The Chief Constable himself issued a writ. What was happening here? The questions that apparently led to the dismissal seem to have centred on the Chief Constable's receipt of additional payments for watching the River Teifi for poachers and his failure to put in bills on time. The underlying issue was much more significant; it was no less than a question of who really controlled the police. Lewis was an ex-military man, whose politics, it was claimed, were conservative. The matter of watching the river raised starkly the question of who the police existed to serve, the landed individuals who owned the fishing rights or the county as a whole. Similarly, Lewis was criticized in the press over the severity of his conduct in the 'Tithe Wars', which pitted popular, nonconformist farmers against the Anglican establishment. The six JPs on the SJC were Tories, the six representatives of the County Council were Liberals, at least two of whom had had action taken against them in respect of tithes. The Chair, John James a Liberal, had the casting vote.[14] The Home Secretary

13 Emsley, *English Police* p.88; P. Rawlings, *Policing: A Short History*, Cullompton: Willan, 2002, p.183.

14 This account is drawn from contemporary local press accounts, see *The Cambrian News*, 18, 25 October 1889, 20, 21, 28 February 1890, 11, 18 April 1890, *Western Mail*, 28 March 1889. The case stated seems not to have been submitted, *Western Mail*, 11 July 1890. I take the *Cardiff Times'* criticism (25 May 1889) of Lewis to the effect that he needed a cavalry escort to carry out his duties while the Chief Constable of Pembrokeshire needed only one man, to refer to the response to tithe agitation. The 'Tithe Wars' were a series of disturbances connected with payment (of money rather than in kind after the Tithe Commutation Act 1836) originally to the established church, though many of the profits had fallen into lay hands. The payments, and the measures taken to enforce them, were to lead to mass resistance among nonconformists in the 1880s and 1890s: see Ireland, *White Gloves*, pp.65–7.

set up an Inquiry under Captain Elgee, Inspector of Constabulary, to investigate the dismissal, which Elgee declared was unique in his experience, but James refused to cooperate, claiming that it had no right to question the SJC's decision. Lewis was dismissed.[15] The significance of the case was not lost on the *South Wales Daily News*:

> as affording the most practical and decisive proof we have yet had of the immense change in the balance of power which has resulted from the passing of the Local Government Act. . . . The people for the first time begin to feel that the sceptre which had so long been held by the privileged classes has passed to other hands. [16]

Bassett Lewis's proposed successor was Sergeant David Evans, a nonconformist and member of the Cardiganshire force, but at this point central government, apparently after lobbying by the Conservative faction and perhaps itself smarting from the earlier rebuff, again entered the fray. The Home Office refused to accept the nomination, its explanation, at first undisclosed, apparently resting on the fact that he had not held a sufficiently senior position. The SJC were nevertheless intent on proceeding with the appointment, but Evans, obligingly, died in October, thereby heading off, albeit temporarily, another clash.[17]

One of Evans's competitors, the Deputy Chief Constable, Superintendent Lloyd, again entered the lists to succeed him but again failed, according to the *North Wales Chronicle*, because he had seceded from the Calvinistic Methodists.[18] The candidate endorsed by the SJC and eventually appointed was Howell Evans, a farmer's son from North Carmarthenshire who had joined that county's police in 1868 and had risen through the ranks to the position of Detective Inspector. The old rancour had not disappeared; a letter to the *Carmarthen Journal* complained that Evans practised religious bias and favoured men from his own county.[19] Nonetheless he seems to have been very popular with his new force, despite his insistence that all members should wear white gloves in summer and attend a place of worship weekly.[20] He policed the bitter tithe disputes in a spirit of compromise, obtaining a concession from the Home Secretary that the police, though they had a duty to protect distraining bailiffs, were not obliged to facilitate their entry into premises.[21] Such tactics led to accusations both in the press and in the House of

15 *Western Mail*, 5 April 1890. Apparently some SJC members were absent from the dismissal vote, but the fundamental division was maintained.

16 *Western Mail*, 21 February 1890.

17 *South Wales Daily News*, 29 August 1890 (under the subheading 'A Tory job'), *Liverpool Mercury*, 14 August 1890, *Western Mail*, 7 October 1890.

18 *Western Mail*, 23 March 1893.

19 *Western Mail*, 12 December 1890.

20 *General Order Book, Llanbadarn Fawr Station*. Ceredigion Archives ADX/1494, 13 April 1896, 18 May 1903.

21 *Aberystwith Observer*, 27 August 1903, *Cardiff Times*, 29 August 1903.

Commons that Evans was in breach of his duty.[22] Historians of the police, no less than religious dissenters, owe Evans a debt of gratitude; for at the end of 1900, to mark the millennium, he produced a splendid account of the history of policing in the area.[23] He also seems to have felt strongly that promotion within his force should be based upon merit rather than seniority,[24] an issue which was to rise again after his death.

Howell Evans's long and successful tenure of his post might have been assumed to have healed the rift in the county when the question arose of who was to succeed him on his death in 1903. It had not. The *Cambrian News* optimistically suggested that the old cleavage between Liberal councillors and Tory JPs no longer existed, though it conceded that 'There are conflicting interests and much wire-pulling'. It also expressed its belief that a majority of the SJC would not think it wise

> to put at the head of the Cardiganshire Police either a retired officer of the army or a decayed aristocrat. The course that would give most satisfaction to the people of the county would be to appoint one of the present officers of the force . . . [25]

The SJC, now numbering 24, but still split along the same lines as before and dependent on the casting vote of the council side, interviewed six candidates out of a field of 23. All were questioned about their ability to speak Welsh, and in particular about their ability to give evidence in that language. It may be noted in parenthesis that legal proceedings were supposed to be conducted in English, the question thereby confirming what other sources tell us, namely that at least at a summary level this requirement was, more than 450 years after its enactment, still being ignored. After a first ballot threw up two frontrunners in the Deputy Chief Constable David Williams (an Anglican) and Sergeant Richard Jones (a non-conformist). The votes in the second ballot were even and the casting vote went to the junior man. Inside Lampeter Town Hall an intention to refer the decision to the Home Secretary was immediately announced by the irate Reverend Griffiths, outside the townspeople cheered and 30–40 telegrams and 70–80 letters of congratulation were reportedly sent to the victor.[26]

22 *Morning Post*, 2 June 1893, *Western Mail*, 23 August 1893, *Huddersfield Daily Chronicle*, 7 September 1893. Evans was not subsequently averse to mass action, drafting in officers from Glamorgan and Carmarthenshire in 1895, but calling for discussion with agitation leaders subsequently to avoid a repetition, in *Standing Joint Committee Minutes*, 1895, Ceredigion Archives.

23 Dated 31 December 1900, in *SJC Minutes*, 1900–01.

24 See, e.g. General Order Book, 16 February 1897.

25 General Order Book, 4 September 1903.

26 SJC Minutes 30 October 1903, *Cambrian News* 6 November 1903, *Weekly Mail*, 7 November 1903. Richard Jones was the son of a farmer from Penwch who had trained as a teacher. He had learned fingerprinting at Scotland Yard and had made the first successful use of the technique in the county in the year of his election, see R. W. Ireland 'Caught on Camera: Cardiganshire Criminal Portraits in Context' *Ceredigion*, 2006, vol. xv, 19–21.

The appeal by the Tory faction to a Tory Home Secretary achieved the result for which its promoters hoped and Sergeant Jones's election was not approved on the grounds echoing the parallel case thirteen years earlier that Jones had not held a sufficiently senior position. The Liberal members of the SJC were incensed and seriously raised the question of the 'total emancipation' of the force from the Home Office, one stressing the constitutional significance of the intervention; 'It was a grave matter of principle whether the Home Office were to govern the county or whether the people were to do it'.[27] Similarly the decision drew the wrath of the *Cambrian News*, notwithstanding the fact that it favoured the losing candidate, its editorial is remarkable. To some it may seem mere bluster, but to those who have studied the operation of the law in rural Wales it strikes (as does the reference above to the use of Welsh in courts) a note of robust authenticity. 'The HOME SECRETARY', it announced:

> will ultimately find that it is far easier to get into the sort of mess he has floundered into than to get out of it with credit, for Cardiganshire is not a compliant county as those who know it best are well aware, and the public bodies of that county care just about as much for the HOME SECRETARY as they care for the man in the moon, or for any other purely mythical personage.[28]

Rather than proceed with Richard Jones's appointment the Liberals swapped their allegiance to another candidate who had been originally shortlisted, Edward Williams, an Inspector from the Liverpool force, while the Tories persisted with the Deputy Chief Constable as their candidate. Predictably the vote again resulted in a twelve–twelve split, with the casting vote of the Chairman (Councillor Edward Jones) going to the Liverpool man.[29]

It is as well to stop our narrative here, not only because of limitations of space but also, wearying of these parochial political concerns and the apparently endless procession of those named Jones, Evans and Williams in whom they are exemplified, the reader is entitled to ask why he or she should be bothered by such things. The narrow answer would be that the apparently technical change introduced by section 30 of the Local Government Act 1888 was capable of a much more profound outcome that in Cardiganshire had resulted in a dispute lasting decades raising matters of major constitutional importance. But the whole story also depends on an essential proximity, in a small, rural, integrated community, between the police and those who lived in that community. The challenge of policing in such circumstances was to remain until the circumstances, either of the community or of the police, themselves changed. The remainder of this chapter will focus on the controversies rather later in the twentieth century which repeat these concerns.

27 *Cambrian News*, 11 November 1903.

28 *Cambrian News*, 4 December 1903. See also *SJC Minutes*, 10 December 1903, 14 January 1904.

29 *SJC Minutes*, 14 January 1904.

An invitation to a dance, a pig and the last waltz

The picture drawn in the last section placed local politics in the foreground, but many of the people involved in the scene, those who cheered in the streets and prayed in the chapels as well as those who sparred in meetings, knew each other and knew, or knew of, the Chief Constables themselves. As the Chief Constable of Gwynedd stated in 1957, the requirement that those who held the office in Cardiganshire should be Welsh-speaking necessarily limited the field from which recruits could be culled.[30] The merits of localism were to be closely examined in the 1940s and 50s.

A Home Office letter in 1941, recorded by the SJC of Cardiganshire, addressed the issue of the use of police cars for non-police purposes. Cardiganshire had ordered three new ones, two Humber Snipes and a Sunbeam Talbot, only a few months earlier.[31] By the end of the year it was clear that some controversy was in the air. In January 1942 a Sub-Committee of the SJC investigated claims of impropriety against the Chief Constable, J. J. Lloyd Williams. The evidence suggested that a taxi had arrived to take two young ladies, one the step-daughter of a Senior Naval Officer, from the Chief Constable's house in Aberystwyth to a nearby dance. The driver had been sent away when a police car had arrived to perform the duty. The investigation found that although the procedure had been undesirable the use of the police car had been paid for. The matter dragged on for over a year, eventually resulting in the Home Secretary appointing a Committee of Enquiry and the resignation of Lloyd Williams. One observation made before the 1942 Sub-Committee is worth pausing over: 'the matter had become generally known throughout Aberystwyth and caused great resentment amongst taxi-drivers'.[32] Even in the midst of the Second World War it seems that the wrath of the West Wales' cab trade was capable of ousting the head of the constabulary.

It was this atmosphere of mutual backscratching, of laxity of procedure rather than ingrained corruption, which hovered over the rural fastnesses. The next instance in which it was raised has nothing directly to do with the police but merits attention as indicating an area of concern to central government which is not far removed from that which was to touch the force a little later. In 1946 the Justices of the Peace for Aberaeron in Cardiganshire dismissed a case involving the slaughter of a pig contrary to food regulations. The defendant occupied the positions both of Food Executive Officer and Clerk to the Justices. Lord Chief Justice Goddard expressed himself shocked and a public inquiry was set up under Lord Justice Tucker to investigate the case. Notwithstanding the general

30 *The Times*, 18 December 1957.

31 See *SJC Minutes*, Finance Committee 19 December 1940. The Committee seems to have been pleased with the terms of the part-exchange deal, resulting in a bill of £600, half of which they anticipated would be paid by the Treasury. One of the older cars had been destroyed in the works at Coventry (by bombing presumably) the other two were 'worn out'. West Wales had a strategic importance in the war, due to fears of invasion via Ireland.

32 See *SJC Minutes*, 19 December 1940, 25 June, 24 October 1941, 17 January 1942, 8 July 1943.

exoneration of the magistrates it might be suggested that in the aftermath of the national sacrifice of wartime issues which smacked of local favouritism, abuses of power were beginning to cause rather more concern than once they had.[33]

The last of the instances to be related here may also draw on this changed perception of the responsibility of local agencies, but its essence inevitably reminds one of those Victorian and Edwardian disputes already considered. Again the events turned on a promotion, in this instance to the position of Deputy Chief Constable of the Cardiganshire force, whose incumbent retired in July 1956 after 42 years' service, yet the consequences displayed, in the words of the subsequent *Report of Enquiry*, 'the unhealthy atmosphere surrounding promotion in a small force in a parochial community'.[34] The Chief Constable, W. J. Jones (who had taken over from Lloyd Williams) wanted to appoint Inspector R. E. Davies to that position but required the approval of the SJC. The two policemen had incurred the displeasure of some on the Council in a dispute over civil defence the previous year. The SJC declined to endorse the appointment of Davies and then, following an exhaustive trawl for evidence by one of the rivals for the post, decided to initiate disciplinary proceedings against the Chief Constable himself. Allegations were made over a variety of matters (including, ironically in the light of the circumstances of his appointment, the misuse of a police car) which revealed a split between the traffic branch and the CID of the force, the latter believing that the former had received preferential treatment. This sentiment was fed by the failure of the Chief to take action in two instances of misconduct against traffic officers which provoked moral outrage, or at least the affectation thereof. In one, two members of the force were found to have stayed overnight at the Glyndwr, Machynlleth, with women who were not their wives, while the second involved the pregnancy of a WPC as a result of the attentions of a traffic officer (it is unclear whether the two allegations arose from the same misconduct).

A solicitor reviewed the allegations before being passed on to an Inquiry in January 1857 before J. Scott Henderson QC, the Recorder of Portsmouth, sitting with Sir Henry Studdy, Chief Constable of the West Riding of Yorkshire.[35] Scott Henderson, the findings of whose report were apparently not initially made public on the advice of the Home Office,[36] recommended that Jones should be required to resign as an alternative to being dismissed, though that punishment was varied on appeal to the Home Secretary to a reprimand. Subsequently, the whole proceedings were reviewed, at the insistence of the SJC, by H. J. Phillimore (with

33 See R. Jones, 'The strange case of a wartime pig and a judicial inquiry into the conduct of a Cardiganshire bench', *Ceredigion*, 2004, vol. xiv, p.123. The *Tucker Report* 1947 Cmmd.7061.

34 The fullest account of the details is to be found in the Report of Enquiry into the Administration and Efficiency of the Cardiganshire Constabulary and the State of Discipline in the Force 1956–7 Cmnd 251, 'The Phillimore Report', p.13.

35 *Cardigan and Tivy-Side Advertiser*, 26 January 1957.

36 *Cardigan and Tivy-Side Advertiser*, 19 April 1957. The Scott Henderson Report was cleared for public disclosure at the amalgamation inquiry, *The Times*, 17 December 1957.

Francis Armstrong MBE as assessor) who reported in April 1957. Phillimore's final recommendation, to the effect that 'Urgent consideration should be given to the future of the Chief Constable and of the Cardiganshire Constabulary'[37] looks a good deal more anodyne than was its intended effect. The Enquiry had heard accusations of collusion, nepotism and jealousy. Phillimore had seen enough:

> I am satisfied that the Cardiganshire Police Force is too small a force to exist independently in the setting in which it is required to act . . . In a little over ten years two Chief Constables have been involved in disciplinary proceedings at the instance of the Committee [i.e. the SJC] whilst the collection of evidence has been to some extent in the same hands . . . A force of this size gives little scope to the officer of real ability and is at the same time too closely connected with the police authority.

While conceding that a strong Chief Constable could make the force efficient, Phillimore went on to argue that if:

> from age or other reason the Chief Constable falls below the highest standard, such a force quickly becomes a prey to the effect of outside influences or the belief in the power of outside influences, both of which can be equally harmful. In this small community, whose members inevitably know a good deal about each other's affairs and where connections through marriage or business are so far-reaching favouritism or the suspicion of it is bound to affect morale.[38]

The appointment of Davis as Deputy Chief Constable was finally accepted by the SJC and the Chief Constable was notified that he would be required to retire in November 1957.[39]

That the amalgamation of the Cardiganshire force with another should be mooted at this time came as no surprise. The Home Secretary gave notice that he was preparing a scheme for amalgamation under section four of the Police Act 1946, publishing the Phillimore Report as a preliminary to that action.[40] With a total of 77 officers of all ranks including two women, Cardiganshire was the smallest force in England and Wales. Its independent existence had been threatened

37 Phillimore Report, p.17.

38 Phillimore Report, pp.15–16.

39 The *SJC Minutes* of 12 June 1957 suggest that Jones was to be asked to retire; by 11 August 1957 the formulation was 'required to retire'. But Jones could not find an alternative house and was allowed to stay on until the end of that year. One councillor even suggested the resolution that he retire should be rescinded, but the motion was not accepted. The Home Office had informed the SJC by letter of 3 August 1957 that they could appoint no new Chief Constable on Jones' retirement (ibid., 31 October 1957). See also *The Times*, 23 August 1957.

40 *The Times*, 23 August 1957.

before; indeed Phillimore had heard the allegation that the renewal of Chief Constable Jones's position when he reached retirement age in 1954 had been actuated by a desire to make amalgamation more difficult.[41] Other Welsh forces had already combined; Montgomeryshire, Breconshire and Radnorshire to form the Mid-Wales constabulary in 1948, Anglesey, Caernarfonshire and Merionethshire to become the Gwynedd Constabulary two years later.[42] But localism had, for too long, been at the heart of the Cardiganshire Constabulary and of its problems, for talk of a loss of its identity by outside influences to be considered with equanimity. The SJC, it need hardly be said, were opposed to any such move. So too were the SJC of Carmarthenshire, the force with which the proposed union was to take place.

The two local authorities held joint meetings and in November 1957 each had retained the services of eminent Welsh lawyers to argue their opposition to amalgamation, Edmund Davies QC for Cardiganshire and Elwyn Jones QC for Carmarthenshire, and they were deployed in a local inquiry held on 16 December before H. I. Nelson QC. Despite objection to the 'high-handed' actions of the Home Office in attempting to create a 'Carmardigan' force the evidence of two Inspectors of Constabulary who favoured the process was powerful, and in February 1958 the Home Office declared its intention to proceed with the merger.[43] Still the local authorities refused to concede; a joint deputation of the MPs for the counties and the chairmen and clerks of both SJCs met unsuccessfully with the Home Secretary in March, and a motion to oppose the implementation of the scheme was moved in the Commons by Lady Megan Lloyd George (Carmarthenshire) and seconded by Roderick Bowen (Cardiganshire) but defeated, despite the support of some notable Welsh MPs. The Carmarthenshire and Cardiganshire Police Authority first met on 8 July 1958.[44]

Conclusion

What this chapter has provided is an account of some disputes concerning the appointment and actions of Chief Constables within one county, and a remote and poor one at that. It does not even extend to consideration of the whole of Wales, and the experience of Wales, even as such a whole, is easy to overlook. Yet there are elements in this account which deserve consideration by those who are interested in the leadership of the police more generally.

Let us begin with a truism about the 'new police' of the nineteenth century England and Wales which almost escapes critical notice. The police begin in the metropolis and gradually spread to boroughs and to counties until the new structure

41 Phillimore Report, p.6.

42 Ireland, *White Gloves*, p.93.

43 See *SJC Minutes*, 15 November 1957, 20 February 1958, *The Times*, 17 18 December 1857.

44 *SJC Minutes*, 7, 27 March, 8 July 1958 *Hansard HC Deb*, 16 June 1958, vol.589, cc.826–52.

covers the whole of the jurisdiction.[45] This diffusion seems natural and unexceptional. But before 1851 most people in Britain lived in the country rather than in towns.[46] The profound effects of industrialization and urbanization and the ease of movement created by the railway age did not affect all areas of the country simultaneously and to the same effect, in the way that Acts of Parliament might be expected to. New structures were being grafted onto old communities as well as new, and there is an argument to be made that these were necessary because they sought to devolve to discrete professional agencies within those new communities powers of observation and social control which were entrenched, amateur and socially diffused within smaller, more intimate ones.[47] It is now well known that there was opposition to the introduction of the new police in some areas,[48] but in others the response might be seen more accurately as incomprehension. Hettie Davies of Cardiganshire's question of 1894, 'Plismon yn wir, be mae nhw'n feddwl ydym ni?' ('A policemen indeed, what do they take us for?') can be read in a number of ways, but it clearly refers to a perceived unnecessary intervention in the accepted social order.[49] And, however it might be read by us, it could not have been read at all, untranslated, by the Home Secretary.[50] The village of Bow Street in Cardiganshire, (where once I lived), was a long way away, geographically, culturally and linguistically, from the thoroughfare in which the Fieldings had first experimented with their force of 'Runners'.

If the police themselves were regarded as an import from a different sort of world what are we to make of the position of those who managed them? The first matter to be determined, of course, is that of who actually *did* run them. This chapter started with the contention that the Chief Constable occupied an intermediate position, one with responsibilities as well as powers. This chapter has demonstrated that the exact nature of the nexus between these different agents was something which might need to be worked out, a process which could be both protracted and

45 The reality is, of course rather more complex. It ill behoves one who writes about one country, the policing history of which is routinely subordinated to the English paradigm, to ignore those of other countries, which may have different and earlier experiences. For Scotland see A. Dinsmor and A. Goldsmith, 'Scottish Policing: A Historical Perspective' in D. Donnelly and K. Scott (eds) *Policing Scotland*, 2nd edn, London and New York: Routledge, 2011. For Ireland, S. Palmer, *Police and Protest in England and Ireland 1780–1850*, Cambridge University Press, 1988. Nor do I wish to suggest that in England and Wales the process of expansion from the centre was either uniform or uncontested. For more on the English experience see D. Phillips and R. Storch, *Policing Provincial England 1829–1856*, Leicester University Press, 1999.

46 See the discussion in R. W. Ireland 'Why everything that we think we know about criminal justice history is wrong', *Law, Crime and History*, 2015, vol.1, p.140.

47 Ibid., p.141.

48 See, e.g. Rawlings, *Policing*, pp.142–3.

49 Quoted in G. Williams 'The disenchantment of the world: innovation, crisis and change in Cardiganshire c1880–1910', *Ceredigion*, 1983, vol. ix, p.313. See for a discussion Ireland, *White Gloves*, p.75.

50 Paradoxically I think that it could have been by the Home Secretary from 1954–57, Gwilym Lloyd George!

painful. Chief Constables were originally answerable in their localities to JPs at Quarter Sessions. The evidence adduced however shows that this might be a matter not only of administrative convenience but of profound political significance, and one which conceivably played a greater role in the appointment of early Chief Constables than is generally acknowledged: the ex-army officer may not simply have experience of 'controlling men' but also be (socially, politically) 'one of us'. The Local Government Act 1888, ostensibly so anodyne in its rearrangement of administrative structure, revealed the chasm in Cardiganshire between the traditional power-holders, the Tory landed gentry, and the elected representatives of the county; Liberals who took their religion from the chapel, often in Welsh, and whose doctrinal and, I suggest, national self-identity might resist expectations of deference. This trend is evident too in the unease and even hostility to interventions by the Home Secretary, particularly a Conservative Home Secretary, in matters which were believed to be of local concern. The expansion in the nineteenth century of the power of central government and the consequent increased intervention of the criminal law (both in scope and enforcement) in the lives of communities with their own traditions of regulation did not simply fall unnoticed on an apathetic population. It is interesting to note that the complaint of the arrogance of the Home Office is being voiced in 1957 as it had been in 1903. In such power struggles the position of the Chief Constable became central to the question of how far other forms of 'localism' should be allowed to enter into public office, notions of helping one's friends, for example, or of ignoring formalities.

The character and goals of individual Chief Constables might clearly influence their style of policing and their priorities. If I have not given sufficient attention to individual traits in this chapter it is not because I think them unimportant: the difference between Glamorgan's Lionel Lindsay, presenting a miniature truncheon as a gift in the aftermath of the Tonypandy riots which had been suppressed with lethal force, and Cardiganshire's Howell Evans refusing to open the gates for bailiffs seeking to distrain on dissenters' belongings is clear.[51] I have concentrated here, however, on the structures which surrounded the office, on the way appointments were made and terminated. The events I have described took place in one county and I do not maintain, even if we restrict our gaze only to Wales, that the county can be seen as 'typical' in any sense. Yet the issues which they raise are not merely a parochial oddity. Questions of who it is the Chief Constable serves and to whom he should be answerable remain central to the historical development of the role.

Afterword

When this chapter was originally planned it was to have had a rather different content and a co-author; my former colleague Dafydd Llywelyn. Before we could

51 See Ireland, *White Gloves*, p.91.

begin to write it, however, Dafydd was elected Police and Crime Commissioner for Dyfed-Powys Police (the Carmarthenshire and Cardiganshire force merged with Mid-Wales and Pembrokeshire in 1968, taking the new name in 1974 and in the process ironically becoming the geographically largest police area in England and Wales).[52] When I was working on this material it became a cause of some humour between us that he is a Welsh speaker from a nonconformist background, hailing from the small Carmarthenshire town of Newcastle Emlyn. The pressure of his workload unfortunately meant that he was unable to contribute to the chapter. One of the tasks which took up his time was the appointment of a new Chief Constable. The coincidence (and certainly I must stress that not for a moment do I wish to suggest it was more than that) of the successful candidate's place of birth, though he was appointed from another force, is entertaining. He lived for some time in Newcastle Emlyn!

52 Ibid., p.93.

7 'The best police officer in the force'[1]

Chief Constables and their men, 1900–39

Joanne Klein

Introduction

During the early twentieth century, police views shifted on who made the best Chief Constables. In the nineteenth century, most policemen were from the lower working class and not sufficiently educated to rise to the top ranks. As highlighted in previous chapters, forces recruited Chief Constables from the military, the colonial police, and the Royal Irish Constabulary (RIC).[2] The passage of the Police Act 1890 granted pensions to policemen, a rare benefit for working-class occupations at that time.[3] This attracted a better quality of policemen with better educations. Constables now could have strong enough credentials to support ambitious goals. By the 1910s, constables began to insist that only career policemen understood policing well enough to lead forces. The Police Act 1919 introduced even higher standards, creating a supply of internal Chief Constable candidates which were eventually relied on exclusively. Complicating this transition were 'clerk constables', men who spent most of their careers behind desks at headquarters. They might have risen from the ranks but the men who walked the beats viewed them with suspicion. Many policemen insisted that education alone was not enough; only Chief Constables who had 'tackled the rough side of his work' understood the realities of policing.[4] By the 1940s, hiring Chief Constables who had risen through the ranks of British police forces became the new standard.

Both the old and new kinds of Chief Constables served side-by-side during this transition. This allows for a close comparison of relationships between Chief

1 'In the case of a Chief Constable who is the head of a Police Force it ought naturally to follow that he is the best Police Officer in the Force of which he is the head', cited in 'The qualifications of a Chief Constable: Our reader's opinions', *Police Review*, 26 May 1916, p.248.

2 See H. Shpayer-Makov, *The Making of the Policeman: A Social History Of A Labour Force In Metropolitan London, 1829–1914*, Aldershot: Ashgate Publishing, 2002, p.29.

3 See P. Thane, 'The experience of retirement in Britain, past and present', *Austrian Journal of Historical Studies*, 2011, vol.22:3, 13–32.

4 'The qualifications of a Chief Constable: Our readers' opinions', *Police Review*, 26 May, 1916, p.248.

Constables and their men, who were also evolving to meet higher education and training standards. This chapter compares leadership in Manchester, Birmingham and Liverpool. John Nott Bower[5] (Liverpool, 1881–1902), Charles Rafter (Birmingham, 1899–1935), Leonard Dunning (Liverpool, 1902–12), and Cecil Moriarty (Birmingham, 1935–41) all began in the Royal Irish Constabulary. Francis Caldwell (Liverpool, 1912–25) was a clerk constable. Robert Peacock (Manchester, 1898–1926) and John Maxwell (Manchester, 1926–42) began their careers as beat constables. These men roughly match Robert Reiner's categories of 'Barons, Bobbies, Bosses, and Bureaucrats'.[6] Rafter was a baron, military in experience and style, while Nott-Bower and Dunning were bosses with a top-down approach. Peacock was a bobby with working-class roots. Maxwell and Moriarty were bureaucrats, professional and diplomatic. However, Reiner did not have a clear category for clerk constables; Caldwell aspired to be a boss but never achieved it. Peacock was one of the first Chief Constables who had begun his career walking a beat, another as Cox outlines in Chapter 2 was Henry Goddard (Chief Constable of Northamptonshire Police 1840–9). Peacock joined up in Bradford in 1878, heading the Canterbury police in 1888, the Oldham police in 1892, and the Manchester police in 1898. He provides the clearest contrast to the older types of Chief Constables who served alongside him.

Defining Chief Constables

A Chief Constable shaped the character of his force, for better or worse. His treatment of his men set the standard for how superior officers treated constables. If he remained inaccessible to constables at police headquarters, his constables were left without recourse if their Inspectors and Superintendents proved to be unreliable. A common complaint from constables was inadequate communications between Chief Constables and the ranks, a factor in poor morale and mistreatment of constables. Constables did not need to like their Chief Constable but they needed to respect and trust him. They frequently voiced strong views about their Chief Constables within the pages of the *Police Review and Parade Gossip*, founded in 1893.[7] Their letters to the editor stressed that a good Chief Constable must be accessible and an experienced policeman. Constables wanted their Chief Constables to be seen outside of headquarters, building connections with their men and improving conditions of service for all ranks. He needed to listen to their

5 Liverpool had Head Constables until 1919, when they became Chief Constables.

6 R. Reiner, *Chief Constables: Bobbies, Bosses, or Bureaucrats?* Oxford University Press, 1991, pp.306–8.

7 For examples, see *Police Review*, 9 February 1900, pp.64, 66; 12 April 1900, p.175; 3 May 1901, p.207; 10 October 1902, p.483; 13 February 1903, p.75; 7 April 1905, p.163; 1 June 1906, p.261; 31 July 1908, p.363; 29 January 1909, pp.57–8; 10 September 1909, p.442; 8 July 1910, p.319; 26 July 1912, p.352; 13 February 1914, p.75; 26 May 1916, p.248; 11 March 1927, p.182; 10 March 1933, p.183.

concerns, help them in their careers, and lead them rather than rule them. A well-informed Chief Constable promoted competent men and surrounded himself with efficient superior officers. He created a sense of common purpose and understanding, grounded in open communication. Constables argued that Chief Constables isolated at headquarters had little understanding of the ranks. Their remoteness allowed favouritism to flourish, and could lead to poor promotion decisions and inferior senior officers. The consensus from these letters was that practical experience as a street patrol officer was key to effective leadership.

When the founding of the *Police Review* in 1893 gave them a forum, constables published adamant views that Chief Constables should be policemen with significant beat experience. The Royal Irish Constabulary and the military had their merits, but neither were British beat policing. A 1916 *Police Review* article, 'The qualifications of a Chief Constable: On the beat' asked, 'here are men in the Service who, though self-educated, possess brilliant abilities . . . Shall these men be turned down at the behest of systems that encourage the appointment . . . of men with certain social standing and influence?'[8] Constables disliked clerk constables even more than they disapproved of outsiders, complaining that too many clerks were counterfeit policemen with no practical experience patrolling the street. 'T.W.' declared, 'Let the Chief Constable of the future be a man who has walked a beat; any scholar can drive a pen.'[9] However good classroom training might be, men learned policing on the job. 'Metro. Sergeant' argued,

> How can a Policeman respect his Chief when he knows that he, as a man on the beat, can tell his superior many things about Police Duty that his Chief does not know, but at the same time is paid to know?[10]

'Semper Fidelis' still favoured military officers, primarily arguing that 'patrol men as a rule are too old when they get to the higher ranks that qualify for Chief Constables'.[11] But by the 1930s, military officers as Chief Constables no longer made sense. A lead editorial in the 1932 *Police Review* maintained that taking on the position of Chief Constable 'is asking a lot [of military officers] even if Police duty was as simple and straightforward as it was regarded in the days of long ago. To-day it is asking for the impossible.' A modern police service, the editors argued, needs 'men who have given their lives to the study of Police work.' [12] This editorial was written in support of the appointment of Chief Constable Peel of Essex, who had joined the force as a constable in 1920 and earned rapid promotion. By the 1930s, the 1919 Police Act generation of constables, such as Peel, had demonstrated their ability to serve well in the office of Chief Constable. Now that

8 *Police Review*, 26 May 1916, p.248.
9 Ibid.
10 Ibid.
11 Ibid.
12 'Police service as a career', *Police Review*, 10 March 1933, p.183.

police forces had ample qualified internal candidates for Chief Constable, the nineteenth-century model of appointing leaders from outside the British police was not required.

Better educated constables were central to promoting police candidates to the highest ranks, as well as to the increasing duties of policemen more generally.[13] Dunning observed in 1905, 'The standard of education has risen very much during the past 10 years or so, as it is absolutely necessary for enabling the police to cope with their duties, increasing as they are both in numbers and intricacy.'[14] Despite this insight, Liverpool did not develop an education tradition, possibly due to promotion being too linked to favouritism for education to seem worthwhile for many men.[15] Peacock and Rafter became the pioneers in educating their men, though adopting different approaches to motivating them. Peacock believed that 'An ignorant policeman is not a credit to himself, to his uniform, or to the town in which he serves'.[16] He understood that having constables attend evening classes with civilians created conflicts of interest as well as embarrassing comparisons, and he arranged for classes to be held at police stations, showing consideration for his men. Convincing constables to take advantage of these opportunities could be uphill work. Rafter hounded his men, often expressing deep frustration with those not attending classes. In 1904, he wrote, 'the young man who refused to take advantage of a hint to the effect that a course of instruction would be beneficial, is not of the type likely to make headway in the Police Force'.[17] Peacock adopted a more helpful tone, explaining that constables eager for promotion could improve their chances with a better education. Rafter also linked education to advancement, but in a more threatening manner: 'In future men with a low standard of education will have little chance of promotion.'[18] His constant badgering convinced enough men to cooperate that Birmingham became known for its good training and penmanship. When Moriarty took over, he adopted a more tempered approach, making it clear that he shared the police belief that practical experience on a beat is what made a man a policeman. But he also wrote, 'The responsibility for an instructed police force rests at first on those in command; later on, it devolves in some measure on the men themselves, whose efforts towards improvement should be encouraged and supplemented by their superiors'.[19] While all three Chief Constables supported education, Peacock and Moriarty used persuasion rather than hectoring their men. The 1930 Chief Constables' Conference

13 See J. Klein, *Invisible Men: The Secret Lives of Police Constables in Liverpool, Manchester, and Birmingham, 1900–1939*, Liverpool University Press, 2010, chap.2.

14 Liverpool City Police Annual Report (LAR), 1905, p.6.

15 See Klein, *Invisible Men*, pp.123–6.

16 R. Peacock, *Police Constables' Duties: Addresses by Robert Peacock, Chief Constable, City of Manchester*, Manchester: Henry Blacklock, 1900, p.4.

17 'Educating the Birmingham police', *Police Review*, 23 September 1904, p.459.

18 Birmingham City Police Orders (BPO), 21 July 1927, p.13108.

19 Cecil C. H. Moriarty, 'The police recruit', *Police Journal*, 1929, vol.2:3, p.454.

reflected their approach, stressing that Chief Constables must inspire their men to be the best policemen they could be.[20]

Chief Constables and scandal

Two Chief Constables, Peacock and Dunning, were appointed to clean up forces after embarrassing police scandals. Both scandals involved senior officers corrupting junior officers, primarily through recruiting them to participate in illegal activities, and punishing any junior men who defied them. None of the junior men dared to report senior officers, later complaining that their Chief Constables were inaccessible to them. Both Peacock and Dunning inherited demoralized forces. When Peacock became Chief Constable of Manchester in 1898, he succeeded in transforming the force and making it one of the most successful in England. Conversely, when Dunning became Chief Constable of Liverpool in 1902, he failed to root out the favouritism networks behind the scandal and left the force for his successor much as he found it. These scandals had substantially different outcomes. Peacock quickly perceived that the scandal had its roots in the lower ranks being blocked from communication with the Chief Constable, particularly when they needed to report their own senior officers. He made a point of declaring his open-door policy and then carried it out, restoring the confidence of his men. In contrast, Dunning failed to grasp the magnitude of Liverpool's problems with obstructed communication. It cannot be shown conclusively that the different social backgrounds of Dunning and Peacock shaped their ability to lead police forces. However, Dunning attended Eton and Oxford University, setting him apart from his working-class policemen and perhaps impeding his ability to understand their concerns. Peacock, on the other hand, was the son of a miner and began his career walking a beat. This gave him better insights into what problems he needed to resolve.

The Manchester scandal exposed a fundamental breakdown in force discipline, reinforced by an interfering Watch Committee. In the 1890s, Superintendent Bannister of D Division ran brothels in his division, and recruited constables and sergeants under him to protect his brothels from prosecution.[21] Despite his links to these disorderly houses, he convinced many Watch Committee members that he was innocent of any misconduct. Chief Constable Wood recommended that Bannister be dismissed, but the Watch Committee overruled him. Finally, in 1897, rumours of Bannister's brothels and the prevalent drunkenness of the officers he supported were too rampant to be ignored. The Lord Mayor appointed Dugdale QC to investigate. Bannister quickly signed a resignation letter, which was accepted by the Watch Committee and enabled him to avoid serious consequences for his actions. Dugdale found a poor relationship between the Watch

20 '*The President's Address*', *Chief Constables' Association Annual Report*, 19 June 1930, p.16.

21 For a full account, see E. J. Hewitt, *A History of Policing in Manchester*, Manchester: E. J. Morten, 1979, pp.96–101.

Committee and the Chief Constable, with Wood too often ignored by the Committee. Discipline in Bannister's division was bad: constables feared to go against Bannister who took punitive actions against anyone who tried to report his brothels. Constables repeatedly testified that they had no confidence in Bannister but that reporting him was futile since they would only get into trouble. Dugdale concluded that the Watch Committee was largely to blame:

> if you have men in a high position in a Force such as the police Force, where strict discipline must be maintained, of Bannister's character, there is no doubt it is difficult for an officer to resist the influence such a man may bring to bear upon him.[22]

Dugdale also found that Wood was too inaccessible to men trying to report problems. As a result of the inquiry, fourteen constables from D division resigned, twelve were ordered to resign, and thirteen were dismissed. Wood resigned, citing exhaustion. In elections, Watch Committee membership largely changed. The new committee recommended that policemen should have the right to make confidential reports to their Chief Constable since a key factor in this scandal was that sergeants and constables who wanted to report Bannister had no means to do so.

Peacock, appointed in 1898, found Manchester to have low morale, both from the Bannister scandal and poor conditions of service. He quickly made himself accessible to all ranks, resolving the most serious problem. His men appreciated this, declaring, 'No one is more eager to see a P.C., on any subject whatever, than Mr. Peacock is.'[23] He rooted out bad practices, particularly men making false statements to hide breaches of discipline. He made it clear that, 'The Chief Constable hopes that this reprehensible practice will be discontinued for instead of lessening a man's punishment it will only increase it.'[24] He also changed the roles of Inspectors, employing them to supervise constables on patrol and essentially restoring them to their original function. He cleared out poor senior officers and promoted good ones. Even policemen tainted by the Bannister scandal did well if they accepted the new regime. He improved daily conditions, granting men travelling expenses and rent allowances, and setting up regular meal breaks. Some older men grumbled but most preferred Peacock. When men hired later complained about Peacock's high standards, veterans retorted:

> If some of the men had worked under the conditions existing before our present C.C. took the reins, they would appreciate the improved conditions and give

22 In the Matter of an Inquiry re The Efficiency and Discipline of the Manchester Police Force. Before J. S. Dugdale, Esq., QC, Commissioner. At the City Sessions Court, Minshull Street, Manchester, On May 24th, 25th, 26th, 27th 28th, 29th, and June 14th, 15th, 16th, 17th, 18th, 1897. From the Shorthand Notes of Mr. Frederick William Baber, York Chambers, 27, Brazenose Street, Manchester. John Heywood, Typo., 1897, p.41.

23 'Manchester Police', *Police Review*, 9 February 1900, p.66.

24 Manchester City Police General Orders (MGO), 13 July 1900.

> credit where due . . . We have a lot to thank our C.C. for, and the men would do well to appreciate the same.[25]

Peacock's efforts to wipe out corruption and clean up disorderly houses faced resistance from magistrates and city councillors. In 1901, two magistrates tried to dismiss cases of disorderly conduct at public houses. Peacock refused to drop the charges, obtaining Home Office support, and the magistrates resigned. His men noted his willingness to fight for what was right. One wrote, 'Inspector Whitehead, Superintendent Watson, and the Chief Constable of Manchester are deserving of the Victoria Cross . . . for their splendid action in successfully fighting the two Magistrates who tried to use their influence in preventing them from doing their duty.'[26] Next, city councillor Clyne accused Peacock of criminal conspiracy, alleging that Peacock had a liquor licence application refused based on false accusations of prostitutes frequenting the venue. Peacock was soon exonerated when Clyne could not present any evidence to support the conspiracy charge, and in 1905 Manchester citizens presented Peacock with a testimonial of support.[27] Peacock's hard work transforming the Manchester police was grounded in his careful study of what his men required and his ability to convince the Watch Committee to support his changes.[28]

The Liverpool scandal ended less happily. It grew out of entrenched favouritism, a force-wide problem that Chief Constables had failed to resolve. During the 1890s, Superintendent Sperrin, Superintendent Irvine, and Inspector Strettell groomed Constable Welsh to pilfer items from the Liverpool docks on their behalf. They wrote letters to Welsh, making regular orders for tobacco, liquor, and corn sweepings to feed their chickens, and Welsh wrote back when their orders were ready to arrange delivery. Welsh became an effective scavenger, creating relationships with ships stewards and bond warehouse men. In reward, he was promoted to sergeant and detective sergeant, despite being a poor officer.[29] When Sperrin became third in command of the Liverpool City Police, he decided that Welsh had become a liability and had to go. Welsh fought back replying that 'what he had done at the docks, he did at the bidding of others, and he had letters to prove it'.[30] Sperrin and Strettell responded harshly, arresting Welsh and committing him to a lunatic asylum. His wife finally freed him after three days and Nott-Bower put him on a disability pension, even though he was neither ill nor insane. Despite his unsavoury dealings, Welsh gained widespread sympathy both in and out of the force for his treatment at the hands of his superiors. He successfully sued the Liverpool City Police for false imprisonment. The resulting trial captured public

25 'Manchester Police Supervision', *Police Review*, 26 July 1912, p.352.
26 'Manchester Justices and the Chief Constable', *Police Review*, 3 May 1901, p.207.
27 Hewitt, *A History of Policing*, pp.107–9.
28 'Presentation to the Chief Constable of Manchester', *Police Review*, 9 March 1917, p.76.
29 'Liverpool Police Action', *Liverpool Mercury*, 15 May 1902, p.9.
30 *The Catholic Herald* (Liverpool), 8 November 1901, p.16.

attention, and produced pages of witness testimony that did much to damage the reputation of the police.[31]

Liverpool's Chief Constables seemed aloof from the disreputable behaviour of their senior officers. In the middle of the trial, Chief Constable Nott-Bower left to become Chief Constable of the City of London. This appointment was based on his reputation as an innovator, particularly Liverpool's ambulance service. However, by leaving before the scandal was resolved, he created an impression among the ranks that his career took precedence over the well-being of his men. He was replaced by Leonard Dunning, his second in command. After the trial, Dunning launched an internal investigation and concluded that Sperrin and Strettell had not done anything illegal. He reprimanded them and reduced them in rank but they continued to serve as senior officers. Dunning did not extend this mercy to Welsh and considered revoking his disability pension, arguing that Welsh was not entitled to it since he was not suffering from lunacy. Dunning ignored the fact that senior officers had groomed Welsh into being their personal thief, showing how deeply he was affected by the prejudices of rank. Like the Manchester scandal, no one dared report senior officers, with Welsh believing that Nott-Bower would have ruined him if he had shown Nott-Bower the letters. Unlike Peacock, Dunning failed to correct the rampant favouritism underlying the scandal. Instead, he used Liverpool as a stepping-stone to a long career in the Office of Inspectors of Constabulary, similar to how Nott-Bower left for the City of London.

Favouritism thrived when men felt cut off from their Chief Constables. If corruption or neglect existed, constables often had only their Chief Constable for support. If they could not reach him, they had to learn to live with corruption or leave the force. As one man put it, 'Every constable with a little service knows that [favouritism] is the curse of the service.'[32] Favouritism remained a deep-seated problem in Liverpool that Chief Constables disregarded or ignored. Anti-Catholic and anti-Irish prejudice was rife. Constables were vulnerable to senior officers who could inflict both minor and harsh punishments. Men feared crossing senior officers even in electing members of charitable committees. One man complained:

> the Sergeants and P.C.'s dare not vote contrary to the opinions of their superior Officers . . . who take care when the election of the Committee takes place not to favour the candidature of a Sergeant or P.C. unless he is a man that will twist in any direction that suits them.'[33]

Clerks who had close access to senior officers were promoted over better qualified men. Men protested that:

31 *Liverpool Echo*, 10 May 1902, pp.5–6; 12 May 1902, p.4; 21 May 1902, p.5; 28 May 1902, p.3; 29 May 1902, pp.4–5; 31 May 1902, p.5; 5 June 1902, p.5; 12 June 1902, p.4; 17 June 1902 p.5; 24 June 1902, p.5; 2 July 1902, p.3.

32 'Service Conditions: Birmingham', *Police Review*, 13 February 1914, p.75.

33 'Liverpool Police Orphanage', *Police Review*, 13 February 1903, p.75.

> It is deplorable to see how matters are conducted by some of these Superintendents who have sat on office stools all their life, and then been suddenly placed in charge of a Division over the heads of Inspectors who have been in charge of Divisions week after week.[34]

Liverpool was not alone in suffering these problems, even while holding the dubious distinction of being the most corrupt force. Rumours of freemasonry affecting promotion existed everywhere. In Birmingham, Inspector Hay maintained that promotion came in three ways: 'having the same religion as the Chief Constable; marrying into a police family, preferably a superintendent's daughter; and if all else failed, working hard and coming to the superintendent's notice'.[35] Another accused Superintendents of promoting sons of gamekeepers in return for a day's shooting. Men expressed disappointment that Rafter publicly advocated for promotion based on education but still made decisions based on influence.[36] Manchester had religious prejudice problems but Peacock worked to stop them.[37] Complaints about favouritism appeared regularly in the *Police Review*, one outlet that policemen could use to vent their frustrations.

Chief Constables and strikes

Scandals and favouritism came back to the fundamental need for Chief Constables to listen to men of all ranks. The police transformation that produced qualified internal senior officer candidates created a workforce demanding more input into their occupation. During the 1919 police strikes, men who trusted their Chief Constables to take their concerns seriously were less liable to strike than men who did not. Before 1919, petitioning was the primary means policemen had to make concerns known to Watch Committees and Chief Constables. Such petitions often made the case for improving police pay but rarely met with success. Even quite detailed petitions could be left to lay upon the table. During the First World War, wages eroded so severely that policemen could not cover their basic expenses. When efforts to increase pay failed, the Metropolitan and City of London police went on strike in August 1918.[38] Caught off-guard despite clear warning signs, the Government granted a pay increase and a parliamentary investigation into their grievances. The unofficial union behind the strike, the National Union of Police and Prison Officers (NUPPO), grew rapidly as a consequence, claiming membership from across the country. During the following year, NUPPO branches

34 'Alleged Favouritism in Liverpool', *Police Review*, 9 February 1900, p.64.

35 B. Weinberger, The Best Police in the World: an Oral History of English Policing, Aldershot: Scolar Press, 1995, p.55.

36 *Police Review*, 10 October 1902, p.483.

37 Ibid.

38 See J. Klein, 'Blue-Collar Job, Blue-Collar Career: English Policemen's Perplexing Struggle for a Voice in the Early Twentieth Century', *Crime, History & Societies*, 2002, vol.6:1, 5–29.

appeared in Manchester, Birmingham, and Liverpool. While pay remained a key issue, union members also focused on promotion, favouritism, and their right to confer over conditions of service. The outcome of this fervent union activity varied dramatically according to the effectiveness of force leadership.

During the 1918–19 police upheavals, Peacock came across as a considerate leader while Rafter sounded autocratic and Caldwell weak. In all three cities, Watch Committees and Chief Constables expressed surprise that local police unions existed. They often took similar actions, yet created quite different impressions. Peacock met with his force to review pay and conditions in October 1918 and gave permission for all ranks to meet and discuss issues.[39] Caldwell also allowed men to meet but included rather fretful reservations regarding mass meetings.[40] Rafter did not bother to hold a meeting, calling the 1918 police strike a national disgrace and the NUPPO socialists, pacifists, and anarchists.[41] Instead, he had the Watch Committee create a permanent elective committee to which the ranks could elect members.[42]

When the national government recommended that forces set up representative boards as an alternative to the NUPPO, Birmingham men set up the boards, knowing that Rafter would never support the union. But when the Home Office called for a conference including the Birmingham Police Representative Board, Rafter failed to pass this message on to the board, instead sending men he thought appropriate.[43] Caldwell held an election to let men decide if they wanted a representative board; 449 voted in favour and 738 against.[44] Caldwell let the matter drop, rather than recognizing the danger signal that most men saw the board as useless. In Manchester, their board was organized and active, but it became frustrated that the Watch Committee did not take its members seriously. They declared it disbanded and supported their NUPPO branch. Peacock reacted quickly to this setback, reassuring men that their grievances on pay would be addressed immediately rather than waiting for Parliament. Simultaneously, Caldwell told his force that the Watch Committee would not address pay until Parliament acted.[45] Under Peacock, even when his policemen disagreed with him, they felt confident in their ability to reach him. When the strike call came in August 1919, they remained on duty. Birmingham policemen had less confidence in Rafter who refused to concede that his men had serious grievances. While only about ten per cent of them officially struck, more snuck back onto duty when it was clear the strike had failed. Conditions broke down entirely in Liverpool. Half the force

39 MGO, 2, 8, October 1918.

40 Liverpool City Police Chief Constable's Orders (LCCO), 3 September 1918.

41 Birmingham City Police Superintendents Reports and Confidential Letters R Div, 26 November 1918, p.504.

42 BPO, 7 October 1918, pp.257–8.

43 J. W. Reilly, *Policing Birmingham*, West Midlands Police, 1989, p.72.

44 LCCO, 18 November 1918, p.62.

45 LCCO, 19 February 1919, p.112.

walked out, their main grievance being that 'More promotions were made by the back door than the front'.[46] Caldwell thanked the men who stayed but failed to consider why so many long-serving policemen felt compelled to strike.

The 1918 and 1919 strikes underscored that policemen could no longer tolerate being ignored by Chief Constables and senior officers. As the men patrolling their cities, they believed that they should be involved in determining police policy, including their conditions of service. The Police Act 1919 required higher qualification standards for constables, resulting in constables becoming even more unwilling to have no voice in their work. Successful leaders took petitions seriously, paid attention to representative boards, and supported the Police Federation, created in 1920 as an official association for policemen. Yet after the strike, old patterns continued. The Manchester Federation was effective but the Liverpool one withered away. In Birmingham, Rafter supported its charity actions but otherwise ignored it. Clearly, the character of the Chief Constable was critical to the Federation's success or failure. Peacock regularly listed Federation resolutions in General Orders. When he was unable to follow their requests, he was careful to explain his reasoning. For example, when the Federation requested that band members work all shifts, he spelled out how band duties did not make this practical.[47]

His successor, Maxwell, was even more responsive. When the Federation complained that collar numbers on new uniforms chafed, Maxwell quickly fixed them.[48] He researched the impact of traffic duty on the men, both physically and mentally, recognizing its serious health impact and adopting automatic traffic signals.[49] The Birmingham Federation was less effective. While Rafter lived, it mainly raised money for charitable causes. When they tried to get Rafter to change from split four-hour shifts to continuous eight-hour shifts, he refused.[50] As soon as Moriarty became Chief Constable, they tried again. This time, it worked.[51] Under Moriarty's leadership, the Federation became more active. In Liverpool, the Federation languished: 'Few saw the Police Federation in any way as having the strength to articulate the problems and stresses of street duty'.[52] They briefly won the right to smoke while off duty in uniform, since the Metropolitan Police and the military allowed this, only to have this disallowed four months later for giving men a slovenly appearance.[53]

Liverpool police had so little faith in the usefulness of the Federation that its board often had vacancies. When Wilson became Chief Constable in 1935, he was

46 'The Police Union', *Police Review*, 18 October 1918, p.334.
47 MGO, 31 March 1921.
48 MGO, 20 December 1927.
49 MWCM, September 13, 1928.
50 BPO, 30 January 1928, 13779–80.
51 Birmingham Watch Committee Minutes, 7 April 1938, report no.5, p.4.
52 M. Brogden, *On the Mersey Beat: Policing Liverpool between the Wars*, Oxford University Press, 1991, p.156.
53 Liverpool Watch Committee Minutes, 21 February 1922, pp.360–1; 28 June 1932, p.667.

shocked to learn that five seats on the board were vacant and appealed to the men to take the Federation seriously.[54] But federation branches could only be successful if leadership took them seriously. Both Peacock and Maxwell had started as beat constables and they supported the Federation. Moriarty learned from Rafter's mistake and supported it as well. But the Liverpool police had so little confidence in their clerk constables that their Federation dwindled away.

Chief Constables and their men

Effective Chief Constables provided their men with the tools to be successful, including training, education, and opportunities for advancement. They rewarded achievements, advised the uncertain and disciplined fairly. Rather than demanding perfection, they created a range of acceptable behaviours that allowed for human foibles. Chief Constables needed to walk a careful line between imposing strict discipline and making allowances for discretion and human flaws. The most common infractions were neglect of duty, which required senior officers to help men focus on their jobs. Realistically, they aimed for keeping behaviour within certain limits rather than requiring complete obedience. Even the best constable sometimes took an unofficial break or sat down on the job, regardless of regulations. Smoking and gossiping were banned, but everyone knew that both continued. Regular reminders that they were banned kept constables discrete and within acceptable limits.

Chief Constables issued annual warnings against drinking during the holidays to keep it minimal rather than eliminate it entirely. Rafter's usual Christmas homily against drinking warned young men that many 'who may be enjoying their Christmas Festivities think it is an act of kindness to the Officer doing duty on the Beat outside in the cold and inclement weather, to wait for him and give him various drinks.' While meant as a kindness, Rafter reminded them to be on their guard against such impulses.[55] Within a few paragraphs, he paid tribute to public kindness, acknowledged the temptation, and reminded men of their duty. Peacock took this a step further and set up a reward system; divisions with no holiday infractions received four hours off duty. During the war, manpower shortages suspended it. One of the first Manchester Federation actions was to ask for it to be reinstated in 1921.[56] His goal was to support constables in their work and weed out men who could not adapt to the job.

Most Chief Constables focused on bigger issues and delegated many responsibilities to Superintendents and Inspectors. Rafter, however, had a deserved reputation for intervening in the most trivial issues. This had mixed results. His men certainly knew that he was paying attention to every level of their lives, though

54 LCCO, 24 July 24 1935.
55 BPO, 24 December 1920, p.3031.
56 MGO, 31 March 1921.

he might have been better served to leave minor concerns to his officers. He was a fiend for order, reminding men that 'Bicycles must not be stacked in the halls and passages leading to the Chief Constable's Offices.'[57] His rules for station houses were strict and did not change over his long career – no gambling, no smoking, no drinking, no noise, and inspections for cleanliness and tidiness.[58] He gave advice on how best to clean station toilets, and delivered lectures against practical joking at station houses. He warned men not to leave money around carelessly, as well as not to borrow or lend money to each other, 'If an Officer gets into financial difficulties he should consult his superior Officers.'[59] He cautioned against 'silly conduct from time to time on the part of individual officers. Many of the complaints could be avoided with a little tact and common sense'.[60] He lectured against gambling:

> No man can afford to lose his wages in this way and the Chief Constable hopes that the good sense of the majority of the members of the Police Force will prevail, and put an end to any tendency towards this vice which can only lead to the ruin of those who take part in it.[61]

More seriously, he warned against officers leaving the city without permission: 'It is essential that all Officers . . . desiring to leave the City should notify their Superintendents. It would be impossible otherwise to conduct the business of the Police Service'.[62] To his credit, he usually combined his condemnations with explanations, using them to educate men in good police conduct. Probably the Birmingham policemen perceived these constant admonishments as white noise after a while.

Even quite minor disciplinary concerns revealed how Chief Constables understood policing. For 35 years, Rafter waged an unsuccessful campaign against gossiping. He objected to the image of constables chatting with civilians, and did not understand its purpose in gathering information. He issued repeated orders demanding that it cease and that Superintendents enforce regulations against it. He lamented that 'whilst the abuse of gossiping continues as bad as ever, no Constables are brought before the Orderly room on account of it'.[63] He even had to rebuke men for gossiping outside his office door in what he labelled 'a kind of "gossip club"'.[64] But his men ignored these orders, knowing that they needed to get acquainted with citizens on their beats so they could distinguish the normal

57 BPO, 8 October 1918, p.259.
58 BPO, 27 April 1904, pp.161–3; 19 November 1937, pp.29223–4.
59 BPO, 19 November 1934, p.22936.
60 BPO, 4 August 1933, p.20989.
61 BPO, 11 December 1913, p.23.
62 BPO, January 1, 1934, p. 21592.
63 BPO, 15 August 1902, p.183.
64 BPO, 8 May 1926, p.11271.

from the unusual. In testimony to the Desborough Committee in 1919, constables stressed that learning local conditions was crucial to effective policing, including 'conversation with the average man in the street'.[65] Constables needed to talk to each other to share information as well.[66] With his martial style, Rafter failed to appreciate that much of this talk was central to policing. In contrast, Peacock waged a successful campaign against tardiness for duty. He created a scale of fines, sixpence for every half hour before the First World War and every fifteen minutes afterwards. Offenders had to explain themselves to their superior officers. Their reasons were commonplace, including faulty alarm clocks, misread schedules, domestic emergencies, and missed buses. Men quickly learned to make punctuality a priority. While lateness seemed minor, Peacock used it to train his men to be reliable in their duty.

Beginning in the 1920s, the growing number of automobiles, motorcycles and lorries became a new challenge for police forces.[67] New traffic divisions were needed. Men were trained to direct traffic and to enforce traffic laws. Traffic accidents created an explosion of new paperwork to satisfy insurance companies. Chief Constables continually had to urge their men to avoid carelessness in reporting road accidents since incomplete reports had serious consequences both for drivers and the police. Men were reminded that, 'Police Officers should not decide that any occurrence reported to them is too trivial to make a note of, take the names and addresses of the persons concerned, and make a report of'.[68] For the first time, working-class constables encountered members of the middle and upper-classes as lawbreakers rather than civilians (see Rowbotham Chapter 8). Unsurprisingly, this created resentment and confusion for drivers and pedestrians unused to police notice. Unfortunately, the growth in traffic coincided with youthful police forces. After the war, forces needed to replace men who did not return due to death, injury, striking, or disinterest. Having so many new recruits was bound to create rough periods while men adapted to their new occupation.

During the interwar period, Chief Constables regularly had to remind their men to be civil to drivers no matter how rude drivers might be to them. How Chief Constables chose to frame their comments shed light on how police leadership changed in the early twentieth century. In 1929, Rafter set out one of his standard pronouncements:

> the Chief Constable has always pointed out that where Police Officers forget themselves and enter into unseemly arguments with members of the public

65 Report of the Committee on the Police Service of England, Wales, and Scotland, Evidence, 1920, Cmd. 874, vol.xxii, 573, p.75.

66 See Klein, *Invisible Men*, ch.7, for an analysis of police-civilian fraternization.

67 See J. Klein, 'Traffic, telephones and police boxes: the deterioration of beat policing in Birmingham, Liverpool and Manchester between the world wars', in G. Blaney (ed.) *Policing Interwar Europe: Continuity, Change and Crisis, 1918–1940*, Aldershot: Palgrave Macmillan, 2007, pp.215–36.

68 BPO, 14 July 1931, p.18323.

> whilst performing their duties they place themselves in quite a wrong position, which is undefensible; whilst if they carry out their duties with a firm but seemly manner, they will always obtain the support of the Chief Constable and of the Watch Committee.[69]

He distanced himself from his men with his formal tone; his disappointment in his men's failings is clear. His successor, Moriarty, lamented that traffic encounters kept ending in public slanging matches:

> A prominent gentleman resident in the City has supplied the Chief Constable with examples of offensive bad language recently used, in his hearing, by Constables of this Force stationed on Traffic Duty. This language included the following:- 'You aint bloody well blind nor deaf are you'. . . . The Chief Constable is very disappointed that police officers . . . should use such language to members of the public.[70]

While still formal, he presented his case as a story, introducing the gentleman and including the bad language. His approach brought his concerns closer to the men, who no doubt had been provoked into similar language when dealing with traffic problems. But Chief Constable Maxwell perhaps understood the strains best, as well as recognizing the class differences that often intensified these clashes. During an address to the force he:

> appealed particularly to the younger members of this Force to remember the old maxim about the 'soft answer' . . . As one grows older in the Service, [he maintained] one sees the wisdom of handling situations calmly & dispassionately, remembering that you are simply a paid officer of State, whose duty it is to enforce the law & regulations in the interest of the general community, & one can easily do that without losing one's sense of humour & good temper.[71]

Trained in the Peacock tradition that emphasized good public relations, he acknowledged the difficulties traffic enforcement created. He made his point in a friendly way, referring to himself as just another policeman.

Conclusion

So, what made a good Chief Constable at this moment in police history? Forces succeeded or failed based on connections between policemen and their Chief

69 BPO, 4 February 1929, p.15052.
70 BPO, 20 December 1937, p.29382.
71 *Police Review*, 10 September 1937, p.234.

Constables. Peacock was the most successful. He was accessible, respected, strict but fair, and supported his men. His strong ethics were grounded in his working-class background, giving him a shared cultural context with his men. They had confidence in his concern for their welfare; as one man explained, 'They believe you are just, and they have had several chances of testing your goodwill. You do not suffer fools gladly, and while you will not stand nonsense you are quick to reward common sense.'[72] Shortly before his death in 1926, Peacock explained his philosophy: 'It has ever been my desire and ambition to improve the efficiency of the Manchester Police Force, to make it more of a social than a repressive Force, and to gain the confidence of the community.'[73] His leadership carried his force away from nineteenth-century scandal and towards valuing close ties with the community. He trained generations of men in the Peacock tradition: 'In times when the public temper has been strained confidence that the Manchester Police would do the fair and proper thing has had a wonderful reassuring effect upon all sections of the community.'[74]

Moriarty and Maxwell were experienced and professional leaders. Maxwell started as a constable in Manchester, and continued the Peacock tradition. While not as personable as Peacock, he had the men's confidence. Moriarty learned from Rafter's mistakes, leading with courtesy and professionalism. Rafter had a strong military bearing, insisting on regular drill to the despair of his men. He lectured and organized, and rewarded men publicly and regularly for good work. He held himself apart but the men knew that he was paying attention to their conditions of service. These Chief Constables all enjoyed success in their different ways, though Rafter was less accessible and so not as effective. Dunning and Caldwell of Liverpool were ineffectual. Dunning was too culturally removed from his men, coming out of Eton and Oxford. He did not address or perhaps understand the entrenched favouritism, and his philosophical style was not welcomed by his men. His privileged background did win him favour at the Home Office; his long service as an Inspector of Constabulary fit his thoughtful character better than leading in Liverpool. Caldwell was one of the loathed clerk constables. He was isolated at headquarters and looked weak; he did not root out fundamental problems. Both Dunning and Caldwell were too insulated from the men on the streets, failing in the key requirement of accessibility. By 1939, new Chief Constables were career police rather than military or RIC. Any police officer might aspire to become Chief Constable. When Chief Constables changed from outsiders to insiders, this created a fundamental change in dynamics. Police officers could take for granted that Chief Constables understood life as a patrol officer. However, this also created a new insularity, with police forces increasingly inward looking.

72 'An open letter to the Chief Constable of Manchester', *Police Review*, 26 August 1910, p.400.

73 'The history of the Manchester City Police', *Police Review*, 22 October 1926, p.605.

74 *Police Review*, 11 March 1927, p.182.

8 'A nice old boy'

Characterizing the Chief Constable role in detective fiction c.1890–1960

Judith Rowbotham

Introduction

This chapter focuses on the presentation of Chief Constables as characters in detective fiction. Generally bit-part players, their contributions to a better understanding of the policing of communities should not be dismissed, given the insights they provide into community-police relations. This is, though, mainly a twentieth century development. Late-Victorian detective tales primarily featured private detectives and paid the police scant attention except as stock figures to show up private detective brilliance. Though authors including Conan Doyle, L. T. Meade, Robert Eustace and Grant Allen regularly included a cast of police characters, these rarely included Chief Constables, especially identified by name. This rank, it would seem, held little relevance to their narrative focus where private detectives busily uncovered predominantly working class (or foreign) villainy. These Victorian and Edwardian authors preferred to focus on the lesser ranks, police constables or sergeants, and detectives of varying ranks. Their well-bred private or amateur detectives related to the police largely through demonstrations of superior competence, followed up by delegation to the police of the mundane tasks of coping with the messy details associated with mopping up after villainy and instituting court processes.

In the twentieth century, however, things changed substantially because of a shift in relations between respectable society and the police. Fictional Chief Constables began to assume greater importance to the messages conveyed by fiction, even while mainly remaining minor characters in the unfolding of the plot. Generally, twentieth-century British authors of detective stories were both familiar with the presence of the police at crime scenes and broadly supportive of the institution. They were consequently prepared to feature them, and to use their hugely popular genre to convey positive, if not totally uncritical, messages about the police as a feature in the criminal landscape.[1] Within that landscape, Chief

1 See C. Rzepka, *Detective Fiction*, Cambridge: Polity Press, 2005; H. Worthington, *The Rise of the Detective in Early Nineteenth Century Popular Fiction*, Basingstoke: Palgrave Macmillan, 2005; L. Landrum, P. Browne and R. Browne (eds) *Dimensions of Detective Fiction*, New York: Popular Press, 1976; A. E. Murch, *The Development of the Detective Novel*, New York:

Constables were, especially interwar, 'fingered' to play the role of mediators between respectable society and the police by being 'nice'. Rarely young, they used their social circles and habits of command of the lower classes to promote good public-police relations. Fictional conversations with members of the public, interpreting police actions, were intended to ensure that a necessary level of community support for the police was sustained; reflecting a real-life challenge as everyday police pursuit of lawbreakers had now extended to include respectable society to hitherto unprecedented levels, thanks to a rise in regulatory offences. This chapter uses fictional Chief Constables to illuminate the shifts in public expectations of that rank and attitudes towards the police from the 1890s on.

Chief Constables *in absentia*: early detective fiction

When the rank was first established in England and Wales in 1835 there were already expectations of how Chief Constables would and should act to improve the efficiency of their forces and strengthen relationships between the police and the rate-paying community.[2] The office was of real importance to local politicians and ratepayers in terms of the successful management of a police force.[3] By the 1880s, borough Chief Constables were generally either career policemen or lower middle-class men who had been in white-collar jobs associated with local administration, ensuring shared experiences with local community leaders. The nuances of the power relationships between Chief Constables and local authority always involved tension and provided a potential for dispute, as highlighted in the first part of this book. By contrast, county Chief Constables were generally retired officers of rank (colonel or above, or naval captains) who came from educated upper-middle-class or gentry backgrounds, again ensuring a shared background with rural and small town elites.[4] Few things better underline the distinctions perceived by Chief Constables themselves about the differences in both interests and class between heading county or borough forces than the County Chief Constables Club, founded in 1858, and the later creation (in 1896) of the Chief Constables Association of England and Wales, catering for the urban forces.[5]

However, the local politics of policing held little interest for nineteenth and early twentieth-century authors. Where tension, especially class-based tension, existed

Philosophical Press, 1958; M. Dalziel, *Popular Literature 100 Years Ago: An Unexplored Tract of Literary History*, London: Cohen and West, 1957.

2 For example, 'Rural Police Act', *The Times*, 21 October 1839; 'Introduction of the Rural Police Bill into West Riding', *Leeds Mercury*, 2 August 1856.

3 For instance, the comments accompanying the resignation of the Lancashire Chief Constable after 17 years: 'Resignation of the Chief Constable of County of Lancaster', *Morning Post*, 7 August 1856.

4 See B. Caless, *Policing at the Top: The Roles, Attitudes and Values of Chief Police Officers*, Bristol: Policy Press, 201, p.182; P. Rawlings, *Policing: A short history*, Abingdon: Routledge, 2012, pp.133–8.

5 Rawlings, *Policing*, pp.183–4; M. Brogden, *The Police: Autonomy and Consent*, Amsterdam: Elsevier, 2014, pp.155–6.

in the pages of their fiction, the focus was on that between the socially superior private sleuth and the less well-bred and educated policemen, especially after the establishment of a specialist detective branch to policing, which brought the amateurs and professionals head-to-head.[6] In late Victorian and early Edwardian detective tales, class was established as being at the heart of relationships between the official arm of the law and the private detective. This was expressed primarily through depictions of the superior moral sense of responsibility for delivering 'justice', shown to be a quintessentially upper and middle-class phenomenon enhanced by education, as opposed to the 'letter-of-the-law', rule-bound perspective of the ordinary policeman.[7] Coming from a humbler social background, with all the implications that had for a lack of cultivated imagination, the stereotypical policeman was also expected to show due deference to the higher social orders. As any reader of Conan Doyle's Sherlock Holmes stories is aware, the relationship between Holmes and police detectives was rooted in his superior intelligence, honed by education, and the way in which this evoked the frustration, resentment and also admiration of figures like Inspector Lestrade.[8] Consequently, there was no need for a fictional Chief Constable to play some instrumental part in explaining the role of the police in a narrative: the detective did that.

Changes in respectable middle-class attitudes to policing

What was required to ensure that Chief Constables received more than a passing mention in detective fiction was the development of a new, and potentially uneasy, relationship between the respectable middle and upper-classes and their local police forces in real life. This impelled a new focus on how the police were presented fictionally. As Brogden has commented, in real life, the traditional respectable perspective on the police was rooted in 'generalised approval for a servant institution . . . [which] ensured the maintenance of legally ordained privilege'.[9] For borough police forces, Watch Committees were, until after the Great War, traditionally packed with members of the local middle-class communities, representing their interests when setting local policing priorities. Equally, counties were dominated by local gentry priorities, even after the development of the county councils in 1888.[10] Thus especially in rural areas and small towns with borough police forces, the expectation of a deferential hierarchy had traditionally been crucial to relations between local police and the community. By the interwar period, that expectation was being challenged.

6 For the history of the police detective, see H. Shpayer-Makov, *The Ascent of the Detective: Police Sleuths in Victorian and Edwardian England*, Oxford University Press, 2011.

7 Angus Hawkins, *Victorian Political Culture: 'Habits of Heart and Mind'*, Oxford University Press, 2015 pp.243–4.

8 Ibid. pp.245–50.

9 Brogden, *The Police*, p.184.

10 C. Emsley, *The English Police: A Political and Social History*, Abingdon: Routledge, 2014 pp.88–9.

It had long been recognized that villainy was not the sole purview of the lower orders and that it was not uncommon for individuals from the respectable middle and upper-classes to find themselves suspected (and convicted) of law-breaking. Generally, however, offending by such individuals was regarded as being minor by respectable society. Many young men from good social backgrounds could be expected to have brushes with the police in their wilder (usually university) days.[11] With the exception of a few rotten apples, the middle- and upper-classes expected to be *victims* of crime, not perpetrators. Even where respectable individuals were arrested pre-war, there was still (as the detective fiction of the day emphasized) an expectation of deference even after detention. Grant Allen insisted that 'the police are always considerate to respectable-looking prisoners'.[12]

A shift in such certainties of due deference began to manifest itself from the start of the twentieth century, as a result of changes in two areas involving an impact of local policing on respectable society. One was tangible. The twentieth-century rise in prosecution of regulatory offences, especially motoring ones, meant that members of the respectable middle- and upper-classes, accustomed to identifying themselves as law-abiding, found themselves instead regular targets of police attention. The other was less tangible, being part of a general decline of the supposed intrinsic working-class deference displayed to their social superiors, especially within the local community. In the immediate post-Great War period, there was also a time when the police were regarded with misgiving by respectable society because of the police strikes in 1918 and 1919 as outlined by Klein in Chapter 7. Relatively few policemen actually joined in, but the strikes created a new suspicion that, as an institution, the police were no longer dedicated to the maintenance of a traditional class hierarchy as an intrinsic element in the maintenance of an orderly society.[13] This combined with the rise of a new political party, rooted in the working class, the Labour Party. It all promoted fears that the police, emboldened by a new class-based hostility towards the respectable middle and upper-classes, would dispense with the intrinsic deference associated with traditional social hierarchies.[14] An apparent manifestation of this came with challenges to the traditional dominance by the middle and upper-classes in local politics stemming from the success of local Labour party candidates in local government elections.[15]

The impact this all had on attitudes towards the police was significant. One way in which this regularly manifested itself was through comments from the

11 Oxford and Cambridge universities had their own police forces and summary courts, and the policing of undergraduates was shared between the town and gown's forces and courts.

12 G. Allen, 'The gold wulfric', *The Beckoning Hand and Other Stories*, London: Chatto and Windus, 1887.

13 For more on police strikes, see Emsley, *English Police*, pp.132–5; 146–8.

14 For discussion of the Labour Party's slow infiltration of Watch Committees and its general impact on local politics, see B. Doyle, *Urban Politics and Space in the Nineteenth and Twentieth Centuries. Regional Perspectives*, Cambridge: Cambridge Scholars Publishing, 2009, pp.68–76.

15 Ibid.

respectable general public highlighting their expectations of Chief Constables and reflecting on their success in managing their forces in the 'best interests' of the community. In 1928, the Home Secretary made a 'pressing personal appeal' to Chief Constables throughout England and Wales, tacitly acknowledging the potential for 'new and damaging confrontations' between the police and the middle classes. He pleaded with them to urge moderation on their men, including when encountering the public on the roads.[16] This gives a clear hint about the new need for Chief Constables to be prepared to act as an emollient in community-police relations.

Regulatory offences and the new criminality

The call for moderation was also recognition of the new need for police forces to have to work to sustain middle-class support for the police, instead of taking it for granted. There had long been respectable resentment of the police issuing summons to enforce local regulations. In 1870, a case brought against Walter Michell for riding a bicycle on the footpath in contravention of the City's by-laws was heard by the Oxford town magistrates, chaired by the Mayor. The delinquent was the schoolboy son of Reverend Dr Michell, Principal of Magdalen College, Oxford. Dr Michell appeared on behalf of his son (back at Wellington College) to protest both the charge and the manner of the summons. In a bad-tempered exchange with the Bench, Michell protested the unfairness of the case, to be told that it was 'The duty of the police to proceed against everybody who commits the offence, whether a boy or a man.'[17] However, that resentment had generally been occasional and not defining. In the twentieth century, that changed.

One early fictional depiction of a growing respectable hostility towards the police in the performance of their duties which was rooted in resentment of the rise of police prosecutions of the respectable classes for regulatory offences is contained in Kipling's 1914 short story, 'The Village That Voted the Earth Was Flat'. It presented a late Edwardian/early George V scenario, when the narrator (clearly a man of substance and position), a newspaper proprietor, a rising young journalist, an MP and a theatrical entrepreneur were all 'caught' speeding near the Sussex village of Huckley. It turned out, to their great chagrin, that the local village constables and the local landowner (also an MP and JP) were in cahoots to catch motorists, and not only fine them but also to use the occasion of their appearance before the Bench to mock them. They hatched a plot to turn the tables on Sir Thomas Ingell, MP, Chairman of the local Bench, making him a laughing-stock and figure of scorn not only in his own locality but nationally, in the press and the House of Commons. Tellingly, when one of the anti-Ingell cabal, the MP Mr Pallant, made a reference to the local Chief Constable, and asked 'What on

16 Emsley, *English Police*, p.148.

17 'Oxford City Court', *Jackson's Oxford Journal*, 29 January 1870.

earth was the Chief Constable thinking of' in letting the case proceed, the response was that he was 'a friend of Sir Thomas's.' A further revealing passing comment was that 'They are all Rads who are mixed up in this – from the Chief Constable down'.[18]

The importance of this comment is twofold. First, the automatic acceptance by Kipling (clearly based on his own experience of living at Batemans and forming part of the local community there) that a rural Chief Constable was an intrinsic part of the local society which his force policed.[19] This makes it unsurprising that he also depicted Pallant as making (unchallenged) assumptions about the political proclivities of both Ingell and the Chief Constable. Second, it supported Kipling's underlying theme throughout, that Ingell was betraying his own class, by colluding with his fellow magistrates and (with the consent of the Chief Constable) the local police to trap and criminalize motorists which by default, given the cost of motoring pre-war, were inevitably his peers. Though the cars involved were driven not by the car owners but by their motor men, the police summonses were issued against the owners. Shockingly, Ingell was overheard informing his fellow magistrates that he and the local constabulary were making a regular business out of trapping motorists: 'We rooked seventy pounds out of 'em last month.'[20] This also explains the condemnatory comment aimed at the Chief Constable. He deserved blame because he had allowed his men to participate in this inappropriate challenge to the status of solid members of the middle-class whose reputations were potentially damaged by the embarrassment of being summonsed by the police to answer for their actions, something described in the text as a 'serious business'. *And* they were held up to public ridicule before the working classes.[21]

The slow emergence of the literary Chief Constable

The longer background context framing an emergence of fictional Chief Constables as important contributors to a narrative's reception relied on the popular appetite for 'realistic' crime stories where, for verisimilitude, a police presence would necessarily be a feature of a crime landscape, including interacting with private detectives. Kipling's unnamed county Chief Constable was a rarity. In late-Victorian and Edwardian tales, the few fictional Chief Constables who did

18 R. Kipling, 'The village that voted the earth was flat', *A Diversity of Creatures*, 1915, at www.telelib.com/authors/K/KiplingRudyard/prose/DiversityOfCreatures/villagevoted.html. 'Rads' stood for Radicals, who were, in Kipling's terms, those responsible for promoting temperance and other forms of social management or over-zealous community control.

19 Another Kipling short story reveals his awareness of how local society in rural England operated, and the closeness of ties between local gentry/landowning families. R. Kipling, 'An habitation enforced', *Actions and Reactions*, London: Macmillan, 1909.

20 Kipling, 'The Village That Voted the Earth Was Flat'.

21 The local reporter took pains to reassure the motorists, insisting that the local paper 'never reported Sir Thomas *in extensio*', only the charge and the fine albeit in itself embarrassing enough. Ibid.

figure were almost universally borough police Chief Constables. Depicted as men with personal detective experience, and so recruited from the ranks of career policemen, they were implicitly lower class or lower bourgeoisie in origins. Their fictional presence was invoked largely because they had the authority to order certain actions or involvement by the local police constables, over whom they had authority.

One detective fiction author, spanning the late-Victorian and Edwardian decades, who occasionally did give a Chief Constable a useful (but usually unnamed role) in some of his short stories was Robert Barr. Barr (the first parodist of Sherlock Holmes as Sherlaw Krombs, in 1892) favoured private detectives like Eugène Valmont, who cast a wry look upon establishment British society.[22] As part of that sardonic commentary on Britishness, Valmont's adventures included an encounter with a local Chief Constable where the main point seemed to be to show up the stolidity of British policemen of all ranks. Valmont's description of an unnamed borough Chief Constable labelled him as 'a solid, taciturn person' and an 'unimaginative man', who was of little use in solving an ingenious puzzle. Tellingly, though, the Chief Constable did want to help Valmont because it was a case involving the local aristocracy, 'so great was his inherent respect for the nobility'.[23] It turned out that the supposedly haunted Ramtremly Castle contained a secret room, where the last Earl of Ramtremly had immured his son and heir who had married to disoblige him. On those grounds, the Chief Constable was prepared to do the physical hard work of bashing down a wall to enable them to rescue the rightful Earl (a distant cousin of his had taken the title, because it was believed the real heir had died, instead of being imprisoned by his father).[24] The characteristics and behaviour of the Chief Constable depicted by Barr provided an indication to readers of his being someone risen up from the ranks, and also possessed of a traditional deference to a higher social class. But a new set of characteristics were woven into the depictions of well-bred (but not necessarily intellectually bright) Chief Constables featuring in tales from the so-called Golden Age of detective fiction.

Golden Age detective fiction: the continuation of police incompetence?

On a qualitative survey of the best known fictional detectives, the majority in interwar narratives remained private sleuths from upper or upper-middle-class backgrounds. True amateurs, they rarely (unlike Holmes and his rival Martin

22 Barr was Scots-Canadian. Valmont has been dubbed a precursor to Hercule Poirot, but with a French, not Belgian, scorn for the British.

23 R. Barr, *The Triumphs of Eugène Valmont*, London: Hurst and Blackett, 1906, www.online-literature.com/robert-barr/eugene-valmont/6/, see chap.6 'The ghost with the club foot'.

24 Meaning, of course, the Lord Ramtremly who had hired Valmont was not, in fact, the new Earl, but Valmont was paid by the man he liberated.

Hewitt) looked for any remuneration for their detective efforts, coming from monied as well as socially secure backgrounds.[25] Instead, they were attracted to the task of uncovering criminality as a validation of their higher social standing, sending a message thereby that they were not just products of privilege. As with their predecessors, their superior education, enhancing the natural inborn insight of the upper-classes, equipped them to solve crimes baffling to the 'ordinary' working-class policeman. It was therefore their moral duty to employ those skills, out of a sense of social responsibility, to deliver justice on behalf of the community.[26]

A number of male Golden Age detective authors produced a range of gentleman detectives demonstrating these traditional amateur characteristics, notably an educated ingenuity. They included Cecil Day-Lewis' creation, the gentleman poet and detective Nigel Strangeways. These novels were often a hook for wider political beliefs and sympathies with national or international perspectives or relatively straightforward adventure stories.[27] The male detectives created by women authors partook broadly of the qualities established by their predecessors. These detectives included Dorothy Sayers' Lord Peter Wimsey and the reinvention of Eugène Valmont in the shape of Christie's Hercule Poirot. However, at least as popular were their updating of the indomitable female sleuths also created in Victorian detective tales.

Prominent among them were Christie's Miss Marple, Wentworth's Miss Silver and Gladys Mitchell's indomitable if unattractive Mrs Bradley. Generally, it was the female authors who were more explicitly concerned with the domestic details and nuances of local community power relations in their novels, including how respectable society related to the police and vice versa through Chief Constables. Partly this was because (in the interests of 'realism'), their female sleuths had a harder time in winning police respect for both their ingenuity and right to authority. As irritating as male amateurs, they lacked masculine authority and conviction in the eyes of the police. What (again stereotypically) these women had in common, in class terms, is that they were all genteel, having some independent means. Miss Marple and Miss Silver avoided challenging gender stereotypes by being elderly spinsters, while the more challenging figure of

25 Holmes, as consulting detective, and his *Strand Magazine* rival, Arthur Morison's Martin Hewitt, clearly valued the fees they received for their sleuthing. Hewitt commented that he insisted on being 'commissioned in a regular manner', with the fee settled, before he 'took up a case'. Arthur Morrison, 'Martin Hewitt: Investigator. The Quinton Jewel affair', *Strand Magazine*, July 1894, vol.viii at http://freeread.com.au/@rglibrary/ArthurMorrison/MartinHewitt/MartinHewitt Investigator.html. Cecil Day-Lewis, writing as Nicholas Blake, provided one exception, with Nigel Strangeways being a professional private detective, R. James, *Great British Fictional Detectives*, Oxford: Casemate, 2009, p.192.

26 Their assistants were now frequently loyal servants or working-class disciples, reinforcing the social hierarchy involved. See J. Clarke, 'The pleasures of crime: interrogating the detective story', in J. Muncie and E. McLaughlin (eds) *The Problem of Crime*, London: Sage, 1996, pp.71–106 at 74–5.

27 For a more extensive survey, see L. Horsley, *Twentieth Century Crime Fiction*, Oxford University Press, 2005.

Mrs Bradley was fortunately widowed. A number of other female sleuths, such as Christie's Tuppence Beresford and a range of Wentworth heroines typically worked in association with interesting young men, adding a romantic dimension to their sleuthing. Thus these women, if usually less socially prominent and wealthy than their male counterparts, still inhabited the same social world. Equally, they shared the same sense of moral responsibility explaining their need to deliver justice in the wider interests of social stability and community happiness.[28] Regardless of gender, these private or 'amateur' detectives all found it more necessary to work with the police than their predecessors had, if only because the vast majority of Golden Age detective fiction featured plots focused exclusively on murder. The wider range of plots (including theft and fraud), which had framed the puzzling crimes presented to earlier generations of readers, had narrowed. The dominant position of the police in both solving and prosecuting such crimes ensured that the involvement of the police was taken for granted by the interwar period.[29]

Murder was the most popular form of criminal puzzle presented in the Golden Age texts. Typically, the deceased were those of the wealthy or socially prominent, or linked to them in some way. This related to a growing class insecurity interwar, leading to a sense of social vulnerability. Underlying the apparent cosiness of the detective fiction of the interwar period was, then, a real unease arising out of the lack of confidence in their class-based financial and cultural superiority.[30] Another insecurity revealed in Golden Age detective murder plots arose out of the perception that the police themselves were part of the threat. No longer could they be relied on to assume working-class villainy at work when it came to crime, but instead seemed almost to prefer looking for perpetrators among their social superiors. Wentworth's Inspector Crisp, appearing in several Miss Silver novels, was described as being 'afflicted with class-consciousness . . . [which] provided him with a conviction that a section of his fellow citizens were out to down him', notably his social superiors.[31] Equally, in *Miss Silver Comes to Stay*, the well-born Chief Constable of Ledshire, Randal Marsh, was dismissive of a subordinate's insistence on the guilt of his childhood friend, the equally well-born Miss Rietta Cray. Superintendent Drake's resentful and class-based response was graphically depicted: 'Class-consciousness rose in him, bitter as brine . . . All these people

28 M. Reddy 'Women detectives', in M. Priestman (ed.) *The Cambridge Companion to Crime Fiction*, Cambridge University Press, 2003, pp.191–208.

29 The automatic involvement of police in the detection and prosecution of crime, even summary crime, interwar was not automatic before 1914.

30 See A. Light, *Forever England: Femininity, Literature and Conservatism Between the Wars*, London: Routledge, 1991, especially pp.6–11; 24–5; 33–4; 63–6; 79–80; 99–108. Also J. Scaggs, *Crime Fiction*, Hove: Psychology Press, 2005, pp.46–9, making the point that the middle and upper-classes feared that their own social destruction could, indeed, come from a 'rottenness' within.

31 P. Wentworth, *The Brading Collection*, London: Hodder and Stoughton, 1950, at www.amazon.co.uk/Brading-Collection-Miss-Silver-Mystery-ebook/dp/B0043VD61W. Though published after the interwar period, it continues the series and social attitudes found between the wars.

hung together'.[32] This fiction gives an insight into the reality that the longstanding middle-class reliance on a stereotype where the working-class policeman's lack of insight was remedied by his deference to social superiors was seriously shaken interwar.

This unease also helps to explain the positive reader reception of a new type of hero: the police detective who combined his official role with an upper-class background – the best of both worlds. There had, from Charles Dickens on, always been 'heroic' fictional working-class police detectives in British literature. During the Golden Age, prominent police characters of this type included Christie's Superintendent Battle, as well as Leo Bruce's Sergeant Beef and Mary Fitt's Inspector Mallett. But the interwar police detective could also be superlatively well-born and socially responsible. One of the best known of these remains Ngaio Marsh's Roderick Alleyn, who strode aristocratically onto the scene in 1934. Other favourites coming from socially impeccable backgrounds include Wentworth's two regulars, Randal Marsh and subsequently, Frank Abbott. Typically, such men were revealed in the narratives to be superior, in their powers of detection, to the less socially well-born policemen with whom they worked. Frank Abbott was there both to provide a conduit between the police and Miss Silver and act as a foil to Earnest Lamb, her decent but relatively dim working-class detective. A consistent social message could thereby be underlined: it took breeding as well as well-educated brains to solve a tricky murder case.[33]

What is interestingly informative about the nuances visible in interwar respectable attitudes to the law and policing is that these fictional amateur sleuths were happy to be lawbreakers when it suited not just the needs of the plot but also as a demonstration of their refusal to be constrained by pettifogging regulatory laws when catching 'real' lawbreakers. The males especially regularly took advantage of the stereotype of police incompetence to perpetrate an amount of law-breaking, snapping their fingers at regulatory crime, notably if motoring was involved.[34] Along with British adventurers like Bulldog Drummond and Simon Templar, aristocratic, socially responsible (and patriotic) detectives like Peter Wimsey and Allingham's Albert Campion cheerfully drove fast cars and broke speed limits, relying on police incompetence to fail to catch them breaking the law in this way, or alternatively, to turn a blind eye because of who they are. Even Buchan's more proletarian, but still naturally noble, Dickson McCunn was scornful of the regulatory aspects of the law, and perfectly ready to disregard and break such 'petty' restrictions in the interests of a higher justice.[35] The reality in the interwar period was very different to this fictional depiction of motoring

32 P. Wentworth, *Miss Silver Comes to Stay*, London: Hodder and Stoughton, 1948, at www.bol.com/nl/p/miss-silver-comes-to-stay/9200000034191962.

33 Scaggs, *Crime Fiction*, pp.46–9; 91.

34 D. Taylor and K. Laybourn, *The Battle for the Roads of Britain: Police, Motorists and the Law, c1890s to 1970s*, 2016, http://library.wur.nl/WebQuery/clc/2119404.

35 K. MacDonald, *Novelists Against Social Change: Conservative Popular Fiction 1920–1960*, Basingstoke: Palgrave, 2015, pp.45–6; 149–50.

insouciance unaccompanied by consequences. As Taylor and Laybourn point out, 'traffic offences' including speeding and dangerous driving, 'accounted for over 40 per cent of all criminal offences' prosecuted in the courts by 1931. By 1938, 'almost two-thirds of those found guilty of a criminal offence were guilty of a traffic offence', and came predominantly from respectable society.[36] This is underlined by regular correspondence to the press, with one motorist insisting that breaching speed regulations did not amount to an offence: instead motorists were victims of police oppression and tyranny. He warned that such policing created 'a contempt for the law' which was dangerous to national social stability.[37] Fictional Chief Constables never seemed to insist on prosecutions of private sleuths for speeding or reckless driving, even when they were fully aware of it within a detective story. Genuine Chief Constables were concerned, not only because of road safety but also because of the negative impact of rising numbers of motoring prosecutions on the support of the respectable classes for policing.[38]

Accurate detail about police forces and individual ranks within them did not concern interwar detective writers, making their depictions of policing less realistic than that provided by Victorian authors. Writers like Dickens and Wilkie Collins had taken pains to understand the police properly, as a new factor in the social landscape of community cohesion in the face of the disorder represented by crime. At a time when counties and boroughs were debating whether or not to invest ratepayers' funds in the new uniformed police, with a Chief Constable at the head of a force, Dickens had been sure of engaging his audience when he explored the benefits of the uniformed police (including detectives) in a series of short stories from the 1840s onwards. By the time he created Inspector Bucket (*Bleak House*, 1852) Dickens had a sophisticated comprehension of the ways in which policing worked, allied to an admiration of what the police could realistically achieve.[39]

By the turn of the century, the real policeman (including the detective) had become a figure whose presence was largely accepted as beneficial, removing the need to explain and justify them through fiction. The nuances of police procedures and organization became largely taken for granted and glossed over in fact and fiction. A side-effect of this was the growing acceptance of the police as default prosecutors on behalf of the community. The focus of interwar public discussion about the police had shifted to consideration of their perceived effectiveness when responding to regular public calls on them.[40] Correspondence in the interwar press demonstrates the range of criticisms levelled at the police at a time of rising crime rates.[41] Still suffering from being stereotyped as both less imaginative and insightful

36 Taylor and Laybourn, *Battle for the Roads*.

37 Anonymous, 'A Motorist: My Grouse Against the Police', *Saturday Review*, 15 December 1928.

38 Taylor and Laybourn, *Battle for the Roads*.

39 S. Mitchell (ed.) *Victorian Britain. An Encyclopaedia*, London: Routledge, 2011, p.526.

40 For more on these contemporary debates see J. Carter Wood, 'Press, public and the "police-public" debates in the late 1920s', *Crime, History and Societies*, 2012, vol.16:1, 75–98.

41 Ibid.; also H. Taylor, 'The politics of the rising crime statistics of England and Wales, 1914–1960', *Crime, History and Societies*, 1998, vol.2:1, 5–28.

and less educated than their middle-class critics,[42] the police were blamed for either failing to do what was expected of them, or for stepping beyond what the public considered the proper boundaries for policing the community.[43]

Detective writers cheerfully relied on superficial popular stereotypes about the police, framing their fictional policemen as part of a broad scenario where most individual policemen were fundamentally honest but also incompetent when it came to criminal insights into a sophisticated puzzle that did not involve one of their own class, in the shape of the everyday working-class petty criminal as perpetrator. Their lack of engagement and interest in the details of policing must be held to echo the attitudes of the readers of these popular productions, who do not seem to have complained about inaccuracy.[44] Ngaio Marsh, for instance, never seemed quite sure whether Roderick Alleyn was an Inspector Detective, or a Detective Inspector in her early fiction. Her copy-editors and publishers did not clear up the confusion either and I have found no critical mention of this before the late twentieth century.

This all had an effect on a public comprehension of the point of a Chief Constable and consequent expectations of his role. The fictional focus was increasingly on either county or small borough Chief Constables, because the majority of their murders outside London took place in rural surroundings or small towns (London automatically brought in Scotland Yard and dispensed with any other senior police officers). Few interwar authors clearly understood the difference between county and borough or urban Chief Constables. Getting such petty details right did not matter to authors: what was important was to establish the relevant stereotype for Chief Constables. They had to be the socially acceptable face of policing for local communities. Often retired military officers and/or local gentry reflecting their real life counterparts as already discussed in a number of previous chapters in this volume,[45] manners were more important than mental abilities or actual policing competence. In Wentworth's *Dead or Alive*, when cursing a Chief Constable's inefficiency, the Foreign Office brains, Colonel Frank Garrett, was entirely muddled (or rather, Wentworth was) about whether or not the target of his criticism, Chief Constable Murray, was a county or borough figure. On the one hand, Murray was in charge of men from what was, from other evidence in novels, clearly a borough town, Ledlington, because one of his 'bright lads' (a clearly sarcastic descriptor as they had previously been described as 'beef-witted') had spotted one of the villains while patrolling the streets there. On the other, the hero, Bill Coverdale, described Garrett's arrival as him being 'embedded, so to speak, in a solid mass of County constabulary'.[46] Not that it seemed to matter.

42 Shpayer-Makov, *Detective Police Sleuths*, pp.249–62; 291.

43 See J. Rowbotham, K. Stevenson and S. Pegg, *Crime News in Modern Britain: Press Reporting and Responsibility*, Basingstoke: Palgrave Macmillan, 2013; Emsley, *English Police*, p.116.

44 Nor was it part of the literary criticism of the day, as a survey of reviews reveals.

45 See especially Stevenson Chapter 5, also Cox, Chapter 2, Ireland Chapter 6.

46 P. Wentworth, *Dead or Alive*, London: Hodder and Stoughton, 1936, at http://ibooklibrary.net/DEAD-ALIVE-PATRICIA-WENTWORTH.html.

Garrett, in his criticisms, lumped all Chief Constables together. Murray, a 'damned fool' was at fault for letting the villains escape, but then he acknowledged that he had never known 'a Chief Constable yet' who was not one. Garrett also described Murray as 'an old woman', afraid to tackle a crime he suspected was being committed because he wanted to avoid scandal and upset.[47]

Christie's Colonel Melchett, featuring in works including *The Body in the Library*, was another such stereotypical Chief Constable, 'a nice old boy' but out of his depth with any criminal occurrence that upset his equilibrium by being out of the ordinary. More active than some in detective fiction, Melchett was clearly identified as in charge of a county force (Radfordshire). Stereotypically, he was also a conservative man, inefficient at helping his force to solve a crime like murder, especially where he was appropriately embarrassed by it intruding (as it did in *The Body in the Library*) on his own social milieu. Though he insisted on becoming involved in such crimes, the purpose revealed through dialogue with other characters was, substantially, to reassure his fellow members of the county set that he was not just leaving it to subordinates who might take the chance to 'have a pop' at their social superiors. Melchett had neither the training nor instincts of an effective detective. Where he excelled was in being a 'decent chap' on whom his social peers could rely, unlike working-class police characters such as Inspector Slack. Melchett's social background meant that he was able to recognize a member of his own social order who had inherent detective instincts, in the shape of Miss Marple, and to force resentful figures like Slack to take account of her insights.[48]

In both fiction and reality (the latter as discussed by Morris in Chapter 9), one of the regular roles of a local Chief Constable was to make a decision to summon in 'higher authority', usually in the shape of Scotland Yard. Often perceived by police subordinates as being a pusillanimous choice, it was revealed to readers in particular as a shrewd strategy to maintain local smooth police-public relations. In one Basil Thompson novel, the Chief Constable of Devon requested the involvement of Scotland Yard to decide whether or not a fatal motor accident was, in fact, murder because he did not wish to upset the local gentry by relying on his 'limited staff' in terms of both experience and numbers.[49] Chief Constable 'Sir Joseph' was summoned to a house-party in Michell's *Speedy Death* to conduct an 'informal enquiry' into whether two deaths might be murder, before a decision would be taken formally to involve the police, so as not to alarm the neighbourhood.[50] Some policemen were shown as recognizing the value of a Chief

47 Ibid. Interestingly, the key villainess in *Dead or Alive*, Maud Millicent Deane, was eventually captured in a later Wentworth novel, *Miss Silver Intervenes*, owing to the superior insights and detective powers of Miss Silver.

48 E. F. Bargainnier, *The Gentle Art of Murder: The Detective Fiction of Agatha Christie*, Bowling Green, OH: Popular Press, 1980, pp.69–70; Agatha Christie, *The Body in the Library*, London: Collins, 1942.

49 B. Thompson, *Richardson Solves a Dartmoor Mystery*, London: Eldon Press, 1935. Now available as B. Thompson, *A Dartmoor Enigma*, London: Dean Street Press, 2016.

50 Gladys Mitchell, *Speedy Death*, London: Victor Gollancz, 1929.

Constable's ability to do this. In Wentworth's *The Watersplash*, the shrewd local police Superintendent informed his juniors that he was requesting the Chief Constable to call in Scotland Yard because 'Nobody's going to give us any black marks once the Yard has been called in'. The sensitivities of a murder where local magistrates and other dignitaries were taking an interest, guaranteed that it was important for the local policemen to 'Get out of harm's way and stop there'.[51] It was all a matter of tactics when managing police-community relations positively.

Chief Constables and class-associated competence

The traditional Chief Constable appointed to county forces, as already discussed, was not likely to be a traditional career policeman. From the start he was likely to have been a local dignitary or to have connections which would make him acceptable in some other way to local elites. Appointments to county posts were, until post-1945, usually in the hands of local magistrates and other prominent county figures, including those who served post 1888, as county councillors. Many of the early figures appointed to county forces had a 'professional' background as retired military or naval men and so were considered by those local elites as used to command of their social inferiors. Fictional characters with military titles like Colonel Melchett mirrored real life, where the real figures often had significant local links to their appointments, as highlighted by Stevenson in Chapter 5.[52]

Interwar, a new type of county Chief Constable was introduced in fiction to echo the real life entry into policing as a career of educated middle and upper-class men. Always aiming for the detective branch in literature, like Allingham's Roderick Alleyn, these figures were professional policemen but also, always, something more, explaining why some of them at least rose to the rank of county Chief Constable. These competent interwar fictional Chief Constables qualified for their post not only because of their appropriate social backgrounds, combined with some actual policing experience (including military or colonial policing) but also because they shared many of the qualities of the private sleuths discussed earlier. Professional policemen of this type, like Wentworth's Randal Marsh, the Chief Constable of Ledshire, were reassuring figures as they understood the importance of stepping outside the constraints of formal police procedure. Even if subtly done, it would be discreetly known in the 'right' local social circles, as when Marsh involved Miss Silver in his cases. In *Poison in the Pen*, his wife invited her to tea, ostensibly to see the Marsh children, but really to discuss the murders going on in the village of Tilling.[53]

51 P. Wentworth, *The Watersplash*, London: Hodder and Stoughton, 1951, at www.download-books.com/patricia-wentworth-collection/.

52 An Irish connection was also valued. Mr Valentine Goold, the first Chief Constable of the Somerset Constabulary was appointed in 1856 from his previous position as Sub-Inspector in Ireland.

53 P. Wentworth, *Poison in the Pen*, London: Hodder and Stoughton, 1957 at http://izakayamblog.com/poison-in-the-pen-by-patricia-wentworth/. Mrs Marsh was formerly Rietta Cray. The Marshes had married after Miss Silver assisted in clearing Miss Cray of murder. See *Miss Silver Comes to Stay*, 1948.

This underlines that respectable society's core expectation of a county Chief Constable was that he operate to allay their fears in relation to crime. Such fears related to the threat posed both by crime itself, and by the potential that an increasingly less deferential police force would use the opportunity provided by crime to destabilize their 'natural' authority. Few Chief Constables did this more effectively than the only Chief Constable who combined this role with being the detective hero. Sir Clinton Driffield, created by J. J. Connington in 1927, appeared in a series of seventeen further detective novels up to 1947.[54] Driffield was less obviously socially emollient than Wentworth's Randal Marsh or the Chief Constable Sir Leo Pursuivant in Allingham's Campion novels. Typically, Pursuivant was described in *The Late Pig* as 'an extremely nice old boy' in that he was magnificently eccentric and quintessentially a decent British gentleman, a typical county squire.[55] Driffield, by contrast, was more the police professional, as well as being acerbic and scientific. However, his companion and neighbour, Squire Wendover, could explain Driffield to the rest of the county, as he shared the stereotypically eccentric and sociable decency of men like Pursuivant.

The reader in *Murder in the Maze* learned that Driffield had held 'a big post in the police' out in colonial South Africa, returning for family reasons and taking up the county office out of a sense of duty.[56] Thus established as a gentleman who has both experience and the right kind of socially responsible instincts, Driffield revealed himself to be no formal police detective, being no respecter of the letter-of-the-law school of policing. His methods were more idiosyncratic than bureaucratic and resembled the approaches pioneered by Holmes: featuring scientific logic and deduction. When explaining to Wendover and a small audience of male social peers the solution to the crimes committed in the Maze, he referred to criminology and the typecasting of murderers in that field of academic study. In this case, he was looking for a murderer impelled by financial motivation stressing that criminology revealed such killers were 'clever enough' but not of 'a very brainy type'. Such murderers, he opined, frequently resorted to serial killing in order to clear the path to their financial goals, but lacked the imagination to be creatively variable, as well as having a tendency to betray themselves when covering up their crimes before an elite interrogator like Driffield.[57]

However, having solved the murder mystery he proceeded to act completely outside the boundaries of police procedure and the expectations of the criminal justice process. Driffield explained that as the murderer was clearly insane, he intended to risk the charges that might arise of 'police inefficiency' in his force to cover up the 'best' and most just solution. Admitting that he 'could have arrested

54 Connington was the pen-name of Professor Alfred Stewart, a scientist who ended up holding the Chair of Chemistry at Queen's University, Belfast. He died in 1948.

55 Margery Allingham, *The Case of the Late Pig*, London: Hodder and Stoughton, 1937, at www.overdrive.com/media/1219122/the-case-of-the-late-pig.

56 J. J. Connington, *Murder in the Maze*, London: Ernest Benn, 1927, at www.bol.com/nl/p/murder-in-the-maze/9200000009716741/.

57 Ibid.

the brute' and proceeded to trial, Driffield pointed out that the accused's surviving family would 'have been branded as the relatives of a murderer'. He had avoided this by delivering his own form of justice, 'making Ernest Shandon his own executioner'. His audience of social peers agreed about the value of preventing 'an innocent family' from suffering 'through no fault of their own'. There would be some talk, but Sir Clinton was right to claim his conscience was clear. Driffield had also saved the public from 'a big bill for his prosecution'. He congratulated himself that in terms of talk, 'we've stilled that as far as we possibly could' (amounting, strictly, to a misuse of police resources), and in respect of the wider social ramifications, 'the reporters got so little that the thing was hardly talked about in the papers'.[58]

The significance of this aspect of Driffield's tactics and their endorsement by his peers, is that he was a character represented by his author as someone of sufficient social class and inherent authority to comprehend how important it was to ensure that the policing of the community and the delivery of justice were not inappropriately constricted within the boundaries of formal rules and regulations, especially when eluding them discreetly assured the maintenance of community cohesion. The message particularly apparent in the Driffield novels was that policemen from the ranks of the lower classes needed the discipline provided by the rules. They were not possessed of the self-discipline that came with good breeding and an education from the 'right' type of school. The interwar popularity of Connington's perspective on the police among respectable readers lay in the reassurance it provided that the police as an institution need not be perceived as automatically hostile to them, even if ordinary police constables *did* still arrest members of the middle and upper-classes for speeding. Chief Constables, still coming from the 'right' background, could be relied upon to understand both the need for middle- and upper-class support for the police on the one hand, and on the other, the need to at least appear to temper the rigours of the law in relation to a section of society that was instinctively law-abiding.

Conclusion

Throughout his fictional career, and with an equally clear conscience to that established in *Murder in the Maze*, Sir Clinton Driffield doled out solutions to crimes that threatened his social peers. This meant he was cheerfully prepared to tweak the formal processes of the criminal justice system in order to deliver a version of justice delivery that, he and his social circle agreed, best suited the broader interests of the upper and middle classes. Driffield was an extreme example of a Chief Constable in his sensitivity to the concerns of his social peers about the injustice of a strict observance of the law, representing wishful thinking on the part of his author and audiences. More realistically, Randal Marsh was

58 Ibid.

conscious of a need to observe police proprieties publicly even when he bent them privately. But Driffield was more popular with the reviewers of his day than figures like Marsh, or Pursuivant. Connington's tales have, for reasons including changing attitudes and expectations of the police post-war, stood the test of time less well than Allingham, Christie and Wentworth. His maverick tactics and overt insistence on preserving traditional social values presented a more egalitarian society with a problem in perceiving him as a positive representation of policing. These tales do, however, provide a useful insight into the pressures on interwar Chief Constables, above all the need to ameliorate the fears of respectable society about the propensity of the police to challenge the respectable social status quo of the day by criminalising the law-abiding instead of 'real' criminals.

The structures of individual police forces, including the official remit for Chief Constables, have changed. But has the need for them to be perceived by the public as a reassuring conduit to the law-abiding in society changed? It seems unlikely that there is not still a need for a sense of good will towards today's version of respectable society to emanate from the police, given how difficult it can be to avoid actual law-breaking due to the apparently inexorable rise in regulatory offences. Popular television dramas like *Midsomer Murders* still frequently feature detectives like Jim Barnaby being hauled before a Chief Constable and told to tread warily, lest they offend the socially prominent members of a local community. Thus the twentieth-century detective genre provides an interesting accompaniment to the narratives of the challenges faced by both rural and borough Chief Constables in asserting their authority, especially in the decades running up to and in the first decade or so after the Second World War.

9 What the Met brought to the party – reinforcement, colonization, specialization and fusion

Robert M. Morris

Introduction

From the beginning the Metropolitan Police was, and remained, by far the largest of the police forces established from 1829. With the exception of the Birmingham, Bolton and Manchester forces set up for three years by temporary Acts in 1839, it was the only force that for 170 years answered directly to the Secretary of State for the Home Department and a senior member of the Cabinet. The Home Secretary appointed the force's Commissioner and most senior officers (whose numbers were limited by statute), and answered for its conduct directly to Parliament. When the County and Borough Police Act 1856 made the establishment of forces compulsory with government funding dependent on inspection, the Metropolitan force was exempted from inspection and had itself received government subsidy since 1833.

When the Central Conference of Chief Constables for England and Wales got underway from the end of the First World War, the Commissioner himself did not attend: he was instead represented by officers below even Assistant Commissioner rank that he deemed sufficiently equivalent even to Chief Constables of the largest provincial forces. Whereas the latter tended to recruit mostly from their own localities, the Metropolitan drew in recruits from all over the United Kingdom as well as from the rapidly growing population of its own district.

Despite somewhat *d'haut en bas* attitudes, the Metropolitan force interacted with other forces as they did with each other but the relationship was never an equal one and nor was it consistent. What follows will chart its ebbs and flows concentrating on two dimensions: personnel and services. To what extent, and to what effect, was there interpenetration of personnel between the Met and other forces; and what transfers of expertise and services did the Met develop to offer the other forces?

Reinforcement

Not only was the Met the largest 'modernized' force in 1829, for some years it was the only such force.[1] Its quickly established reputation for disciplined control and intelligent management by the Commissioners, Charles Rowan and Richard

Mayne, led to calls for assistance of various kinds. Some calls were for temporary local reinforcement to deal with public order crises. The Huddersfield election 1837[2] and the Birmingham Chartist riot of 1839 are the best known (see Channing, Chapter 10). The longest and most extensive of the deployments was in West Wales sent intermittently during 1839–44 for the 'Rebecca riots', a series of agrarian disturbances rooted in agricultural depression and targeted on the gates of local turnpike trusts.[3] In all these cases the Met was deployed where local policing was inadequate for the task and where the military were still deployed in support.

More important in aggregate were the extensive if piecemeal Met deployments in order to assist with new policing arrangements outside London. In such situations the Met was asked to provide officers to assist in establishing and/or supervising forces constituted under a number of expedients ranging from private Improvement Acts, through the adoptive Lighting and Watching Act 1833 to private subscription forces and, briefly until declared *ultra vires*, forces financed by the poor law rates.[4] In addition, the Municipal Corporations Act 1835 empowered borough councils to establish forces under Watch Committee control. In this period of experimentation, the Whig government had considered how best to extend stable, modernized systems nationally[5] and the Home Secretary during 1835–9, Lord John Russell, had instituted in 1836 a Constabulary Royal Commission chaired by Owen Chadwick. It was the settled policy of all Home Secretaries to reduce the former reliance on resort to military units to keep the peace.

This was for two reasons. First, military deployment once committed was difficult to control and risked disproportionate use of force. Home Secretaries

1 This is not to argue that the Met came from nowhere: see E. A. Reynolds, *Before the Bobbies: The Night Watch and Police – Reform in Metropolitan London, 1720–1830*, Stanford: Stanford University Press, 1998. Nor is it to overlook the important functions of the Bow Street 'Principal Officers'. From their establishment in 1792 to the transfer of their responsibilities (but not immediately all their functions) to the Met in 1839. They frequently operated on an individual basis outside London to an extent little realized until investigated by David Cox. See his *A Certain Share of Low Cunning: A History of the Bow Street Runners 1792–1839*, Abingdon: Routledge, 2012, especially chap.5. There is also the sense in which the two Metropolitan Police Acts 1829 and 1839 can be seen as the resurrection (without including the City of London) of much in Pitt's abortive London and Westminster Police Bill 1785. See R. M. Morris (ed.) *Reforming the Police in the Nineteenth Century*, London: Pickering and Chatto, 2014, p.xi.

2 See letter 30 July 1830 from a Mr Laycock reporting on Sergeant George Martin's condition in hospital, TNA HO61/19.

3 See D. J. Jones, *Rebecca's Children: A Study of Rural Society, Crime and Protest*, Oxford University Press, 1989. The Met detachment was led by the then Inspector George Martin, a Welsh speaker. Shortly after his return to London, he was recommended to succeed Inspector Browne, F Division, who had been appointed as head of the Sunderland force where he stayed until 1855: TNA HO61/19 letter 18 September 1837 and M. Stallion and D. S. Wall, *The British Police Forces and Chief Officers 1829–2012*, (2nd edn), Hook: Police History Society, 2011, p.187.

4 The character and extent of these initiatives is discussed in D. Philips and R. D. Storch, *Policing Provincial England 1829–1856: The Politics of Reform*, London: Leicester University Press, 1999, pp.92–110 and Appendix B, pp.237–44.

5 Philips and Storch, 'Whigs and coppers: The Grey Ministry's National Police Scheme, 1832', *Historical Research*, 1994 vol.67:162, 75–90.

would have had in mind the mayhem of the yeomanry cavalry's dispersal in 1819 of a large political demonstration at St Peter's Fields, Manchester, which resulted in fifteen deaths with several hundred injuries, known in dire, parodic reference to Waterloo as the 'Peterloo Massacre'. Ministers also became much preoccupied with how to cope with disorderly resistance to the new Poor Law from 1834, and the threat of violence from Chartism, a popular movement aimed at the extension of the electoral franchise and popular political control. Secondly, governments wanted change for cost reasons. The cost of military deployment fell wholly on central government and it was all too easy for local magistrates to call for military reinforcement at no cost to the locality.

It followed that Russell was keen to respond to requests for Met assistance whether for advice on setting up local forces or for reinforcing localities in crisis, in all cases on condition of cost repayment.[6] Initially, the Commissioners seem to have had no objection since such requests boosted their force's reputation and influence. Commissioner Rowan was, after all, a member of the 1836 Royal Commission, which recommended in 1839 a scheme that would have effectively 'metropolitanized' the whole of England and Wales. For Russell's government or, indeed, any government of that time, that was not a practical proposition and Russell pursued the voluntary scheme for counties embodied in the Constabulary Act 1839 asking Mayne (in another example of a Met contribution) to draft the regulations to be made under the Act.[7]

However, the sheer scale of the physical demands on the Met regardless of cost neutrality began to perturb the Commissioners because it conflicted with their primary responsibility for London. In 1835, they were requesting an augmentation to replace the four from S and T Divisions on loan to the Birmingham Railway Co. who wanted to keep the men on.[8] Successive statements from the Commissioners showed the growing extent of the burden. In July 1837, the Commissioners listed 64 places where the Met had helped establish forces. Most locations were in the midlands and the south but there were also locations in Yorkshire and Wales as well as deployments to Dublin and Haddington, East Lothian.[9] The same return also included a separate list of officers 'sent permanently to establish a police in the country'. The number but not the names of the places amounted to 88 and the number of officers totalled 132: 5 Superintendents, 21 Inspectors, 41 Sergeants and 65 constables. In addition it was claimed that 2,140 constables since June 1830 had been sent to different places 'for the preservation of the peace and apprehension of offenders'.

6 Sometimes Met officers lent elsewhere had to resign first. See the applications for reinstatement from Sergeant Goodyer who had been sent 'on special duty at Wymondham' and Inspector Mallalieu whose appointment as Inspector General of a new Barbadian force was terminated when the colony's legislation was voided by London: TNA HO61/15, Commissioners' letters 20 January 1835 and 20 July 1835.

7 TNA HO65/13 Phillips to Mayne 31 August 1839.

8 TNA HO61/15, letter 6 October 1835.

9 TNA HO61/19, 'Return of Places where a Police has been established, with the aid of the Metropolitan Police', 26 July 1837.

Two later returns showed the demand growing. At the beginning of 1838, there were said to be 111 places where police bodies had been established with Met help, the number of officers totalling 167, and the number sent for policing purposes having risen to 2,246. This was an average since June 1830, the Commissioners pointed out, of upwards of 300 men a year.[10] The next return showed the Commissioners' concern put so baldly that they were required to withdraw their covering letter the contents of which we have to rely on the summary prepared by a Home Office clerk, Samuel Redgrave.[11]

On this occasion, the statistics were set out in four tables. Table A showed the number of constables sent to the country for temporary purposes from June 1830–1 November 1838 (3,010) showing a steep increase from 444 in the whole of 1837 to 764 for the first ten months of 1838 Table B showed the cumulative number of places (136) where forces had been established with Met assistance provided by 221 officers; Table C was a list of places where officers (444) had been sent for temporary purposes in 1837; and Table D gave a similar list for the 764 officers in the first ten months of 1838.

Redgrave's summary of the withdrawn letter recorded:

> They state that this practice has been detrimental to the Force – and that new arrangements of considerable detail have become necessary. They therefore feel it their duty to bring the subject distinctly under Lord John Russell's consideration.

The Parliamentary Under-Secretary, Fox-Maule, minuted that he had not asked for or expected the letter which he did not think tended 'to the good of the service', and thought it possible that the Commissioners 'will have it moved for in the HC', that is published by the House of Commons under Parliamentary privilege. Russell was firm: 'They had better withdraw it. It must otherwise be refuted, which is very easy – See within return.'

Previous writers have been understandably puzzled by what the returns indicated. It is clear they did not show wholesale Met aid to the 1835 boroughs. Jenifer Hart concluded that, of the total number of 136 places outside London listed up to 1 November 1838, only 34 were boroughs or roughly one-fifth of all the boroughs up to 1838.[12] It is not possible even to establish which officers of which seniority

10 TNA HO61/20, 'Return of Places where the Police has been established with the aid of the Metropolitan Police up to 31 January 1838', 31 January 1838.

11 TNA HO61/21, returns of 14 November 1838.

12 J. Hart, 'Reform of the Borough Police, 1835–1856', *English Historical Review*, 1955, pp.411–27 at p.421. She was responding to an earlier claim that implied a greater extent of Met help to boroughs by assuming all the officers sent out of London assisted boroughs: C. Reith, *The British Police and the Democratic Ideal*, London: Oxford University Press, 1943, p.198. These issues were also interrogated by Critchley who, although agreeing with Hart as to the boroughs, chose to raise additional questions about the returns foreshadowing the more complete analysis of Phillips and Storch summarized above. See T. A. Critchley, *A History of Police in England and Wales 1900–1966*, London: Constable, 1967, fn pp.145–6. For a criticism of Hart's view of the *rate* at

went to which boroughs. While it is known, for example, that Superintendent Joseph Bishop, the longstanding Superintendent of V or Wandsworth Division, both recommended the organizational structure of the new Bristol force and became its head in 1836,[13] there is no collected record of other Met contributions. In the case of York, while it was a Met officer, Inspector Stuart, who undertook a survey in 1836 of what was required, his services were not continued as head of the new force. On the other hand, it was a Met officer, Chalk, who was appointed as the second head in 1841 serving for 20 years.[14] Another long-serving Met appointee was Inspector J. T. Enright who was Southampton's chief officer 1836–1868.[15] On the other hand, the Met officer, Sergeant John Redman, who was first appointed in 1834 to head the 1833 Act force at Newport, Monmouthshire, survived only a year after being appointed to head the new 1835 Act force. His next but one successor, Stephen English (1848–52),[16] was also a Met officer who went on to command the Norwich (1853–9) and Leeds (1859–63) forces.[17]

As Jenifer Hart went on to point out, it follows that the majority of Met force establishment help was in practice sought for relatively small rural locations. Further, whatever the Commissioners came to think, deploying officers outside London predominantly for public order purposes, a point made in an important study of Chartism,[18] was not from any Home Office Minister's point of view a waste of effort. The deployments spanned serious public order problems like the Rebecca and Birmingham riots at one extreme through assisting railway companies keen to protect their property and have order kept within their workforces to comparatively trivial and very localized situations at the other. Politically all were important. A Sussex MP's request received on 21 November 1835 for a Sergeant to implement a Lighting and Watching Act 1833 scheme in Steyning was acted

which boroughs responded to the 1835 Act, see D. S. Wall, *The Chief Constables of England and Wales: The Socio-Legal History of a Criminal Justice Elite*, Aldershot: Ashgate, 1998, pp.32–4.

13 R. Walters, *The Establishment of the Bristol Police Force*, Bristol: Bristol Branch of the Historical Association, 1975. Bishop died in 1838, his place was taken temporarily by Inspector Mallalieu of the Met, see PP, 1853, *Second Report of the Select Committee on Police*, Evidence, QQ 2833–5. The next three heads of the Bristol force up to 1894, Fisher, Handcock and Coathupe, were also Met officers.

14 Wall, *The Chief Constables of England and Wales*, pp.27–9 and 120–1.

15 A. Cookes, *The Southampton Police Force 1836–1856*, Southampton: City of Southampton, 1972, p.25.

16 I. Bale, *Through Seven Reigns: A History of Newport Borough Police 1836–1959*, Pontypool: Newport Police, 1959, pp.21–4 and 47–8. See also Stallion and Wall, *The British Police Forces and Chief Officers 1829–2012*, pp.224–5.

17 It seems possible that the Commissioners did not always register all the locations they assisted. Horncastle, for example, set up a Lighting and Watching force under the 1833 Act with some, initially grudging, Met assistance but the town is not apparently included in the Commissioners' returns. See B. J. Davey, *Lawless and Immoral: Policing a Country Town 1838–1857*, Leicester University Press, 1983. Davey's describes how the state of public order in the town was the prime motivation of the resort to the 1833 Act.

18 F. C. Mather, *Public Order in the Age of the Chartists*, Manchester University Press, 1966, pp.105–6.

on with alacrity that day, a minute recording 'Col. Rowan verbally authorized to send a serjeant, the Parties paying all expences [sic]'.[19]

That Met help was given for such events as race meetings and even at the Three Choirs festival might seem insignificant but could mean a lot to the recipients. Real improvements to the local quality of life were not be sniffed at and ministerial sponsorship helped cumulatively to set new standards for public conduct and social order. As to the Commissioners' concerns, the effects of the significant increase in the size of the force from the extension of the Met police district due in 1840,[20] the maturation of the borough forces and the gradual effects of the establishment of county constabularies from 1839 led to a decline in the demands placed on Met strength. By late 1839, the Home Office seemed confident enough about the situation to dismiss out of hand a Shoreditch vestry resolution against sending Met officers to deal with public order events outside London.[21]

Most of the approaches up to 1839 for inclusion in the Met from parishes neighbouring the original metropolitan police district of 1829 were concerned as much with public order and civility as with crime in the sense now understood.[22] Publication in 1857 of the first set of criminal statistics made possible by the Police Act 1856 gave the Home Office clerk, Samuel Redgrave,[23] an opportunity to reflect on what had been achieved. Taking no rosy view of the state of the smaller borough forces – 'a great want of system and efficiency'[24] – he looked forward to the disappearance of 'a constitutional jealousy of police systems'. In evangelizing, aspirational terms, he argued such systems:

> will act for the removal of all demoralizing influences, for the better maintenance of public order and decorum . . . they will interfere to prevent the drunken brutality of the strong against the weak, and promptly assist in many ways in obtaining justice for the poor, whose material improvement they will greatly promote.[25]

19 TNA HO61/15, minute of 21 November 1835.

20 Involving an extra Superintendent, seven Inspectors, 88 Sergeants and 589 constables, memo March 1840, papers in TNA HO61/25.

21 TNA HO61/24, letter 9 October 1839.

22 See TNA HO61 series generally for petitions, for example letter of 23 August 1839 HO61/23 from the Rector of Tottenham urging that the Home Secretary should include Tottenham in the imminent extension of the Met district 'as I am thoroughly convinced that the moral improvement of a large and rapidly increasing population is closely interwoven with the decision of his Lordship'. Tottenham ratepayers had earlier in January 1838 (TNA HO61/13) petitioned for inclusion: attempts to adopt the 1833 Act had twice failed and the petitioners were 'now convinced that the good order and security of the neighbourhood cannot be maintained without the introduction of a well-regulated system of Police, under the direction of persons not locally connected with the Parish'.

23 Samuel Redgrave (1802–76), Home Office clerk 1818–60. Secretary to the Constabulary Commission 1836–9. Keeper of the Criminal Register 1841–60. In his private life, he was a significant art historian: see his Oxford Dictionary of National Biography entry.

24 *Judicial Statistics 1857*, PP 1857/8, vol.lvil, Introduction dated 29 May 1857, p.v.

25 Ibid. p.vi.

One of the Met's other contributions to organizing policing improvement was the dissemination of the various editions of its Instruction Book. This is what Joseph Bishop took with him to Bristol and which he adapted for local circumstances. In an unpublished lecture, Joanne Klein has shown the extent to which these Met documents were circulated outside London. The surviving example of the manual issued by Bishop in Bristol shows clearly its provenance with the addition of the fruits of his own experience.[26] Other examples of what the largest force could accomplish for general benefit were the Met's taking over from Bow Street and transforming the *Police Gazette* in 1883, and Howard Vincent's *Police Code.* Originally published in 1881 and maintained by the Met for over 20 years following Vincent's death in 1908, it was an accessible manual of policing law replaced eventually by Moriarty's *Police Law* from 1929. Similarly, it was the Met that edited three updating editions of Gross's *Criminal Investigation: A Practical Textbook*, first published in English translation in 1924 and the leading textbook of its age.[27]

Reinforcement, including under mutual aid arrangements for particular occasions, did not extend only to provincial forces but also to the policing of government establishments. Thus, the Met took on the naval dockyards at Deptford and Woolwich in 1841 and from 1860 a fuller range of naval and army establishments well beyond the Met's London district. Under arrangements that lasted until 1934, the Met provided four Superintendent-led forces at Woolwich, Devonport and Chatham with an Inspector led contingent at Pembroke Dock plus smaller detachments to army depots. By 1914 this deployment consisted of over 2,000 officers most of whom were in units considerably larger than the local constabularies. During the First World War the deployment was extended to Rosyth in Scotland. These arrangements, where the Met was reimbursed by the other government departments, relieved the ordinary civil police of a potential burden it would have been onerous to assume and at the same time preserved a situation where the policing, gradually taken over by defence established forces, was carried out under the auspices of a responsible minister.

Colonization

The establishment of the Police College at Hendon from 1934 was the outcome of a very personal attachment on the part of its founding Commissioner, Trenchard, to improving the standard of senior officers in the Met. It also had the effect of spreading Hendon-trained officers throughout the police service. Just as Met

26 Rules, Orders and Regulations framed by the Watch Committee of the Borough and City of Bristol and County of the same City for the guidance of the Officers and Constables of the Police appointed to act in the said Borough, under 5 and 6 of HM K William IV, chapter 7, Bristol: Bristol Watch Committee, 1836. See for example the entry on Superintendents, p.3.

27 The nearly 2,000 page Met commissioned compendium by W. F. A. Archibald, *The Metropolitan Police Guide*, London: Metropolitan Police, 1891 and regularly updated, found its way to other forces because of its pragmatic ordering of police relevant public law.

officers had assisted nascent provincial forces so in Hendon's case was the diaspora not originally intended. Coming in the wake of a failed Home Office attempt to secure agreement with other police authorities for a rather different central police training establishment where failure had been occasioned partly by the austerity policies of the day, Trenchard's college was, and in many ways remains, controversial in the police service. This was principally because it challenged the fundamental understanding that promotion through the ranks should start from the bottom: experience, in other words, was more highly prized than capacity for 'leadership'. The fact that room would be made for direct entrants to the College with no police experience at all was the clearest possible signal that old orthodoxies were to be challenged. As the principal mouthpiece of the rank and file put it commenting on the original White Paper proposals, they would have 'the inevitable result of creating an officer class distinct from the rank and file of the Police. . . . The chances of promotion from the ranks will in consequence be diminished.'[28]

When it was revealed that College entrants would have to equip themselves with dinner jacket, four dress shirts and patent shoes, there was laughter in Parliament and elsewhere, duly noted in Jack Hayes's column in the *Review*. But Hayes went on to criticize the scheme's age limits which put the experience and its advantages beyond the reach of in-service officers over 26: 'A grave injury is being done to many individual officers whatever may be the measure of its effects on the Service generally'.[29] The fact, too, that the scheme to accommodate graduates' expedited promotion meant delaying and/or preventing the promotion of others beyond the rank of Inspector was a defect from the beginning. This actuarially worsened during the scheme's life and was one of the reasons why the College could not have survived in its original form had it not been stood down because of the onset of the Second World War in 1939.[30]

For many, but not all, graduates of the College, the experience opened up careers formerly unimaginable. Hitherto, the very senior ranks above Superintendent had, from the Met's inception, been, with very few exceptions, filled overwhelmingly by direct entrant navy and army officers. It was an article of political faith, endorsed by the Committee set up following the Pall Mall riots of 1886, that those ranks and what they could aspire to should be filled by officers of good social standing.[31] This created a system that was closed not only to all more junior

28 *Police Review*, 19 May 1933.

29 Ibid. 15 December 1933. Jack Hayes (1887–41) a former Met officer from a Midland police family and last secretary of the unrecognized National Union of Police and Prison Officers responsible for the 1918 and 1919 police strikes. He was MP for Edge Hill, Liverpool, 1922–31 and for a long while on the editorial board of the *Review*.

30 K. A. L. Parker, 'Hendon and after', *Police Journal*, July 1980, pp.219–32, especially pp.222–3.

31 *Report of the Committee to inquire into the Administration and Organisation of the Metropolitan Police Force*, C. 4894, 19 June 1886. The class politics behind this system are discussed in R. M. Morris, 'The Metropolitan Police and Government 1860–1920', Ph.D. thesis, Open University, 2004, pp.17–52.

members of the Met but also to members of other forces except in the rare event of a provincial candidate qualified under the 1886 criteria. As one of the early Hendon graduates noted:

> it had been rare indeed for a Metropolitan officer to be selected for a senior post in the Provinces, and any influx from the opposite direction, from Provinces to London, had been non-existent. . . . Within ten years, more than half the total police strength outside London was commanded by Hendon men.[32]

In less celebratory tones, this view was both corroborated but also qualified by Wall:

> Considering the relatively short period in which the Metropolitan Police College existed, its legacy as a source of police officers was considerable. Two quite contradictory issues stand out: on the one hand, any success that the Hendon scheme had achieved in creating future senior officers was offset by the fact that it took place at the expense of the rest of the police. Not only did morale drop within the Metropolitan Police during its existence, but the quality of recruits entering by the normal procedures also fell.[33]

A review undertaken in 1965 of the positions that Hendon graduates had achieved in the Service is summarized in Table 9.1 below.

Further analysis of these data showed:

> that the pool of Hendon graduates enabled the provincial police authorities, particularly in the counties, to select people with similar social qualities to those of their previous, externally appointed, Chief Constables and at the same time comply with the principle of appointing career police officers.[34]

Table 9.1 Senior posts held by Hendon graduates 1965[35]

Metropolitan Police	
Commissioners/Deputy Commissioners and Assistant Commissioners	6
Chief and Assistant Constable equivalent	5
HM Inspectors of Constabulary	5
Provincial forces	
County Chief Constables	19
Borough Chief Constables	6
Assistant Chief Constables (all Provincial)	3

32 R. Bacon, 'Hendon: Historic milestone – A student looks back', *Police Journal*, 1980, pp.15–23 at p.19.

33 Wall, *The Chief Constables of England and Wales*, p.214.

34 Wall, ibid., p.218.

35 A. L. Dixon, *The Home Office and the Police in England and Wales between the Two World Wars*, 1966 (typescript, Home Office Library), Table 4, p.216 (adapted) and Wall, ibid., Table 10, p.217.

However, this did not mean that all the Hendon graduates had social backgrounds to which county police authorities could instantly relate or that they ignored merit, as the career of Graham Rutherford shows.[36]

Hendon graduates certainly shook up provincial and, in the end, national policing. Ted Dodd (1909–66) became a Met constable in 1932 after a career in the merchant navy and was one of the first to join the Hendon course. Having become a Met senior sub-divisional Inspector, he was appointed aged 31 to the Birmingham force as an Assistant Chief Constable (ACC) in 1941 and became its Chief Constable in 1945. His genial but firm and determined manner raised standards not only in his own force but in all those surrounding Birmingham in the west midlands, which became known in police circles as 'Dodd's own country'.[37] Among his achievements was the formation of the Midlands Regional Crime Squad and Criminal Record Office. The Squad included all forces in Warwickshire, Staffordshire and Worcestershire, and by 1960 Leicestershire and Rutland. This initiative was the precursor of a system that went national from 1964. In his 1960 annual report to the Watch Committee he claimed that the initiatives had 'done a great deal to overcome the problems of geographical boundaries between forces in relation to the investigation and detection of crime'.[38] He became HM Chief Inspector of Constabulary (HMCIC) 1963–6 and did much to develop the role and capacity of the Inspectorate.

Eric St Johnston (1911–86), accepted at Hendon from the Scotland Yard *civilian* staff, became Chief Constable of Oxfordshire aged 29. After important service involved in the reconstruction of policing in Europe after the War, he became Chief Constable first of Durham and then from 1950 of Lancashire, at the time the largest force outside London. In all his postings, if without Dodd's likeability, he showed energy and innovatory ability, famously for his development of mobile policing. He followed Dodd as HMCIC 1966–70.

While the unintended exodus of Hendon men to provincial forces could be said to have disadvantaged the Met, numbers returned with horizons widened by wartime and provincial experience. 'Rasher' Bacon (1906–88) after Provost wartime service was Deputy and then Inspector General of the Ceylon Police and afterwards spent 14 years as Chief Constable of Devon before returning to the Met in 1961 to serve as Assistant and then Deputy Commissioner. Peter Brodie (1914–89) also spent time in the Ceylon police before becoming Chief Constable of Stirling and

36 H.G. Rutherford (1908–2003), Consett Grammar School; Barrister, Gray's Inn 1941. Selected for first Hendon course winning prize for 'Police Duties and Procedure'. After war service in Africa, Sicily and the Allied Military Government, he was successively Chief Constable of Oxfordshire (1945–54), Lincolnshire (1954–6) and Surrey (1956–68).

37 Dodd's dominance was signalled by the fact that the Chief Constable of Dudley 1946–66, C. W. Johnson, could never bring himself to address Dodd as other than 'Mr Dodd'. (Interview with Lord (Philip) Knights, 19 August 2010).

38 TNA HO272/86. Dodd's appointment as HM Chief Inspector of Constabulary (HMCIC) in 1962 was marked by unusually warm appreciative minutes of the Birmingham Watch Committee of 5 December 1962 and in its report to full Council of 23 July 1963 (Birmingham City Archives).

Clackmannan 1949–56 and succeeding another Hendon graduate, G. C. White, at Warwickshire 1958–66. After a spell in the Inspectorate, he returned to serve as a Met Assistant Commissioner 1966–72. John Waldron (1909–75) also undertook wartime service in Ceylon and after returning to the Met became Assistant Chief Constable in Lancashire 1951–4, then Chief Constable of Berkshire 1954–8, returning to the Met in 1959 to serve as an Assistant Commissioner, Deputy and finally Commissioner 1968–72.

Specialization

The sheer size of the Met tended to precipitate specialisms which developed into service functions available to other forces. Initially, the process was anything but linear or intended since regard had to be paid to the interests of the London ratepayer, any programmatic approach was not encouraged by the fiscal framework. The Commissioners' insistence on repayment inhibited requests for assistance from, for example, thinly financed provincial forces and higher Met salaries.[39]

In practice, the most important specializations were related to crime control, less in investigation itself than in the bureaucracy of identification. Customarily, much attention is given to the initially small group of central detectives acknowledged to operate at Scotland Yard from 1842. Among other things, these officers undertook investigations when invited to do so by provincial police authorities. This was work hitherto undertaken by the Principal Officers attached to the stipendiary Police Offices set up by the Middlesex Justices Act 1792 and mostly, but not exclusively, from the Bow Street Police Office.[40] This service was ended in 1839 when all the small magisterial police forces attached to the 1792 Act's stipendiary courts were abolished and their role not immediately taken up by the Met which was, after all, thought of as a preventative rather than a detective force. In practice, however, most of the officers, such as Inspectors Nicholas Pearce and John Haynes plus the majority of the sergeants, nominated to the new detective department in 1842 had been engaged in plain-clothes investigation for some time.[41]

Because the Met detectives were full-time investigators they were able to develop expert knowledge of criminal and court procedure as well as investigative skills and were not in fact called upon by provincial forces all that often. Apart from the inhibition of expense, forces were reluctant to recruit them because to do so underlined local failure. In turn, this meant officers being summoned often sometime after the discovery of the offence when trails were already cold. The successes of these detectives were celebrated in the press and in their memoirs; their failures appeared in the former but not the latter. What an experienced officer

39 Birkenhead Police failed to recruit a Met Chief Detective Inspector in 1904 because they could not afford to match his salary, S. P. Thompson, *Maintaining the Queen's Peace: A Short History of the Birkenhead Borough Police*, (Birkenhead: Birkenhead Police), 1958, p.5.

40 See, Cox, *A Certain Share of Low Cunning*, pp.39–40.

41 B. Cobb, *The First Detectives*, London: Faber, 1957, especially Chapters 12 and 13.

could achieve remains celebrated even now. The classic case of the murder of a young boy in Road, Somerset, in 1860 continues to fascinate[42] and the surviving contemporary papers show an intelligent and thorough operation where the investigating officer, Jonathan Whicher (one of the original detective sergeants appointed in 1842), demonstrated considerable psychological insight.[43] One of the reasons why the Yard's reputation grew was because for much of the nineteenth century provincial forces did not generally possess detective departments and, where they did, the number of detectives was small. The Met, on the other hand, grew not only its central detective department but also from the late 1860s set up divisional detective units.[44]

These factors helped the Met to develop collective detective experience and investigative routines that included crime scene preservation and scrupulous maintenance of evidence sequences. Such sophistication was beyond much smaller forces at a time when, by 1901 for example, the strength of only fourteen of the 125 non-London borough forces in England and Wales exceeded 200 as against the Met's nearly 16,000. Sent to Salisbury (police force of 40 men) in 1908 to investigate the stabbing murder of a twelve-year-old one-legged boy, Inspector Dew found that, by the time he got there, the body had been washed and an attempt – not quite determined enough – had been made to clear up the bloodstains on the premises. Against the weight of the evidence Dew was nonetheless able to assemble, the mother was acquitted. One result was a Home Office circular enjoining provincial forces to call for assistance more promptly.[45] At the other end of the spectrum of difficulty was a Monmouthshire case in 1920. A fifteen-year-old girl, used as a skivvy by better-off family members including at the house of a widowed aunt, had sensationally clubbed the aunt to death. A Met detective Inspector and Sergeant were sent to assist the county force to *process* rather than to investigate the obvious culprit: no doubt her youth was thought to call for a degree of experienced handling not within the local force's capacity.[46]

The challenge of Irish terrorism provoked further specialization within the Met detectives by the establishment of the Irish Special Branch in 1883, later known as the Special Branch (see Malcolm, Chapter 4). This led on terrorism of all kinds and from 1909 acted as the operational arm of the counter-espionage functions of MI5 while until 1992 retaining its lead on Irish terrorism when that role was ceded to MI5.[47] These were national services supported by provincial officers in

42 K. Summerscale, *The Suspicions of Mr Whicher or The Murder at Road Hill House*, London: Bloomsbury, 2008.

43 MEPO 3/61, murder of Francis Saville Kent.

44 For an account of detective developments generally, see B. Morris, 'History of criminal investigation' in T. Newburn, T. Williamson T. and A. Wright A. (eds) Cullompton: Willan, 2007, pp.15–40.

45 MEPO 3/187, murder of Teddy Haskell.

46 MEPOI 3/270, murder at Rose Cottage, Llanvetherine.

47 Much to the chagrin of the Branch, R. Wilson and I. Adams, *Special Branch: A History 1883–2006*, London: Biteback, 2015, pp.375–91.

collaboration with Special Branch who also actually manned operations at the main ports and, later, airports.

Detective operations fascinate where the bureaucracy of identification does not, though it is arguably the latter that catches more criminals than the former. How to be certain of the identity of a suspect or those found guilty at trial was a crucial requirement of crime control. Without secure identification no one could be linked to previous or other outstanding offences, possible accomplices and modes of operation. Arising partly from concern focused on the more serious offenders who after the ending of transportation remained in the country, the Habitual Criminals Act 1869 required details of all convicted persons to be recorded on a register to be maintained by the Met.[48] The amount of detail, including photographs, increased over time. Attempts to achieve a reliable system of identifying people coming before the courts experimented with a French system of anthropomorphic measurement, the Bertillon system, but culminated in the system made possible by the invention of a workable scheme of fingerprint classification. This was the work of the Met Commissioner, Edward Henry (and a rare example of a former member of the Indian Police Service at the Met), whose system became operational from 1901.[49] Still at the Yard, the system gradually developed, including with the introduction of automatic fingerprint recognition, into the National Investigation Bureau, a facility for national use. It was also under Home Office auspices that the Police National Computer Unit was instituted in collaboration with the Met within the Hendon training school site, going live in 1974. Subsequently, the Met has ceased to host these national functions which have both developed new capacities (DNA recording, for example) and become organized and reorganized in a series of autonomous statutory service bodies.

These were by no means the only forms of Met specialisation. Other examples included what became a joint Met and City Fraud Squad, and expert units on currency fraud and crimes involving fine art and valuable antiques. There was even a special cohort of Met detectives located from the 1840s in the Post Office dedicated to the pursuit of offences against the mail and, later, telephone services. There being no practicable way to allocate the costs of the benefit of these services to provincial forces, the Metropolitan Police Act 1909 initiated a Treasury grant to the Met 'for imperial and national purposes' to mitigate costs that would otherwise have been part funded by the 50 per cent of total Met expenditure provided by London ratepayers.

Fusion

Robert Mark's memoirs describe the hostile reception he experienced when inserted by the Home Secretary into the Met as an Assistant Commissioner in 1968.

48 See T. Stanford, 'Who are you? We have ways of finding out! Tracing the police development of offender identification techniques in the late nineteenth century', *Crimes and Misdemeanours*, 2009, vol.3:1, 54–81.

49 D. E. Luke, *Criminal Record Development*, Godalming, self-published (ISBN 0907204015), 1980.

Although most of its former Commissioners were men without previous police experience, the then Commissioner Joseph Simpson was the first to have joined as a constable and risen through the ranks. Moreover, he was a Hendon man surrounded by Hendon men who had come to regard the Met as their own property.[50] This clannishness was one of the downsides of the Hendon system which had often, though not invariably, identified and developed a new, and not to be repeated in that way, cohort of competent police leaders.

What is in comparison notable about the present most senior Met officers at the time of writing is that only one started their career in the Met. In addition, an unscientific perusal of *Who's Who* shows that in recent decades it is evident that officers have been building careers by leaving the Met for provincial experience and returning to more senior posts or seeking higher posts in provincial forces. Similarly, there have been growing numbers of provincial force officers taking senior Met posts. Statistically as opposed to impressionistically, Wall's study of the 1,485 officers who between 1836 and 1996 held chief officer posts has shown that Met penetration of provincial forces has been greater than, say, Bacon's understanding that movement outwards from the Met was rare. While this may have been truer in the period up to the Hendon college, it is nonetheless the case that for the 1,485 cohort as a whole the Met 'was the singular most popular' force that the Chief Constables entered upon joining the police. Moreover, 'almost a third (30 per cent) of the Chief Constables appointed since the 1974 configuration of forces first joined the police through the Metropolitan Police'.[51]

The principal reason for these changes is the greater degree of relative equality between individual forces. The service had grown piecemeal during the nineteenth century. By the end of the First World War, it was pointed out that among 'the 129 separate City and Borough Forces there were still 50 with under 50 men'.[52] The average size of forces continued to be low. Out of the total number of 188 forces, including the Met, in 1910, only 25 had more than 200 men. In 1939, the by then 180 forces had 39 with more than 200 officers. Following the rounds of amalgamations initiated by Home Secretary Roy Jenkins and forced under procedures contained in the Police Act 1964, a substantial reduction in the number of forces in England and Wales was achieved from 116 forces in 1965 to 44 in 1969. This outcome was further sealed by the Local Government Act 1972 coming into force in 1974. Of the 43 forces that resulted, only two, the City and Wiltshire, were under 1,000 strong in 1992. At present 21 of the 42 forces have more than 2,000 officers and two, again the City and Wiltshire, have fewer than 1,000.[53]

50 R. Mark, *In the Office of Constable*, London: Collins, 1978, pp.78–87. Philip Knights, then Chief Constable of the West Midlands and aware of Mark's reception, declined to be considered as Mark's replacement in 1976 because he thought it unwise to take on the role without previous service in the Met which, however painfully, Mark had acquired (Interview 19 August 2010).

51 Wall, *The Chief Constables of England and Wales*, pp.250–1.

52 Dixon, *The Home Office and the Police in England and Wales between the Two World Wars*, p.1.

53 C. Emsley, *The English Police: A Political and Social History*, (2nd edn), London: Longman, 1996 Appendix 1, pp.262–8.

While the Met at 31,000 officers remains by far the largest, it is no longer as absolutely dominant as it once was.[54] Some provincial Chief Constables are now commanding larger numbers than their Met counterparts. This change in relative status is evidenced in two other ways. First, at the time of writing, the proportion of chief officers who had served in the Met has declined from the 40 per cent of Reiner's 1991 study, through the 30 per cent in 1996 who had started in the Met observed by Wall, to 19 per cent now, a fall of almost 50 per cent over 25 years.[55] Secondly, it is observable that the careers of members of the leadership teams in provincial forces are generally more regionally based than may be recollected of the more fragmented service of the pre-1974 period where promotion more often required a greater degree of relocation because posts were more scattered across the UK.[56] At the same time, however, it can be observed that, of the eight present provincial Chief Constables who began their service in the Met, five head Home Counties forces and it would therefore appear that a form of regionalization has taken place of which the Met is the centre.[57] Indeed, a few years ago a Home Office initiative of the then Home Secretary, Charles Clarke, suggested a pattern of fifteen regional forces which his successor, John Reid, discontinued.

Fusion has also extended more purposefully to the creation of nationwide police operational units rather than treating metropolitan capacity as recognized by the Metropolitan Police Act 1909 – as a surrogate for centralized national units. Examples include taking the responsibility for identification services out of the Met, the creation of the one-time Police Information Technology Organization and, most important of all, the establishment of the National Crime Agency (NCA). Its lineage goes back to the crime squad coordination of the 1960s through the amalgamation of the National Crime Squad and the National Criminal Intelligence Service into the Serious and Organised Crime Agency (SOCA) in 2005. There followed the further incorporation based on SOCA of investigative functions formerly in the Border Agency with elements of National Police Improvement Agency functions as well to create the NCA. To an extent, the transfer of Home

54 The extension of HM Inspectorate to the Met has thrown up performance issues where the Met has not shone, for example in murder investigation. See 'Met must solve more murders', *BBC News*, 10 April 2003.

55 Latest figures calculated from the biographies of Chief Constables on force websites accessed 16 October 2016. For the earlier figures see R. Reiner, *Chief Constables*, Oxford University Press, 1991, p.76; and Wall, *The Chief Constables of England and Wales*, pp.250–1.

56 Lord (Philip) Knights (1920–2014) as a Superintendent in the Lincolnshire force attended interviews for Assistant Chief Constable posts unsuccessfully at Durham (where the entire police authority attended and he lost by one vote) and Somerset where, after an overnight stay and interviews, the local candidate was selected anyway to the fury of a Manchester force candidate, Robert Mark, who resolved to avoid such charades in future, (Interview 19 August 2010).

57 Though such apparent regionalization matches a common-sense appreciation that officers would prefer to avoid disrupting family life where, in addition, spouses tend more often to be themselves employed, the observation needs to be deepened by a time series to confirm the extent to which the apparent change has been continuous or merely an accident of what are, in fact varying, relatively small numbers.

Office responsibility for the Met to a Metropolitan Police Authority in 2000, and to the Mayor of London and the Greater London Authority in 2012 as the counterpart to the institution of the new Police and Crime Commissioner system, made the surrogate national functions of the Met more obviously anomalous, and this could lead to the Met losing its lead role in counter-terrorism.

Conclusion

Its location, its size and direct central government control meant that the Met was from the beginning in a dominant position. Established at a time when public order and crime control were still seen as predominantly local responsibilities locally financed, it was the decay and inadequacy of those local institutions in a new type of urban agglomeration that lacked effective metropolitan agency that forced government to innovate and create its own. In turn, responding to its circumstances, the Met developed or sophisticated pre-existing order and crime control procedures, which invariably, were not of immediate, useful applicability to provincial forces. It is significant too that, although Met advice was widely sought in the 1830s, their officers were not imported frequently into chief officer posts.

In that respect, the Hendon diaspora was exceptional and for special contemporary reasons. The College was generally not favoured by Home Office officials because it was not a solution to the long-term problem of leadership in the the police service in England and Wales which was what the failed Hendon project had been created to address. Having joined the Home Office in 1934, Philip Allen, 60 years later reflected 'though it lasted only until 1939, it did irreparable damage after the War so far as securing agreement to higher training was concerned.'[58] The perceived elitism of the College and the high-handed denial of preferment to non-College officers meant that any successor project, however different, faced deep suspicion and hostility in the service.

As to services, the Met did not make 'corporatization' of the police service inevitable but it did pilot much of its content. While it was not responsible for the centralization which grew after the First World War, it was a standing example of how larger forces could command greater internal specialization and develop a professionalism not easily otherwise obtained.

58 Interview 17 July 1997 with Lord (Philip) Allen of Abbeydale (1912–2007), PUS Home Office 1966–72.

10 Chief Constables and public order

Tensions between discretion and consistency

Iain Channing

Introduction

Public order offences range from high-level disorders such as riot and violent disorder to low-level offences such as causing harassment, alarm or distress. While these offences can happen within a multitude of scenarios and environments, this chapter is concerned with how Chief Constables have led their respective forces when disorder has been anticipated in relation to riot and unlawful assembly.[1] Many of the incidents discussed involved facilitating or restricting political activism and public protest which frequently called into question the partiality of the police responses. Throughout the nineteenth and twentieth centuries, public order has been regulated by a combination of both statutory and common law powers. Such powers, especially those related to the breach of the peace doctrine which are derived from the common law have always been ambiguous and actions taken by the police to prevent or restore order have often been contentious. Since the formation of modern provincial police forces in the nineteenth century, the individual leadership, background, and personality of Chief Constables has played a significant role in how public disorder has been policed. The inconsistencies in police practice in relation to different political groups have frequently been explained in terms of police prejudice.[2] Other explanations have highlighted that such prejudice was not always so habitual and activists from opposite ends of the political spectrum may face differing police treatment dependant on temporal and geographic permutations.[3] Yet, what this research has not questioned is the influence that individual Chief Constables may have had on their respective force responses.

1 Before the enactment of the Public Order Act 1986 riot and unlawful assembly were both Common Law offences.

2 See K. D. Ewing and C. A. Gearty, *The Struggle for Civil Liberties: Political Freedom and the Rule of Law in Britain, 1914–1945*, Oxford University Press, 2004. For the immediate post-war period see D. Renton, *Fascism, Anti-Fascism and Britain in the 1940s*, London: Macmillan Press, 2000.

3 I. Channing, *The Police and the Expansion of Public Order Law in Britain, 1939–2014*, Abingdon: Routledge, 2015.

Body-Gendrot makes the salient point that in cases of public disorder, police officers are enemies to some and saviours to others.[4] Moreover, the wide discretion available in public order policing does not guarantee an activist's estimation of the police as being either positive or negative. The influence of individual Chief Constables towards a force's response to political activism and protest has had a significant impact on the relationship between the police and the policed. This chapter critiques events which include the Chartist activism in 1839, the unemployed workers march in 1908, the activism of the British Union of Fascists (BUF) in the 1930s, and the inner city riots and protests of the 1980s, and illuminates the influence of certain Chief Constables behind the variety of tactics employed.

Birmingham and the Chartists

The Chartist related disorders in 1839 starkly demonstrated the deficiency of the peace-keeping arrangements in Birmingham. The attempts of the magistracy to prevent Chartist agitation, which included the employment of London's Metropolitan Police officers, only antagonized the disenfranchised groups of activists and protesters.[5] With anti-police sentiment high, coupled with the magistrates' orders to the Metropolitan Police officers to arrest any Chartist addressing a crowd, a series of pitched battles and disorders ensued, culminating in the Bull Ring Riot in the summer of 1839.[6] The violent suppression of Chartist activity also provided the Chartists with the opportunity to claim that the establishment were unsympathetic to public expressions for democracy.[7] In response to the growing Chartist activity, the Whig government established police forces in Birmingham, Bolton and Manchester, which remained under the control of the Home Secretary until 1842.[8] In Birmingham, Francis Burgess was appointed Commissioner following the Act for Improving the Police in Birmingham 1839. Burgess was a barrister, but had also served as a captain in the Battle of Waterloo, and effectively became the first leader of the 'new' police in Birmingham. The Birmingham Town Council had previously been bound to establish an adequate police force under the Municipal Corporation Act 1835, following the Charter of Incorporation 1838. However, with legal doubts over whether the Council had the powers to levy such rates, a police force was not established.[9]

With the prospect of further Chartist demonstrations ahead, Burgess had to ensure that the new Birmingham Police Force under his command demonstrated

4 S. Body-Gendrot, *Public Disorder and Globalization*, London: Routledge, 2017.

5 F. C. Mather, *Public Order in the Age of the Chartists*, Manchester University Press, 1959, p.13.

6 M. Chase, *Chartism: A New History*, Manchester University Press, 2007, p.81.

7 Ibid., p. 82.

8 C. Emsley, *The English Police: A Political and Social History*, 2nd edn, Harlow: Pearson Education Limited, 1996, p.41.

9 C. C. H. Moriarty, Birmingham City Police Centenary, 1838–1939: The Formation of the Force, and Its Present Organization, Birmingham Watch Committee: Birmingham, 1939, p.9.

legitimacy in its operations and gained public confidence and support. In Moriarty's history of the Birmingham Police Force, which was written to celebrate its centenary, he claimed that although there were many more Chartist demonstrations between 1839 and 1842, 'there were no riots and no conflicts between the police and the public.'[10] As early as 12 March 1840, Burgess had even been so bold to write to the Home Secretary claiming his force had been successful in 'pacifying the Town protecting property and reducing crime' and claimed that the force's popularity was increasing daily.[11] Although Burgess' eulogizing assessment of their own progress is questionable as he also requested extra funds from the Home Office in the same letter, Weaver highlights that by 1842 'Burgess had made progress toward gaining acceptance for his force'.[12]

While Burgess had been successful in preventing serious disorder, there was still evidence of resentment towards the police. His achievement in quelling disorder largely lay in his dedication to allow peaceful political activism by negotiating with the Chartists. The level of dialogue between the police and activists has been seen to be critical in recent public order literature.[13] The release of the Chartist John Collins, following twelve months' imprisonment, illustrates this liaison. His liberation was a cause for celebration and bands playing music escorted him through Birmingham 'in a triumphant manner'. The procession ended with Collins addressing the 'immense' crowd.[14] Where such radical martyrdom was displayed and anti-Government speeches delivered, previous policing arrangements would have attempted to quash such activism. Conversely, Burgess supplied his assurance to the committee organising the demonstration that 'unless the peace was disturbed the police was not to interfere with their proceedings.'[15] The *Warwick and Warwickshire Advertiser* stated that the 'arrangements made by Police and Magistrates were in all respects admirable' and that Burgess had assured the committee that they would not need to pay the police for their services, and if he believed there would be any disorder he would supply officers without charge.[16]

A militant wing of the Chartists was still active in the period under Burgess' tenure. Although his leadership can take some credit for the reduction in disorder, the local split in the Chartist movement itself also played a part. For instance, after Collins had distanced himself from the more militant Chartists, Burgess' correspondence with the Home Office identified that it had the effect of reducing

10 Moriarty, Birmingham City Police Centenary, p.22.

11 TNA HO 65/10, Letter Book (Birmingham), letter dated 12 March 1840.

12 M. Weaver, 'The new science of policing: Crime and the Birmingham Police Force, 1839–1842', *Albion: A Quarterly Journal Concerned with British Studies*, 1994, vol.26:2, 289–308, p.308.

13 H. Gorringe, and M. Rosie, '"We *will* facilitate your protest": Experiments with liaison policing', *Policing*, 2013, vol.7:2, 204–11; C. Stott, M. Scothern, and H. Gorringe, 'Advances in liaison based public order policing in England: Human rights and negotiating the management of protest?' *Policing*, 2013, vol.7:2, 212–26.

14 *Newry Examiner and Louth Advertiser*, 5 August 1840.

15 Ibid.

16 *Warwick and Warwickshire Advertiser*, 1 August 1840.

their attendance to between 300 and 150 people. The letter also indicated that Burgess had employed reliable surveillance sources admitting he had 'good intelligence' of their proceedings.[17] Burgess had a clear grasp of crime prevention strategy and championed it as key to effective police work. He utilized a strong police presence at public meetings where crowds gathered, resulting in the *Birmingham Journal* (which frequently criticized the new police force), to claim that it was the number of police on duty at these events that caused the worst obstruction of the streets.[18] This included the use of plain-clothed officers at Chartist gatherings, as well as other events that drew crowds such as music festivals and the annual horse fair. Burgess successfully established a police force in a town that largely opposed its formation. Not only did he play a part in reducing Chartist disorder, but he managed to convince critical ratepayers and local politicians that the force could provide value for money.[19]

Early twentieth century inconsistencies

The radical change in approach instigated by Burgess in 1839 was a complete departure from the previous tactic of the robust suppression of Chartist activism. However, the breach of the peace doctrine was ambiguous enough to support both approaches. Before the Human Rights Act 1998 incorporated the European Convention on Human Rights into UK law (which includes Article 10 the right to freedom of expression and Article 11 the right to freedom of assembly), if a police officer was of the opinion that a speaker threatened a breach of the peace by their activity they could ask them to cease addressing the crowd. Subsequently, if they did not they could be arrested for the obstruction of a police officer in the course of their duty.[20] The inconsistency in approaches to the policing of political activism continued into the early twentieth century. These differences were notable in both indoor and outdoor meetings.

With regard to indoor meetings, the Public Meeting Act 1908 addressed the growing problem of suffragette militancy that began to interrupt political meetings (a genuine public order concern given that Mrs Pankhurst's bodyguard were trained in ju-jitsu as referenced in Silvestri, Chapter 11). Political violence and rowdiness was not uncommon at such meetings in the Edwardian era, and letters published in *The Times* underline the view that the interjections made by suffragettes were 'no more than ordinary interruptions made by men at political meetings for which they are never thrown out'.[21] In 1905, Christabel Pankhurst and Annie Kenney

17 TNA HO 45/52 Disturbances, letter dated 14 January 1841. 'Good' underlined in original document.

18 *Birmingham Journal*, 28 Nov 1840, cited in Weaver, 'The new science of policing'.

19 Ibid.

20 The most famous case where this course of action was supported by the judiciary was *Duncan v Jones* [1936] 1 KB 218. See also, Channing, *The Police and the Expansion of Public Order Law*.

21 *The Times*, 8 December 1908.

were ejected from the Free Trade Hall, Manchester when Liberal MP Sir Edward Grey refused to answer their questions on female suffrage which were ruled out of order. Following Pankhurst's cry of 'Treat us like men!' the two agitators were forcibly removed by the police.[22] The following 1908 Act was mandated to prohibit disorderly conduct at a public meeting that was for the express purpose of preventing the transaction of business. The limitations of this Act were highlighted at a Liberal meeting in Ingatestone, Essex later that year. Following information that their meeting was to be interrupted, a request was made by the Liberal agent, Mr Martin, for the police to attend. But Sergeant Willsmer of the Essex Constabulary refused the request stating that the police were not allowed to be present in the hall and it was up to the organizers to keep order at their own meeting.

It was reported that the meeting was forcibly entered by 50 youths who threw aside the doorkeepers and violently ejected the Liberals inside. Martin was carried out to the street but dropped along the way, and was rescued by friends who took him into a side room of the hall where he fainted.[23] The public meeting was abandoned at the last moment. Liberal Unionist Austen Chamberlain asked the Home Secretary, Herbert Gladstone, whether he knew that different police forces in the country held different views of their duties regarding the preservation of order at public meetings, suggesting that a committee should be appointed to inquire into the conduct of the police. Subsequently, a Departmental Committee was set up to review the duties of the police at public meetings and revealed the variations of police practice.

The Minutes of Evidence included the examination of Captain Showers, Chief Constable of Essex, who reiterated Willsmer's report that the police did not enter indoor public meetings and the standard practice was that they stationed two police constables outside the meeting. Showers highlighted his 25 years' experience of police work which included appointments as Superintendent at Devon County Constabulary and Chief Constable of Exeter City Police, claiming that this was the standard practice in all forces.[24] Defending the view not to station police officers inside the hall, Shower stated, 'I think it would be most irritating to those people inside, and more likely to incite a row than to quell it.'[25] The Committee also called on evidence from Robert Peacock, the Chief Constable of the City of Manchester. The practice there was to provide police officers in either uniform or plain clothes inside the meetings if requested by the organizers. They would then pay for the services on a scale adapted by the Watch Committee.[26] Leonard Dunning, the Liverpool Chief Constable, thought the onus was on the organizers

22 *Daily Express*, 16 October 1905.

23 'Report of the Departmental Committee on the duties of the police with respect to the preservation of order at public meetings. Volume 1: Report and appendices', 1909, Cd.4673, p.22.

24 'Departmental Committee on the Duties of the Police with respect to the Preservation of Order at Public Meetings. Volume 2: Minutes and Evidence', 1909, Cd.4674, p.7.

25 Ibid.

26 Ibid., p.13.

rather than the police, arguing 'if you consider that your meeting is going to be disrupted by fifty roughs you must have seventy-five roughs who can throw them out.'[27] Jon Lawrence has argued that these views are typical of the pre-war political culture in which the 'old ways' of party politics and the disorder that occurred are referred to as a 'form of sport'.[28]

In total, the Committee interviewed the Metropolitan Police Commissioner, four Chief Constables from county constabularies and six Chief Constables from large borough forces. It determined that the varying practices of the Chief Constables could be classified by three distinct principles:

(1) That it is unwise for the police to interfere inside political meetings any further than they are bound to do in order to prevent actual breaches of the peace;
(2) That it is expedient to assist the promoters of public meetings to keep order inside, but that this is a special duty of the police which must be paid for by the persons desiring their assistance;
(3) That keeping order inside public meetings is part of the ordinary duties of the police, for which no payment ought to be asked.[29]

Despite the large variations of practice, the Committee did not advocate any action to bring uniformity of police practice to public meetings, stating that the three different systems 'have in each case been adopted either in consequence of, or with the sanction of, the public opinion in each locality.'[30]

The Departmental Committee also provided an opportunity for Chief Constables to provide their feedback on the Public Meeting Act. Shower commented that he had little knowledge of it as 'We very seldom get copies of Acts sent to us for a long time afterwards.'[31] There was consensus among the Chief Constables that the Public Meeting Act 1908 was a weak statute that did not confer any additional powers or impose any additional duties on the police. With barely any exception, the Chief Constables would not direct the police to prosecute interrupters, but would require that the charge sheet was signed by the promoter or a steward of the meeting. Chief Constable Dunning expressed his dissatisfaction that such a short Act of Parliament had too many pitfalls. In his questioning, it is established that if the police were to bring a prosecution under this Act, they would first have to prove that it was a lawful public meeting; second, that there was a disorderly act by someone in preventing the transaction of the business for which the meeting was called; and third, they would have to prove the intent of the person was to obstruct the meeting. Because of the wide discretion involved, Dunning explained that the Public Meeting Act should only be instigated by the injured person and

27 'Departmental Committee: Minutes of evidence, Volume 2', p.22.
28 J. Lawrence, 'Fascist violence and the politics of public order in inter-war Britain: The Olympia debate revisited', *Historical Research*, 2003 vol.76:192, 238–67.
29 'Report of the Departmental Committee, Volume 1', p.15.
30 Ibid.
31 'Departmental Committee: Minutes of evidence, Volume 2', p.8.

not the police. He further clarified that there was no power of arrest under the Act if the disorderly person refused to give their name to the police.[32] This was an important oversight which helps explain the police reluctance to use this legislation.

The ambiguity of police powers in regards to meetings held in public places was also contentious. Chief Constables were able to use their own autonomy to provide distinct instructions for their forces. Although there was no legal protection of the right to public meeting, different forces provided varying levels of commitment to such freedoms. In Plymouth, Chief Constable Sowerby instructed his force to prohibit any person holding a meeting in Market Place if they did not obtain the Chief Constable's permission beforehand.[33] This legally dubious order was amended the following month with a resolution by the Council that only one meeting at a time may take place in Market Place and Sowerby's order obligated the police constable on duty there to prevent any second meeting from forming.[34] Sowerby's initial order is consistent with his ambitious crime preventive strategy, which has been associated with early forms of what has more recently been referred to as zero tolerance policing as analysed by Stevenson in Chapter 5. Although controversial, his public order strategies also won plaudits. His 'clever' arrest of Mrs Pankhurst in 1913 thwarted the Suffragette activists waiting for her arrival in Plymouth on-board the liner *Majestic*, and he was praised for preventing a riot.[35]

Chief Constables in other provincial forces also adapted a zero tolerance approach when involving political activists that were considered to be radical or extreme. Birmingham's Chief Constable, Sir Charles Haughton Rafter, was experienced in managing riot and disorder. A report on his death in 1935 highlighted how he was remembered for dressing David Lloyd George in a police uniform at a Liberal meeting in 1901 so he could be escorted away from Birmingham Town Hall without being seen by the 'excited mob' outside who were angry over his anti-Boer War stance. In the confusion, a police baton charge was ordered and one youth was killed as the 'innocent as well as guilty persons suffered'.[36] Rafter (profiled by Klein in Chapter 7), who also served as a District Inspector of the Royal Irish Constabulary (RIC) was adept at managing disparate communities. His experience of working within a more militarized police culture is also evident in his writing of the RIC *Drill Book* which was published the year after his appointment as Birmingham's Chief Constable.[37] His evidence to the 1908 Departmental Committee also highlighted how he differed from many of his

32 Ibid., p.23–4.

33 South West Police Heritage Trust, 1973.0001.001, 'Plymouth Constabulary general orders, 1907–1916', Order from Chief Constables Office, 6 October 1911.

34 Ibid., Order from Chief Constables Office, 22 November 1911.

35 J. Rowbotham and K. Stevenson, 'A point of justice – Granted or fought for? Women's suffrage campaigns in Plymouth and the South West', *Plymouth Law and Criminal Justice Review*, 2016, vol.1, 84–98.

36 *Warwick and Warwickshire Advertiser*, 31 August 1935.

37 C. H. Rafter, *Drill Book for the Royal Irish Constabulary, Containing Manual & Firing Exercise, and Company Drill, &c.*, Aldershot: Gale & Polden, 1900.

contemporaries and favoured having police officers attend public meetings and support the stewards in the eviction of any disruptive audience members.[38] Rafter revealed to the Committee that all sorts of public views were aired at the Bull Ring (likening it to Hyde Park in London) and stated that even the extreme views of anarchists are expressed without disorder as the people of Birmingham were tolerant of the views of others.[39] Although, in 1908 when a procession of the unemployed from Manchester passed through Birmingham, they were not provided the same hospitality.

When the Manchester men arrived at Birmingham, they were warned by the police that they could not hold a procession through the streets to the centre of the city, or hold an open air meeting there. It is unclear what legal authority was used, but it is likely that the police order was a 'loose' interpretation of the common law power to prevent a breach of the peace. Despite this, the leaders of the march declared their 'intention of asserting their rights of free speech' by insisting to the police Inspector, 'I tell you frankly that there will be a meeting.'[40] The leaders also attempted to meet with the Mayor to resolve the issue but had been hindered by the police who refused them entry to 'Mansion House'.[41] Undeterred, the procession which consisted of flags, banners and a hand cart carrying the petition for local people to sign proceeded and was met by a 'strong force of police'. After unsuccessful negotiations, the unemployed began to advance, the police obstructed their progress, and 'a scene of extraordinary violence ensued'.[42] The *Manchester Courier* attributed the cause of the violence to the unemployed men stating, 'A riot, which nearly attained the most serious proportions, occurred . . . owing to the aggressive attitude which was displayed by the body of Manchester unemployed.'[43]

After failing to penetrate the police cordon, many of the unemployed marched on to Coventry. Others persisted in attempting to break through the police lines and four men were arrested during the disorder. Two were released on the undertaking that they would leave the city, and the other two men were charged with disorderly conduct at the police court. They were subsequently discharged by the magistrates under the assurance that they would leave the city and join the rest of the group. When the unemployed men reached Coventry on Saturday evening they were 'well received by local labour men'. The Chief Constable in Coventry was Charles Charsley, who had risen rapidly through the ranks of the police force after joining the Birmingham City Police at the age of 21. Within a few years he was a Chief Inspector and was appointed Chief Constable of Coventry in 1889 at the age of 34. He was later a footballer of international standing after

38 'Departmental Committee: Minutes of evidence, Volume 2', pp.29–34.

39 Ibid. at p.34.

40 *Manchester Courier and Lancashire General Advertiser*, 31 January 1908.

41 Ibid. The newspaper report's reference to Mansion House was more likely to mean the Council House which contained the Mayor's Suite.

42 *Lichfield Mercury*, 31 January 1908.

43 *Manchester Courier and Lancashire General Advertiser*, 31 January 1908.

being capped for England in 1893.[44] The Manchester marchers were provided with sleeping quarters for two nights at the Clarion Club and given three meals on Sunday, including one hot meal. The police were also hospitable, and allowed the unemployed to hold public meetings, and make collections.[45] Charsley has been noted locally for his commitment to facilitating controversial protests. During the Great War, he facilitated anti-war protests in Coventry when other provinces saw them as illicit. However, he also showed his pragmatic leadership by allowing them on the condition that a collection was made among the audience for the Coventry Police Fund to aid the families of officers serving in the war.[46]

These contrasting examples illustrate the spectrum of police responses to the facilitation of public meetings in two cities just 20 miles apart. The different tactics employed by each force demonstrate the autonomy of the Chief Constable to assert their own agenda on public order responses. Yet, such public order scenarios which contain a strong element of political activism frequently test the impartiality of the police. Rafter's autocratic position was clear, and shows consistency with Klein's research in Chapter 7 where she revealed Rafter's attitude towards the National Union of Police and Prison Officers as socialists, pacifists, and anarchists.[47] Additionally, the influence of the Watch Committee will also have authority here. Philip Clay, the Chief Constable of Nottingham (1892–1912), highlighted the influence of Watch Committees over their respective Chief Constables in quite exacting terms. In 1899, he stated that it was the Chief Constable's role to 'carry out all orders and regulations' of the Watch Committee and that all orders and regulations deemed expedient to the Chief Constable, were also 'subject to the approval of the Watch Committee'.[48]

The interwar years

In an era when the political cultures outside the mainstream had become so polarized through the activism of both fascist and communist movements, police responses became highly scrutinized. Organizations such as the National Council for Civil Liberties (NCCL) recognized the frequent abuse of police power and campaigned for the political liberties of freedom of expression and assembly.[49] The NCCL became predominantly associated with left-wing politics and defended political speakers in high-profile appeals such as *Thomas v Sawkins*[50] and *Duncan*

44 *Coventry Evening Telegraph*, 11 January 1945.
45 *Lichfield Mercury*, 31 January 1908.
46 P. Walters and Culture Coventry, *Great War Britain Coventry: Remembering 1914–1918*, Stroud: The History Press, 2016.
47 Birmingham City Police Superintendents Reports and Confidential Letters R Div, 26 November 1918, p.504.
48 P. S. Clay, *Police Instructions for the Government and Guidance of Police Forces*, Nottingham: James Bell and Son, 1899, p.3.
49 The NCCL was formed in 1934 and is today known as Liberty.
50 *Thomas v Sawkins* [1935] 2 KB 249.

v Jones.[51] Respectively, these cases challenged the police tactic of entering private premises when a breach of the peace was anticipated and protecting the residual freedom of speakers to hold a peaceful public meeting without police interference. Both appeals were dismissed. The NCCL purposely did not defend abuses against fascist activism, a standpoint that was highlighted by Sylvia Scaffardi, a co-founder of the Council, who argued that fascism represented 'the thunder of brute force [that threatened] to trample and overrun the sensitive humanitarian world.'[52] Therefore, fascism itself was a threat to civil liberty so the NCCL did not use its legal resources to defend such a political agenda.

The provincial policing practices varied widely and the influence of Watch Committees becomes quite evident. For example, the increased presence of the Labour Party in local government in the years following the First World War led to an increase in political battles between police authorities and their Chief Constables. When such tension arose, Chris Williams has highlighted how the Home Office frequently favoured the Chief Constables over the Labour-dominated local authorities.[53] The anti-fascist nature of some Watch Committees became particularly prominent in this era. For example, the Manchester Watch Committee revelled in the conditions placed upon the BUF procession in the city. The BUF application for a public procession in Manchester on 19 July 1936 was initially and controversially declined by the Manchester Watch Committee under section 213 Manchester Police Act 1844 due to the provocative nature of the Blackshirt uniform. The BUF then tested the reason for the prohibition by responding that they would march without their uniform. The BUF march proceeded and the Assistant Chief Constable of Manchester highlighted that the removal of the provocative uniform had aided the successful policing of the procession.[54] In this instance the Watch Committee and the local police leadership agreed on the methods of reducing the provocative nature of fascist activism. At the Labour Party Conference in Edinburgh on 6 October 1936, Alderman Joseph Toole of Manchester seconded a motion for the prohibition of political uniforms, highlighting the BUF's recent plain-clothed march stating:

> Mosley came to Manchester a month ago. We allowed his procession, but the Watch Committee insisted that uniforms should not be worn. I moved that myself, because I wanted the public to see what Fascists were like without Uniforms. (Laughter.) And what a motley crew they were. (Laughter.)[55]

51 *Duncan v Jones* [1936] 1 KB 218.

52 S. Scaffardi, *Fire Under the Carpet: Working for Civil Liberties in the 1930s*, London: Lawrence and Wishart, 1986, p.49.

53 C. Williams, 'Rotten boroughs: The crisis of urban policing and the decline of municipal independence 1914–64', in J. Moore and J. Smith (eds) *Corruption in Urban Politics and Society, Britain 1780–1950*, Aldershot: Ashgate: 2007, p.161.

54 S. Cullen, 'Political violence: The case of the British Union of Fascists', *Journal of Contemporary History*, 1993, vol.28, p.256, quoting from HO 144/21061, 692, 242/172.

55 *The Manchester Guardian*, 6 October 1936.

However, police responses to fascist activism and related disorder have varied. Richard Thurlow highlighted that under Home Office advice, the Metropolitan Police were more cautious in policing the BUF than some provincial police forces. He argued that, despite the Home Office view that the police had no power to inhibit legal public processions, the interference of Chief Constables outside the Metropolitan Police district had 'only avoided legal setback because no one had challenged their instructions.'[56] A further example of this occurred in Exeter, where Chief Constable Frederick Tarry prohibited BUF speaker Captain Hammond from addressing any meetings in public spaces apart from an open space known as the Triangle where it was thought he would cause less provocation. The BUF never challenged this proscription but the Home Office believed that Tarry had overstepped his legal boundaries.[57]

Watch Committees were not always so keen to interfere with public order policing. For instance, in Liverpool when disorder arose from Protestant and Catholic meetings being provocatively held in or near each other's communities, accusations of police bias were levelled at Chief Constable Dunning in 1908, although he was exonerated by a Commission set up under the Police (Liverpool) Enquiry Act a year later. In Liverpool, the emphasis on policing religious disorder remained an issue the Watch Committee avoided and in 1938 the Chief Constable wrote to the Home Office declaring the Watch Committee 'did nothing in the way of making regulations' and have continued to 'evade the issue'.[58] The emphasis then rested on the Chief Constable to make controversial decisions relating to the proscription of meetings and processions. This raises questions about how partiality may be maintained with such wide police discretion. The notion of impartial policing has been criticized by Tony Jefferson as an 'impossible mandate' as the decision-making process of Chief Constables is influenced by a range of factors such as limited knowledge and restrictions on time and resources; let alone personal prejudice that may be conscious or unconscious.[59]

In Manchester, the Watch Committee's desire to stifle the BUF was supported by its Chief Constable, John Maxwell. Following the controversial restrictions imposed on the BUF's procession noted above, Maxwell and prominent members of the Manchester Watch Committee consulted with the Home Secretary, Sir John Simon, in a deputation on 23 October 1936. For the Home Office, the timing of the meeting was critical as they had just begun to draft the Public Order Bill.[60]

56 Thurlow, *The Secret State*, p.198.

57 T. Gray, *Blackshirts in Devon*, Exeter: The Mint Press, 2006, p.177 citing HO 144/21064.

58 TNA HO 144/21037, Disturbances: Police arrangements to prevent disorder at public meetings in Liverpool, Letter dated 27th June 1938.

59 T. Jefferson, *The Case against Paramilitary Policing*, Buckingham: Open University Press, 1990, p.47.

60 Although the fascist and communist related disorder had occupied Parliamentary debates in previous years, the urgency to act was now intensified following the 'Battle of Cable Street', where thousands of anti-fascist protesters clashed with police in their attempt to prevent a BUF procession proceeding through East London. See Channing, *The Police and the Expansion of Public Order Law*.

The mutual support between Chief and Watch Committee was highlighted during a discussion on the potential powers that could be provided to Chief Constables to prevent disorder. In the deputation, Alderman Williams of the Manchester Watch Committee stated, 'I see the difficulty in handing over, not to our Chief Constable, but some Chief Constables, the power. We have absolute trust in our Chief Constable.' Maxwell reciprocated this trust by suggesting the local authority could 'always put the Chief Constable on the spot'.[61] The deputation also highlighted the public order issues raised by the BUF and the difficulty the authorities had in policing them. Maxwell, who clearly saw them as an unwelcome nuisance, despite suggestions that he was sympathetic to the BUF, highlighted some of their tactics which helped them avoid police attention. This included how Blackshirts would cause trouble after their official meetings by going to other districts in small groups and creating disturbances, or by the BUF newspaper sellers 'deliberately going into the streets and sections of the city where they are likely to meet Jews and if there is no policeman about there is always trouble'.[62] These instances are particularly pertinent here. This is because they fall outside the general remit of public order policing arrangements which focuses on the demonstration itself. Maxwell highlighted that he had successfully managed meetings and processions by keeping opposing factions apart, but when the activities of the far right became more sporadic and less predictable, it problematized the police response.

Harry Herman, the Chief Constable of York City Police during the interwar years (1929–55), has been accused by Dorril of being a 'BUF supporter' but did not provide any evidence for this claim.[63] While his sympathy for the fascist movement may be questioned, his aversion towards the political left was not in doubt. This is clearly demonstrated by his obstruction of a Hunger March in 1936. The hunger marches organized by the National Unemployed Workers Movement in 1936 were associated with the Communist Party of Great Britain and a memorandum by the Home Secretary demonstrates the Home Office's attempt to discredit the march and its organizers.[64] While the marchers were well received in some towns and cities, with provisions such as food and lodgings provided for them, in York there was very little hospitality. Chief Constable Herman was said to have met the marchers on the outskirts of the city ordering them to march around the perimeter despite friends of the march having made preparations for receiving them in the city. Although arrangements had been made for them to receive hot food on their passage through the city, Herman rerouted them to the workhouse where they were only provided with bread and margarine.[65] In a scenario reminiscent of the Manchester

61 TNA HO 144/20159, Notes of a deputation from the Manchester Watch Committee to the Home Secretary on Friday, 23 October, 1936.

62 N. Todd, *In Excited Times: The People Against the Blackshirts*, Tyne and Wear: Bewick Press 1995, p.66.

63 S. Dorril, *Blackshirt: Sir Oswald Mosley and British Fascism*, London: Viking, 2006, p.307. See also, Todd, *In Excited Times*, p.66.

64 TNA CAB 24/264, March of the Unemployed on London: Memorandum by the Home Secretary (1936).

65 HC Deb 26 November 1936 vol.318 cc.594–5.

unemployed experiences in the West Midlands in 1908, the operational discretion of the Chief Constable was again demonstrated through the variance of approaches. Subsequently, the legality of Herman's approach was questioned in the House of Commons by Conservative MP Earl Winterton.[66] The issue remained unresolved and Ellen Wilkinson, Labour MP for Jarrow, highlighted that the matter needed to be taken to the House of Lords to challenge the Chief Constable's action, but as the people involved in the march were so poor, there was no chance of that happening.[67]

The views of Chief Constables become more overtly displayed when in consultation with the Home Office about their public order powers. Prior to the Public Order Act 1936, the Home Office consulted with Chief Constables across England and Wales on recent fascist disorder. First, they were questioned on their powers relating to disorder at indoor meetings. The ambiguity surrounding such powers that were highlighted in the 1908 Departmental Commission arose again in 1934 when the Metropolitan Police did not enter the BUF meeting in Olympia despite the evident disorder inside. Eight of the twelve Chief Constables questioned favoured an amendment in the law to allow them to provide police at meetings without invitation. Only the Chief Constable of Newcastle, Frederick Crawely, rejected such an amendment stating that it 'enlarges on general good sense and tolerance of our population'.[68] However, Crawley was not a fascist sympathizer, and his political outlook held distaste for both the far right and the far left. In a letter to Vernon Kell at the Home Office, he referred to fascism as an ideology of 'strange gods' and stated it was 'too foreign for this Northern Public to assimilate'.[69] He also ordered a baton charge against unemployed workers when he was Chief Constable of Sunderland in 1921, and again against trade unionists during the General Strike in Newcastle in 1926. The treatment of anti-fascists in Newcastle bucked this trend; despite the rough treatment of anti-fascists across much of the nation, one anti-fascist remarked that in Newcastle 'the police were courteous to us' and anti-fascists in Newcastle were rarely charged.[70]

Regarding open air meetings, the Chief Constables' suggestions to the Home Secretary revealed a desire to be able to prohibit meetings or processions if they were likely to cause either an obstruction or a breach of the peace. The Chief Constable of Plymouth went even further advocating for the power to prohibit an assembly if it were likely to lead to the 'annoyance or danger' of the public. The term 'annoyance' is particularly ambiguous here. A recurring desire of the Chief Constables was that the power should reside with them to 'sanction' a public procession, and without such they should be proscribed. In addition, when they are sanctioned, many argued that the Chief Constable should then be empowered to route the procession. Although the draft Bill that was created after this consultation

66 Ibid., at 595.

67 Ibid.

68 MEPO 3/2490, Fascist and communist activities: Measures to deal with disturbances.

69 Todd, *In Excited Times*, p.63.

70 Ibid., pp.61–2.

was never introduced, the subsequent Public Order Act 1936 which followed two years later held some of the hallmarks of the Chief Constables' requests. For instance, the Chief Constables could prescribe the route of a procession or prohibit it from entering a specified public place under section 3(1). They could also apply through their respective council to the Home Secretary to prohibit all processions within a specified area for up to three months under section 3(2). Although some Chief Constables had previously taken such controversial steps, such as in Manchester, the introduction of the statutory powers removed the legal ambiguity that was prevalent when relying on their Common Law powers of breach of the peace. The interwar era demonstrates the variety of tactics implemented by Chief Constables, as well as their position being instrumental in public order operations. Their influence on subsequent national legislation should not be discounted either, as a move towards the uniformity of public order powers became more centralized it also began to limit the range of approaches of preventing disorder.

The turbulent 1980s

In the post-war era the foundation of the Association of Chief Police Officers (ACPO) in 1948 gradually increased the collective influence of Chief Constables on policy and legislation. An important aspect of public order policing was the development of Special Patrol Groups (SPGs) which established paramilitary policing units within the police. Although initially dressed in traditional police uniform when they were established in the 1970s, the SPGs quickly became associated with paramilitary crowd control methods, such as aggressive dispersal techniques and the use of snatch squads.[71] This is emblematic of the ascendancy of the police over the military as regards the growing primacy of the role of protecting civil order.[72] The disorders, protests and riots that featured heavily in the early 1980s have again shown that the leadership of Chief Constables can have a significant impact on the style of policing applied. This is not only important in relation to the way they lead, but the different personalities who have occupied the positions is particularly illuminating. On the one hand, liberal Chief Constables such as John Alderson of Devon and Cornwall Police promoted the strategy and philosophy of community policing. On the other, Chief Constable James Anderton's style was epitomized by reactive policing. These two strategies were highlighted in the House of Commons by Labour MP Alex Lyon who criticized the development of Special Patrol Groups, which he associated with reactive policing, stating they 'have done their work ham fistedly. That has resulted in complaints, sometimes in injury, and even, in one case, death'.[73]

The style of policing, and who sets the agenda for it, became a major political issue in the late 1970s and early 1980s. After three years of relative political harmony

71 Jefferson, *The Case against Paramilitary Policing.*

72 R. Vogler, *Reading the Riot Act: The Magistracy, the Police and the Army in Civil Disorder*, Buckingham: Open University Press, 1991, p.108.

73 HC Deb 25 January 1980 vol.977 cc.892–902, at 894.

with his predominantly Conservative police committee, in 1979 Anderton faced the prospect of a Labour majority following the local government elections. As the debate on police accountability heightened, Anderton was alleged to have criticized 'political factions' whose agenda was the creation of a 'totalitarian one party state' rather than the improvement of policing.[74] In 1981 Anderton debated the accountability of Chief Constables with the MP Jack Straw. This culminated in Straw arguing, 'whether an area is policed by a "community policing" approach or the reactive "fire brigade" approach is too important to be left to Chief Constables.'[75]

With regard to the liberty to protest, Alderson's approach was particularly progressive. Even before the Human Rights Act 1998, his commitment to allow peaceful protesters the freedom of assembly in legally dubious circumstances was noteworthy. For instance, when anti-nuclear power protesters in Luxulyan, Cornwall prevented the Central Electricity Generating Board (CEGB) from completing a survey of the site for a power station, Alderson supported his officers present who facilitated the protest and only considered it their duty to intervene if a breach of the peace occurred or was anticipated. The protest lasted six months and the police response was criticized by the Divisional Court when the CEGB sought an order of mandamus to require Alderson to order his officers to assist in the removal of the protesters. Despite the criticism of Alderson's position, the CEGB was unsuccessful as Lord Denning declared that 'I would not give any orders to the Chief Constable . . . the police should decide on their own responsibility what action should be taken in any particular situation.'[76] Ian Welsh identified that the facilitation of the protest was important for Cornish identity and helped strengthen community bonds, but this communal link also extended to the police, and following a meeting with Alderson the protesters left peacefully taking their rubbish and belongings with them.[77]

In contrast to Alderson's liberal leadership, Chief Constables James Anderton and Kenneth Oxford demonstrated their tough crime control response during the Toxteth and Moss Side riots in 1981. The robust tactics used at Toxteth, which included the use of CS gas and police vehicles to disperse crowds, were described by Oxford as 'positive police policy'.[78] Even after the death of a disabled man who was hit by a police Land Rover that was driven into the crowd, Oxford's hard stance was evident as he commented, 'They can see the vehicles coming and they know what will happen if they get in the way.'[79] Due to the mutual aid agreement, Manchester officers were drafted in to support the Merseyside Police at Toxteth. Anderton highlighted

74 J. Alderson, *Law and Disorder*, London: Hamish Hamilton Ltd., 1984, p.108.

75 Ibid., p.105.

76 *R v Chief Constable of the Devon and Cornwall Constabulary, ex parte Central Electricity Generating Board* [1982] QB 458, at 472.

77 I. Welsh, *Mobilising Modernity: The Nuclear Movement*, London: Routledge, 2000; Alderson, *Law and Disorder*, p.188.

78 P. Scraton, *Power, Conflict and Criminalisation*, Abingdon: Routledge, 2007, p.27.

79 R. Hobbs, 'Oxford, Sir Kenneth Gordon (1924–1998)', *Oxford Dictionary of National Biography*, Oxford University Press, 2004, available online at www.oxforddnb.com/view/article/71283.

how this influenced his tactics when riots broke out in Moss Side, Manchester weeks later. He was particularly critical of having lines of police officers with riot shields who were fairly immobile thus becoming a target for missiles. As many of his officers were injured at Toxteth, he favoured having officers deployed in vans, which were 'extremely fast and flexible', disorientating the rioting crowd and providing the officers with the ability to arrest many offenders.[80] Anderton also highlighted the benefit of protective crash helmets that gave the officers confidence and that plans were being made to buy protective overalls in the police colours to retain the 'traditional police image'. However, this measure, despite his assurances, was still one step towards a more paramilitary image. In the following underlined sentence in his report, Anderton stated, 'There are no plans whatsoever to acquire water cannon, CS gas, or plastic bullets.'[81] By 1985, Anderton defied his police authority by acquiring plastic bullets and riot guns on loan from the Metropolitan Police. The Labour-controlled police committee had ordered Anderton to dispose of them.[82] Two years later, the Court of Appeal upheld a Chief Constable's right to bypass police authorities to acquire plastic bullets and CS gas, ruling that the Home Secretary had a statutory power under the Police Act 1964 to issue such supplies, as well as a duty to promote police efficiency. Croom-Johnson LJ emphasized that, 'The judgment of what is an emergency must be within the operational powers of the Chief Constable unsubjected to any control on the part of the police authority.'[83]

The influence of Chief Constables on force policy had increased and was gaining the support of the Home Office. Although their views were important to the Home Office in the 1930s regarding the fascist related disorder, by the 1980s the institutional presence of the ACPO 'enabled them to have a determining role in the production of legislation'.[84] However, this influence was not always so unidirectional. In the following decade, the passing of the Police and Magistrates' Courts Act 1994 provided the Home Secretary with the power to set national objectives which increased the central influence on the police.[85] In addition, there were statutory requirements for local authorities to produce local policing plans. The Act also required the local police authorities to publish an annual local policing plan which detailed both national and local objectives and performance targets. Despite the Chief Constables' ability to consult the police authority about their local policing objectives and to draw a draft of the plan, the Act instigated a shift in the Chief Constable role which had a greater emphasis on the management of their staff and budgets.[86]

80 TNA HO 266/136, City of Manchester: report Civil Disturbances Employment in Moss Side: Hytner report Moss Side enquiry panel, Report of the Chief Constable, 4 September 1981, p.4.

81 Ibid., p.7.

82 *The Times*, 30 November 1985.

83 *The Guardian*, 19 November 1987.

84 R. Vogler, *Reading the Riot Act*, 1991, p.107.

85 D. Gilling, *Crime Prevention: Theory, Policy and Politics*, London: UCL Press, 1997, p.103.

86 T. Jones, 'The accountability of policing', in T. Newburn (ed.) *Handbook of Policing*, 2nd edn, Abingdon: Routledge, 2011, pp.693–724.

Conclusion

The role Chief Constables play in the present era regarding public order operations has been reduced. The operational responsibilities are now largely the duty of Gold or Silver Commanders who have received specific public order training which is accredited by the National Police Improvement Agency. The function of the Chief Constable more generally relates to post-operational reviews, but they also play a significant role in national operational decision-making. For example, the Police National Mobilisation Plan, which is in place to coordinate mutual support between forces, was agreed upon by Chief Constables in 2006.[87] Chief Constables have been particularly adept at stamping their own authority on public order policing. However, now the operational tactics are the remit of public order Commanders, and the position of such officers are significantly filled from officers under the ACPO ranks, the influence of leadership has markedly shifted.[88] The Chief Constable is now more unlikely to lead a public order operation, and with the prospect of having to take control as the highest ranking officer in the event of disorder, they are even unlikely to attend incidences of civil unrest. Their position of direct control may have diminished, but as they are still held to account for their force's actions; their influence in setting the culture of their respective force is still alive.

The differences in operational philosophies between Alderson and Anderton typify the range of approaches and the importance of leadership when setting a force culture for the policing of public order. Where the Chief Constables have enjoyed the support of their Watch Committee (and the political allegiance of the Chief has also been reciprocal), the use of discretion in setting operational priorities or strategies has been substantial. For example, the policing of the BUF in Manchester was particularly noteworthy for its systematic obstruction of their activities. Even the legality of the breach of the peace power to prohibit a BUF public procession on account of the provocation caused by the uniform in 1936 was questionable, but was never challenged because of the BUF's decision to march without their Blackshirt uniform. Other actions taken (or supported) by Chief Constables also highlight that discretion used to avert or reduce anticipated disorder was often legally dubious. Actions such as those taken in Exeter which prevented the BUF's Captain Hammond speaking at certain areas in the city, would be even more contentious now in the post-Human Rights Act era. It is also noteworthy that Chief Constables had the autonomy to utilize diverse tactics in public order scenarios showing different levels of commitment to freedom of political expression. In addition, as was noted with the Departmental Committee of 1909, the different approaches were all seen as legitimate, and it was not until the greater centralization of powers in the 1990s that the autonomy of the Chief Constables was reduced. Although direct control of public order operations may now be the remit of accredited Commanders from the lower ranks, the influence Chief Constables have had in shaping both public order tactics and legislation should not be underestimated.

87 Her Majesty's Inspectors of Constabulary (HMIC), Adapting to Protest: Nurturing the British Model of Policing, 2009, p.96.

88 Ibid., p.98.

Section 3

Twentieth-century Chief Constables

11 Pioneering women police chiefs

A tale of conflict and cooperation

Marisa Silvestri

Introduction

The arrival, in Lancashire, of Pauline Clare in 1995 as Britain's first female Chief Constable has routinely become a starting point for analyses of women and police leadership. Constructed as a watershed moment in the history of women in policing, her appointment has been described as signifying the end of the 'traditional symbolic male dominance of the office of Chief Constable' together with the 'end of patriarchy'.[1] Readers may therefore question the inclusion of women into this collection of historical works on Chief Constables as arguably there were no 'official' women Chief Constables in post before 1995. This chapter argues that such a reading represents a serious misunderstanding of women's engagement with police leadership roles over time. Women have been present in the work of policing and police leadership for over a century now and while they have been documented in police scholarship in relation to understanding the campaign for women police, they are a neglected aspect of scholarship on police leadership.

One of the key aims of this chapter then is to redress this and insert early policewomen undertaking leadership roles into the mainstream narrative of police leadership. Doing so also affords a greater context within which to situate the contemporary intense scrutiny of police leaders and police leadership. Conceptualized as 'new' concerns, the police organization faces mounting criticism over the need to develop greater diversity within its leadership ranks. In relation to women the underlying message offers a fairly syllogistic reading with the recruitment of more women to police leadership constructed as an opportunity to secure 'different' and more 'sensitive' policing.[2] A second key aim of this chapter is to debunk the idea that such concerns are new. Although not described using the language of diversity or equality, the call to diversify policing through the presence of women was very much present over a century ago, as was the idea of women's engagement

1 D. S. Wall, *The Chief Constables of England and Wales: The socio-legal history of a criminal justice elite*, Aldershot: Ashgate, 1998, p.6.

2 M. Silvestri, S. Tong, and J. Brown, 'Gender and police leadership: Time for a paradigm shift', *International Journal of Police Science and Management*, 2013, vol.15:1, 61–73.

with an altogether different form and style of policing. A third and final aim of the chapter is to draw out some of the continuities of women's experience over time. I have argued elsewhere that contemporary women police leaders experience considerable difficulty and resistance in being heard and accepted in positions of authority.[3] Such resistance is best understood alongside that encountered by their historic counterparts.

While this chapter reflects upon the years following the formal integration of women into policing in 1973 and beyond, it focuses predominantly on the first half of the twentieth century. It is here that we can begin to get a sense of the aspirations and challenges faced by early women leaders in the fight to achieve the formal recognition of women police. At the heart of this, a number of prominent women can be identified as holding police leadership roles. Through an exploration of the experiences, motivations and actions of some of these women, including: Nina Boyle, Margaret Damer Dawson, Mary Allen, Sofia Stanley, Dorothy Peto and Barbara de Vitre, this chapter gives voice and presence to a much neglected area of study within police leadership. These women led extraordinary lives and there is much to reflect upon about the important ways in which the 'personal' (sexuality, class and political leanings) has shaped their engagement as police leaders. The chapter does not adopt a strict chronological approach to understanding women's roles nor does it provide in-depth biographical accounts of the women considered. Rather, it provides an overview into some of the key developments that led to the official establishment of women in policing and brings to light their modus operandi in their work.

It is prudent here to remind readers that scholarship on the history of women in policing is neither extensive nor comprehensive. Often overlooked in mainstream accounts of women police for example, are those women working as police officers on the railways. We know that the Great Eastern Railway Police recruited at least six women police officers (one of them as a sergeant) in 1917, and that the North East Railway Police had seventeen women employed by 1918, led by Sergeant M Roberts at York. These women were employed as police officers and were sworn in as constables and so could arguably claim the title of Britain's first 'official' women police.[4] I am therefore mindful of the partial insight being provided in selecting and focusing on some women; there have undoubtedly been many other women who have played significant yet less documented roles in police leadership. The chapter draws on a range of secondary data including oral testimonies, biographies, autobiographies and documentary sources in order to develop its arguments. With memoirs, often 'heroic' in style and subject to exaggeration and historical inaccuracy, some caution is needed in their interpretation. Mary Allen, for example, has been heavily critiqued by

3 M. Silvestri, '"Doing" police leadership: Enter the "new smart macho"', *Policing and Society*, 2007, vol.17:1, 38–58.

4 British Transport Police, Policewomen on the railways, www.btp.police.uk/about_us/our_history/policewomen_on_the_railways.aspx.

scholars for her unashamed search for self-promotion and publicity, forcefully articulating her active and single-handed mission to increase the representation of women police.[5] That said, Louise Jackson reminds us of the value of such personal testimonies in treating them as 'forms of self-presentation that are located within a wider cultural field'.[6] Given the relatively recent appointment of women as Chief Constables, with the exception of Alison Halford (the first woman to reach the rank of Assistant Chief Constable in a UK force in 1983) there are no published personal memoirs of senior women to reflect upon. Given the high visibility of contemporary women chiefs and the ongoing employment of women in these roles, the chapter does not develop its analysis of named contemporary chiefs but rather reflects on earlier anonymized interviews I have conducted with women police leaders.[7]

Made up of three parts, the chapter emphasizes the complex terrain that women chiefs faced in undertaking their roles, paying close attention to the ways in which they actively engaged in the construction and negotiation of their identities and place in the organization. I have argued elsewhere that contemporary senior policewomen are engaged in considerable performance work in *doing* gender in undertaking their roles; this is also true of their historical counterparts. [8] In this chapter I draw out the various and differing ways in which women emphasized both femininity and masculinity in the presentation of the 'self' as leaders. In the early part of the twentieth century, there were a number of different and parallel groups claiming authority as women police. With each group distinct in its remit, motivation and leadership, the chapter emphasizes some important points of conflict and collaboration between and within these groups. Working in a separate sphere to their male counterparts, women's remit within policing was clearly defined in relation to providing 'specialist' work with vulnerable women and children in need of rescue from 'moral' danger.[9] Tasked with this, there is evidence of strong ideological differences in the ways in which the various women police organizations and their leaders perceived this task. Such differences led to considerable disagreement and rivalry between women themselves about how best to *do* policing and how to progress in developing their roles. The differences between how these women police leaders viewed vulnerable women and their involvement tells us as much about their own personal motivations as it does about their campaign to recruit more women into policing. It also highlights the uneasy relationship that women police leaders have had with the idea of feminism over time.

5 M. S. Allen, *The Pioneer Policewoman*, London: Chatto Windus, 1925 and *Lady in Blue*, London: Stanley Paul, 1934.

6 L. Jackson, *Women Police: Gender, Welfare and Surveillance in the Twentieth Century*, Manchester University Press, 2006, p.11.

7 M. Silvestri, *Women in Charge: Policing, Gender and Leadership*, Cullompton: Willan, 2003.

8 M. Silvestri, '"Doing time": Becoming a police leader', *International Journal of Police Science and Management*, 2006, vol.8:4, 266–81.

9 F. Heidensohn, *Women in Control: The Role of Women in Law Enforcement*, Oxford University Press, 1992.

With the campaign for women police inextricably embedded in the history of first-wave feminism in the UK, the first part explores the origins and challenges faced by these early police women leaders against a wider political context of women's suffrage and fight for equality. Indeed, many of the police leaders reviewed were entangled and invested in the political movement to secure greater freedoms for women more broadly. Often finding themselves in direct opposition with mainstream policing, those women police involved in the suffrage movement encountered significant challenges in negotiating the uneasy relationship in building an identity as an 'insider'. Focusing on Nina Boyle, Margaret Damer Dawson and Mary Allen, this part draws on the considerable tensions and conflicts that characterized the years 1914–18. The second part takes the establishment of the Metropolitan Women Police Patrols in 1918 as its starting point and ends in 1973. A rather expansive period to cover, it focusses on the contributions of Sofia Stanley, Dorothy Peto and Barbara de Vitre. With a concerted shift away from the masculine and militarized style that so characterized their predecessors, to a greater feminization of women's presentation and styles of engagement, these women played an important role in the eventual acceptance and formal integration of women into mainstream policing in 1973. The third and final part contextualizes the experiences of these early police women leaders alongside their more contemporary counterparts from the post integration period. Connecting the past with the present in this way enables a space within which to better reflect upon both change and continuity.

Pioneer policewomen: a time of suffrage

Women were present in policing and undertaking a range of policing functions in the late nineteenth century. Employed as police matrons and later as policewomen in a voluntary capacity thereafter, the end of the nineteenth and the first half of the twentieth century is an important time in the campaign for women police. Described by many as a time of considerable resistance towards women police in Britain, it is worth remembering that such a reality has been documented across the world.[10] Though countries vary in the dates that women were admitted into the police, there is a strong consensus that suggests that opposition to their entry and integration was almost universal.[11] In making sense of this opposition, Brown and Heidensohn point to a combination of paternalistic concerns to protect women and patriarchal exclusion of women as being unsuitable for the 'rough and dirty tasks' required by policing.[12] Characterized by a strong gendered masculine social order in which men were dominant, women in late-Victorian and Edwardian society were characterized as weak, inferior and subordinate, confined to a separate domestic and private sphere with its attendant responsibilities of domesticity,

10 D. Schulz, *From Social Worker to Crime Fighter: Women in United States Municipal Policing*, Westport, CT: Praeger, 1995.

11 K. Segrave, *Policewomen: A History*, Jefferson, NC: McFarland, 1995.

12 J. Brown and F. Heidensohn, *Gender and Policing*, London: Macmillan, 2000.

family life and motherhood.[13] Everyday violence and brutality encountered and enacted by policemen at the time were central elements in the formation of a dominant 'physical police masculinity'.[14] It was here from the very outset that the role and identity of the police officer was firmly located within men's domain and associated ideas of masculinity.

Alongside the entrenched views of women as inferior, the second half of the nineteenth century was a time of 'vigorous, diverse and prescient' feminism and by the turn of the twentieth century the suffragette movement was in full swing in the race to secure greater freedoms for women in society.[15] Many of the prominent women police chiefs featured here were active in the suffrage movement and as such were to encounter a complex set of relationships in negotiating their desire to join the police ranks. Subject to considerable police brutality and violence, the policing of suffragettes makes for uneasy reading. Viewed as 'dangerous troublemakers', Sophie Jackson reminds us of the difficult and ironic position occupied by early policewomen who had gone to great lengths to 'mock, deride and denigrate the male police' and yet at the same time 'desired to join the police force'.[16] An appreciation of this backdrop makes the achievements of early women police leaders even more remarkable. The First World War was to bring about a significant shift in the fortunes of the campaign for women police and the shortage of men during the outbreak of war enabled women to enter a wider range of occupations, including policing. While the absence of men in such roles certainly made it easier for women to take up policing roles, it was a broader concern about the need to control female sexuality and the moral danger posed by female immorality, prostitution and venereal disease during wartime that took ascendancy.[17] The ensuing growth in the number of groups of women coming together to police 'wayward' women resulted in considerable misunderstandings and a mixed economy of responsibility, leading Edith Tancred in 1911 to denounce the general confusion as evoking a 'mixed multitude' of pseudo-policewomen.[18] Faced with conditions which offered both a challenge and an opportunity, two separate schemes for the organization and employment of women on police duties were promptly launched: the National Union of Women Workers (renamed the National Council of Women in 1919) and the Women Police Volunteers (renamed the Women Police Service in 1915). What follows is an appreciation of the motivations, conflict and internal rivalries of their respective leaders.

13 A. Vickery, 'Golden age to separate spheres? A review of the categories and chronology of English women's history', *The Historical Journal*, 1993, vol.36:2, 383–414.

14 F. Dodsworth, 'Men on a mission: Masculinity, violence and the self-presentation of policemen in England, c. 1870–1914' in D. Barrie and S. Broomhall (eds) *A History of Police and Masculinities, 1700–2010*. 2012, Abingdon: Routledge, 2012, pp.123–40 at p.131.

15 P. Levine, *Feminist Lives in Victorian England: Private Roles and Public Commitment*, Oxford: Blackwell, 1990.

16 S. Jackson, *Women on Duty*, London: Fonthill Media, 2014, p.18.

17 Levine, *Feminist lives in Victorian England.*

18 Ibid., p.65.

Enter Nina Boyle, Margaret Damer Dawson and Mary Allen

In 1914, soon after the outbreak of the First World War, Nina Boyle (1830–69), advertised in *The Vote* for women to offer themselves as volunteer police in response to Sir Edward Henry's (then Chief Commandant to the Metropolitan Police) broader call for the recruitment of special constables. A strong supporter of women's suffrage, Boyle was active in the Women's Freedom League (WFL), a militant organization that was willing to break the law for its cause. In 1912, she became head of the WFL's political department, and wrote extensively for the WFL's newspaper, *The Vote*. Taking a strategic and leading role in campaigns and demonstrations, Boyle was arrested and imprisoned on several occasions. She campaigned against the unfair and harsh conditions and treatment that she and her fellow suffragists had experienced at the hands of a male criminal justice system and brought with her strong opinions on the empowerment of women in society, protesting vociferously on the deplorable and unjust treatment of women and children by the law. Concerned with male violence against women, Boyle emphasized the 'male peril' and the need for women to protect other women, holding that men were the 'prevailing danger'.[19] In present-day society, Nina Boyle would in many ways be considered to be closely allied to a radical form of feminism. Evidence of her active and strategic approach to leadership can be seen in the following excerpt in which she carefully notes her motivation for securing a long-term role for women in policing stating that:

> If we now equip every district in the country with a body of women able and willing to do this class of work, it will be very difficult for the authorities to refuse to employ women in such capacity after the war.[20]

Attention to Boyle's militancy and association with women's suffrage (and feminism) is an important dimension in understanding her eventual demise, and others' subsequent rise. Considered by Sir Edward an 'intransigeante and in opposition to constituted authority' Boyle's offer to recruit women as volunteers was officially refused, with Sir Edward declaring that only men were suitable.[21]

Around the same time, Margaret Damer Dawson, approached her friend Sir Edward Henry about forming the Women Police Volunteers (WPV). Born to wealthy parents, Damer Dawson (1873–1920) was an educated woman who became involved in various philanthropic activities. Both 'wealthy and well connected', Lock describes her as 'a curious mix of a woman in both her interests and character'.[22] Driven by a desire to fight white slavery and champion animal welfare, her independent income enabled her to move in well-to-do circles

19 N. Boyle, 'The male peril', *The Vote*, August, 27 August1915 p.727.

20 N. Boyle, 'Recruitment details', *The Vote*, 21 August 1914 p.311.

21 J. Lock, *The British Policewoman: Her Story*, London: Robert Hale, 1979, p.21.

22 Ibid., p.19.

conducting her activities on an international stage, becoming the organizing secretary of the International Animal Protection Societies in 1906 and later awarded silver medals by Finland and Denmark. Serving on the Criminal Law Amendment Committee[23] in 1914, she had become friends with Nina Boyle. Unlike Boyle, however, Damer Dawson was less concerned about the suffrage movement and with the ideas of feminism. Upon hearing of each other's intentions to develop the role of women in policing, they decided to join forces in developing the WPV with Damer acting as chief and Boyle her deputy. The transformative effect of Damer Dawson's presence as leader has been well documented by Douglas who notes that her influence radically transformed the WPV 'from a largely nominal body into a viable and active organization, providing it with more attention, more energy but also the financial support of affluent friends'.[24] Damer Dawson's respectability and personal connections no doubt served her well in her strategic interactions with those in power. It was during this time that Mary Allen (1878–1964) joined the WPV. Stemming from a traditional middle-class family, Allen was inspired to join the Women's Social and Political Union (WSPU). As an ex-militant suffragette with a 'strong rebellious streak', records show a considerable history of clashes with the police, a catalogue of police arrests and hunger strikes during her time in prison.[25] With suffrage militancy put on hold during wartime, Allen agreed to give full support to the British war effort, she also used this time to rethink her role. Allen 'wanted action' and was hugely attracted to a role in uniform. It was at this time that Allen heard news of Nina Boyle and her intention to establish a voluntary women police force.[26] We return to Mary Allen shortly as she emerges as a police leader in her own right.

Despite sharing a strong motivation to develop the role of women within policing, it was a fundamental ideological difference between Damer Dawson and Boyle in their quest to recruit more women police that was to result in an important point of conflict, difference and split between these leaders. Increasingly concerned about the repressive ways in which the law was being used towards women, Boyle saw the establishment of women police as an opportunity to challenge male control and practice of the law. Outraged at the events in Grantham in 1914 where women police volunteers were tasked with the imposition of an all-night curfew on other women, Boyle campaigned against the penalization of working-class women through the Defence of the Realm Act 1914. On the contrary, for Damer Dawson,

23 The Criminal Law Amendment Committee joined forces with the National Vigilance Association to press the Home Office to appoint women police officers on an equal status to men to take depositions from women and children in cases of immorality as a means of increasing prosecutions, see K Stevenson, '"Not just the ideas of a few enthusiasts": Early twentieth century legal activism and reformation of the age of sexual consent', *Journal of Cultural and Social History*, 2017, online doi/full/10.1080/14780038.2017.1290999 1–18.

24 R. Douglas, *Feminist Freikorps: The British Voluntary Women Police, 1914–1940*. 1999, Westport, CT: Praeger, 1999, p.12.

25 Jackson, *Women on Duty*, p.24.

26 Lock, *The British Policewoman*, p.20.

having a separate group of trained professional women was an important step in dealing with what she perceived to be a pressing need to control the vices, loosening morals and worsening behaviour of young women in wartime Britain. Although 'protective' towards women, Boyle found such notions of protection to be ultimately patriarchal and overly repressive. In 1915, a vote was taken and Boyle was overwhelmingly defeated, winning only two out of 50 votes. Damer Dawson took control, ended all links with the WFL and went on to change the name of the Women Police Volunteers reforming the group as the Women Police Service (WPS). With Damer Dawson at the helm as Commandant, Mary Allen assumed the position of her Sub-Commandant.[27]

This phase in the history of the WPS was to take on a distinctly 'masculine' leadership outlook and style. Strongly militarist in its discipline, practice and hierarchy the WPS leadership developed and operationalized the male titles of Commandant, Sub-Commandant Superintendent, Inspector, Sub-Inspector, Sergeant and Constable in the organization of its members. It also adopted the behaviours of a bureaucratic hierarchy in its approach to its training regime with its workers receiving instruction in first aid, drill, the art of self-defence (ju-jitsu) and police court procedure.[28] Indeed, the use of ju-jitsu had become an established feature of the suffragette fighting force, with Mrs Pankhurst's 'bodyguard' formed of 20 women carrying wooden clubs under their skirts and trained in ju-jitsu tactics.[29]

In relation to the presentation of the 'self', much has been written about the masculine appearance of its leaders, with both Allen and Damer Dawson adopting close cropped military-style haircuts and trousers beneath their military-style great coats. Sophie Jackson suggests that: 'There was no denying that Margaret and Mary and their fellow officers went out of their way to appear masculine and this troubled the sensibilities of conservative souls'.[30]

Infamous for her uniform, including breeches, cropped hair and a monocle, Laura Doan emphasizes Allen's image and dress in unpacking the cultural codes surrounding lesbianism in the 1920s and 30s. Much has been written about the close professional and personal relationship, with the two leaders living together in London between 1914–20.[31] In her own memoirs, Allen writes that her meeting with Margaret, 'struck an immediate spark, and began a period of close association and intimate friendship'.[32]

27 J. Carrier, *The Campaign for the Employment of Women as Police Officers*, Aldershot: Avebury Gower, 1988.

28 Ibid., p.46.

29 J. Rowbotham and K. Stevenson, 'A point of justice – Granted or fought for women's suffrage campaigning in the West Country', *Plymouth Law and Criminal Justice Review*, 2015, 84–95 at p.98.

30 Jackson, *Women on Duty*, p.50.

31 L. Doan, *Fashioning Sapphism: The Origins of a Modern English Lesbian Culture*, New York: Columbia University Press, 2001.

32 M. S. Allen, *Woman at the Cross Roads*, London: Unicorn, 1936, p.22.

Working in strong unison, accounts show that this new combination of leadership was grounded in the belief that they had a duty to protect women from their own 'foolishness and the base desires of men' if they were to ever achieve full suffrage and female emancipation. Given this, it is perhaps not so surprising to note the ease with which this new leadership team were happy to pursue a 'war of moral purity', acquiescing to the new regulatory requirements, conducting searches of lodging houses and expelling those suspected of immoral behaviour. The clamping down on 'immoral women' by Damer Dawson and Allen has been described as a strategic leadership decision, as 'a means to ingratiate themselves with male authority, thereby increasing the likelihood of policewomen being retained after the war'.[33] In fact Allen was hopeful that Grantham would be a proving ground for women police, where they would be tested and 'acquire merit'.[34] While this strategy did have some traction in the first instance, in that the success of Grantham quickly created demand for the services of the WPS and saw Edith Smith appointed as the first woman police constable in England with full power of arrest in August 1915, such success was to be short-lived. By the end of the First World War, there were over 357 members of the Women's Police Service. Commandant Damer Dawson and Sub-Commandant Allen, asked the Chief Commissioner, Sir Nevil Macready, to make them a permanent part of his force. He refused, noting that the women were 'too educated' and would 'irritate' male members of the force. Macready's intense dislike of suffragettes and his distaste for female homosexuality no doubt informed his decision to 'eliminate any women of extreme views – the vinegary spinster or blighted middle-aged fanatic'.[35] Ill-health forced Damer Dawson to retire in 1919 (dying of a heart attack a year later) and she was replaced as Commandant of the WPS by Allen. The WPS continued as a voluntary service and in 1920 became the Women's Auxiliary Service. Mary Allen went on to become a controversial political figure during the 1930s declaring herself a supporter of Oswald Moseley's British Union of Fascists.[36]

Despite not realizing their aim of being established as the official national women's police service, the achievements of these women leaders should not be underestimated. Between 1914 and 1920 the WPS had trained over a thousand women and policewomen were on duty in cities across the country. Alongside this, their leadership approach had demonstrated a strong capacity to garner patronage, support and influence from the great and the good in power. This is reminiscent of the often overlooked effective activism and networking alliances formed by different women's voluntary organizations in mid-twentieth century Britain.[37]

33 Jackson, *Women on Duty*, p.63.

34 Ibid.

35 N. Boyd, *From Suffragette to Fascist*, Gloucestershire: The History Press, 2014, p.76.

36 See Boyd for an insight into her life beyond this, ibid.

37 C. Beaumont, *Housewives and Citizens; Domesticity and the Women's Movement in England, 1928–64*, Manchester University Press, 2013.

Damer Dawson and Allen lobbied hard and used their influential friends to gain support in promoting the recruitment of women, writing letters and giving interviews to the national, local and women's press.[38] Adopting an international dimension to their leadership they worked tirelessly to build alliances with other policewomen across the world in Germany, Sweden, Australia and the USA. It was through the establishment of international links and presence that pioneer policewomen were able to best achieve a 'critical mass' of colleagues with whom to network and gain support from. They were so effective at this that Frances Heidensohn compares the skills of these pioneer policewomen to those of 'present day spin doctors'.[39] Despite these strong leadership qualities, the aspirations and the 'radical pedigree' of the WPS leadership led to them being overlooked. This was to give way to an altogether different leadership approach and style that was to take root and establish itself over the course of the twentieth century.

An age of feminization: enter Sofia Stanley, Dorothy Peto and Barbara De Vitre

With the WPS side-lined, Commissioner Macready turned to Sofia Stanley, supervisor of the 'Special Patrols' set up under the National Union of Women Workers (NUWW). By the end of 1917 London had 55 full-time Special Patrols and around 5,000 voluntary 'women patrols' across Britain. Their relationship with the Metropolitan Police was complicated and anomalous, donning uniforms with warrant cards but with no powers of arrest.[40] It was from these ranks that Britain's first official women police force, the Metropolitan Police Women Patrol, was established in 1918. That said, I remind readers here of the contested nature of this given the presence of sworn in women as police constables on the railways in 1917. It was the leadership approach adopted by Sofia Stanley that was to have lasting influence in the permanent establishment of women police. Unlike the WPS, whose origins lay in the suffrage movement, and sought a separatist and independent organization for women police, the NUWW patrols were a 'largely middle-class organization in no manner associated with militancy'.[41] Married to a member of the Indian Civil Service, Stanley had an ambition to see its part-time paid patrols become full-time policewomen who would be an integral part of the police service while remaining under the authority of male Chief Constables. More sympathetic to men than her rivals in the WPS, Stanley has been described as a 'charming and clever woman', with both 'sex appeal' and 'common sense'.[42]

38 Douglas, *Feminist Freikorps*, p.29.

39 F. Heidensohn, *Sexual Politics and Social Control*, Buckingham: Open University Press, 2000, p.57.

40 Carrier, *The Campaign for the Employment of Women as Police Officers*.

41 P. Levine, 'Walking the streets in a way no decent woman should: Women police in World War 1', *The Journal of Modern History*, 1994, vol.66:1, p.39.

42 Lock, *The British Policewoman*, p.59.

In making her case for women police, Stanley went to great lengths to downplay any opposition that her patrols may have faced. Despite much evidence of male hostility and discrimination towards women police, Stanley was keen to paint a picture of harmony. In her evidence to the Baird Committee in 1920, she emphasized an unproblematic relationship between male and female police, declaring that 'there had been no friction whatsoever'.[43]

In contrast to the styles exhibited by Damer Dawson, Allen and Boyle, Stanley went to considerable lengths to restate the importance of men in occupying a primary and dominant role in policing, noting that:

> Even training, she felt, was better done in the company of male police rather than with the voluntary patrols, since the work was quite different. Startlingly, she considered the power of arrest 'quite unnecessary for patrols in general', since they could always call on a policeman. She went further and said that the work was better done by patrols in co-operation with the police, than by policewomen'.[44]

Such an approach and leadership style posed little if no threat to the idea of policing or to men's role and authority within it. With the status quo maintained, women were able to establish a place within policing, albeit remaining on the periphery. By 1920, with 110 policewomen attached to the Metropolitan Police, policewomen had become an intrinsic part of wartime life and government could no longer ignore them. Yet despite praise for their work, their continued presence and future remained uncertain. In 1922, tasked with addressing the post-war recession, the Geddes Committee recommended the total disbandment of the Metropolitan Women Police Patrols. Following a vigorously fought campaign in Parliament, policewomen were retained, though their numbers were drastically cut to 24.[45] Besieged by a series of scandals in the late 1920s, including accusations of perjured testimony and corruption,[46] it was the harsh interrogation methods adopted by London's Metropolitan Police in the Savidge case in 1928 that was to result in an increase in the power and status of women police. The (male) police mishandling of a case in which Sir Leo Money (an elderly writer) and Miss Irene Savidge (a young, single woman) were acquitted of indecent behaviour aroused much political and public interest. It resulted in a tribunal inquiry in which the case for female police to be present at such interviews was emphasized. This case led to the Royal Commission on Police Powers and Procedures 1929, from which the power and status of women police was to improve drastically. In October 1931, the Home Office established an institutional framework and set of regulations

43 Ibid., p. 112.

44 Ibid., p.85.

45 T. A. Critchley, *A History of Police in England and Wales*, London: Constable, 1978.

46 J. C. Wood, 'Press, politics and the "police and public": Debates in late 1920s Britain', *Crime, History and Societies*, 2012, vol.16:1, p.75–98.

which standardized the pay and conditions of service for women officers wherever and whenever they were employed.[47]

Despite a considerably improved landscape, the decision to recruit women into policing remained grounded in the principle of Chief Constable (male) discretion. This condition remained the case for the next 40 years or so. Neither 'separatist' nor 'fully integrated', Chief Constables encouraged the development of separate structures and hierarchies within forces, later developing into Policewomen's Departments' in urban areas in the 1930s and 40s. Often described as a period of latency in the history of women police, Louise Jackson's analysis suggests the opposite, noting that pioneer policewomen such as Dorothy Peto and prominent inside/outsider Barbara de Vitre worked relentlessly to build policing as a profession for women.[48] As the number of women continued to grow slowly, the idea of difference and their specialist 'expert' contribution in working with women and children become more pronounced. In order to negotiate identity, gender and their place in the organization, appointed women 'did not seek for equality with their male colleagues but rather stressed gender difference and integrated difference as a part of their own identity'.[49] Alongside this, the association with feminism and the campaign for equality took a back seat. Feminists within the police movement were either silenced or discredited and the association of policewomen with militant politics was even used as a 'weapon of ridicule and marginalisation' by mainstream opinion.[50] This lack of association with feminism did not rest solely with policing but was characteristic of a number of well-known voluntary organizations in the 1920s and 1930s. In her analysis of the Mother's Union, the Catholic Women's League, the National Council of Women, the National Federation of Women's Institutes and the National Union of Townswomen's Guilds, Caitríona Beaumont argues that these organizations presented themselves as 'avowedly non-feminist and non-party-political' in order to attract a broad base and mass of women.[51]

With her origins in the NUWW patrols, in 1930, Dorothy Peto was appointed staff officer for Women Police and was the most senior policewoman in the country as head of the Metropolitan Women Police Branch from 1930–1946. Described as determined with a strong will, the success of Dorothy Peto has been emphasized as an outcome of her avoidance of overtly feminist statements and through her 'careful balance of the rhetoric of both equality and femininity'.[52] Despite emphasizing women's 'specialist' role in working within child protection in making her case for the recruitment of more women police, she simultaneously

47 Carrier, *The Campaign for the Employment of Women as Police Officers*.

48 Jackson, *Women Police*, p.22.

49 K. Davey, 'Women's accounts of organizational politics as a gendering process', *Gender, Work & Organisation'* 2008, vol.15:6, p.655.

50 Levine, 'Walking the streets', p.64.

51 Beaumont, *Housewives and Citizens*, p.9.

52 Jackson, *Women Police*, p.23.

worked to extend the remit and perception of policewomen's duties. Joan Lock confirms the strong working relationships that Peto had with men, noting that 'despite the fact that she was tall, masculine and increasingly eccentric, the men also liked her.'[53] During her term of office, she was called upon to advise the Home Office on child welfare policy and on the training of other women and was able to persuade the Assistant Chief Commissioner to allow either one or, if necessary, two female officers to do the job of escorting women prisoners instead of the previous ruling of one female and one male. The far-reaching effects of Peto's leadership style can be seen in the considerable increase from 52 to 152 women working in the Met's Divisions. Her active leadership in the restyling of the overall image of the policewoman as modern, professional while simultaneously feminine fitted neatly with the wider promotion of 'beauty as duty' during the Second World War.[54] Indeed, in 1946 Peto's successor at the Met, Elizabeth Bather reemphasized this post-war image of women officers as 'sensible and fresh-faced heterosexuality associated with middle-class respectability'.[55]

Of notable influence during the first half of the twentieth century and often overlooked and neglected in the history of women police is the role played by non-police female staff who worked with great vigour as leaders to influence change. Lady Nancy Astor (Conservative), Mrs Margaret Wintringham (Liberal), Ellen Wilkinson (Labour), Eleanor Rathbone (Independent), Megan Lloyd George (Liberal) and Edith Picton-Tubervill (Labour) were all present in lobbying for a permanent role for women police.[56] In 1945 Barbara de Vitre was appointed the Police Staff Officer to assist Her Majesty's Inspectorate (HMI) with the inspection of all provincial women police in England, Wales and Scotland. Previously a police sergeant in Leicester and Head Constable in Cairo's Women Police, de Vitre had set up the First Provincial Policewomen's Conference in March 1937, attended by 36 women from 26 forces. De Vitre carefully persuaded Chief Constables, Watch Committees (in boroughs) and Standing Joint Committees (in counties) of the need for a regular establishment of women. Moreover, de Vitre and her successors, Kathleen Hill (1960–68) and Jean Law (1962–76) 'turned the position of Assistant HMI into a high-profile and extremely influential one, from which they were able to advise Chief Constables and to create professional networks of police women, facilitating the exchange of knowledge and information'.[57] By the 1960s, the work of the Policewomen's department was increasingly becoming decentralized and the British Policewomen's Department, as a central office with its own structure had ceased to exist; by 1969 the 'demise of "women police

53 Lock, *The British Policewoman*, p.179

54 P. Kirkham, 'Fashioning the feminine: dress, appearance and femininity in wartime Britain' in C, Gedhill and G. Swanson (eds) *Nationalising Femininity: Culture, Sexuality and British Cinema in the Second World War*, Manchester University Press, 1996.

55 Jackson, *Women Police*, p.55.

56 Heidensohn, *Women in Control.*

57 Jackson, *Women Police*, p.27.

work" was a function of its success'.[58] As part of this, the role of the senior policewoman was to become redundant with the operational management of female staff passing to male station inspectors. At the same time, women's distinctive role of dealing with 'wayward' women and children and young people was increasingly being absorbed and carried out by male officers and other specialists, including social workers and probation officers. Against a backdrop of emerging equalities legislation in the 1970s, the final dissolution of the Metropolitan Women Police Branch and the formal integration of male and female officers took place in 1973. In other forces, policewomen's departments were disbanded overnight when the Sex Discrimination Act came into operation in December 1975.

Post integration: change and continuity

The idea that integration would automatically improve women's situation and bring about equality did not materialize. Hailed as a moment of 'progress' and 'gain' in the journey towards gender equality, commentators have observed the considerable and simultaneous losses experienced by women police leaders who were now forced to relinquish their leadership ranks as they joined forces with men.[59] Together with this, integration also brought a considerable loss of expertise, with the move towards integration described as 'the striking of a somewhat Faustian bargain' and the price of admittance resulting in a loss of a radical agenda and the acceptance of male definitions and methods of control.[60] Relatively little was done to prepare the police service to become a gender-integrated organization in the aftermath of the Sex Discrimination Act 1975 and much has been written about the disjuncture between policy and practice in the decades that followed, with research reporting discrimination and sexual harassment as consistent features of policewomen's experiences. Sexist jokes, the use of derogatory language, differential deployments, blocked promotions, and the allocation of 'safer' station assignments are all indicative of women's discriminatory experiences of policing over the course of the twentieth century.[61] The high-profile case of Assistant Chief Constable (ACC) Alison Halford is perhaps noteworthy here. In 1983, following competition with three male Chief Superintendents, Halford became the highest ranking woman police officer in Britain, taking up her post as ACC in Merseyside. In 1990, after a series of nine failed promotions, she took the police authority to court for sexual discrimination (see also Brain Chapter 14). In her memoir entitled *No Way Up the Greasy Pole*, Halford recounts being vilified, humiliated, alienated and subjected to considerable sexual discrimination. In line with the heroic narratives of her early historical counterparts, Halford emphasized her pioneering status describing herself as 'forging ahead as a single woman in a man's world' and finding herself as an 'icon of thwarted female potential' following the launch

58 Ibid., p.201.

59 Schulz, *From Social Worker to Crime Fighter*.

60 Brown and Heidensohn, *Gender and Policing*, p. 4.

61 S. Jones, *Policewomen and Equality*, London: Palgrave Macmillan, 1986.

of her sex discrimination case.[62] Despite describing herself as 'no ardent feminist' she underlines the ways in which many of her male colleagues perceived her as a 'woman with a high feminist profile who wanted to stir things'.[63] Halford's Equal Opportunities Commission Tribunal continued for two years, attracted considerable publicity and was finally settled out of court.

There remain remarkable parallels and continuities in the concerns of early police women leaders and their contemporary counterparts. The observations that follow are based on interviews I carried out with 30 senior women in 2001, and while there has been much scholarship on women in policing over the past 30 years or so,[64] this remains the only published study focused on women as police leaders in the UK. Given the high visibility of these women, confidentiality was assured at the time of interview and so no named chiefs are featured. Many of these women remain in leadership posts and have continued to climb the organizational ladder – for an in-depth account of their career reflections see the original study.[65] The following discussion draws out in brief some of the key continuities over time in relation to: the concept of the 'pioneer' police woman; the incompatibility of policing with womanhood; the discourse of difference; the presentation of the self and women's relationship with feminism.

Pioneers

The concept of the 'pioneer' is a recurring theme in the lives of contemporary senior policewomen. All of the senior women interviewed drew on the construct of the 'pioneer' to describe their careers, being the 'first' at something, be it rank, role, position or area. Unlike their historic counterparts however, being the 'first' and in many cases the 'only' was less about emphasizing a heroic identity of accomplishment but rather was expressed in relation to feelings of considerable anxiety, isolation and pressure that accompany the high visibility in being a pioneer. The pressure to 'fit in' and achieve a sense of 'organizational belonging' play a significant role in women's engagements with pushing forward the campaign for women police more broadly. Standing as beacons for all women's achievements and their failures, was not a position with which most felt comfortable, with one respondent nothing that 'The last thing you need is an ACC (Assistant Chief Constable) who is female and useless'. At the time of writing, on 22 February 2017, following the retirement of Sir Bernard Hogan-Howe, Cressida Dick was appointed Metropolitan Police Commissioner. Such an appointment is hugely significant, in that the Metropolitan Police Service has never had a woman as Commissioner in its 188-year history. It is also worth emphasizing that the competition for this post was played out with a gender balanced shortlist – two men

62 A. Halford, *No Way Up the Greasy Pole*, London: Constable, 1993, p.9.
63 Ibid., p.7.
64 P. Dick, M. Silvestri and L. Westmarland, 'Women police: Potential and possibilities for police reform' in J. Brown, (ed.) *The Future of Policing*, London: Routledge, 2014.
65 Silvestri, *Women in Charge*.

(Mark Rowley and Stephen Kavanagh) and two women (Cressida Dick and Sara Thornton) were in the frame for leadership (see Introduction to this volume).[66]

Doing difference

Despite women's integration into mainstream policing, the idea that women are better suited to 'specialist' policing in relation to women and children remains a persistent one. In relation to women leaders, the discourse has been less about specialism and more about 'difference'. Indeed the broader campaign to recruit more women to leadership ranks has been dominated by the idea of difference with women being afforded the capacity to bring about an altogether alternative style of leadership. While there was evidence within my own study of women enacting more transformational styles of leadership than their male counterparts, the significance for this analysis is that the idea of difference still heavily marks and shapes messages about women's contributions to the project of policing. In line with their historical counterparts, contemporary policewomen face a landscape in which their presence is being justified through ideas of 'difference' rather than as a matter of simple social justice and legitimacy – this is a precarious strategy to ensuring the future and full participation of women in policing.

Incompatibility of policing with womanhood

While the incompatibility of being a woman and a police officer has lessened over time with women now working across a range of previously exclusively male designated roles such as firearms, women working in leadership remain heavily constructed by a narrative that constructs them as 'unsuitable' to the demands of police leadership. Despite much organizational change, police organizations remain bound by traditional leadership notions and a leadership identity founded upon ideas of command and control. In this way, women leaders interviewed describe being positioned by their male counterparts as being 'too sensitive', 'too soft', and 'unable to withstand the rigours and demands of twenty-first century policing'. The idea of incompatibility is further compounded by the 'irreconcilable conflict' experienced by women in balancing family commitments with a career in police leadership.

Presentation of the Self

In the same way that historic pioneers dedicated considerable time to managing their bodies in the presentation of the self, a concern with body image is an important feature in contemporary women's understandings of how best to navigate and communicate messages about power and authority. Senior women interviewed were heavily involved in the management and cultivation of their own body image

66 'Cressida Dick appointed first female Met police commissioner', *The Guardian*, 22 February 2017.

and their stories tell us much about the conscious decisions made in balancing visible and socially constructed ideas of femininity and masculinity. While some senior women transgressed their gender boundaries by rejecting the so-called trappings of femaleness in self-presentation, others emphasized their female appearance. Above all else, they remained conscious of the degree of femininity and masculinity exposed, perhaps best encapsulated by the following officer when she notes that being a successful leader requires 'just the right amount of lippy'.

Feminist identity

I have already highlighted the uneasy and complex relationship between feminism and early women police leaders. The extent to which women in such roles allied themselves to the ideas of feminism is central to unpacking the acceptance and progress of women within policing. This complexity remains some hundred years later with this dimension perhaps having the most marked resonance for contemporary women leaders. Few of the women interviewed associated themselves with feminism; in fact the majority of them were hostile to the concept and actively dissociated themselves from it, avidly demonstrating distaste for feminist aims, strategies and actions in challenging the gendered inequalities, noting that 'feminism is a dirty word in policing'. Women held overwhelmingly negative images of feminism, equating it with radicalism and with that a strong awareness of the ruinous effects of identifying as a feminist in the climb to the top of the police hierarchy, suggesting that 'You cannot be outspoken about women's issues. You'll just never get anywhere'. Even those women who were engaged in pro-women initiatives articulated that feminism had no place in the modern police organization. Unlike, their historic counterparts, women interviewed showed little evidence of working together in collaboration with each other as women in driving forward the campaign for more women police. Even where common views and experiences were expressed there was little evidence of a shared consciousness or of an overall solidarity, perhaps best described by one woman when she notes that, 'It's like being in the sisterhood with no sisters.' Driven by external organizational pressures and individualist considerations, contemporary women leaders overwhelmingly accept policing in its current form and work within existing frameworks of male power. While sisterhood may not characterize women's working relationship with one another, there was a strong sense of 'sibling rivalry'. Here, women find themselves working in a situation of increased competition with other women (and men) over a diminishing number of senior level jobs.

Conclusion

This chapter has sought to extend and reposition the story of women's participation in early policing into scholarship that focuses on police leadership. Women leaders at the beginning of the twentieth century played an enormously important role, both in leading the campaign for women police as well as carrying out central functions of policing. Any appraisal of their work would be incomplete without a very real appreciation and acknowledgement of the hugely unequal and tumultuous setting they operated within. Faced with a landscape that positioned all women as 'lesser' and as occupying a 'separate' sphere to men, their capacity to establish a permanent place for women within policing make their achievements even more remarkable. The women featured here fought hard to carve out their own identities as police chiefs. The arguments presented above demonstrate the ways in which women used their authority and presence to influence and negotiate an expanded role for women in policing. Although differently positioned in relation to their views about other women and men, the coming together of women in the campaign for the employment of women police is a testament to their strength and tireless determination. At the heart of this chapter then is a celebratory appreciation of the ways in which women seized and capitalized upon opportunities that presented themselves to use their power and status as leaders to work strategically, drawing on their authority and influence to drive forward the campaign for the acceptance of women police both on a national and international stage.

The chapter has also emphasized that the concerns expressed by contemporary women in police leadership and policing more generally are not new concerns, but rather can be located in the experiences of their historic counterparts. Frances Heidensohn refers to the history of women and policing as being 'highly instructive and laden with messages and symbols about the nature of social control and of gender . . . [for] women in the early twentieth century'.[67] I would add that it also provides important and instructive lessons for those engaged in the contemporary call for more women to join policing and for more women to take up police leadership roles. Understandably the need to come together as women is less obvious in the twenty-first century. Drawing on official accounts, the battle for equality has been won and there are no structural obstacles to prevent women's participation and progression within policing. Indeed, the number of women in leadership roles is at its highest, standing at 23 per cent for chief officers[68] and women occupy key positions in a host of law enforcement and related organizations, with Cressida Dick as Commissioner of the Metropolitan Police; Chief Constable Sara Thornton leading the National Police Chiefs Council, Dame Anne Owers, Chair of the Independent Police Complaints Commission; Chief Constable Lynne Owens, Director General of the National Crime Agency; Alison Saunders, Director of Public Prosecutions and Amber Rudd as Home Secretary. At the same time, we know that the story of gender equality within policing is best understood as one of simultaneous progression and regression, of gain and of loss.[69] The challenge for contemporary policing and its leaders (both women and men) will be to identify the inconspicuous yet deeply entrenched forms of gender discrimination that continue to be present.

67 Heidensohn, *Women in Control*, p.42.

68 J. Hargreaves, J. Cooper, E. Woods and C. McKee, *Police Workforce, England and Wales, Statistical Bulletin 05/16*, London: Home Office, 2016

69 M. Silvestri, 'Gender Diversity: A hop, skip and a jump forwards and back', *Policing: A Journal of Policy & Practice* 2015, vol.9:1, 56–64.

12 Leading through conflict and change

Chief Constables in Northern Ireland

Joanne Murphy

Introduction

Reflecting on the challenge of making sense of Ireland's fractured and contested past, the poet Louis MacNeice observed: 'History never dies, at any rate in Ireland.'[1] The Janus-faced nature of police leadership in Northern Ireland is similar to that of other divided societies: permanently facing both the challenge of the future and the legacy of the past. Bearing in mind the ever-present weight of history, it is not surprising that there has been a long held and common perception that the role of Chief Constable in Northern Ireland is one of the most challenging and high-profile of all senior policing positions in the UK. While there is a significant body of work around police leadership generally and policing in Northern Ireland specifically, there is much less scholarship which turns its attention to the intersection of police leadership and conflict in Northern Ireland.[2] What work does exist focuses on change and the intersection of politics, policing

1 T. Walker, *Louis MacNeice and the Irish Poetry of his Time*, Oxford University Press, 2015. p.26

2 For police leadership see, J. A. Schafer, 'Effective leaders and leadership in policing: Traits, assessment, development, and expansion', *Policing: An International Journal of Police Strategies and Management*, 2010, vol.33:4, 644–63; B. Caless, *Policing at the Top: The Roles, Values and Attitudes of Chief Police Officers*, Policy Press, 2011; J. Fleming (ed.) *Police Leadership: Rising to the Top*, Oxford University Press, 2015. For Northern Ireland policing see, A. Mulcachy, *Policing Northern Ireland*, Cullompton: Willan, 2006; M. Downes, 'Between symbolism and substance: police reform in post conflict contexts' in J. Doyle (ed.) *Policing the Narrow Ground: Lessons from the Transformation of Policing in Northern Ireland*, Dublin: Royal Irish Academy, 2010; G. Ellison, 'Police-community relations in Northern Ireland in the post-Patten era: Towards an ecological analysis' in J. Doyle (ed.) *Policing the Narrow Ground: Lessons from the Transformation of Policing in Northern Ireland*, Dublin: Royal Irish Academy, 2010; M. Gethins, *Catholic Police Officers in Northern Ireland: Voices Out of Silence*, Manchester University Press, 2011; G. Ellison and N. Pino, *Globalization, Police Reform and Development: Doing it the Western Way?* Basingstoke: Palgrave Macmillan, 2012; A. McInnes and T. Meaklim, 'Leading the Police Service of Northern Ireland: Ten years and beyond', *International Journal of Leadership in Public Services*, 2012, vol.8:1, 39–58; J. Murphy, *Policing for Peace in Northern Ireland: Change, Conflict and Community Confidence*, London: Palgrave Macmillan, 2013.

and peace.[3] It is perhaps useful to pause and reflect on some of the factors that make this a difficult subject to address and therefore a complex area to research.

The first relates to the circumstances of Northern Ireland itself. As a small place, with a total population of around 1.8 million, it has a single police service and a highly developed, if provincial, body politic. Policing in Northern Ireland is by its nature personal, highly connected to other parts of civil society and as such, subject to all the limitations, risks and issues of proximity that such an environment cultivates. While there may be similarities with other largely rural regions, the divided history of Northern Ireland and the segregated nature of its education and public housing add to the potency of politics and the legacy of the past to normal community and cultural interactions. The second significant point is that of the role of Chief Constable, a position which has changed over time, and has been impacted upon and determined by the identity and the leadership practices of the individual who held or holds it. This makes it a peculiarly personal subject to write about because, in such a closely-knit environment where continuity and change bookend the journey, personal agency and individual decision-making will always matter.[4] The third is the development of the role which mirrors the history of Northern Ireland, its conflict and its still unsettled peace. At an event held at Queen's University, Belfast on 3 November 2016 to mark the fifteenth anniversary of the Northern Ireland Policing Board, the current Chief Constable, George Hamilton, spoke about the need for 'policing to stay out of politics, but politics to be engaged in policing'.[5] This may not be an unusual refrain in modern-day UK policing as services struggle to navigate the present challenges of a changing institutional landscape, but within Northern Ireland, where for a long time policing was deeply and contentiously embedded in politics, the statement was an important one. There is nowhere in the UK where policing is subject to more significant scrutiny or individual police leaders are more heavily monitored. Their personal views, and in some cases, their personal lives, have become a part of a larger public narrative. The role itself is a leitmotif of change. This chapter will therefore explore the experience, challenges and shifting nature of what it has meant to lead the police in Northern Ireland. What follows is as much as is possible, an organizationally focused and role-orientated narrative, centred on the three themes of continuity, conflict and change. These themes also serve to temporally

3 D. Morrow, B. McAllister, J. Campbell and D. Wilson, 'Mediated dialogues and systemic change in Northern Ireland: Policing our divided society' (PODS) 1996–2003', *Journal of Mediation and Applied Conflict Analysis*, 2013, vol.1:1; A. Mulcachy and H. Orde, 'Police leadership in fractured societies', in J. Fleming (ed.) *Police Leadership: Rising to the Top*, Oxford University Press, 2015; J. Murphy, 'Tracking change in Northern Ireland policing: Temporal phases and key themes', *Policing: An International Journal of Police Strategies and Management*, 2015, vol.38:1, 117–31.

4 A. Pettigrew, 'Strategy as process, power and change' in S. Cummings and D. Wilson (eds) *Images of Strategy*, Cambridge MA: Blackwell, 2003, pp.301–30.

5 *Irish News*, 'PSNI Chief George Hamilton urges progress on Troubles' legacy issues', 2 November 2016,

bracket the development of Northern Ireland policing, and helpfully demarcate a complex history.[6]

Continuity: an institution of the state

The story of police leadership in Northern Ireland is a story of institutional development going back over a hundred years, but in these early stages of police leadership a paradox is evident; while change is occurring all around, it is continuity which is most prized. Amid the restructuring of partition, a concern to preserve and conserve the established policing order was most keenly reflected in the choice of senior officers in the fledgling Royal Ulster Constabulary, established in 1922.[7] The first of these and an almost embodiment of the colonialism of the time was Lieutenant Colonel Sir Charles George Wickham, a former British Army officer with a career that included a period with the Mounted Infantry in the Second Boer War, and another with the British Expeditionary Force sent to aid the White Movement forces in Russia. Wickham was Inspector General (Chief Officer) of the Royal Ulster Constabulary from 1922–45, through a period where the new unionist dominated institutional fabric of Northern Ireland was evolving and becoming increasingly intertwined with the organization itself. Having gained the confidence of Northern Ireland's first Prime Minister Sir James Craig,[8] the culture and edifices of built-in majority rule and political partisanship that characterized the structures of government in the emerging state were welcomed into the evolving police force. The long customary ban on members of the police joining the Protestant and Unionist Orange Order was lifted, and the Sir Robert Peel Orange Lodge was established in 1923 at the same time as Catholic membership of the force reached its notable peak of 21.5 per cent.[9]

This political pattern of what Brewer refers to as 'dominant-subordinate'[10] relationships reinforced the perception of the RUC as 'the armed wing of unionism'.[11] It also illustrates the strength of the bond between the political ruling ideology and the police as an agent of that socio-political position, and therefore police leadership as its essential personification. Wickham's tenure was followed by that of Captain Sir Richard Pike Pim, a former British civil servant and naval officer. Inspector General from August 1945 to January 1961, his previous career as the supervisor of Churchill's cabinet map room had an iconic relevance to the

6 A. N. Langley, C. Smallman, H. Tsoukas and A. H. Van De Ven, 'Process studies of change in organisation and management: Unveiling temporality, activity and flow', *Academy of Management Journal*, 2013, vol.56:1, 1–13.

7 J. D. Brewer and K. Magee, *Inside the RUC*, Oxford University Press, 1991.

8 C. Ryder, *The RUC 1922–2000: A Force under Fire*, London, Arrow Books, 2000.

9 J. Brewer and K. Magee, *Inside the RUC*.

10 J. Brewer, A. Guelke, I. Hume, I. E. Moxon-Browne, R. Wilford, *The Police, Public Order and the State*, 2nd edn, Macmillan, London, 1996, 50–1.

11 Ibid.

history of the time. Pim had remained at Downing Street during the course of the war and upon his return to Northern Ireland was appointed RUC Inspector General, a post he held until his retirement in 1961. At this stage the 'old' IRA campaign was petering out, but new political sands had begun to shift. Pim was followed in his role by his deputy Albert Kennedy, the first senior officer in the Force to rise through the ranks. The elevation of Kennedy to the top job coincided with the beginning of a shift in the political environment, including the doomed tenure of Northern Ireland Prime Minister Terence O'Neill and the rise of the Reverend Ian Paisley. The increasing disillusionment of Northern Ireland's Catholic community at the slow pace of reform put in place the foundations for the next phase; that of outright violence and conflict.[12]

Conflict: the third community?

The first phase of the RUC's lifetime was dominated by an organizational desire to retain what had been the status quo of the old Royal Irish Constabulary. This in turn strengthened and gave increased weight to growing community divisions a fluid and unsettled political environment. These organizational decisions, which we need to assume were the result of a complex political and organizational interaction of both RUC Inspector General's with the leaders of local unionism and government in London, sowed the seeds of the political and social conflagration which encompassed Northern Ireland from the late 1960s to the mid-1990s. Policing was at the very heart of the conflict, caught in a symbiotic relationship of mistrust and missed opportunities in an increasingly volatile and unstable environment.[13] Mulcahy comments that 'Policing itself constituted a major axis of division, and shaped the social and political landscape within which it operated'.[14] In many ways the continuity of the early part of the century was the prelude to the storm of this second phase; a period of active conflict and in many ways horror, for the people of Northern Ireland and for the policing community which was threaded through it. The 'Troubles' as they are generally known, were a catastrophe in every sense, and a particular disaster for its police service. This is a contentious period and one which tends to elicit polarized views from both commentators and police alike. There is, however, no doubt that leading any organization in such an extreme environment represented an immense set of almost daily challenges. The emerging conflict's ethno-political status and the reality of Northern Ireland's deeply divided society becomes even more evident in this period as we see one leader after another struggle and fail to engage meaningfully in a deteriorating security situation.

The evolution of the RUC's identity and culture as an embedded institution of the Northern Ireland state was to have significant consequences for both Northern

12 J. Bardon, *A History of Ulster*, Belfast: Blackstaff Press, 2005.

13 G. Ellison, and J. Smyth, *The Crowned Harp: Policing Northern Ireland*, Pluto Press, 2000.

14 E. Mulcachy, *Policing Northern Ireland*, Cullompton, Willan, p.3.

Ireland society and the organization itself. It is in this period that we also begin to see in a meaningful way the personal and professional agency of individual chief officers. This phase begins with the brief tenure in 1969 of Anthony Peacocke. One of Peacocke's first actions as Inspector General was to make public his assessment that the IRA were actively involved in the civil rights campaign,[15] a statement which seems to convey a serious misjudgment of both the relationship between the Catholic community and the police, and indeed the State itself.[16] As the security situation deteriorated and the policing response became more aggressive, the environment on the streets of Derry and Belfast deteriorated to an almost catastrophic extent. Having initially resisted the deployment of the British Army, the Inspector General appeared to have badly underestimated the seriousness of the situation and the significant risk to life and property. Between July and August 1969, ten deaths had resulted from rioting and civil disturbances, 179 premises had to be demolished, mainly Catholic-owned and the fear garnered by the violence resulted in the movement of over 40,000 people from their homes in what is still the largest single displacement of people in the history of Ireland.[17] The extent of disorder in Northern Ireland prompted the commissioning of the Hunt Report[18] hastily published against a backdrop of growing civil and increasingly entrenched unrest. Peacocke's short tenure ended in resignation and on his departure in October 1969, he became the last Inspector General of the RUC.

The Hunt Report and its recommendations centred around the basic premise that there was a need to separate out the twin roles of policing and security policy.[19] This point is significant, because it begins to define the role and practice of the senior officers through the remainder of this period. Its aim was to civilianize policing along the lines of the rest of the UK and while the Committee's main proposals were accepted against strong opposition from unionists, the ambitious civilianization strategy was continually undermined by a steady deterioration in the security situation. It was, however, the first occasion when it is possible to detect a shift in focus and a recognition that change is overdue. In November 1969 Arthur Young, Commissioner of the City of London Police, was seconded to the role and became the first Chief Constable of the Royal Ulster Constabulary, implementing the revised rank system among other Hunt reforms. Known as 'softy, softly Young' with regard to his articulated strategy to get police officers back into what had become 'no-go' Catholic areas, Young was viewed as an unpopular

15 C. Ryder, *The RUC 1922–2000: A Force under Fire.*

16 Ibid.

17 P. Conroy, T. McKeaney, Q. Oliver, *All over the Place: People Displaced to and from the Southern Border Counties as a Result of the Conflict 1969–1994*, Ralaheen Ltd Dublin with EXPAC Monaghan and Stratagem Belfast, commissioned by Area Development Management and Combat Poverty Agency within the European Union Peace II Programme, 2005.

18 Baron Hunt, CBE, DSO, Report of the Advisory Committee on Police in Northern Ireland, Presented to Parliament by Command of His Excellency the Governor of Northern Ireland October 1969. Belfast: Government of Northern Ireland, 1969.

19 Brewer and Magee, *Inside the RUC*, p.50.

reformer,[20] and moved quickly through his brief, task-orientated tenure to engage so-called community 'defence committees' and publicly disarm an organization severely tarnished by the conduct of some of its officers and the decisions of its leaders. His return to London in November 1970, after the disbandment of the notorious B Specials[21] in April that year and the implementation of the Hunt committee's proposals, saw organizational change in response to extreme environmental difficulties, but no real external alignment which may have allowed the organization to develop along a different path.

This period of time also saw a shift in activity away from the long-established IRA to the Provisional movement and the beginning of the long, violent road of the Troubles. Young's managerially focused tenure was followed by the appointment of his deputy Graham Shillington, Chief Constable from 1970 to 1973. The early 1970s is regarded by most commentators as one of the most volatile and dangerous in the history of Northern Ireland.[22] The combination of a horrifically degenerating security situation with escalating tension and an increasing unease in the command relations between the police (who were now operating in an increasingly anti-terrorist role) and the British army led to not just instability but also a sometimes chaotic approach to security and intelligence gathering. The rearming of the RUC in 1971 after a number of police fatalities in shooting incidents further militarized the Force as violence intensified. While Shillingham spoke of consolidating and building on progress that had already been made in his initial statement[23] the words rang hollow against a backdrop of increasing alienation of the minority community against the police and what they had come to represent.

The introduction of internment (administrative detention) in 1971 reinforced this still further, as flawed intelligence resulted in the widespread round-up of suspects. Subsequent abuse of prisoners increased the risk of the radicalization of whole communities. The imposition of direct rule in 1972 was the British Government's response to a security situation that seemed to be spiralling out of control as the power-sharing executive, which had been established earlier in the same year, collapsed after five months.[24] Shillingham himself secured some progress and at least a reduction in the mounting death toll from 1972–3. He did, however, begin to articulate a message which has become a theme among RUC Chief Constables since, the vocalization of a belief that the organization could at some point be allowed to carry out its work with an expectation that it was both fair and impartial, and that reform was neither necessary or wise, even with its

20 E. Mulcachy and H. Orde, *Police Leadership in Fractured Societies*, in J. Fleming, *Police Leadership: Rising to the Top*, Oxford University Press, 2015, p.172.

21 The B Specials were the only remaining component of the original Special Constabularies and had a particular reputation for sectarianism and violence, see J. Murphy *Policing for peace in Northern Ireland*, Basingstoke: Palgrave Macmillan, 2013, p.11.

22 T. Hennessey, *A History of Northern Ireland*, New York: St. Martin's Press, 1999.

23 Ryder, *The RUC 1922–2000: A Force under Fire*.

24 Bardon, *A History of Ulster*.

partisan history and in the context of a divided society. When James Flanagan took over as Chief Constable in 1973, the first Catholic to hold the rank, he continued to defend the organization in relentless terms while at the same time making significant organizational gestures to the Republic of Ireland's Garda Síochána in relation to the sharing of intelligence and patrolling of the border.

As the death toll of the Troubles mounted, political initiatives such as a short IRA ceasefire and the power-sharing Sunningdale agreement faltered in the increasingly fragmented and bitter discord of local politics.[25] A further attempt in the form of the constitutional convention of 1975 also failed. The 1975–6 Bourne Ministerial Working Party on Northern Ireland police and security paved the way for a new doctrine of 'police primacy'. This resulted in the expansion and reequipping of the RUC, its partial remilitarization, the end to detention without trial, and the phasing out of 'senior category' status for those convicted of terrorist offences.[26] Flanagan retired in 1976 and made way for his deputy, Kenneth Newman, who held the post to 1980. Previously a member of the police in British Mandate Palestine, Newman is best known for ensuring that the Royal Ulster Constabulary replaced the British Army as the dominant security force in Northern Ireland and for a significant reorganization of police headquarters, putting it on a much more reliable organizational footing. Newman went on to become Commissioner of the London Metropolitan Police.

John Charles Hermon, commonly known as Jack Hermon followed Newman, and was Chief Constable from 1980–89. Priding himself as 'holding the line' against both republican and loyalist paramilitaries, Hermon was a staunch advocate of force discipline and an equally strong defender of the organization in the face of increasing criticism including the notorious shoot to kill controversies of the 1980s.[27] Faced with appalling atrocities and extreme loss of life including the murder of nine members of the RUC in a motor attack on a police station in Newry, his time in office saw the twin policies of police primacy and Ulsterization progress steadily. As well as 900 deaths in the Troubles, including infamous incidents such as the Enniskillen bombing, the killings of IRA volunteers in Loughgall and Gibraltar and the murders in Milltown cemetery,[28] Hermon had to deal with an organization that seemed to exist within a constant state of alert and was becoming increasingly insular. The perception that the RUC was 'organically' drawn from the Protestant community and that many members of that community considered the organization 'our police' became increasingly ingrained in the general body politic.[29] In one often quoted remark, the Deputy Leader of the

25 Ibid., pp.707–8.

26 Brewer and Magee, *Inside the RUC*.

27 Ryder, *The RUC 1922–2000: A Force under Fire*.

28 For a comprehensive analysis of events during 'The Troubles', see S. McKay, *Bear in Mind These Dead*, London: Faber and Faber, 2008.

29 G. Ellison, 'Police- community relations in Northern Ireland in the post-Patten era: Towards an ecological analysis' in J. Doyle, *Policing the narrow ground: Lessons from the transformation of policing in Northern Ireland*, Dublin: Royal Irish Academy, 2010.

moderate Social Democrat and Labour Party (SDLP) referred to the RUC as '97% Protestant, and 100% Unionist'.[30] This perception was reinforced during Hermon's tenure despite his not inconsiderable attempts to modernize and professionalize the Force, and his own belief that the police constituted a third community.[31]

Change

For communities that had been through over 20 years of political violence, polarization and alienation from the state and each other, the unstable paramilitary ceasefires of 1994 represented the end of one journey and the beginning of another. For the leadership of the RUC and the Chief Constable Hugh Annesley, the ceasefires were first and foremost the beginning of a process of environmental and organizational change which sat outside the realm of existing organizational experience. Annesley himself was extremely cautious, going as far as to comment publicly:

> I do not accept the change argument. I do not believe that there is anything inherently wrong with the RUC that needs to be changed. I do not accept that the organisation is wrong and needs to be fixed.[32]

Most scholarship on the policing change process that followed the ceasefires and includes the shift from the Royal Ulster Constabulary to the Police Service of Northern Ireland dates the period of transition from the Good Friday Agreement 1998 and its follow-on, the Independent or Patten Commission on Policing.[33] While this juncture matters enormously and forms the political piece of the change jigsaw, it does not take account of activity within the organization, and leadership decision-making at a much earlier stage. Looking at the process through a different lens, we see that activity such as the instigation of the Fundamental Review process and increased engagement with external organizations and community representatives, generated by Annesley[34] and his senior officers had a cascading effect that became significant both inside and outside the organization. By instigating the RUC's own 'Fundamental Review', under the control of the then acting Deputy and future Chief Constable, Ronnie Flanagan, the RUC leadership began to explore the reality of life after conflict with the development of three possible

30 M. Smyth and R. Moore, *Policing and Sectarian Division*, Derry: Templegrove Action Research, 1996 p.2.

31 Brewer and Magee, *Inside the RUC*.

32 M. O'Rawe, 'Transitional policing arrangements in Northern Ireland: The can't and won't of the change dialectic', *Fordham International Law Journal*, 2002, vol.26:4, p.1031.

33 G. Ellison, 'A blueprint for democratic policing anywhere in the world?' *Police Quarterly*, 2007, vol.10:3, 243–69.

34 This period coincides with the significant external engagement of senior officers with the nationalist community and the commissioning of a 'Fundamental Review' of the RUC in light of the ceasefires (1994). The Fundamental Review document has never been published in full.

environmental 'realities' and organizational responses.[35] While Annesley himself appeared sceptical about the prospect of sustained peace[36] and defensive in relation to the organization itself, it is possible to see the RUC leadership actively looking at defensive strategies to both engage in welcome change, but hold off its unwelcome elements. It is also important to remember that much of the pressure which brought about the Fundamental Review was financial in origin.[37] While the Review made 189 recommendations for change, it stayed firmly distanced from the symbolic issues of name, badge and flag, and even more so from the concrete issues of recruitment and reform of 'Special Branch'.[38] It also followed on from other community engagement strategies, such as the instigation in 1993 of the 'Policing Our Divided Society' programme of the community mediation service, Mediation NI.[39] By 1996 Mediation NI had established a community awareness programme in Foundation Training but withdrew when they found themselves at odds with the RUC over their work as mediators in the emerging parades conflict. Annesley himself faced widespread criticism over his decision to reverse the ban imposed on an Orange Order march proceeding down the Garvaghy Road, Portadown against the wishes of local nationalist residents. In the same period the police were establishing links with the media and in particular with well-known Catholic journalists and commentators in an effort to move forward. 'Future Ways' a University of Ulster based think-tank using an early form of their organizational learning and community relations methodology 'Equality, Diversity and Interdependence' (EDI) was also beginning to work internally with the organization, in conjunction with Mediation NI.[40] All of this activity demonstrates a leadership and an organization that are aware of both their own central position in the emerging peace process and their vulnerability to aspects of the external change agenda. They were also increasingly aware of the consequences of change for members of an organization who were used to high stress, long hours with considerable overtime and appropriate recompense. The reality of peace meant a reduction in both with financial and other consequences for the RUC and its members.[41] Flanagan's appointment as Chief Constable in 1996 was a high-profile endorsement of him as an organizational leader, and more importantly a recognition that his formidable media skills were in demand at the highest level in the organization. Intense political negotiations culminated in the Belfast or Good

35 Murphy, *Policing for Peace in Northern Ireland*, p.47.

36 Mulcachy, *Policing Northern Ireland*, p.110.

37 Murphy, *Policing for Peace in Northern Ireland*, p.46.

38 RUC, *A Fundamental Review of Policing*. Belfast: RUC, 1996; O'Rawe, 'Transitional policing arrangements in Northern Ireland'.

39 D. Morrow, B. McAllister, J. Campbell and D. Wilson, *Mediated Dialogue and Systematic Change in Northern Ireland: Policing our divided society (PODS), 1996–2003*, Belfast, Community Relations Council, 2014.

40 K. Eyben, D. Morrow and D. Wilson, *The equity, Diversity and Interdependence Framework: A Framework for Organisational Learning and Change*, Belfast: University of Ulster, 2000.

41 Murphy, *Policing for Peace in Northern Ireland*.

Friday Agreement of 10 April 1998 and moved the police resolutely from possible change to certain change, with all of the leadership challenges and organizational concerns that such change brings. This was a period of huge uncertainty, but also a time when the Chief Constable himself became enormously important as an embodiment of both the past and the future.

When the Patten Commission reported in September 1999 it made 175 recommendations, the most controversial of which was a change of name, badge and uniform. Patten had been very clear in his view that a change in the RUC needed to be deep rooted and transparent to those who were looking at the organization from communities who had mistrusted it deeply:

> The 'significant change' in policing should not be a cluster of unconnected adjustments in policy that can be bolted or soldered onto the organisation that already exists. The changes that we propose are extensive and they fit together like the pieces in a jigsaw puzzle. We believe that we have met the argument of the former Standing Advisory Commission on Human Rights that 'holistic change of a fundamental nature is required'.[42]

The British Government's general acceptance of Patten's Report to the fury of unionists in Northern Ireland lit the torch paper on the pace of transformation. In response, the RUC leadership accepted the recommendations and began the process. Flanagan's significance as Chief Constable at this juncture, is difficult to underestimate. While there is no doubt that some in the RUC embraced change and understood how necessary it was within the extended history of policing in Northern Ireland, others, including those politically aligned to unionist parties, actively and aggressively resisted. In this Flanagan's qualities as an articulate and intelligent advocate for a yet unknown future came to the fore. While he himself had concerns, he was also able to argue internally for flexibility and externally for understanding. His political skill and that of those around him meant that the severance package negotiated for members who chose to leave the RUC, rather than engage in a career in the PSNI was at a level previously unprecedented in policing or in public service generally. Having, like many Chiefs before him, carried the coffins of murdered colleagues, he was also in a strong position to rebut criticism. These qualities were well known already and were the key reasons why he had secured the Chief Constable position in the first place. Personable, articulate and charismatic, he was both a 'cop's cop' and an organizational advocate, even before the political bifurcation of the ceasefires and his own elevation to the top job. One of his colleagues commented of his frequent television appearances and his ability to talk meaningfully about the murders of colleagues:

42 International Commission on Policing for Northern Ireland, *A New Beginning: Policing in Northern Ireland*, Belfast, HMSO, 1999.

> Ronnie Flanagan – he humanised the face of policing. He brought into people's homes that these were real people. You haven't just killed an 'apparatus of the state'. He was great at that. He was well loved for it. (Chief Superintendent Interview with the author, 13/02/2004)

His ability and willingness to communicate was key to this at a time when police officers at senior levels in the RUC were with good reason, often reluctant to appear on camera or to be publically identified. Another former colleague observed:

> When Ronnie came in we'd gone through a period of criticism after criticism after criticism and nobody seemed to really stand up for us but Ronnie was up for it. Ronnie went on the TV programme. Ronnie did the face to face interviews. Ronnie did the one to ones and he won them because he was such a good communicator. Everybody in the organisation just was in awe of Ronnie Flanagan. (Assistant Chief Constable, Interview with the author, 07/12/2005)

Others spoke about his inherent credibility with both the pro-change and anti-change advocates within the organization itself:

> He had a massive credibility in the organisation and was very highly regarded. He was very very popular within the organisation as well and was regarded in policing terms as a real sort of cop's cop type of thing and I am sure you have heard that term before. Actually the fact that and I think a key part of the selling or the marketability of the bulk of the Patten recommendations had been actually that most of them were fundamental review recommendations which his fingerprints were all over because he was the driver behind the fundamental review. Which added a sense – at the level that I was at that stage, a degree of organisational credibility'. (Assistant Chief Constable, Interview with the author, 29/11/2007)

Flanagan's history and his association with its tarnished past had a significant impact on how he continued to be regarded within the nationalist community. Controversy around intelligence failings regarding the Omagh bomb and the subsequent investigation were to lead to a serious dispute between the police and the Police Ombudsman and had important ramifications for Flanagan professionally. Having started his career in the RUC, he retired as the first Chief Constable of the PSNI, acting as a bridge between the old RUC and the new beginning of the Police Service of Northern Ireland.

The period between March and May 2002 was one of stasis and anticipation for the newly established Police Service. Deputy Chief Constable Colin Cramphorn took over the position of acting Chief Constable, but only temporarily. Cramphorn was popular internally, but the task ahead was enormous and he stated early in the process that he was not interested in becoming Chief. Hugh Orde, Deputy Assistant Commissioner of the Met and the man responsible for the Stevens enquiry into RUC collusion concerning the murder of the Belfast solicitor Pat Finucane, was appointed Chief Constable of the PSNI in 2002 amid allegations of political manoeuvring. The 'new broom' of Orde was controversial: clearly well acquainted with what nationalists referred to as the 'dark side' of policing in Northern Ireland, the new Chief Constable was the choice among a raft of candidates from the old, established order. Unionists, however were unhappy.[43] Unable to argue with his distinguished policing credentials, they instead chose to absent themselves from the press conference that made the announcement. The veteran Ulster Unionist and member of the Policing Board, John Taylor, Lord Kilclooney, went as far as to describe the decision to appoint Orde as both 'surprising' and 'political'.[44]

The absence of a honeymoon period for the new Chief Constable was compounded in October of that year with the PSNI raid on Sinn Fein's Stormont offices. Allegations of 'intelligence gathering' and the arrest of three Sinn Fein employees including Denis Donaldson, their Head of Administration (later uncovered as a British 'agent') resulted in the collapse of the fledgling power-sharing administration in Stormont. The Assembly elections of 2003 saw the Democratic Unionist Party (DUP) and Sinn Fein returned as the largest parties for the first time. Tentative progress to engage Sinn Fein within the policing process culminated in the first meeting between Sinn Fein President Gerry Adams and Hugh Orde in November 2004, but hopes for an immediate breakthrough were dashed soon after when the PSNI named the IRA as the group behind the Northern Bank heist and the theft of £26.5m. This was followed by the murder of Belfast man Robert McCartney with significant allegations of republican involvement. In September of that year, General John de Chastelain and his colleagues in the Independent International Commission on Decommissioning (IICD) reported that they were 'satisfied that the arms decommissioned represent the totality of the IRA's arsenal'.[45] At the same time, and after much discussion, the PSNI established the Historical Enquiries Team as an attempt to answer some of the questions around historical investigations and unsolved murders of the Troubles.[46]

The first five years of Hugh Orde's tenure were marked by below the radar engagement and political rankling. The decision to move away from the Patten espoused 28 policing districts to a Review of Public Administration inspired eight Districts (two to cover Belfast) required very significant reorganization in both human resources and structures. The change went live on 1 April 2007, just as the political focus returned to the NI Assembly and Executive. In addition, Orde had to contend with the regular and often adversarial meetings with the Northern Ireland

43 'Met man is new NI Chief Constable', *BBC News Northern Ireland*, 30 May 2002.

44 'Unionist unease over new Chief Constable', *BBC News Northern Ireland*, 30 May 2002.

45 'IRA arms decommissioned', *The Guardian*, 26 September 2005.

46 The Historical Enquiries Team was established in 2004 to attempt to 'help people bereaved by the Troubles by answering their questions'. (www.psni.police.uk/historical-enquiries-team). It looks at each historical case with a view to bringing forward any new or remaining evidential opportunities. It is an independent police team and reports directly to the Chief Constable on operational matters.

Policing Board – a body which was established to 'hold the Chief Constable to account' and to represent a real and substantive challenge to any drift towards what had been for so long the default in Northern Ireland: damagingly political policing. For a significant period of this time the Policing Board itself was the main arena for political dialogue in Northern Ireland, as the institutions of government stuttered and stalled through political infighting and a series of significant divergent concerns. Orde however, seems to have managed the Board very effectively. One Policing Board Officer commented on Orde's skilful management of the process in a blatantly confrontational environment:

> Orde conveyed a sense of confidence. Certainly had respect. No one ever really landed a punch on Hugh Orde. He got the politics. His time on Stevens saw to that. He didn't have the baggage that makes it difficult for others, particularly indigenous police officers. He recognized that the Policing Board is important, which is ingenious in itself because the Policing Board can be a pain in the backside for police officers'. (Interview with author 11/10/2011)

In a parallel development, a new group was established, headed by Lord Eames and Dennis Bradley, to begin the slow process of contemplating how NI should best 'find a way forward out of the shadows of the past'.[47] This consultation and the conclusions it reached were ultimately to prove too controversial for both Governments and some political parties to stomach. Little of significance has emerged from it since and it remains the great challenge of conflict transformation. Orde himself made a significant attempt to move on the same issue through the 'historical enquiries team'.[48] Such initiatives are extraordinarily difficult to manage or embark upon in a society emerging from conflict.[49] As an organization, the RUC and its successor the PSNI have both had to contend with the challenge of 'living with the dead', both in relation to their own members and those in the society around them that suffered and died through the conflict. A relatively stable security situation and ongoing political progress resulted in the end of Operation Banner, the official name of the British Military Campaign in Northern Ireland in July 2007. But the relative calm of the time became punctuated more and more regularly with dissident republican activity. Serious and sustained rioting blighted Craigavon in August 2008 amid then in March 2009 the self-styled 'Real IRA' murdered two soldiers outside Massereene army base and went on to kill Constable Stephen Carroll – the first PSNI officer to be murdered. These tragic events came close to the end of Orde's tenure as Chief Constable.

47 R. Eames and D. Bradley, *The Report of the Consultative Group on the Past in Northern Ireland: Second Report of Session 2009–10*; Report, Together with Formal Minutes, Oral and Written Evidence, Stationery Office, 2009, p. 4.

48 Murphy, *Policing for Peace In Northern Ireland*, pp.127–9

49 S. McDowell and M. Braniff, *Commemoration as Conflict: Space, Memory and Identity in Peace Processes*, Basingstoke: Palgrave Macmillan, 2014.

The departure of Orde in 2009 saw a hiatus in which Northern Ireland saw a shift in the role for the first time. The appointment of Judith Gillespie as acting Chief Constable from August 2009 to September 2009 saw a temporary female Chief and some appreciation of how the male-orientated and male-dominated organizational culture was unhelpful to women seeking senior roles. Gillespie had risen through the ranks herself and had been identified at an early stage through the Policing Our Divided Society programme as a significant talent, but decided not to apply for the Chief Constable post.[50] The appointment of Matt Baggott, (formerly Chief of the Leicestershire Constabulary) in September 2009 saw the new Chief inherit a host of problems, including a renewed dissident threat and increased financial pressures. Baggott was a compromise appointment, with a significant background of community policing but little of the nuanced political experience which had marked out his predecessors. He was also an evangelical Christian and President of the Christian Police Officers' Association. This detail, while insignificant in many contexts is unusual in Northern Ireland, where the nature of community division means that such manifest identification with a particular religious or political perspective seems at best risky and at worse profoundly dangerous with regard to how the individual and the role is perceived. Baggott appeared to be significantly challenged by the overt politics and the level of contestation presented by police oversight in Northern Ireland. He was also reluctant to engage in the frequent discourse around what is often called 'dealing with the past'. In particular, his mishandling of the police response to the enquiry into one of the most notorious bombings of the Troubles, was roundly condemned by nationalists.[51] A Policing Board member, who was highly critical of his tenure, commented privately:

> He doesn't get the politics. He doesn't take the time to understand the politics. There is a disconnect between the leadership needed and what there is. It doesn't take many incidents for the confidence in the Chief Constable to erode. McGurks bar, Loughinisland, the Historical Enquires Team. He conveys an arrogance which is completely misplaced. (Policing Board member, Interview with the author, 7 January, 2012)

These comments and the emotion behind them reflect the significance and necessity of the detailed political knowledge within the still divided environment of Northern Ireland. As much as there has been a clear and identified requirement to separate politics from policing, there is still a clear need that policing must

50 Gillespie was not technically eligible to apply as she had not served the requisite 2 years outside Northern Ireland, but a consultation to amend this criteria was underway as she departed, see 'I'm leaving PSNI on my own terms, insists Deputy Chief Constable Judith Gillespie', *Belfast Telegraph*, 13 March 2014.

51 'McGurk's bomb ombudsman report: Baggott criticized', *BBC News Northern Ireland*, 22 February 2011.

acutely understand the politics of division, if only to avoid the inevitable criticism of political policing. While Baggott diligently focused his attention on community policing, his lack of this awareness and his unwillingness to engage on these terms was fundamentally damaging to his position and his legacy within the Catholic community. His tenure saw the murder of PSNI Constable Ronan Kerr in April 2011. A Catholic Patten recruit, and active Gaelic Athletic Association (GAA) member, Kerr's death reinforced the seriousness of the difficulties that still exist in relation to policing in Northern Ireland and the significant danger which still confronts members of the organization on a daily basis.

Baggott was followed by the appointment of George Hamilton in May 2014, who had previously served as Assistant Chief Constable with responsibility for rural policing. The least controversial Chief Constable since the Good Friday Agreement, Hamilton is also the first since Ronnie Flanagan to have served in the RUC. Perceived as an authentic leader of an organization to which he is deeply connected, Hamilton has also been the Chief Constable who has been most able to pursue an agenda of community based policing, in a political environment which has generally been in his favour. Well regarded and organizationally focused, Hamilton has been resolute in his concern for 'what we do and how we do it' (Interview with the author, 17th May 2016) but has also urged local politicians not to stall on new structures to deal with the legacy of the troubles. Commenting recently, he clearly identified the issue of confidence in the police with an effective management of the historic legacy of division and conflict within the region: 'In the absence of any alternative political and societal resolutions, these issues continue to be left at the door of policing and the broader criminal justice system. They sap community confidence and drain budgets'.[52]

Conclusion: the Chief Constable as an agent for change

This chapter has attempted to draw together the history and activities of leadership in Northern Ireland policing, from the partition of Ireland to the present day – with a focus on the three themes of continuity, conflict and change. All of the individuals mentioned are significant figures and all have attempted to carry out difficult roles in complex and often dangerous environments. Operating in such environments is challenging and certainly for the early occupants of Inspector General and Chief Constable positions it is difficult to fully appreciate the decisions and pressures that must have been brought to bear. For more recent appointments, it is easier to appreciate what were sometimes invidious decisions, with high stakes. It is perhaps useful to reflect on what we learn by looking at the role of individuals such as these and individual decision-making within such environments. The organizational scholar Andrew Pettigrew expresses very well what is to be gained by these types of studies:

52 'PSNI Chief George Hamilton urges progress on Troubles' legacy issues', *Irish News*, 2 November 2016.

> My interest is in the dynamic of human conduct in organizational settings. Thus, I have been preoccupied with how decisions are made, how power is won and lost, how organizational cultures are created and maintained and the juxtaposition of continuity and change over time.[53]

One thing that is clear from the intertwined histories above is that the role of the Chief Constable is one of an agent for change in an environment and organization still undergoing transition. Another is the persistent significance of political skill as a mediating factor for policing change itself, particularly within a fractured political and community environment of Northern Ireland.[54] The role of Chief Constable in Northern Ireland illustrates too, the role of police leadership in other divided societies, as well as other policing reform or change processes, and gives us a particular insight into leading public institutions through conflict and building peace. In the later stages of the RUC story and the beginning of the PSNI experience we see an organization and a leadership which understands its role and its central position within a nascent peace process, and moves carefully to protect both the process and the organization itself. This demonstration of acute organizational and political skill is significant, and appears as a central component of effective, politically tied change.

53 Pettigrew, 'Strategy as process, power and change' p.5.
54 Mulcachy and Orde, 'Police leadership in fractured societies'.

13 'Seirbheis Phoilis na h-Alba' Police Scotland

The rationalization of Chief Constables

Gareth Addidle

Introduction

In 2011, Kenny MacAskill, the Scottish Cabinet Secretary for Justice, described the pre-existing police system, consisting of eight separate police forces, as 'unsustainable' and proposed a vision for a new centralized police service expected to result in savings of £1.1 billion by 2026.[1] Confronted with cuts in public spending determined by Westminster, the Scottish Government had its overall funding reduced by almost 11 per cent between 2010/11–2015/16. As a (by) product of this political reality, the Police and Fire Reform (Scotland) Act 2012 (the Reform Act) was granted Royal Assent on 8th August 2012, with the Police Service of Scotland (PSS), coming into existence on 1 April 2013.

The Reform Act abolished the pre-existing governing bodies and the Scottish Crime and Drug Enforcement Agency. It also laid down substantial requirements for the modernization of Scottish policing through the creation of a national system of police governance, providing new arrangements for the delivery of local policing and the maintenance of a range of local police accountabilities alongside the enunciation of a new set of policing principles. The stated aims of the Act proposed by the Scottish Government were 'to protect and improve local services . . . create more equal access to specialist support and national capacity . . . [and to] strengthen the connection between police services and communities'.[2] The purpose of this chapter is not to provide a comprehensive overview of these reforms, as they have been ably set out elsewhere but to explore the developments and the potential impacts for local policing that have arisen from the creation of a national police force run from corporate headquarters in Stirling.[3] It will examine

1 The Scottish Government, Police Officer Quarterly Strength Statistics Scotland– www.scotland.gov.uk/Resource/0039/00394382.pdf.

2 Audit Scotland, *Police Reform: Progress Update*, Edinburgh: Audit Scotland, 2013.

3 See K. Scott, 'A single police force for Scotland: The legislative framework (1)', *Policing*, 2012, 7:2, 133 and 'A single police force for Scotland: The legislative framework (2)', *Policing*, 2013, 8:2, 140; N. R. Fyfe and K. B. Scott, 'In search of sustainable policing? Creating a national police force in Scotland' in N. R. Fyfe, J. Terpstra and P. Tops (eds) *Centralizing Forces? Comparative Perspectives on Contemporary Police Reform in Northern and Western Europe*, The Hague: Eleven International Publishing, 2013, 119–35.

the relationship between politics and the police, the effectiveness of the new accountability mechanisms, the balance between local and national priorities, and the Chief Constable's arguable 'Post-Met enforcement' approach to policing and leadership. To this end, the chapter largely deals with how Sir Stephen House, the Chief Constable of Strathclyde (and formerly a senior officer of the Metropolitan Police) became the first Chief Constable of Police Scotland. Lastly, the chapter analyzes the developments and issues identified, drawing upon Loveday's concept of a 'professional model of policing', and their relationship to the eventual resignation of the first Chief Constable of Police Force Scotland, which brings us to the present day.

Reform: push and pull

The decision to create a single police service followed a period of public consultation on the future of Scottish policing. [4] In February 2011, the Scottish Government launched the first of two consultation exercises to seek views on how to protect and improve the police service and increase partnership working with other organizations.[5] Interestingly, the findings from the first consultation provided rather mixed views on how the police should be structured. A number of respondents, especially among police bodies, supported retaining the existing eight forces in a modern form with increased collaboration.[6] Similar views were also found in a later consultation carried out in June 2011, with two principle responses: 'the current system works well and could be built on (i.e. through increasing collaboration between forces) without the need for major restructuring (mentioned by 20 respondents); and the need for communities to have local police forces with local knowledge and/or the importance of having locally managed forces to reflect the diverse needs of the Scottish population' (ten respondents).[7] It was also argued that 'one size does not fit all' and that different approaches are required in

4 This move to a national police force is not a new idea. From a proliferation of 89 separate police forces in 1859, the number had been reduced to 48 by 1949 and eight in 1975. The idea of a 'single' or national force was mooted from the 1850s onwards in moments of unrest, disorder and emergency, but for most of the twentieth century it remained an anathema. For further discussion, see N. Davidson, L. Jackson, and D. Smale, 'Police amalgamation and reform in Scotland: The long twentieth century', *Scottish Historical Review*, 2016, 95:1, 88–111.

5 Consultation typically included police and fire bodies, voluntary sector, national and local partnerships and other national entities. See L. Nicholson, 'Keeping Scotland safe and strong: A consultation on reforming police and fire and rescue services in Scotland', Research Findings No.36, 2011. Available at: www.scotland.gov.uk/Resource/Doc/365341/0124238.pdf Interestingly, the consultation did not include a 'public' consultation, see N. R. Fyfe, 'A different and divergent trajectory? Reforming the structure, governance and narrative of policing in Scotland', in J. Brown (ed.) *The Future of Policing*, London: Routledge, 2016, 493–506. The idea of a public consultation may not be as 'public' as the consultation process suggested.

6 Nicholson, 'Keeping Scotland Safe and Strong'.

7 R. Bryan, S. Granville and S. Sizer, *Research Support for a Consultation on the Future of Policing in Scotland*, Scottish Government: Edinburgh, 2011, p.28.

different areas across Scotland, based on local knowledge and community policing. Pre-reform force areas in Scotland covered 'a unique mix of urban and rural communities with very different policing needs'.[8] Stephen Curran the (then) convenor of Strathclyde Joint Police Authority in 2010, noted that different areas could be contained within pre-reform force areas arguing that 'Strathclyde covers 44% of the Scottish population in an area running from Tiree to Ballantrae, so we know all about preserving local accountability. . . . If it can be done within Strathclyde, it can be done within Scotland'.[9]

Nevertheless, the Scottish Government published a business case for police reform in September 2011. The report argued that although the police were performing well in Scotland, with low levels of crime and high levels of public satisfaction 'in the face of unprecedented cuts to public sector budgets, the Scottish Government wished to protect this level of performance. It is not possible to meet that challenge in the current structure and organization of policing in Scotland'.[10]

While the report considered three different restructuring models as per previous consultations, a single force was ultimately the Scottish Government's preferred option.[11] The report set out that a single force offered the greatest potential to generate efficiencies based on the following justifications:

- Total net present value £1,364 million over 15 years and annual recurring cash savings estimated at £106 million from the end of the programme of change;
- requires up to £161 million one-off transitional investment over the programme of change;
- would best deliver non-financial benefits in improvements to service delivery and policing outcomes with the removal of internal boundaries which would facilitate specialist resources being deployed flexibly across Scotland as required, and national capacity to tackle threats such as terrorism and serious organised crime where it is needed;
- The single service model presents the best opportunity to drive out duplication, ensure consistency, and rationalise existing systems and structures as far as possible. Efficiencies should be realised through economies of scale, with expertise, capability and budgets pooled at a national level then targeted to local need.[12]

There were also other potential benefits that the Scottish Government had been keen to highlight. A national force would, they argued, create more equal access

8 Her Majesty's Inspectors of Constabulary (HMIC), *Independent Review of Policing*, 2009 available from: www.scotland.gov.uk/Publications/2009/01/23133505/5

9 R. Dinwoodie, 'Scotland's police chiefs take first merger steps', *The Herald*, 14 September 2010.

10 Scottish Government, Police reform programme: Outline business case, Edinburgh, September 2011.

11 Other models were an enhanced eight forces model and a regional police model. Scottish Government, A consultation on the future of policing in Scotland, Edinburgh, 2011, p.30.

12 Scottish Government, *Police Reform Programme*.

to specialist support and expertise and, through the arrangements for local policing, strengthen the connections between the police service and communities.[13] It seems central arguments for the introduction of a national police force were therefore based on the likelihood of substantial cuts to police funding and the need to make savings while at the same time protecting police establishment and its performance.[14] This was supported by the 'pro-national' (then) Chief Constable of Strathclyde, Sir Stephen House, who publicly stated that a national police force would protect police numbers as a result of savings made on infrastructure.[15] House also stated:

> I doubt that anyone can argue against the often quoted notion that if we were sitting with a blank sheet of paper deciding how to police Scotland, we wouldn't come up with a model that has eight forces supported by national agencies. It doesn't make financial sense, nor does it make operational sense.

He said the real benefits would be felt across Scottish communities, adding: 'A single force would mean that policing would be directed nationally, but delivered locally'.[16] More broadly, House believed Scotland's single force would be a model for the 'inevitable' mergers of England and Wales's 43 forces. It is a proposal that has been vigorously resisted by English and Welsh Chief Constables and local councils,[17] but any success for Police Scotland could embolden the Home Office to try again.[18] Before looking more closely at the impact and leadership practices of the eventual first Chief Constable of Scotland, we need to consider his influence alongside other senior Strathclyde police officers in the development and reform process leading to a national police service.

The Strathclyde effect

While initial planning for the reformed police service was to be the responsibility of the Scottish Government, it was devolved in early 2011 to the Scottish Police College who then commissioned the Sustainable Policing Project Team to take this

13 Fyfe and Scott, 'In search of sustainable policing?'

14 B. Loveday, Evidence submitted to the SIPR Review of police structures and governance, Dundee: SIPR, 2015.

15 Fyfe, Terpstra and Tops, *Centralizing Forces?* p.126: The protection of police numbers (the addition of 1,000 extra police officers) was a key SNP government pledge when they came into office in 2007 and one they were determined to carry through. Especially, as they used this as a major political move to draw comparisons with England and Wales where numbers had been falling over the last decade see 'Police numbers fall to 11-year low', *The Telegraph*, 29 January 2014.

16 S. House, 'Top officer calls for single Scottish police force', *STV News*, 13 January 2011.

17 Also see Lord Stevens, *Policing for a Better Britain*, Independent Police Commission, 2013 for further discussion and debate of how developments in Scotland have given rise to considerations of a national police service for England and Wales.

18 S. Carrell, 'Scotland's new unified police force replaces eight regional constabularies', *The Guardian*, 1 April 2013.

forward.[19] The Team was led by Neil Richardson Deputy Chief Constable (DCC) of Strathclyde Police.[20] With the support of his Chief Constable, Sir Stephen House, Richardson drafted the Sustainable Policing Project report which again explored the three options for reform. It came to the clear conclusion that a national force would maximize operational benefits as well as secure significant financial savings supporting the Scottish Government's position as set out in its business case. The DCC then continued to play a pivotal role within the National Police Reform Team once the decision to establish a national force had been taken.[21]

In contrast to these views of support, Loveday observed that professional opinion as to the value of a national force was to prove divided (much like the views expressed in the consultations of the future of Scottish Policing).[22] Many Chief Constables heading up the threatened eight forces did not share the optimism of either the Scottish Government or fellow Chief Constable of Strathclyde as to the benefits of the merger. They argued instead for a regional structure to allow for local demands and differences[23] and had strong concerns about political interference. For example, Grampian Police Chief Constable Colin McKerracher told BBC Scotland he was in favour of some kind of restructuring, but feared a single force could mean funding issues. Adding to this he stated, 'A few of my Chief Constable colleagues are concerned about political interference in policing.'[24]

The political narrative focused on the economic rationale for reform, need to deal with national challenges to safety, strengthening local connections and protecting performance levels. It seems that the concerns highlighted in the consultation exercises and by many Chief Constables were largely ignored. This reflected, as has been argued by observers, a decisive move to centralizing policing and was fully intended to represent a clear break from the past.[25] There was also a particularly influential role over the direction of national reform played by senior police officers from Strathclyde Police. This may be indicative of what Loveday contends, that 'the professional solution to new challenges always appear to be based on ever larger units of policing'.[26]

19 The focus of the work of the Sustainable Policing Project was an assessment of the operational and financial implications of three options: enhanced collaboration between the existing eight police forces; the creation of three or four large regional forces; or the establishment of a single police service for the whole country.

20 Fyfe, 'A different and divergent trajectory?'

21 The reform team was initially led by the Association of Chief Police Officers in Scotland (ACPOS). Latterly, the police led team became known as the National Police Reform Team.

22 Loveday, Evidence submitted to the SIPR Review.

23 Fyfe, Terpstra and Tops *Centralizing Forces?*

24 'Scottish Police Force merger plan outlined', *BBC News*, 12 January 2011.

25 Fyfe, Terpstra and Tops, *Centralizing Forces*, p.126.

26 B. Loveday, 'Workforce modernisation in the police service' *International Journal of Police Science and Management*, 2008, 10, 136–44. There are ongoing debates about the impact of police force sizes, structures and mergers as police organisations attempt reductions in their budgets and deal with changes in patterns of criminality. See J. Mendel, N. R. Fyfe and G. den Heyer, 'Does police size matter? A review of the evidence regarding restructuring police organisations', *Police Practice and Research*, 2017, 8:1, 3–14.

As Scotland's largest police force prior to reform, it is therefore not surprising that former senior officers of Strathclyde Police comprise the largest constituent element of Police Scotland with its former Chief Constable assuming the same role for all Scotland and Neil Richardson as Deputy Chief Constable. However, at the time of the appointment of Sir Stephen House in September 2012, only the chair of the Scottish Police Authority was in place and all other members and officials of the Authority had still to be appointed. Although the circumstances were unique, it does raise concerns about the potential for political influence in the selection process. It seems that the reform process was largely controlled by the police, and by Strathclyde in particular, which has further contributed to two concerns as set out by Loveday:

> First the plans arising from the Sustainable Policing project appeared to demonstrate a traditional police objective which has been, where possible, to remove their service from effective local oversight and accountability. This has been a long term feature of police interpretations of effective policing. Based on a 'Professional Policing Model' it has, as its objective, a significant enhancement of police operational autonomy.[27]

These are important issues for consideration for the remainder of this chapter and will frame some of the key issues that are examined in relation to the leadership of Sir Stephen House as Chief Constable of Police Scotland.

Governance arrangements: centralism v localism

Policing in Scotland has 'always been a local service, locally delivered and locally accountable'.[28] Under the previous arrangements, set out in the Police (Scotland) Act 1967, local authorities exercised responsibilities for maintaining the eight regional forces, appointing and dismissing Chief and Assistant Chief Constables, employing civilian staff, scrutinizing the Chief Constable's annual report, and requiring additional reports deemed necessary for the maintenance of policing in that area. These functions were carried out within unitary or joint Local Police Authorities (LPAs). This is no longer the case. It is claimed that, one of the most radical changes brought about by the Reform Act was the abolition of LPAs.[29] The main form of statutory governance now operates at the national level via the unelected Scottish Police Authority (SPA).[30] This agency, as per section 5(1) of the Reform Act, 'must comply with any direction (general or specific) given

27 Loveday, Evidence submitted to the SIPR Review.

28 Scott, 'A *single police force* for Scotland: The legislative framework (1)'.

29 Scott, 'A single police force for Scotland: The legislative framework (2)'.

30 Such developments offer a significant contrast to those implemented in England and Wales where direct election has now assumed an ever greater significance in the governance of the police through Police and Crime Commissioners providing balance between the police and elected officials.

by the Scottish Ministers' (with the exception of specific operations) and its members are directly appointed by the Scottish Ministers'. The Authority's main functions are to maintain the Police Service, promote the policing principles, promote and support continuous improvement in the policing of Scotland, and to hold the Chief Constable to account, as set out in section 2 of the Reform Act. However, there are no statutory guidelines that dictate the new body must include elected members of local government. This in turn may give rise to the possibility of local issues not being raised or listened to at a national level.

The new system of police governance came under strain in June 2013 with a dispute over the powers given to the new Scottish Police Authority and the operational independence of the Chief Constable, a battle that the Chief Constable won. The dispute concerned who should have ultimate authority over police civilian staff. Justice Secretary Kenny MacAskill said Stephen House, Chief Constable of Police Scotland, had reached an accord with the Scottish Police Authority (SPA) on responsibility for human resources. The SPA agreed (or rather conceded) that the vast majority of personnel should fall within House's remit while it refocused its efforts on the 'not inconsiderable task' of holding 'a very powerful Chief Constable' to account.[31]

The local accountability that used to exist within policing has been removed, as local authorities no longer contribute in terms of finance. This can be seen as a direct means to undermine local accountability, at least at the local authority level. The new role of local authorities was set out in chapter 7 of the Reform Act (sections 44–7) and framed in terms of 'consultation', providing 'feedback' and 'scrutiny'. This was to be the 'new' mechanism of local governance. How local authorities engage in their 'new' role in scrutiny and engagement was a matter for them as the Reform Act prescribes neither structures nor processes and instead encourages flexibility and the need to be responsive to local conditions. What has transpired is the development of Local Scrutiny Committees (LSCs) in different forms across Scotland to fulfil this role.

A complex landscape: structure and local policing

Although constituting a single police service, the organization is structured around local geographic areas. There are three Police Regional Command Areas: North, West and East, each with an Assistant Chief Constable having oversight of their respective areas. Within these are thirteen Divisions, each with a Divisional Commander of the rank of Chief Superintendent.[32] While this structure for delivering local policing offers a degree of managerial efficiency allowing the

31 'Powerful' Chief Constable given charge of most police personnel', *STV News*, 21 June 2013.

32 This internal structure has been the subject of some change. In 2013, when Police Scotland was created there were fourteen Divisions across Scotland but in January 2016 this has reduced to thirteen with the merger of the Aberdeenshire and Moray Division with the Aberdeen City Division into the North East Division.

national command team to work with thirteen rather than 32 area commanders, from a local authority perspective, this configuration creates a more complex landscape.[33] While some Divisions are coterminous with Local Authority Areas such as the Greater Glasgow Police Division and Glasgow City Council[34] in most instances a Divisional Commander serves more than one local authority and so more than one LSC, each of which might be constituted in a different way. In areas without coterminous boundaries the most senior officer will be a Chief Inspector who is responsible to the Divisional Commander. Terpstra and Fyfe further contend, 'In those areas where local authority boundaries are coterminous with the police division, the local commander has a higher degree of authority to take decisions than in those local authorities which are not aligned'.[35] Thus creating a two tier system[36] which represents a more differentiated landscape across Scotland within which local authorities must interact with the police.

More importantly, the Reform Act did not state the consequences if a local commander were to ignore entirely the wishes of the local authority. It is also far from clear what would happen if a local authority were to refuse to endorse the plan of its local commander.[37] Loveday sees this also as the, perhaps deliberate, work of the Sustainable Project Team, led by Strathclyde Police senior personnel, in terms of ensuring the 'operational autonomy' of senior police officers with lack of coterminous boundaries in places and resultant lack of clear and potential effective local oversight due to the complexities that have prevailed.[38] Thus, providing perhaps the beginning of a model of Professionalized policing at a national level with a focus on centralism and control by the Police.

A further important point of note is that the Chief Constable, Sir Stephen House, had gone further than the legislative requirements and established a policing plan for each council ward in Scotland. There are 353 neighbourhood level policing plans (based on multi-member ward areas) across Scotland. It is argued that this will lead to greater cooperation between local communities to allow them to be better able to provide input into the strategies which play a significant role in how the criminal law of Scotland is administered on a daily basis.[39] This may also be seen as providing a 'softer' form of accountability for the police (or perhaps a tactical decision by the Chief Constable) whereby he was happier for his officers

33 J. Terpstra and N. R. Fyfe, 'Policy processes and police reform: Examining similarities and differences between Scotland and the Netherlands', *International Journal of Law, Crime and Justice*, 2014, 42:4, 366–83.

34 There are five local authority areas across Scotland with coterminous Local Authority Areas.

35 Terpstra and Fyfe, 'Policy processes and police reform'.

36 First tier: local authorities with Divisional Commander responsible and second tier: local authorities with a Chief Inspector who is then responsible to a Divisional Commander.

37 Scott, 'A single police force for Scotland: The legislative framework (2)'.

38 Loveday, Evidence submitted to the SIPR Review.

39 A. Henry, 'The development of community safety in Scotland: A different path?' in A. Crawford (ed.) *Crime Prevention Policies in Comparative Perspectives*, Cullompton: Willan, 2009, pp.86–110.

to be answerable to community participants than through formal accountability to democratically elected representatives. Terpstra and Fyfe contend:

> While this could be seen as adding a further degree of localism and sending a potent symbolic message regarding the local orientation of the national force, it also creates potential for tensions between the priorities set out . . . for each local authority area and those contained within ward level plans.[40]

Adding to this, in their submission to the Justice Sub-Committee on Policing on Local Policing and Police Reform in Scotland, initial findings from the qualitative research conducted by Anderson *et al* highlighted that:

> some of the most significant changes have been experienced by local authorities who, having lost their pre-reform statutory responsibilities for policing, now see themselves in a weaker position to influence what happens locally and are around local scrutiny and engagement, particularly in relation to the production of local police plans.[41]

Anderson *et al.* also found in site two of their research that the style of reporting was a cause for concern for both District Commanders and LSC members particularly due to the nature of the report being a 'formulaic Strathclyde region based style which consists of hard raw facts and no relating introductory narrative.'[42] This was similar to the issues presented by Addidle which found that a lack of understanding of police performance reporting among partner agencies meant that the accuracy of police statistical evidence was (had to be) taken at face value.[43] It could be suggested therefore that the legacy of 'a Strathclyde effect' although largely perceived as having a negative impact, remains prominent.

Policing principles: a new vision

Police reform in Scotland has also been used to articulate a new vision of the purpose of policing. This has been embraced quite explicitly by including a set of Policing Principles within the Police Reform Act which have echoes of the Principles of Policing put forward by Robert Peel in 1829.[44] Section 32 states that:

> a) the main purpose of policing is to improve the safety and well-being of persons, localities and communities in Scotland and b) that the Police Service,

40 Terpstra and Fyfe, 'Policy processes and police reform'.

41 S. Anderson, N. R. Fyfe and J. Terpstra, 'Local policing and police reform in Scotland: Some initial research findings', Evidence submitted to the Scottish Parliament's Policing Sub-Committee, 2014.

42 Ibid.

43 G. Addidle, Community planning, community safety and policing: A local case study of governance through partnership, unpublished PhD thesis, Plymouth University, 2016.

44 C. Emsley, *The English Police: A Political and Social History*, Harlow: Longman, 2014.

> working in collaboration with others where appropriate, should seek to achieve that main purpose by policing in a way which is i) accessible to, and engaged with, local communities [and] ii) promotes measures to prevent crime, harm and disorder.

These policing principles reflect the Scottish ambition to have a community orientated style of policing with a broad view on what policing should be, in close cooperation with partner agencies and communities, and with much emphasis on police visibility and proximity.[45] This view clearly contrasts with the vision of policing being articulated in England and Wales which is strongly focused on crime fighting.[46] This modernized vision of the purpose of policing can also be seen to give clearer guidance to police officers about how they should act and is a useful reminder of key attributes of their office. However, as Fyfe highlights, there is a certain irony that this focus on prevention and partnership in the policing principles have been overshadowed in the first few years of Police Scotland's existence by a strong emphasis on enforcement and 'crime fighting'.[47] It is the actions and leadership of the first Chief Constable, Sir Stephen House, that are significant in this respect.

A professional model of policing – professionalism vs partnership

The stated purpose of the Police Service of Scotland, as defined by section 32 of the Act is to 'improve the safety and wellbeing of people, places and communities in Scotland'. This rather ambiguous phrasing downplays the great discretionary power held by the Chief Constable and law enforcement agencies as a whole. It has been previously stated that 'what emerges from an encounter between a citizen and a law enforcement official often bore little relation to what have been expected from a simple reading of the formal requirements'.[48] The high degree of autonomy of the Chief Constable over the policing in Scotland has meant that he has not only been able to introduce a police structure but a style of local policing that differ in important respects from those envisaged by the legislation.[49] This creates the potential of a growing tension between the 'policing principles' set out in the Reform Act, with their emphasis on partnership, harm reduction and community well-being, and the Chief Constable's leadership and policing practices which appear to place greater emphasis on enforcement over engagement.

45 S. McKenzie and A. Henry, *Review of Community Policing in Scotland*, Scottish Government: Edinburgh, 2012.

46 See for discussion of comparison N. R. Fyfe and A. Henry, 'Negotiating divergent tides of police reform within the United Kingdom', *Journal of Police Studies*, 2012, 25:4, 171–90.

47 Fyfe, 'A different and divergent trajectory?' 493–506.

48 J. Kleinig, 'Handled with discretion: Ethical issues in police decision-making', Lanham: MD: Rowman & Littlefield, 1996.

49 Terpstra and Fyfe, 'Policy processes and police reform'.

In his Annual Policing plan (2013), the Chief Constable made clear that crimes of violence were to be given the highest priority, particularly rape and other forms of sexual violence. One consequence of this was that each local police division throughout Scotland had to establish a rape and sexual violence unit.[50] This in turn led to the displacement of other local priorities, particularly where these relate to property crime, with the result that some pre-reform local initiatives, such as specialist burglary teams, have been abandoned.[51] Such developments can be seen to be representative of Loveday's positioning that 'the new model central direction from the Chief Constable, on operational policing grounds can be expected to override any previously agreed local commitments'. The prioritizing of national police priorities[52] causing the displacement of other local priorities can be seen as demonstrating more of a professionalism approach to 'the enhancement of operational autonomy' over anything else.

Professionalism is also present when we consider that police priorities have been reinforced by a new national performance management system.[53] This system is based around a range of quantitative indicators and key performance targets for predominantly enforcement-led activities such as stopping motorists who are speeding or using mobile phones.[54] This approach to policing and target setting reflects the way that the Chief Constable of Police Scotland delivered policing in his previous role as Chief Constable of Strathclyde Police, dubbed in the media as 'Strathclydisation'.[55] After joining Strathclyde Police in 2007, House developed a reputation for bringing the Met's style of policing to the West of Scotland. What transpired was an apparent 'action orientation' and preference for enforcement and order maintenance. For instance, in 2010 House called for the widespread arming of officers with taser guns. This was piloted with some officers on the streets of Glasgow and Rutherglen but, following condemnation from Amnesty International and Scotland's Commissioner for Children and Young People, Tam Baillie, was never rolled out across the force.[56] Further contentious and high-profile practices

50 Such high priority setting in relation to rape and sexual violence are not only a Police Scotland development, similar moves were part of a national drive following the Stern Review on rape reporting in 2015. However, this may be indicative of House's leadership style whereby certain crimes are given the highest priority, this was the case in Strathclyde see R. Perry, 'Strathclyde Police report drop in violent crime', *The Scotsman*, 7 June 2012 where House was praised for his work in reducing violent crime. This style of leadership is being replicated and rolled out across Scotland.

51 Ibid.

52 The setting of national priorities is not just a development in Scotland as it is also occurring in England and Wales, however it is made more visible perhaps through having a national police service with one accountable Chief Constable.

53 Police Scotland corporate performance management system ScOMIS (Scottish Operational and Management Information System) introduced following the development of the national police service.

54 Terpstra and Fyfe, 'Policy processes and police reform'.

55 'Re-empowering local chiefs', *Herald Scotland*, 26 September 2016.

56 'Police Taser gun trial 'unlawful', *BBC News*, 17 May 2010.

included the increasing use of stop and search powers across Scotland which had intensified from the mid-2000s and by 2010 was nearly four times higher than in England and Wales. This was largely accounted for by Strathclyde Police who were responsible for over 80 per cent of stop and searches that were carried out in Scotland.[57]

Following the establishment of Police Scotland, the use of stop and search tactics had continued to grow as a result of specific national performance targets. It had been estimated that the national rate was 140 stops per 1,000 people in 2013/2014 compared with 86 per 1,000 in 2010.[58] This has meant substantial increases in stop and search activity in many areas of Scotland where previously this tactic had been used less often, with some communities seeing the number of stop and searches increase by over 400 per cent in the period April and December 2013.

Concerns about the long-term consequences of this large increase in the use of stop and search prompted the Scottish Police Authority to focus its first ever scrutiny review on Police Scotland's policy and practice in this area recommending more attention be concentrated on balancing police use of their stop and search powers with the rights of individuals.[59] What is more alarming is the lack of democratic accountability of the Chief Constable for these changes in practice. This builds upon the fear of Christine Graham MSP, the Convenor of the Justice Sub-Committee on Policing, when she noted the 'perception that policing practices are being standardized across the country at the detriment of local flexibility'.[60] Adding to this, Robert Crawford states 'Like good and evil, Glasgow and Edinburgh are often mentioned in the same breath but regarded as utterly distinct'.[61] It is therefore important for the Chief Constable to consider that measures employed in the former are not imposed arbitrarily on the latter, so that policing retains its longstanding local focus and character.

In his first annual Apex Scotland lecture (2013), the Chief Constable of Scotland provided his views on policing raising a number of points relating to partnership working, performance and engagement with partner agencies (among other things). First, he asserted:

> In the context of shrinking budgets, paradoxically, and I'm sure we have all heard this before; actually partnerships are more important, if they are effective partnerships. If they are duplication or triplication then they are not effective and they probably shouldn't endure. But if they are partnerships where,

57 K. Murray, 'Stop and search in Scotland: An evaluation', Scottish Centre for Crime and Justice Research, 2014 online at: www.sccjr.ac.uk/wpcontent/uploads/2014/01/Stop_and_Search_in_Scotland1.pdf

58 Scottish Police Authority, Scrutiny Review: Police Scotland's Stop and Search Policy and Practice, 2014. Online at: www.spa.police.uk/assets/126884/230479/scrutinytaskgroupreport

59 Fyfe, 'A different and divergent trajectory'?

60 Scottish Parliament, 'Local communities asked for their views on the impact of police reform', 4 November 2013, www.scottish.parliament.uk/newsandmediacentre/69425.asp

61 R. Crawford, *On Glasgow and Edinburgh*, Harvard University Press, 2013, p.1.

> coming together of partners actually produces more than the single agencies can on their own, then that is effective, it's efficient, and it should continue to be supported, and we will continue to support those.[62]

This statement suggests that the Chief Constable is not against partnership working but that it must not provide duplication of effort and needs to be effective, even more so, in light of the budgetary positioning. In support of these views, there is a growing body of literature concerned with getting partnerships to work and focusing on addressing such issues.[63]

House goes on to provide examples of good partnership working, highlighting:

> There is a long-standing partnership between the police and Glasgow City Council in what used to be called Glasgow Community Safety Services (GCSS) . . . It is about information sharing, intelligence sharing, joint patrolling, tasking, it's about doing complementary roles. So the officers will attend and deal with the initial anti-social behaviour, perhaps membership of a juvenile gang, but it is officers from the initiative themselves who then go back to the house, talk to the parents about their child's membership of a youth gang and what can be done to overcome it, maybe help them develop some parenting skills to place the proper parental control over child's behaviour. These are the sort of things that police officers are not trained to do, and shouldn't be trying to do, but which our partners do very well. The approach, we think, works.[64]

It seems that the Chief Constable supports this 'type' of partnership working, from his time at Strathclyde Police as he acknowledges that the Glasgow Community Safety Services did play their part 'very well'. However, this leaves the police to do what they do as their 'core' business, one of the reasons being that they are 'not trained to do' other roles and 'shouldn't be trying to do them'. This is further supported by the highly controversial revelation from the lecture that:

> Policing does not solve problems. There used to be a policing philosophy called 'problem solving policing', a few years back now. My view is policing doesn't solve problems. We are not a solutions agency, we are a restraint agency. We can control behaviour, we can rarely change it; sometimes, but it's rare.[65]

62 Apex Scotland, Collaborative working and shrinking budgets: Can we get better value by behaving smarter? Sir Stephen House Annual Lecture, 2013, p.6.

63 For instance, see J. Fleming and J. Wood, *Fighting Crime Together: The Challenges of Policing and Security Networks*, UNSW Press, 2006; A. Crawford and M. Cunningham, 'Working in partnership: The challenges of working across organizational boundaries, cultures and practices', in J. Fleming (ed.) *Police Leadership – Rising to the Top*, Oxford University Press, pp.71–94, 2015; and Scottish Government, *Shaping Up Report*, Edinburgh: Scottish Government, 2010.

64 Ibid., p.8.

65 Ibid., p.9.

In providing context to such a revelation, it is important to note that prior to House's reign in Strathclyde, the police service had a legacy of problem-solving policing dating back to 2002 with 'Joint Problem-Solving' in South Lanarkshire[66] and then Operation Phoenix in 2007.

Problem-solving policing was also presented as a core component of the Strathclyde Policing Model developed in 2009 and was strongly supported by the previous Chief Constable Sir William Rae.[67] Therefore, contrary to the negativity of the 'Strathclyde effect' in terms of increasing centralism and the erosion of local oversight and accountability for the development of Police Scotland, there is another supportive 'legacy' of partnership working and joint problem-solving. The development of Community Planning[68] (with early Strathclyde Police Chief Constable Sir William Rae on the Community Planning Task Force in 2001) has been prominent in recognition of the need to adopt an holistic approach to community safety which is problem oriented rather than organization led.[69]

It seems that Sir Stephen House's views may represent a rather short sighted or narrow view in terms of how to deal with problems that require longer-term and joint solutions. A further contention must be noted in that as a result of the breadth of the police mandate and the fact that the police are a '24 hour' service shaped in response to citizen demands, crime fighting and law enforcement are only a relatively small part of police work.[70] Therefore, such a professional 'operational focused' approach to policing may neglect the issue that a number of the problems the police deal with are in fact 'wicked issues' of community safety that demand the engagement of multiple actors and agencies. 'Wicked issues' are not capable of being managed by organizations acting independently as stated by Kooiman:

> No single actor, public or private, has the knowledge and information required to solve complex, dynamic, and diversified problems; no actor has an overview

66 The Problem-Solving Policing pilot, established across South Lanarkshire (Q Division) during 2002, provided an innovative way in which to tackle community concerns and problems using the Scanning, Analysis, Response and Assessment SARA problem-solving model (Tilley, 2005). The development of this approach was based on: more effective joint partnership working, the sharing of information, more co-ordinated service delivery and greater responsiveness to community concerns.

They used a variety of external and internal consultation measures including: a Citizen's Panel (which surveyed over 1700 residents across South Lanarkshire), Neighbourhood Management Surveys and employed FMR Research Ltd to carry out research throughout South Lanarkshire to inform Neighbourhood Management Plans. The Pilot was nominated for a Tilley Award in 2007.

67 Strathclyde Police, *Strathclyde Policing Model*, Glasgow: Headquarters, 2009.

68 The Local Government in Scotland Act 2003 introduced Community Planning as a statutory responsibility in Scotland. The main aims are described as 'making sure people and communities are genuinely engaged in the decisions made on public services which affect them; allied to a commitment from organizations to work together, not apart, in providing better public services'.

69 A. Crawford, *Crime Prevention and Community Safety – Politics, Policies and Practices*, Harlow: Pearson Education Limited, 1998.

70 E. Bittner, *Aspects of Police Work*, Boston, MA: Northeastern University Press, 1990.

sufficient to make the needed instruments effective; no single actor has sufficient action potential to dominate unilaterally.[71]

While recognizing the need for engagement and partnership as set out in the Reform Act, House seemed to prefer a position whereby partnerships involving the police have the potential to free-up capacity allowing organizations to specialize and focus on their 'core business'.[72] This seems paramount to him but may not deal with issues in the long-term, especially with requirements of 'wicked issues' of community safety.[73] As it stands, it seems partnership working and dealing with broader 'community safety' would remain secondary to the operational and professional drive for enforcement-led policing for the Chief Constable. It was this persistence of an enforcement approach alongside a series of scandals that brought House to receive serious criticism.

The years following the implementation of Police Scotland have further seen a number of high-profile issues emerging which have raised concerns about the efficacy of these new arrangements and the power of the Chief Constable. For example, the routine arming of police officers, the reduction of policing of saunas and the sex industry and the ending of police traffic wardens were understood in some circles, including the Justice Sub-Committee on Policing, to evidence a lack of local consultation and deliberation on matters which have a direct effect on local policing services and the communities they serve.[74] Additionally, concerns about local policing are also given particular emphasis in both the Scottish Labour Party's 2015 review of policing in Scotland[75] and in the SPA's wider review of the governance of Police Scotland.[76] A further crisis of confidence in Police Scotland, which included the death in custody of Sheku Bayoh in Kirkcaldy, as well as the scandal which saw M9 crash victim Lamara Bell spend three days in a car before police responded to a call reporting the accident, came to a head on 27 August 2015 when Sir Stephen House, bowed to intense pressure and announced he would resign early.[77] Walking away with a £500,000 tax-free lump sum and £100,000 per annum from his pension pot and with watchful eyes south of the

71 J. Kooiman, 'Societal governance: levels, models and orders of social-political interaction' in J. Pierre (ed.) *Debating Governance: Authority, Steering, and Democracy*, Oxford University Press, 2000, pp.133–64.

72 J. Fleming and J. Wood, *Fighting Crime Together: The Challenges of Policing and Security Networks*, Sydney: UNSW Press, 2006.

73 These have an impact on the police and what they do alongside that of public confidence and issues relating to fear of crime.

74 For examples, see 'Police Scotland needs to get its house in order', *Daily Record*, 20 January 2016; 'Edinburgh could axe lenient approach to sex saunas', *Edinburgh Evening News*, 7 October 2013; 'Police Scotland faces clampdown on stop and search' *The Guardian*, 3 September 2015.

75 G. Pearson, *The Pearson Review of Policing in Scotland*, Scottish Labour Party, www.scribd.com/doc/288716647/The-Pearson-Review-of-Policing-in-Scotland, 2015, accessed 1 March 2017.

76 A. Flanagan, *Scottish Police Authority Review of Governance in Policing*, Glasgow: SPA, 2016.

77 'Probe commissioned into Police Scotland "failings"', *Herald Scotland*, 20 August 2015.

border looking on to see how a centralized approach to policing in Scotland could work, it is fair to say that the Chief Constable did not cover himself in glory. Adding to this, prior to his resignation, House cancelled 33 appointments he had a duty to attend as Chief Constable with the Force stating in his last few months in office, he was 'working from home'.[78] Perhaps what House was really doing in this time was planning his next moves as it had been reported that he set up a consultancy business 'Sarantium Solutions'. It is not currently known what services the business will provide, but senior law enforcement officials often go on to provide security consulting work to private partners. A policing source explained that House would be 'well placed' to offer such services.[79] House did provide media commentary upon his resignation explaining:

> As the leader of a national organisation that provides a vital public service 24 hours every day of the year, there can never be a convenient time to move on, but after nearly 35 years as a police officer and the last nine as a Chief Constable in Scotland, I believe the time is right for me to take up a new challenge and thereby allow the process to recruit my successor to begin. Much has been achieved since the creation of Police Scotland and I firmly believe that Scotland is better served for it. Not only in managing the changes brought about by reform and substantial financial cuts, but most importantly in the public service we provide.[80]

These sentiments of achievement had not been shared by everyone – especially those in opposition to the Scottish National Party (SNP) government. For instance, Scottish Liberal Democrat leader Willie Rennie, said Sir Stephen's departure would not by itself solve the 'deep-rooted problems' in Police Scotland and that the force needed a 'fresh start'. He added: 'Ultimately the SNP government must accept responsibility for this chaos. They rammed through the centralisation of our police service despite warnings. They set up the toothless Scottish Police Authority. They appointed the Chief Constable.'[81] Scottish Conservative leader Ruth Davidson said Sir Stephen was 'bowing to the inevitable' by resigning, and said it was 'essential that his replacement is up to the task of tackling the problems that have afflicted the single force since its inception'.[82] Scottish Labour's justice spokesman, Graeme Pearson, who was formerly a senior police officer, said the process of reforming Police Scotland 'can begin now if the SNP government are willing to take responsibility for their mistakes'.[83]

78 J. Ferguson, 'Stephen House cancelled 33 appointments before he quit while still raking in £208,000 salary', *Daily Record*, 20 January 2016.

79 P. Hutcheon, 'Sir Stephen House started new company while still Police Scotland Chief Constable', *The Herald Scotland*, 31 January 2016.

80 'Sir Stephen House to quit as Police Scotland Chief Constable', *BBC News*, 27 August 2015.

81 S. Johnson, 'Sir Stephen House quits as Police Scotland chief', *The Telegraph*, 27 August 2015.

82 Ibid.

83 Ibid.

Perhaps in an attempt to move away from the potential lasting imprint of controversy left by House, it is not surprising that his replacement Phil Gormley who was appointed in late 2015 has made his core aim to engage with local government leaders and key partners to hear their views of policing in Scotland and to 'build a service the public can trust'.[84] However, the appointment of Gormley has been labelled 'worrying' by some for sharing a similar career history as former Chief Constable Stephen House. Gormley's background is in counter-terrorism and intelligence in London's Metropolitan Police and the National Crime Agency. His career in policing began in 1985. He served as the Metropolitan Police Service Commander, with responsibility for special branch and counter-terrorism. Gormley was awarded the Queen's Police medal in 2012, and spent two years as deputy director at the National Crime Agency from 2013–15.

MSP John Finnie, justice spokesperson for the Scottish Greens, questioned the appointment of someone with only a 'passing knowledge' of the issues at hand. Finnie's concerns were echoed by Dr Nick McKerrell, a lecturer in law at Glasgow Caledonian University:

> Given the perpetual crisis engulfing Police Scotland it is no surprise that an outside appointment has been made. It's a bit worrying that Gormley has a Met police background as their record on harassment and public order is not great. Stephen House came from the Met as well.[85]

Brian Docherty, chairman of the Scottish Police Federation stated:

> Mr Gormley's entire policing career has been forged in England. In the past we have expressed concerns that policing in Scotland has had its unique identity diminished due to a lack of understanding of our own challenges and issues. We have already met with Mr Gormley and are delighted that he has acknowledged his willingness to listen and learn.[86]

Andrew Flanagan, the Scottish Police Authority's (SPA) chair, claimed:

> From a strong field, I am confident we have found the best candidate to build on the progress that policing in Scotland has made, and to address the issues and challenges that the service faces . . . He has extensive experience in leading law enforcement organisations with diverse workforces, operating across both rural and urban environments, and with local, national and international reach. That mix fits well with the needs of a single service here in Scotland.[87]

84 'New Police Scotland Chief Constable sworn in and promises to "build service the public can trust"', *Daily Record*, 5 January 2016.

85 '"Worry" as another former Metropolitan chief appointed to head Police Scotland', *Common Space*, 3 December 2015.

86 'Former Crime Agency chief Phil Gormley appointed new head of Police Scotland', *BBC News*, 2 December 2015.

87 Ibid.

It may be a combination of both Gormley's experience and his 'openness' to adapt and learn how policing in Scotland can be developed that gave him the advantage over others. In criticisms of House, there were strong sentiments of not understanding what was needed in Scotland. This is also something that has been mentioned repeatedly by politicians, the media and those opposed to House's approach to policing. This sense of the 'Scottishness' of Scottish policing is strong particularly in the current context (with independence still a dominant issue) and perhaps is highlighted so as to represent a constant (and historically laden) comparison to policing in England and Wales. It may also be consistently referred to in making sure that whoever the Chief Constable is, they have the needs of the Scottish population at the forefront of their thoughts. However, this is a debatable point considering the Chief Constable now swears allegiance to the Scottish Parliament rather than the public they serve.

Conclusion

Police reform has brought about a fundamental shift in the relationship between local authorities and the police away from local governance towards what can be referred to as more of a 'scrutiny and engagement' function. Strategic, budgetary and policy decisions are now made more centrally, both within Police Scotland and the SPA and through the Scottish Government with little influence from local authorities. However, as the first few years have suggested, 'control' and 'power' over the police and policing has been a battleground for the Chief Constable and the SPA with the Scottish Government siding with House.

The stated aims established by the Scottish Government were to 'protect and improve local services, create more equal access to specialist support and national capacity' and to 'strengthen the connection between police services and communities'. It cannot be said that the Chief Constable or Police Scotland have fulfilled these aims equally. Following Loveday, there seems to be signs of a professionalized model of policing taking shape, with considerable emphasis on 'operational autonomy' and the removal of any meaningful local accountability by the Chief Constable and senior officers. The arrangements set out in the Reform Act (linking local authority areas directly with the national level) has been modified by the creation of additional layers (lack of coterminous boundaries and accountability to wards) that reduce the scope of most local authorities to engage directly with a single senior local commander. Adding to this, there has been a number of high-profile issues of concern alongside a preference for enforcement-led policing which positions partnership working as a secondary function. The Chief Constable has been shown to represent great influence over these developments and holds strong enforcement tendencies alongside the pursuit of efficiency and a focus on measurable targets. Perhaps this is a result of the need to perform in light of savings.

While the Reform Act is said to strengthen mechanisms of local governance it has been found that this has been implemented with a strong 'master of the police' orientation and control by House. Furthermore, there are parallels with the origins of the Glasgow Constabulary in 1800 as outlined by Smale in Chapter 3 which also tried to establish an innovative blueprint for policing, and promotion of a national police as provided for by List. Lastly, while the Reform Act sets out policing principles as a new normative vision which is broader than that of crime reduction and importantly aligned to key elements of partnership working and community safety, it seems the police focus has tended to be on short-term crime related activities. At the same time, the Reform Act is only a starting point. If it is to succeed in its stated aim of going beyond structural reorganization to a process of reform in Scottish policing, the issues highlighted in this chapter require continuing attention as the Police Service of Scotland develops.

The appointment of Gormley by the SPA can be seen to be a rather bold move in light of the controversies surrounding his predecessor providing the opportunity to make a fresh start and lay down the boundaries for the relationship (or a better one) between the SPA and the Chief Constable. Something it could be argued, they failed to achieve with the previous Chief Constable.

From the above, it seems that Police Scotland are now in a transition period of learning, adapting and consistently under the gaze of those around them. Under House, reform could be best described as 'House rules' or a merger of Strathclyde ideas but with Gormley now at the helm, he will probably be the most politically scrutinized Chief Constable in the history of Scottish Policing. It remains to be seen how he will fare in his new role but there is no question that however he puts his mark on Police Scotland it will have significant consequences for both how policing across Scotland will be developed, and also how those in England and Wales judge the success of police reform at a national level. Clearly, House's leadership of Police Scotland did not make a sufficiently strong case to become the blueprint for an 'inevitable model' for England and Wales. The question now remains, can Gormley make this case?

14 Chief Constables after PACE 1985–2017

The decline of a professional elite

Timothy Brain

The Police and Criminal Evidence Act 1984 was a watershed for the police service in England and Wales in general and for Chief Constables in particular. It coincided with the miners' strike, which represented the pinnacle of professional independence for Chief Constables and political alignment. It also coincided with the service of some of the most professionally dominant characters ever to hold the office of Chief Constable. With hindsight, however, this was a passing moment in police history. Thereafter the organizational and professional independence of Chief Constable was eroded, the result of political intent, changing management doctrines, and the changing culture of the workplace. Landmarks on the journey of that decline include the doctrine of New Public Management, the Police and Magistrates' Courts Act, Fixed-Term Appointments and finally, and most significantly, the Police Reform and Social Responsibility Act 2011. The result has been 'the decline of a professional elite'.

Introduction

On 28 March 1985, some six months after the Police and Criminal Evidence Act 1984 had received its Royal assent, Kenneth Oxford, CBE, (Merseyside, 1976–89) attended a special meeting of the Merseyside Police Authority; special because it was called specifically to seek from him an explanation as to why he had failed to attend a scheduled meeting of the Authority the previous week. He informed them that he had been asked to attend a conference in America by the Home Secretary, Leon Brittan. The majority Labour councillors called upon him to retire. He refused. They had been at loggerheads with Oxford and his abrasive style for some time over issues such as the death in custody of Jimmy Kelly, a local resident; the policing of the ethnically diverse inner city area of Toxteth; his robust handling of the 1981 riots and his supply of Merseyside officers to support other forces in the Miners' Strike (March 1984–March 1985). His absence in March was the final straw. A delegation took its case to Brittan, who listened to them for 90 minutes and then declined their request. That was the end of the matter. Oxford retired in 1989, picking up a knighthood along the way.[1]

1 'Police chief dictated', *The Times*, 14 July 1992 and D. Hobbs, 'Obituary: Sir Kenneth Oxford', *Independent*, 26 November 1998.

Oxford was not the only Chief Officer to face difficulties with Labour-dominated police authorities in the late 1980s. Several faced calls for dismissal or censure, notably James Anderton (Greater Manchester, 1976–91), but only one, Alf Parrish (Derbyshire, 1981–5), was effectively forced out by left-wing elements in the police authority, ostensibly over the unauthorized redecoration of his office but probably in reality over his deployments in the Miners' Strike. Even then, the authority proved unable to legally dismiss Parrish; the Home Secretary, Douglas Hurd, broke the deadlock after seventeen months using his Police Act 1964 powers to retire the Chief Constable in the interests of 'efficiency'.

Almost 30 years later, in May 2013, the Gwent Police and Crime Commissioner (PCC), Ian Johnston, told his Chief Constable, Carmel Napier (Gwent, 2011–13), that he intended to commence dismissal proceedings against her using new powers granted by the Police Reform and Social Responsibility Act 2011 (PRSA). She concluded that she could not win and instantly retired.[2] The difference in the fates of Oxford and Napier could not have been greater. Oxford stood firm in the face of considerable pressure and survived; Napier went without resistance. What had happened to bring about this change in the balance of power? The answer is to be found not simply in differences of character, but in the actions of Chief Constables and the reactions to them of political parties from both left and right in the period under scrutiny in this chapter.

This period, 1985–2016, is a remarkable one for police history. The police had in that time to cope with immense social and political change, a series of extreme critical incidents, and internal and external pressure to initiate and absorb comprehensive organizational change. Approximately 260 men and women held the post of Chief Constable or London equivalent, commanding 43 forces of variable size and nature. The job was difficult, the organizations they commanded large, complex, geographically disparate and subject to changing local and national political policies. Notwithstanding the absence of strict empirical data, the assessment must be that most, not all, discharged their duties diligently, although not always successfully. Products of central selection (Extended Interview) and training (the Senior, latterly Strategic Command Course), all were locally appointed by a police authority or, since 2012, a PCC.[3] To be shortlisted for selection required approval from the Home Secretary, which meant in practice approval by one of the regional HM Inspectors of Constabulary (from 2002 the central Police Leadership Development Board). For much of the period Chief Constables were expected to play a part in the national governance of the service through participation in the Association of Chief Police Officers (ACPO). Chairmanship of one of the major committees brought influence and esteem, possibly leading to the presidency of the association. For some, participation in ACPO became the defining aspect of their career, arguably to the detriment of the leadership of their

2 'Carmel Napier "bullied" into retiring as Gwent police chief', *BBC News South East Wales*, 2 July 2013.

3 The 'police authority' for the Metropolitan Police was the Home Secretary until 2000.

forces. Only towards the end of the period with the creation of such statutory national bodies as the National Policing Improvement Agency (NPIA) and the College of Policing (CoP) did this role significantly diminish. For much of the period Her Majesty's Inspectors of Constabulary (HMIC) were also drawn from the Chief Constable cadre, this changing only towards the very end.

These years can be further divided into four sub-periods. The first, 1985 to 1990, is one of dominating personalities, who in the face of what they saw as a destabilizing challenge from the political left were prepared to assert their organizational independence. The second, 1990 to 2001, is one with an increasing emphasis on management techniques in response to central governments impatient for 'police reform'. The third, 2001 to 2010, one in which Chief Constables collectively sought to impose greater uniformity on the service. Finally, 2010 to 2016, Conservative-led governments consciously sought to impose constitutional change, which increased local political influence at the expense of the status and independence of Chief Constables.

1985–90: PACE and personalities

The Police and Criminal Evidence Act 1984 (PACE) was a watershed in the history of policing introducing new statutory based rules of evidence. The Chief Constables' first task was to implement extensive training and procedural programmes, which they did successfully. Less easy to achieve was the cultural change necessary to adjust attitudes and practices. While PACE was largely of organizational significance, section 106, requiring police authorities to make arrangements for 'obtaining the views' of people in their area about policing and for securing their cooperation, had direct implications for Chief Officers. Some forces, after the 1981 riots, had informally established local liaison committees, but now everywhere had to have some mechanism. Crucially, they were run by the authorities, not the police. In theory, Chief Constables were not obliged to take notice of these committees but in practice there was a moral imperative to act. A small chink in the operational autonomy of Chiefs had opened up.

Implementation of PACE was delayed for a year because of the Miners' Strike which not only represented a significant operational and political issue but also represented the pinnacle of Chief Constable autonomy. The forces directly affected were those with mining districts but the remainder were required to provide mutual aid. Labour-dominated police authorities chafed at not only being unable to directly influence their Chiefs' operational deployments to enforce the anti-secondary picketing sections of the Employment Act 1980, but they also resented having to accept and pay for mutual aid, sought by their Chiefs without the need to seek their prior permission. This compounded what many Chief Constables saw as a pre-existing challenge from the political left to control them. The Home Office backed the Chiefs in a straight challenge over mutual aid, but were unable to help Parrish over the issue of his redecorated office. In the constitutional confrontation between Chief Officers and Police Authorities over who controls the police it was the Chiefs (who in the short term at least) won, but not all were comfortable with the strain this placed on community relations. Colin Sampson (West Yorkshire, 1983–9) publicly expressed his concern about the long-term effects on police-community relations, while many others held a similar view in private.[4] In contrast, Anderton, with typical individual assertiveness, said that few other countries would be prepared to tolerate 'so patiently a politically-motivated industrial mafia at work causing friction between the police and the people'.[5]

It would be wrong, however, to characterize the relationships between all Chief Constables and Police Authorities at this time as confrontational; most Chiefs possessed a positive, if slightly condescending attitude ('my police authority' being a not atypical description).[6] Nor where there was antagonism was this simply a clash of egos. Labour had, to varying degrees, a principled belief that the police should be under direct democratic control, while most Chiefs believed this would compromise operational independence, seeking instead to maintain the arms-length arrangements established in the Police Act 1964. Some Chiefs, probably like Oxford, would have been aware that behind a façade of moderate councillors like the chair of his Merseyside police authority, Margaret Simey, lurked the Marxist entryism of the Militant tendency.

The Miners' Strike was not the only operational test for Chief Constables during this period. This was possibly the period of greatest social tension that the country had seen since before the First World War, with inner city riots occurring in several locations but most severely in Brixton, Handsworth and Tottenham, the latter resulting in the death of a police officer, PC Keith Blakelock. There was industrial disorder in 1986 at the Wapping print plant and anti-'Poll Tax' riots in 1990. At the same time the country continued to face the threat of extreme Irish republican terrorism, the blowing-up of a jet liner over Lockerbie by Middle Eastern terrorists, continued football hooliganism, the breakdown of order in several prisons, a firearms massacre in Hungerford, and in 1989 the Hillsborough tragedy. It was during this time that a series of miscarriages of justice from an earlier period began to unravel resulting in the quashing of convictions in several high-profile cases such as the 'Birmingham Six'. It was hardly surprising, therefore, that there arose genuine questions of confidence in, and legitimacy of, the police mandate to police by consent. The period was also one of seemingly inexorably rising crime that the police seemed powerless to stop while simultaneously the Home Office was adopting a more consciously cost-conscious approach to funding.[7]

The times required strong leadership and received it from some of the most high-profile, resolute and outspoken leaders that the service has ever produced. Chiefs like Anderton, Oxford, the intellectual Sir Kenneth Newman (Royal Ulster,

4 See R. Reiner, *Chief Constables: Bobbies, Bosses, or Bureaucrats*, Oxford University Press, 1991, pp.182–92.

5 *Police Review*, 6 July 1984, p.1303.

6 Reiner, *Chief Constables*, pp.249–300.

7 See Home Office Circular No. 114/1983, 'Manpower, effectiveness and efficiency in the police service', November 1983, passim, and T. Brain, *A History of Policing in England and Wales from 1974: A Turbulent Journey*, Oxford University Press, 2010, pp.158–62.

1976–9, Metropolitan, 1982–7) and the charismatic Geoffrey Dear (West Midlands, 1985–90), were all prepared at various times to defend and champion their forces and the service. The eminent criminologist Robert Reiner compiled a remarkable snapshot of the 43 contemporary Chief Constables, revealing a body of men, largely from working-class backgrounds, who had risen to the top by sheer endeavour. He divided them into four categories: 'Barons, Bobbies, Bosses, and Bureaucrats', with the latter category beginning to become the dominant norm. He did not name names, but to speculate perhaps Anderton was a 'Baron', Oxford a 'Boss', Sir Philip Knights (Sheffield and Rotherham, 1972–4, South Yorkshire, 1974–5, and West Midlands, 1975–85) a 'Bureaucrat' and Charles MacLachlan (Nottinghamshire, 1976–87) a 'Bobby'. Given the scale of their personal achievement and the breadth of their responsibilities Reiner reasonably described them as 'a Criminal Justice Elite'.[8] They were certainly experienced with the average length of service in the rank being five years and seven possessing ten years in the rank by 1990.[9] The paternalistic Sir Stanley Bailey (Northumbria, 1976–91), a strong advocate of crime prevention and community policing, and Anderton both served fifteen years in their respective forces.

This elite may have emerged from the decade with its organizational autonomy intact but there were wider doubts about the degree to which the police had contributed to social tensions by failing to sufficiently adapt to Britain's changing social and ethnic structure, had become too paramilitary in its public order techniques, and had become over identified with the Conservative government. On the other hand, Chiefs had maintained the effectiveness of their forces and developed riot-control techniques that, in retrospect, broadly struck the balance between effectiveness and the principle of policing by consent. They had also begun to develop new management techniques. Maurice Buck in Northamptonshire (1981–6) and Newman at the Metropolitan flattened managerial hierarchies, devolving budgets and other responsibilities to semi-autonomous Basic Command Units (BCUs), but wider take-up was slow and it required pressure from the Audit Commission and HMIC to complete the process by the mid-1990s. Local initiative also saw lay custody visitor schemes, crime prevention partnerships with local authorities and local team policing models, while John Duke (Hampshire, 1979–88) and John Hoddinott (Hampshire, 1988–99) introduced new communication systems and technologies. Hoddinott also experimented in more flexible shift systems.

It was not enough. It was the seemingly inexorable rise in crime, a series of 'miscarriages of justice', the systematic malpractice of the West Midlands Serious Crime Squad (disbanded by Dear in 1989) and the consequences of the Hillsborough disaster (1989) that suggested to a powerful combination of the Home Office, the Home Affairs Committee (HAC) and the prime minister, Margaret

8 Reiner, *Chief Constables*, p.39.

9 Calculated from the force and service profiles presented in M. Stallion and D. Wall, *The British Police: Forces and Chief Officers 1829–2012*, Hook: Police Historical Society, 2011, passim.

Thatcher, a wider failure of leadership. Mrs Thatcher, favoured reintroducing a direct officer entry scheme, but recalcitrance by Home Secretary Douglas Hurd and her ejection from office in 1990 scuppered the immediate prospect.[10] Chiefs did, however, respond, at Hurd's prompting, by reforming ACPO, tightening collective responsibility, increasing the professionalization of the central office, developing national policies, and by commissioning a service-wide review of contemporary policing, the *Operational Policing Review* (1990). A principal product of the latter was the ACPO 'Quality of Service Initiative', which sought to reconcile central government's increasing demand for value for money with expectations of local communities. The 'Plus Programme', introduced by Newman's successor at the Metropolitan, Peter Imbert (Thames Valley, 1979–85, Metropolitan, 1987–93), was its precursor.

1991–2000: New Public Management

Given time these initiatives might have worked but instead they were subsumed by a fundamental change of government strategy. John Major's premiership (1990–97) produced a step-change in public service management. His 'Citizen's Charter' was intended to simultaneously improve the efficiency of public services and their cost-effectiveness. Regulators would ensure value for money and high performance. Targets would be set and monitored; league tables would enable the public, regulators and the government to compare the service of the providers. The umbrella term was 'New Public Management'. The government was not convinced that the service could deliver. In 1991 Treasury minister David Mellor observed that despite having 'thrown money' at the police 'we have the highest level of crime in our history', a view apparently shared by the Prime Minister.[11] The service consequently needed to adapt quickly to the new realities but it was not necessarily equipped to do so. Writing in the early 2000s, Bramshill academic Peter Villiers detected what he considered to be two counterproductive characteristics of contemporary police leadership, the inability to delegate and an 'unwillingness to consider alternatives', itself an adverse by-product of the prevalent task-driven 'can do' attitude, which many would consider one of the most positive of police characteristics at any rank.[12]

Adapting to the new realities would prove painful for many but the most prescient of Chief Constables did not allow the declining political confidence to accumulate. The service, led by John Hoddinott and the ACPO Crime Committee pressed for a 'National Crime Squad' despite reservations at the top of the Home Office. A National Criminal Intelligence Service was introduced in 1992, but it

10 D. Hurd, *Memoirs*, London: Abacus, 1980, p.380.

11 Quoted in K. Baker, *The Turbulent Years: My Life in Politics*, London: Faber and Faber, 1993, p.451.

12 R. Adlam and P. Villiers, *Police Leadership in the Twenty-first Century*, Hook: Waterside Press, 2003, p.26.

was not until 1998 that a National Crime Squad was created. Hoddinott also wrested initiative from the Home Office over the delay in introducing a national Automated Fingerprint Recognition system, establishing a consortium which by-passed the Home Office entirely. Individual Chiefs took the lead in introducing enhanced protective equipment and uniform, with David Shattock (Dyfed-Powys, 1986–9, and Avon and Somerset, 1989–98) and Ronald Hadfield (Nottinghamshire, 1987–90, and West Midlands, 1990–6) leading, respectively, the development of extendable batons and CS spray. Collectively, Chief Constables were also making it clear that they wanted reform of police regulations to enable them to flexibly manage their workforce and to dismiss ineffective and inefficient officers.[13]

Critical operational issues continued to require resolute leadership. Riots continued to occur sporadically, but the techniques, training and experience of the previous decade ensured relative containment. Similarly, the post-Hillsborough experience, together with the move to all-seater stadiums, ensured that the Euro 1996 football cup matches held in England passed off peacefully. IRA resurgence caused periodic death, injury and chaos (notably in Warrington, London Docklands and Manchester), but permanently manned checkpoints around the City of London, occasional armed patrols on English city streets, and several successful investigations contributed to an operational stalemate sufficient for a peace process to take effect and hold. Recorded crime, however, initially continued to increase which represented a poor return for a government that had invested political and financial capital in the police. In the mid-1990s crime began a long-term decline, but as this was apparent only in retrospect, contemporary Chief Constables neither claimed nor were given the credit for it.[14] Major and his home secretaries, Kenneth Clarke (1992–3) and Michael Howard (1993–7), were not content to leave reform to the Chief Constables and therefore forced the pace through two major reports, the Sheehy Report and the Police Reform White Paper (both 1993).[15]

Sheehy sought to sweep away police regulations, introduce pay incentives, thin out the rank structure, and eliminate extended tenure, replacing it with short-term appointments. It produced an unprecedented and unforeseen furore, with the Police Federation vociferously denouncing it. Chiefs realized that Sheehy was going too far too quickly, and several otherwise managerially progressive Chief Constables, including Richard Wells (South Yorkshire, 1990–8), and Paul Condon (Kent, 1989–93 and Metropolitan, 1993–2000), identified themselves with the workforce, while others, like Charles Pollard (Thames Valley, 1991–2002) indicated a selective rather than a comprehensive acceptance. Michael Howard compromised, withdrawing some of the more contentious recommendations and

13 'Anderton's changes puts him at odds with officers', *The Times*, 22 November 1990 and 'Police discipline', *The Times*, 17 December 1990.

14 Office for National Statistics, Crime in England and Wales: year ending Mar 2016, <www.ons.gov.uk/peoplepopulationandcommunity/crimeandjustice/bulletins/crimeinenglandandwales/yearendingmar2016 main-points>.

15 Brain, *A History*, pp.221–8.

incrementally introducing others, but the combined power of the Chiefs and the workforce to defeat a government is likely to have had a long-term adverse consequence, as these events were witnessed at close hand by a member of the Conservative research department, future prime minister David Cameron. Chiefs did not escape without any consequence, however. All were placed on Fixed-Term Appointments (FTAs) of between seven and ten years, generous by private sector standards, but meaning Chiefs would in future be reliant on the good will of their police authorities to ensure their careers were extended.

Chiefs also had to deal with reconstituted police authorities. These became smaller and, with the introduction of independent members, more business-like. This meant focusing on local targets and performance indicators, which, with the support of the Audit Commission and HMIC, proliferated. This was the point at which Chief Constables were required to become truly modern strategic managers, managing devolved budgets, tracking and reporting on performance, developing business plans, and managing forces which themselves had become more devolved. Bramshill supported the transition to some degree, at the same time promoting a more collegiate style of management, arguably at the expense of grip and drive. With little central guidance there was much trial and error with Chiefs and their staff having to learn on the job. Smart Chiefs, like Condon, Edward Crew (Northamptonshire, 1993–6, and West Midlands, 1996–2002), and John Stevens (Northumbria, 1991–6, and Metropolitan, 2000–5) soon adapted, others, slower to adapt, faced more difficult times. There was much local initiative. Pollard promoted 'restorative justice' schemes in Thames Valley, David Philips (1993–2003) 'intelligence-led policing' in Kent, Barry Shaw (1993–2003) experiments in so-called 'zero tolerance' policing in Cleveland, while Brian Hayes (1982–91) and David Williams (1991–7) in Surrey developed early versions of what would become known as 'neighbourhood policing'.[16] The problem was that these were not being developed as a cohesive 'narrative'; indeed, they were often seen as competing techniques. Some Chief Constables remained unconvinced by any of them, particularly the controversial 'zero tolerance', which ran into operational difficulties and never achieved general traction.

The Labour government under Tony Blair, elected in 1997, would prove intolerant of such diversity. Jack Straw, his first Home Secretary, reinforced the Conservative's police reform agenda, but the new government also had its own ideas, summed up in the sound-bite, 'Tough on crime, tough on the causes of crime'. In summary, on the one hand the resources of the police and local government would be harnessed to reduce crime and disorder in statutory local partnerships, while on the other prosecutions and convictions were to increase, either to send more offenders to prison or to one of the numerous diversionary schemes that were being developed. In theory, the crime reduction partnerships

16 For definition of these and other terms see T. Newburn and P. Neyroud, *Dictionary of Policing*, Cullompton: Willan, 2008, passim.

should have reduced the power and influence of Chief Constables, subsumed among other local government executives, but in practice, because of a combination of lack of expertise, competing priorities and some disinterest on the part of local government officials, Chief Constables dominated the local crime reduction scene. Local criminal justice performance was a different matter, with intense interest from the Home and Lord Chancellor's offices in police performance in detecting crime and securing convictions, while the 'Best Value' and 'Crime Fighting Fund' processes signalled a more centrally didactic approach to the use of financial and human resources. For the main, however, in its first term the Labour government was content to work with the police service, a measure of the distance that Blair had brought his party back to the centre ground of British politics from its extremism of the 1980s. Chiefs reciprocated, as was their democratic duty, constructively working with the new political reality.

The single most important issue facing the leadership of the service was that of gender and race equality. In 1990 ethnic minority officers constituted about 1 per cent of police strength, while female officers constituted 11 per cent.[17] There were no ethnic minority officers at Chief officer rank, and just one woman, Alison Halford, a Merseyside ACC (see also Silvestri, Chapter 11). Police leadership was unprepared for the challenges it received from within and without because it had largely ignored the systemic implications of the various pieces of legislation including the Sex Discrimination Act 1975. These required employers to treat their employees equally regardless of race or gender but because officers were not employees and were instead crown office holders it was erroneously assumed the Act did not apply to them. In two high-profile cases Alison Halford, and PC Surinder Singh, Nottinghamshire, took their Chief Constables to an industrial tribunal seeking redress arguing that their careers being blighted by unfair discrimination. Singh won his case but Halford settled out of court and left the service.[18] Both cases were sufficient to shake Chief Constables into a rapid review of their promotion and progression policies. It was a necessary readjustment but it also had the effect of reducing what had until recently been seen as the ultimate right of Chief Constables to promote and deploy whomsoever they pleased. Progress was slow, with female representation increasing to 17 per cent and ethnic minority to 2.3 per cent in 2000.[19] Pauline Clare (Lancashire, 1995–2002) became the first female Chief Constable in 1995, but it was not until 2004 that the first ethnic minority Chief Constable, Michael Fuller (Kent, 2004–10), was appointed.

The single most catastrophic operational failure in these years was the flawed investigation by the Metropolitan Police into the murder of Stephen Lawrence in 1993. It took a prolonged political and media campaign, and a public inquiry led by Sir William Macpherson, to expose the failings. The inquiry went further,

17 G. Allen, Police Service Strength England and Wales 31 March 1977 to 30 September 2000, Research Paper 01/28, London: House of Commons Library, 2001, p.8.

18 'PC's damages', *The Times*, 29 January 1991 and *Police Review*, 24 July 1992, p.1348.

19 Allen, Police Service Strength.

concluding that the whole service itself was institutionally racist. Straw demanded a sweeping response, with new targets, policies, procedures and training programmes. Morale became a serious problem, as most officers and staff did not consider themselves racist and had not engaged in any overt racist acts. The leadership had to reconcile this reaction with the need to respond positively to Macpherson's conclusions and Straw's mandate. Condon accepted the criticism but the most conspicuous Chief Constable who accepted collective blame and the concomitant need to change was Ian Blair (Surrey, 1998–2000, and Metropolitan, 2005–8). The Equalities and Human Rights Commission officially declared that the police were no longer institutionally racist in 2009, although the issue of stop and search would remain a source of criticism while the ethnic profile of the service had not reached even close parity with that of the general population by 2016.

2001–10: New Labour and uniformity

There was an abrupt change of pace and style once Labour had secured its second term in 2001. Labour would invest heavily in the public services, including the police, but in return it would precisely control the way those resources were to be used and would closely measure results. The new Home Secretary, David Blunkett, gave this a personal edge. A determined centralist, he would prove to be impatient with his own civil servants, critical of the constitutional niceties of the 'Tripartite' structure and what he saw as the institutional inertia and parochialism of the Chief Constables. His response was a significant increase in central powers and controls which included a national policing plan with objectives and standards all monitored and enforced by a 'Police Standards Unit' (PSU), together with intensified activity by HMIC and the Audit Commission scrutinizing force and even BCU performance, with powers to intervene and make directions if necessary. A Senior Appointments Panel would guide aspirant Chief Constables to what were considered the most appropriate jobs for them. Above all, there were enhanced powers for the Home Secretary to suspend and dismiss Chief Constables. Blunkett would prove impatient of anyone who suggested that there might be alternatives to his priorities.[20]

Several Chiefs and their forces, notably Stephen Pilkington (Avon and Somerset, 1998–2005), Stephen Green (Nottinghamshire, 2000–8) and Michael Todd (Greater Manchester, 2002–8) found themselves subject to intense PSU scrutiny. Other Chiefs received the personal attention of the Home Secretary for different reasons. Blunkett threatened to suspend Paul Whitehouse (Sussex, 1993–2001) over his controversial promotion of two officers involved in the shooting of an unarmed but considered dangerous suspect, James Ashley, prompting Whitehouse's precipitous retirement. He did suspend David Westwood (Humberside, 1999–2005) for data

20 For Blunkett's own account of his term as Home Secretary see D. Blunkett, *The Blunkett Tapes: My Life in the Bear Pit*, London: Bloomsbury, 2006, pp.267–738.

protection failings in his force that contributed to the chain of events that led to the murder of Holly Wells and Jessica Chapman, in Soham in 2002 by Ian Huntley, but Westwood toughed it out, briefly returning to duty before retiring. He doubted ACPO's reassurances at the time of the terrorist attack on the World Trade Centre on 11 September 2001 and, at the Prime Minister's prompting, used the Cabinet Office's emergency structure ('COBR') to drive through a 'Street Crime Initiative' in response to a rise in street robberies. He even suggested that the Commissioner, Stevens, would have to go if he did not deliver results, although he later indicated this was a misunderstanding.[21] It certainly all amounted to action but the practical results were uncertain. Blunkett departed after a personal scandal in 2004 but centralism continued, albeit with a change of personal style, under his successor Charles Clarke.

Blunkett might have been impatient with ACPO but the organization in fact proved a willing partner in conformity and bureaucracy, promoting the National Crime Recording Standard, the National Intelligence Model and the Neighbourhood Policing Programme, and in effect thereby creating a national police service without the trouble of legislating for one. ACPO itself became more professional, with a president serving a three, later four-year term, and new rules which required even greater conformity with centrally agreed policies, a tendency reinforced by the creation of the NPIA in 2007. It was difficult to argue against conformity but it inhibited local innovation and led to a miasma of intense inspection activity, the benefits of which were, at best, unclear.

Nonetheless the ACPO leadership and the Home Office produced its greatest examples of collusion over policing terrorism and the merger of police forces. There was good reason behind both initiatives, but they were to prove a step too far for centralism. In the autumn of 2005 Britain continued to face a severe Islamist terrorist threat after the atrocities of the previous July, and between the ACPO leadership and the Home Office the view hardened that the period terrorist suspects could be detained should be extended from 14 to 90 days. The evidence for this was not only weak but also politically controversial, especially with Labour MPs. Chief Constables were asked to brief their local Labour MPs to ensure they understood the rationale behind the proposal. It looked like political collusion and a few Chief Constables refused to take part.[22] The tactic became public, producing political backlashes against ACPO, the government and the proposal. There was more success for the Home Office and ACPO in creating regional counter-terrorist units, perhaps a necessary development in the face of an extreme terrorist threat but one which distanced the units from the direction and control of individual Chief Constables and weakened local accountability.

Conformity though had its limits. In 2005 the ACPO leadership responded positively to an HMIC report, *Closing the Gap*, which recommended merging the

21 Brain, *A History*, p.323.

22 I was one.

41 provincial forces to form so-called strategic forces, supposedly more able to address the problems of major crime.[23] In reality *Closing the Gap* possessed significant flaws, but plans were drawn up to create sixteen to eighteen super forces. It received the unequivocal backing of the Home Secretary, Charles Clarke. A few Chief Constables, principally Timothy Brain (Gloucestershire, 2001–10), Paul West (West Mercia, 2003–11) and Michael Fuller, opposed the plans, primarily on the grounds of cost but also on grounds of effectiveness. This was a career-risking move, given the Home Secretary's position. It was, however, illustrative of the discretion available to Chief Constables. Few other public servants would have been able to exercise such freedom of speech. Opposition among police authorities hardened and the scheme collapsed in the early summer of 2006 after Clarke left office over a failure of immigration policy within his department; his successor, John Reid, quickly realized that the plan was not politically or financially sustainable. The rift within ACPO was quickly healed but the sum total of this centralizing activity was to suggest powerfully to the Conservative opposition that, despite the standalone position of a few, collectively police Chiefs had become too closely identified with the Labour government.[24]

This was a time of increasing personal accountability for their actions by individual Chief Constables. In 2003 Condon and Stevens stood trial for health and safety offences, personally being held accountable for specific incidents from which they were operationally very remote. The jury took a pragmatic view and both were acquitted, initiating a change in the law. In 2006 Maria Wallis (Devon and Cornwall, 2002–6) retired early after an Independent Police Complaints Commission (IPCC) investigation into her handling of an internal restructuring. In 2007 Della Cannings (North Yorkshire, 2002–7) stood down after being criticized for spending £24,000 on an en-suite shower for her office. Terry Grange (Dyfed-Powys, 2000–7) stood down after having an affair and irregularities in his expenses claims surfaced, insufficient to merit misconduct proceedings but 'damaging' to the public image of the police service. In 2008 Michael Todd was found dead in Snowdonia; it later emerged that he had had several affairs.[25] It was understandable that Labour Home Secretaries began to look outside their Chief Officer cadre for advice from Bill Bratton, former New York Police Commissioner, Sir Ronnie Flanagan, Chief HMI and a former RUC Chief Constable, and to social welfare specialist, Louise Casey. The sum of advice was, however, conflicting, with Casey favouring more conformity, Flanagan less.

The clearest sign that the political climate might be changing occurred in 2008 with the sudden resignation of Sir Ian Blair, Metropolitan Commissioner since 2005, and conspicuously identified with the Labour policing agenda. He had been

23 Her Majesty's Inspector of Constabulary, Closing the Gap: A Review of the 'Fitness for Purpose' of the Current Structure of Policing in England and Wales, <www.justiceinspectorates.gov.uk/hmic/media/closing-the-gap-20050911.pdf>, passim.

24 Brain, *A History*, pp.350–1 and 364–73.

25 Brain, *A History*, pp.330–2, and 392.

appointed under the mayoralty of Labour's Ken Livingstone, but by 2008 a Conservative, Boris Johnson, had been elected. Blair had achieved much in his career, notably the systematic introduction of Neighbourhood Policing in the Metropolitan, but he never escaped suspicion that he was too close to the Labour government.[26] His reputation for competence suffered a severe setback over his handling of the shooting of an innocent man, Jean Charles de Menezes, in the aftermath of the 7 July 2005 terrorist attacks. He had at first confidently stated that his officers had shot a terrorist but he later had to admit that Mr de Menezes had been totally innocent. Although ultimately cleared of personal misconduct Blair's grip appeared to be in question. His reputation suffered another blow when Flanagan was called in to investigate his inappropriate granting of a police contract to a friend. After a meeting with Johnson in October 2008 Blair decided to walk rather than wait to be pushed. The outcome was of dubious constitutionality but was a summation of the way the office of Chief Constable had been developing throughout the decade.[27] Chiefs could expect increasing scrutiny of their professional and personal conduct. Competent handling of specific major incidents, such as Brain's of the Gloucestershire flooding in 2007, did little to redress the trend.[28]

2010–16: downgrading and politicization

Excluded from power since 1997 the Conservatives under the new and assertive leadership of David Cameron, who had personally witnessed the government's short-term defeat over Sheehy in 1993, determined on a fundamentally different approach to criminal justice and policing to wrest the initiative back from Labour in time for the 2010 general election. Philosophically they became convinced that centralism in all political life, and notably so in policing, was detrimental to social well-being, and that individuals and localities should be given more responsibility. Adopting the principles of 'Civil Society', which owed much to similar political trends in America, they developed a suspicion of professional elites, of which the police, whose leadership had developed out of the workforce, was a notable example. A 2007 report *Policing for the People* promised to dismantle Labour's centralism and increase the local democratic responsibility for policing at the expense of both Chief Constables and the Home Office.[29] By the time of the 2010 general election this policy had crystallized into a manifesto commitment to replace police authorities with a single elected individual. In the resulting Coalition

26 'Ian Blair "too close to Labour"', *BBC News*, 17 November 2007.

27 Brain, *A History*, p.402.

28 This is Gloucestershire, 'Tim Brain looks back on his 31-year career', GloucestershireLive, 3 June 2009 <www.gloucestershirelive.co.uk/dr-tim-brain-looks-31-year-career/story-11934932-detail/story.html>.

29 Police Reform Taskforce, *Policing for the People: Interim Report*, London: Conservative Party, 2007, passim.

with the Liberal Democrats it was Conservative policy which dominated the home affairs agenda. The result was the Police Reform and Social Responsibility Act 2011, the principal feature of which was the replacement of provincial police authorities, considered anonymous and unaccountable, with a single directly elected individual, the Police and Crime Commissioner, a post possessing immense administrative as well as political authority.[30] Great emphasis was placed on the power of PCCs to 'hire and fire' Chief Constables. No longer would there be the backstop of the Home Secretary confirming the dismissal, the feature that had saved Oxford in 1985.[31] Such was the mistrust of the new government in its professional police elite that it preferred the uncertainty of the judgement of locally elected individuals of any party, or even none.[32] As some compensation the plethora of central plans and targets were dismantled, inspections would become less intense, and Chief Constables were given the power to appoint their assistants and deputies.

Some Chiefs did not wait to find out what the new regime was like. Simon Ash (Suffolk, 2007–12) and Tony Melville (Gloucestershire, 2010–12) both left before the November 2012 elections, while Norman Bettison (Merseyside 1998–2005, and West Yorkshire 2007–12) precipitously retired prior to the elections when it became clear that all the West Yorkshire PCC candidates would call upon him to resign because of the controversial role he played some 23 years previously, when a Chief Inspector, in South Yorkshire's follow-up to the Hillsborough disaster. Colin Port (Avon and Somerset, 2005–12) chose retirement when the recently elected PCC declined to automatically renew his FTA, a decision later backed up in the High Court.[33] Nick Gargan (Avon and Somerset, 2012–14) resigned when it became apparent that the Avon and Somerset PCC would initiate dismissal proceedings over lack of confidence following revelations about his private life. The fate of Carmel Napier was, therefore, just one other example of the new reality, although the limits of PCC power were demonstrated by the High Court's reinstatement of Neil Rhodes (Lincolnshire, 2012–16) after his erroneous suspension by the PCC.[34] In a further test of the limits of PCC powers in September 2016 the Chief HMI, Sir Tom Winsor reviewed (as required by the PRSA) the case of David Crompton (South Yorkshire, 2012-date), suspended pending dismissal proceedings because of an alleged lack of public confidence arising from his role presenting the South Yorkshire case in the reopened inquest into the Hillsborough victims. His conclusion was that suspension was 'conspicuously unfair, disproportionate, and so unreasonable' that he could not understand how

30 The Mayor of London became the local policing body for the Metropolitan Police, while arrangements for the City of London were unaltered.

31 Contrast Police Act 1964, section 5(4) with PRSA 2011, section38(4).

32 The 2012 elections resulted in sixteen Conservative, thirteen Labour and twelve independent PCCs being elected; in 2016 the results were 20 Conservative, fifteen Labour and three independents.

33 'Avon and Somerset Chief Constable Colin Port to step down', *BBC News*, England, 22 November 2012.

34 'Chief Constables Neil Rhodes' suspension "irrational"', *BBC News*, Lincolnshire, 29 March 2013.

the PCC had reached his view.[35] Powerful words, but ultimately the last word remained with the PCC. At the time of writing the issue remained to be concluded.

In keeping with its philosophies of 'civil society' and 'localism' the government did not prescribe how each PCC should administer their affairs with the result that there has been a blurring of the lines between the roles of Chief Constables and PCCs, notwithstanding the PRSA notionally protecting the 'direction and control' authority of Chief Constables. A 2013 Home Affairs Committee (HAC) inquiry into the PCC's first year of operation found that those Chief Constables and PCCs that gave evidence were keen to stress either the positive aspects of their relationship or at worst to suggest their relationship was one of creative tension, but the HAC still concluded that there remained a risk to operational independence. In 2015 a Committee on Standards in Public Life report worryingly concluded that there was a confusion among the public, Chief Constables and PCCs themselves 'about roles and responsibilities, especially in relation to where operational independence and governance oversight begin and end'.[36]

The long-term effects of the drive for increased equality from the 1990s onwards had produced a marginally more diverse Chief Constable cadre, with six female Chief Constables in 2016. But there were still no ethnic minority Chief Constables since Michael Fuller's retirement in 2010.[37] The cadre had suddenly become significantly less experienced because of the cumulative effects of the various resignations and the attritional effect of natural retirements at the end of FTAs. By mid-2016, 33 Chiefs had been appointed since 2012, the average length of service in the rank being just 2.9 years, with only one, Metropolitan Commissioner Sir Bernard Hogan-Howe, having over ten years' service.[38] It was this relatively inexperienced and constitutionally insecure cadre that necessarily had to make deep cuts in police personnel numbers, a consequence of the Coalition's response to the 2008 economic recession. After a decade of growth Chiefs now had to slam their organizations into reverse. In just six years 43,000 (or 18 per cent) full-time equivalent posts went.[39] HMIC assessed that Chiefs collectively had handled the

35 'David Crompton: Move to dismiss South Yorkshire police chief "unfair"', *BBC News*, Sheffield and South Yorkshire, 16 September 2016.

36 Home Affairs Committee, *Police and Crime Commissioners: Progress to date*, London: HM Stationery Office, 2014, p.23, and, Committee on Standards in Public Life, *Tone from the Top: Leadership, Ethics and Accountability in Policing*, London: HMSO, 2015, p.9.

37 There was one female and ethnic minority Metropolitan Assistant Commissioner in 2016 (Pat Gallan) but no ethnic minority officer commanding a London or provincial force. Home Office, Police workforce, England and Wales, 31 March 2016: data tables <www.gov.uk/government/statistics/police-workforce-england-and-wales-31-march-2016> and various force websites.

38 These calculations are based on details in profiles on force websites.

39 Home Office, Statistical Bulletin, Police Service Strength England and Wales, 31 March 2010 <www.gov.uk/government/uploads/system/uploads/attachment_data/file/115745/hosb1410.pdf> pp.13, 21 and 22, and Police workforce: England and Wales statistics, 31 March 2016: data tables <www.gov.uk/government/statistics/police-workforce-england-and-wales-31-march-2016>.

loss relatively well, but there was evidence of declining morale.[40] Of even greater significance was the continued decline in recorded crime with measures of public confidence in the police as a whole holding up.[41] However effective they may have been in managing decline, collectively Chiefs were not vociferous in opposing cuts. Was this because opposition would have been fruitless, was it because of behind the scenes influence by PCCs, or was it because of the dissolution in 2015 of ACPO as the Chiefs' representative body, to be replaced by the National Police Chiefs' Council (NPCC)? During its most recent spell in opposition the Conservatives had targeted ACPO as being too close to Labour and its replacement in 2015 with a body with a narrower remit was politically inevitable. Whereas ACPO had the independence to represent Chiefs, the NPCC has a narrower purpose of 'focusing on operational delivery and developing national approaches'.[42] Also many of ACPO's national functions transferred to the College of Policing, which itself had replaced the NPIA. In another constitutional shift, in 2013 the Director of the National Crime Agency formally acquired power to direct and coordinate Chief Constables in certain circumstances.[43]

It is hard to quantify the ways in which the status of Chief Constables as public figures also diminished after 2010. The causes were several. Chiefs became less high profile because PCCs took more of the limelight.[44] With some exceptions, Chiefs did not appear to grip the response to the 2011 riots, allowing them to peter out rather than to contain and suppress them.[45] The growth of collaboration schemes, both between forces and with other organizations, notwithstanding any elusive operational or financial benefits, diminished the significance of Chief Constables as individual leaders of their forces.[46] Collectively, the leadership was unable to take the initiative in the handling of the so-called 'Plebgate' (2012–14) or the phone hacking (2009–11) affairs.[47] Similarly, it struggled to present

40 HMIC, *Policing in Austerity: Meeting the Challenge*, London: HMIC, 2014, pp.33–5, and, Police Federation, Submission to the Police Remuneration and Review Body <www.polfed.org/documents/PFEW_and_PSAEW_PRRB_Submission_FINAL_13-01-2016_v1.pdf>, pp.42–4.

41 'Countering terrorism: Written statement – HCWS116', parliament.uk, 21 July 2016 <www.parliament.uk/business/publications/written-questions-answers-statements/written-statement/Commons/2016-07-21/HCWS116/>, and, Ipsos MORI, Veracity Index 2015: Trust in Professions, 22 January 2016 <www.ipsos-mori.com/researchpublications/researcharchive/3685/Politicians-are-still-trusted-less-than-estate-agents-journalists-and-bankers.aspx>.

42 National Police Chiefs Council, Home <www.npcc.police.uk>.

43 Crime and Courts Act 2013, section 5.

44 For an example of a PCC taking the lead in what might have previously been considered an operational matter see Martin Surl PCC, 'Gloucestershire Police unveil new mounted unit', n.d. <www.policecommissioner.net/gloucestershire-police-unveil-new-mounted-unit/>.

45 T. Brain, *A Future for Policing in England and Wales*, London: Oxford University Press, 2013, p.202.

46 HMIC, *Policing in Austerity: Meeting the Challenge*, <www.justiceinspectorates.gov.uk/hmic/wp-content/uploads/policing-in-austerity-meeting-the-challenge.pdf> p.38.

47 '"Plebgate" row', *BBC News*, UK Politics, 27 November 2014 and I. Chandrasekhar, M. Wardrop, and, A. Trotman, 'Phone hacking: Timeline of the scandal', *Daily Telegraph*, 23 July 2012.

convincing responses to legacy issues such as child and sexual abuse crimes stretching in some cases back to the 1970s, the Hillsborough tragedy or the 1984 Orgreave confrontation in the miners' strike. Individual Chiefs were periodically criticized in the media for their bonus and expenses packages, despite these being within national or local regulations.[48] A series of embarrassments or scandals for some individuals may also have diminished the status of the cadre. Sir Paul Stephenson (Lancashire, 2002–5, and Metropolitan, 2009–11) resigned as Commissioner after his judgement was questioned over hiring a *News of the World* journalist and accepting £12,000 of hospitality.[49] Sean Price (Cleveland, 2003–11) was dismissed for lying about his role in the recruitment of a member of staff, while Grahame Maxwell (North Yorkshire, 2007–12) did not have his FTA extended after inappropriately involving himself in a recruitment drive.[50] Sue Sim (Northumbria, 2011–15) was publicly criticized by her PCC, Vera Baird, for her abrasive management style.[51]

A clear demonstration of this diminution of public status came first in October 2012 when the Home Secretary, Theresa May, appointed Sir Tom Winsor, former Rail Regulator, as Chief HMI, a post previously always held by former senior Chief Constables. Unsurprisingly, given the uncertainty of tenure and diminishment of status, fewer individuals came forward as applicants for vacancies, possibly a contributory factor behind two PCCs in 2016 widening the scope of their advertisement for new Chief Constables in their forces to include applicants from outside the UK, although to date none have been appointed.[52] Sir Bernard Hogan-Howe's (Merseyside, 2004–9, Metropolitan, 2011–17) announcement in September 2016 that he intended to retire some months early in 2017 provided the opportunity for the appointment of a non-UK Metropolitan Commissioner for the first time in its history. But is was an internal candidate, Cressida Dick, who took over.

48 A. Travis, '"Top police officers" allowances and perks boost basic pay by 21%', *The Guardian*, 8 August 2016.

49 'Met Commissioner Sir Paul Stephenson quits', *BBC News*, 18 July 2011.

50 'Cleveland Police chief Sean Price sacked after inquiry', *BBC News*, Tees, 5 October 2012 and, M. Wainwright, 'Chief constable keeps his job after admitting gross misconduct', *The Guardian*, 10 May 2011.

51 W. Metcalfe, 'Northumbria Chief Constable Sue Sim cleared of breaching police standards', ChronicleLive, 11 May 2015 < www.chroniclelive.co.uk/news/north-east-news/northumbria-chief-constable-sue-sim-9234018>.

52 H. Hickey, 'Why does no-one want to be a Chief Constable?', *Police Oracle*, 12 July 2016 www.policeoracle.com/news/Why-does-no-one-want-to-be-a-chief-constable_92318.html and I. Weinfass, 'PCCs advertising abroad in bid to fill Chief Constable vacancies', *Police Oracle*, 20 September 2016 www.policeoracle.com/news/PCCs-advertising-abroad-in-bid-to-fill-chief-constable-vacancies_92964.html. The ability to appoint an 'approved rank' from an 'approved overseas police force' was enacted by the Anti-social Behaviour, Crime and Policing Act 2014, section 140.

Conclusion

It is difficult to conclude other than that by the end of the period the Chief Constable cadre had lost status, authority and power compared to the professional elite described by Reiner in the late 1980s. Some of this has been the result of deliberate erosion by governments (both Labour and Conservative) and some by the cumulative effect of collective and individual failures. The effect of precipitous resignations and natural retirements has weakened the cadre's experience base, and has done so at a critical time. The growing power of PCCs and national policing bodies has further diluted the cadre's authority. The prospect of non-UK citizens becoming Chief Officers, yet to be realized at the end of this survey, will dilute it still further.

Despite this there has over some 35 years been some notable achievements. For most of the period police leadership contained serious disorder and maintained the balance of policing by consent; it had innovated; it contributed to the sustained decline in crime; it had absorbed gyrations in politics, the economy and society and, until the last years surveyed, it maintained its political independence despite huge pressure in the late 1980s. It is ironic, given the pressure that Chiefs withstood from left-wing Labour authorities, that it was a Conservative-led government that ultimately removed the shields against political influence, a probable legacy of how the managerial elite combined with the workforce to delay the implementation of the Sheehy Report in 1993.

Police service leadership was and is highly conspicuous and highly accountable. When surveying the totality of the years from 1985 the judgement must be that the Chief Constable cadre has, on balance, been successful, but its influence, experience and independence has demonstrably declined towards the end of the period. Recognition of its positive achievements – adapting to massive political and social change while maintaining a broad balance in favour of effectiveness and efficiency – has rarely been recognized. The immediate prognosis, however, is that the professional experience, expertise and political independence of the cadre will further weaken as PCCs become more powerful.

Conclusion

Kim Stevenson, David J. Cox, Iain Channing

In November 2016 Andy Cooke, Chief Constable of Merseyside, rather provocatively entitled his first Annual Lecture 'Lions led by donkeys?'[1] This well-known phrase is usually associated with the First World War, but most probably dates back to the debacle of the Crimean War, suggesting that mid-Victorian military senior officers did not possess sufficient intelligence to lead their men. Cooke's choice of title is therefore made more significant and apposite when, as this book has shown, it is recalled that the majority of mid-Victorian Chief Constables were employed from this same cadre of men.

Cooke went on to argue that such a depiction was unwarranted in respect of present-day Chief Constables especially, as Brain's final chapter highlighted, given the complex and challenging nature of the role. We would also conclude that while examples of weak and problematic leadership can be found within most organizations, neither is it an accurate reflection of all the numerous Chief Constables referred to in the book. Several of those profiled carved out highly successful careers as police leaders, diplomatically negotiating the respective minefields of being aware of the social status of their peers combined with a critical consciousness of the behind-the-scenes political machinations of members of the Watch or Finance Committees that ultimately controlled their actions through financial constraints. However, there are also examples of some post-holders who exhibited the kind of blinkered and unthinking state of mind that was later attributed to senior British military officers in the First World War, and others who appear to have been singularly ill-equipped to deal with the minutiae of administrative detail necessary to maintain and develop an effective police force.

The history of Chief Constables in the United Kingdom, as the contributions in this book demonstrate, is undeniably a fascinating but chequered one, littered with many successes and in some cases attracting inevitable controversy. Cooke began his lecture by referring to the fact that currently disciplinary proceedings against senior police leaders are at an all-time high. In support, he cited half-a-dozen examples of newspaper headlines (unsurprisingly tabloid) all of which were

1 Cooke, Chief Constable of Merseyside's Annual Lecture, 28 November 2016.

critical of police chiefs either in respect of their command decisions, performance or individual conduct. This raises a number of questions about the appointment, suitability and integrity of some chief officers reflecting the concerns identified by the College of Policing's *Leadership Review* as highlighted in the Introduction. A perusal of several of the preceding chapters would also find examples of similarly vitriolic sentiments from various sectors of society intent on denigrating the work of Chief Constables throughout the almost two centuries covered in this book. As Brain highlights in the final chapter, the 1980s generation of 'dominating personalities' were among the last to retain the necessary autonomy to ride the contemporary waves of media and political controversy. However, within the last decade there has been a discernible decline of this professional elite and associated evidence of a tension within the higher echelons of policing, despite the fact that most police leaders now have a University education and are certainly not intellectual 'donkeys'. Chief Constables are granted considerable power and authority so should expect to receive constructive critique as an inevitable consequence of the job but disturbingly there is a real sense that the role is becoming an increasingly less attractive proposition to some career-minded individuals.

Chief Constable Cooke was also deeply critical of the fact that, as with many other public services delivery, 'over the last few years policing has been driven by a performance culture', dominated by a politically figures-driven agenda where no senior police leader wants to find themselves under the spotlight. He stated that some Police Authorities had developed into a 'bureaucratic nightmare' with many demanding impracticable and inappropriate 'target-driven' policing plans. The evolving bureaucratic culture that is increasingly encapsulating the leadership role of Chief Constables compels an analysis of the historical development of this rank. The chapters have highlighted the extent of operational control Chief Constables have possessed, from Henry Goddard's involvement in crime solving in the 1840s to James Anderton's and Kenneth Oxford's leadership during the 1981 riots. Yet, it is the strategic concerns that now feature more prominently in the Chief Constable's duties. The current influence of neo-liberal reform that drives the New Public Management ethos noted by Brain as emanating from the 1990s, has injected a market rationality into policing services that continues as an overriding presence today.[2] As such, the prioritization of economy, efficiency and effectiveness has influenced a demise in the operational engagement of Chief Constables and such duties are now more frequently delegated to lower ranks. Furthermore, their autocracy has also been reduced by the drive for efficiency; Reiner and O'Conner argue that the target driven aims imposed have significantly 'eroded the wider independence that chiefs had exercised or sought to exercise in the 1970s.'[3]

2 A. White and M. Gill, 'The transformation of policing: From ratios to rationalities', *British Journal of Criminology*, 2013, vol.53, 74–93.

3 R. Reiner and D. O'Connor, 'Politics and policing: The terrible twins', in J. Fleming, *Police Leadership: Rising to the Top*, 2015, Oxford University Press, p.56.

Additionally, the introduction of Police and Crime Commissioners has changed the landscape significantly. Cooke supported their election hoping that as their position becomes more established it will lead to 'a better and more cohesive arrangement'.[4] Arguably, several authors within this edited volume would be of the opinion that 'plus ça change, plus c'est la même chose'; there has always been the potential for conflict and mistrust between the executive in the form of Chief Constables and the non-executive communities they serve. One key distinction that can be drawn is that while today's Chief Constables are more wary of clashing with public opinion (and perhaps with that of their respective PCC), their Victorian counterparts were always cautious of the constant background presence of the Watch Committee which could more easily exercise its prerogative of dismissal should the Chief Constable countermand their wishes and objectives.

Cooke concluded his lecture by stating that trust – both within the force and outside – is the key to successful future policing. He referred to the recent IPSO MORI Veracity Index 2015: Trust in Professions, in which a cross-section of the British public was asked to rank trustworthiness among professions.[5] 68 per cent of respondents stated that they would trust a police officer, exactly the same figure as the 'ordinary man/woman in the street' category, and, disconcertingly, 1 per cent below hairdressers. This is a somewhat curious computation that not only challenges the historic traditions of policing by consent but demands that Chief Constables need to address the public perception of the police. Trust, Cooke argued, was essential for any Chief Constable; a good police leader needed to gain the trust of his officers and they in turn needed to rely on his trust. But to be a universally effective and well respected police leader it is also imperative, as evinced in a number of chapters here, that a Chief Constable earn the trust of the public. And in this regard it is those individuals who have the strength of character, determination, self-assuredness and innate sense of what they believe and how they can achieve it who have proved themselves more able to generate that trust.

4 Cooke, Chief Constable of Merseyside's Annual Lecture, 28 November 2016.

5 Ibid.

Table of statutes (chronological)

List of Chief Constables/ equivalent titles, mentioned by name

Served as Chief Constable/Commissioner

Serving as Chief Constable/ Commissioner in 2017

Index

(for named police forces, see under individual forces)

For Product Safety Concerns and Information please contact our EU representative GPSR@taylorandfrancis.com
Taylor & Francis Verlag GmbH, Kaufingerstraße 24, 80331 München, Germany

www.ingramcontent.com/pod-product-compliance
Ingram Content Group UK Ltd.
Pitfield, Milton Keynes, MK11 3LW, UK
UKHW022014180926
475701UK00003B/361
9780367227265